BARRON'S

Pass Key to the LSAT

LAW SCHOOL ADMISSION TEST

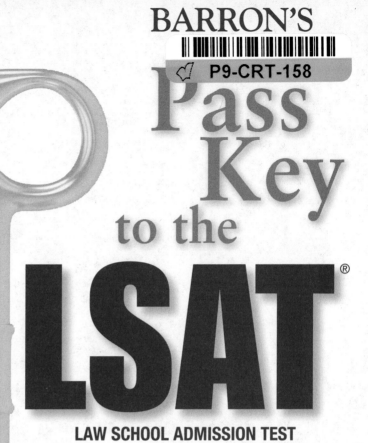

2nd Edition

Jay B. Cutts, M.A.
Director
Cutts Graduate Reviews
Albuquerque, New Mexico

John F. Mares, J.D., M.B.A., M.A.
Attorney at Law
Founder, Mares LSAT Review
Lansing, New York

®LSAT is a registered trademark of Law School Admission Council, Inc.,
which does not endorse this book.

All inquiries should be addressed to:
Barron's Educational Series, Inc.
250 Wireless Boulevard
Hauppauge, New York 11788
www.barronseduc.com

ISSN: 2329-8642

ISBN: 978-1-4380-0913-1

PRINTED IN CANADA
9 8 7 6 5 4 3 2

10%
POST-CONSUMER
WASTE
Paper contains a minimum
of 10% post-consumer
waste (PCW). Paper used
in this book was derived
from certified, sustainable
forestlands.

Contents

Preface

This book is an easy-to-use, compact version of Barron's complete LSAT prep book. You can carry it with you for quick study sessions throughout the day. It is designed to help you, today's law school applicant, master the LSAT and get accepted to law school. Use this book along with actual LSAT practice tests to get your best score, even if your time is limited.

We'd like to share with you some of the elements that make this book uniquely effective. First, Barron's **LSAT** is founded on critical, unique, and highly advanced strategies. These strategies draw on the authors' thirty-plus years of combined experience working hands on with thousands of successful law school applicants. These strategies address timing, test taking, problem solving, and test anxiety, and provide highly systematic and in-depth tools for correctly answering each and every type of LSAT question.

Second, the Barron's staff and the authors share the conviction that this book can best serve the prelaw community by listening to you. We asked a team of nearly 50 current prelaw students to review the book before publication, and their feedback has helped us make sure that the book meets your needs.

Please access the powerful free tools that we have developed to help you succeed. Our LSAT Solution of the Week program e-mails you a complete explanation of an actual LSAT, including how to apply the strategies you are learning in this book. Our weekly study plan helps you organize your prep time. Our forum lets you ask questions, give feedback on this book, and connect with other LSAT students.

We are continually developing new products for you, so please register with us now online. It's free and quick! Go to *www.cuttsreviews.com/prelaw* or use the QR code in the margin.

Take advantage, too, of free materials from Barron's. You can access answer explanations for Test 65, an actual LSAT, at *barronsbooks.com/tp/gd47yw8r/*

On behalf of all of us involved with this book, we wish you success in your pursuits.

Jay B. Cutts, MA
John F. Mares, JD, MBA, MA

Acknowledgments

We would like to thank the following people: Wayne Barr and Linda Turner at Barron's for their kind and wise guidance; our professional consultants Leigh Deusinger (advisor at Washington University), Sara Faradji (Carnegie Mellon), Crystin Immel, Michael Jasso (University of New Mexico), Brein Millea (Harvard), Randy Mink, Catherine Oliver (Oliver-Editorial.com), and Ronak Shah (University of Illinois at Chicago) for contributing according to their areas of expertise; and the prelaw student review panel for their generous feedback.

Introduction to Mastering the LSAT

ORIENTATION TO THE LSAT

Getting into Law School

The goal of this book is to help you get accepted to law school. The Law School Admission Test (LSAT) is one of the most critical factors for admissions. In fact, if your grade point average (GPA) is strong enough, a superior LSAT score can guarantee your acceptance. The information here is based on the authors' multiple decades of hands-on LSAT instruction. The LSAT is learnable. For every LSAT question, there is a specific strategy for answering that question correctly. This book teaches all the strategies that you need, whether you are aiming for a 160 or a 180.

The LSAT

The LSAT is a half-day, paper-based test with four administrations per year: October (or in some years, late September), December, February, and June. The first three are given on Saturday mornings. Saturday Sabbath observers only may register for a non-Saturday test given within a few days after the Saturday test. The June test is on a Monday afternoon. The LSAT is required for admission to all law schools approved by the American Bar Association (ABA). Most Canadian law schools require the LSAT, and many non-ABA-approved law schools also require it. The Law School Admission Council (LSAC), which manages the LSAT, provides extensive information on the LSAT on its website at *www.lsac.org*. Review the information there, including test dates and deadlines.

The LSAT claims to measure comprehension of complex reading selections, organization of complex information, logical and critical thinking, and the ability to evaluate logical arguments. Except for the essay, all questions are multiple-choice, with five answer choices. There is no penalty for wrong answers, so fill in an answer for each question, even if you have not worked on it.

The LSAT contains the following elements, not necessarily in this order:

THE ELEMENTS OF THE LSAT

2 scored Logical Reasoning (LR) sections—35 minutes each

1 scored Reading Comprehension (RC) section—35 minutes

1 scored Analytical Reasoning (AR) section—35 minutes

1 unscored and unreported section of any of the three above types—35 minutes

1 unscored but reported Writing Sample—35 minutes

Logical Reasoning

Each of the two scored LR sections has the following characteristics:

LOGICAL REASONING

25–26 questions

35 minutes

Short passages with 1 question per passage

Each passage includes a partial or complete logical argument that may be valid or faulty. The questions may ask you to strengthen or weaken an argument; identify a flaw, an assumption, or a conclusion; or resolve a paradox. There are other types of questions that an LR passage may ask, and these are covered in Chapter 2.

Reading Comprehension

Each RC section presents four sets of long passages drawn on topics from the natural sciences, humanities, or social sciences. One of the four sets consists of two moderate-length passages.

READING COMPREHENSION

27 questions

35 minutes

3 sets of a single passage with 6–8 questions

1 set of two shorter passages with

   5–7 questions (Comparative Reading)

Each of the three single passages consists of about a half page of text followed by six to eight questions. The Comparative Reading set consists of two shorter passages, each about a quarter of a page, followed by six or seven questions.

Analytical Reasoning

Each AR section includes four game setups, followed by questions.

ANALYTICAL REASONING

23 questions

35 minutes

4 game setups followed by 5–7 questions

The Essay (Writing Sample)

The essay has a 35-minute time limit. The essay requires you to (1) evaluate a brief statement, (2) understand two sides of an issue, (3) understand the criteria used to evaluate a solution, (4) apply the criteria in order to defend one solution as superior, (5) compose a coherent and grammatically correct essay using standard English, and (6) demonstrate a familiarity with the basic elements of legal writing.

LSAT Scores

You receive one total score that reflects your performance on all four scored multiple-choice sections of the LSAT. The unscored section does not contribute to your score. The essay does not receive a score but is forwarded to each school to which you send your LSAT score.

Your score is based on the total number of questions you answer correctly (raw score). There is no penalty for wrong answers and all correct answers are worth the same amount. The raw score is converted to a 120–180 scale (scaled score) according to a curve based on the scores of recent test takers. Table 1 gives an approximate conversion chart for converting raw scores to scaled scores. The actual scale changes slightly from test to test. Notice that one more correct answer often results in a higher scaled score.

Table 1. Converting Raw Scores to Scaled Scores*

Raw Score Range	Scaled Score	Raw Score Range	Scaled Score	Raw Score Range	Scaled Score	Raw Score Range	Scaled Score	Raw Score Range	Scaled Score
0–15	120	30	133	48–49	145	68–69	157	87	169
16	121	31–32	134	50	146	70–71	158	88	170
17	122	33	135	51–52	147	72–73	159	89	171
18	123	34–35	136	53	148	74	160	90	172
19	124	36	137	54–55	149	75–76	161	91–92	173
20	125	37–38	138	56–57	150	77	162	93	174
21	126	39	139	58	151	78–79	163	94	175
22–23	127	40–41	140	59–60	152	80	164	95	176
24	128	42	141	61–62	153	81–82	165	96	177
25	129	43–44	142	63–64	154	83	166	97	178
26	130	45	143	65	155	84–85	167	98	179
27–28	131	46–47	144	66–67	156	86	168	99–101	180
29	132								

*The scaled scores here are approximate. When you use this table to score an actual LSAT, the resulting score may differ by a point or two from the official score; for a simulated test, such as those in this book, the resulting score may differ by 5 points or more from your performance on an actual LSAT.

Score requirements for admission vary widely from school to school. In general, scores of 149 or below are not competitive, though schools may accept a small number of students in this range. Scores in the 150 to 160 range may be competitive at some schools but will not be competitive at many others. Scores of 161 and above will most likely be considered strong by many schools. Students applying to the most competitive schools, however, may need scores above 170.

Canceling Scores and Nonstandard Conditions

At the end of your official LSAT administration you have the option of canceling your test. If you do cancel, you will not find out how you scored. In specific circumstances that have caused you to perform poorly, such as illness, it may be helpful to cancel. However, you also have six calendar days from the date of your test to request a score cancellation. Because test takers' impressions of how they performed are often highly inaccurate on the actual test day, give yourself a day or two to consider whether or not you should cancel.

If you end up with a lower score on record because you did not cancel, most schools do not hold that against you, as long as your score is strong on your next test. In this case you should address, in your personal statement, any reasons that led to your lower score. If you are taking the LSAT on the last acceptable administration for an application year, it may be important to *not* cancel your score, even if the score may not be your best, because getting an official score for that administration will allow you to meet the LSAT requirement for your school. You can then usually take a subsequent LSAT and submit that score as a supplement to your first score. In such a case, send a written note to the schools to which you are applying so that they know to wait for your second score.

If you feel that the testing conditions at your testing center were substandard, you can file a complaint with LSAC. Substandard conditions can include excessive noise, overly cold or hot rooms, failure of a monitor to correctly keep track of time or to enforce quiet in the room, or other actions of the monitor that result in substandard testing, such as not allowing you to use a permitted watch or cutting a break short. If LSAC decides that you were not given standard conditions, it may submit a note to the schools where you are applying. In this case, the schools may take into account that your score was negatively affected.

THE ADMISSIONS PROCESS

LSAT Scores

LSAC provides a database of law schools. You can access the database from the LSAC home page under the link *"Searchable Law School Data and Descriptions."* Many schools publish a grid showing the likelihood of admissions based on LSAT score and undergraduate GPA. Find the school in which you are interested and select the link that says *"LSAC Law School Description."* If the school publishes a grid, it will appear on the last page of the description. Below is an example of part of a grid. For each GPA range, there are two columns. The first shows how many applications (Apps) were received in that range. The second shows how many people in that range were admitted (Adm).

Table 2. Sample Admissions Grid

LSAT Score	3.75+ Apps	3.75+ Adm	3.50–3.74 Apps	3.50–3.74 Adm	3.25–3.49 Apps	3.25–3.49 Adm
175–180	0	0	0	0	0	0
170–174	0	0	1	1	3	3
165–169	2	2	5	4	8	7
160–164	20	16	18	13	16	11
155–159	34	26	54	26	46	21
150–154	29	9	42	11	52	8

Find the column that matches your undergraduate GPA. In calculating your GPA do *not* include any graduate coursework. Then, for each LSAT range, you can determine the relative odds of being accepted. For example, in Table 2, if your GPA is 3.6 and your LSAT score is 156, fifty-four people applied in that range and twenty-six of them were admitted. The relative odds of being accepted in that range, then, were about 50 percent. In other words, one out of two applicants was admitted, and you will be competing with one other person for a spot.

In Table 2, for the top GPA range and for LSAT scores above 154, the school accepted nearly all applicants. If you have a strong GPA, aim for an LSAT score that gives you greater than 90 percent odds of being accepted. Even if you get into this range, take the rest of the application process seriously. A halfhearted application can earn you a rejection despite good test scores.

Acceptance is based on many factors in addition to LSAT score and GPA. However, calculating your odds based on LSAT score and GPA can help you determine how much harder you need to work—both on the LSAT and the rest of the admissions process.

Importance of the LSAT

Law school admissions committees typically make their decisions based on LSAT scores, undergraduate GPA, your personal statement, letters of recommendation, and your academic and professional experience, including graduate-level coursework, internships, and volunteer experiences.

Think of the LSAT and GPA as your first hurdles. If you have a low LSAT score and a low GPA, the committee may not look seriously at the rest of your application. Because the GPA is difficult to increase, a strong LSAT score may be your best chance to be competitive.

Other Aspects of the Admissions Process

During the summer before you apply to law school, as you are preparing for your LSAT, you also need to prepare for other parts of the admissions process. These include a personal statement and letters of recommendation. Check with your adviser to be sure you will graduate on time. Identify the schools to which you will apply and determine the LSAT score you will need to be accepted.

TEST DAY SCHEDULE

The typical test day consists of three sections, a fifteen-minute break, and then two test sections and the essay, in that order. Every test taker receives one test section that is not scored and is not reflected in the score report. This test section is used by LSAC to test and develop new questions. By the end of the test, you will have received either a second section of RC or AR or a third section of LR. However, it is not possible to determine which section is the unscored one, so it is important to work equally well on each section. Typically, you will not receive a second RC or AR section or third LR section until after the break. However, the unscored section has historically been one of the sections given before the break.

HOW TO USE THIS BOOK

You will get the most out of this book if you study the chapters in the order in which they are presented. There is information in some chapters that is important for you to know when you reach subsequent chapters.

Read through the book once, practicing what you learn. This will introduce you to all the insights and strategies that you need. However, you will probably not absorb everything on your first time through the book. Learning the LSAT is like learning a new language. It requires practice, repetition, and review. In order to master the LSAT, review this book three, four, or even five times. Each time you will absorb more of the strategies.

Some of the strategies that you will learn are powerful and intricate. They may not come naturally to you the first time you use them. Some, especially the strategies for logic, require patient practice for you to become comfortable and proficient with them. Read the instruction, practice slowly and carefully with test questions, and then come back and read through the instruction again.

Reference Lists

There are a number of lists and tables in the book that thoroughly break down some of the important complex patterns of the test, such as the types of AR games, patterns for solving games, and types of if/then logic. These lists are *not* meant for you to memorize or read through thoroughly. Treat these lists as you would a dictionary. Glance at them briefly. Then use them as reference tools, coming back to them as you need them when you work on practice problems.

The Practice Test

The answer explanations in the practice test give step-by-step instruction on how to apply the strategies. They reinforce what you learn in the chapters. Read through the answer explanations carefully to learn more strategies.

FOUR-WEEK STUDY PLAN

Here is a plan to organize your studying over four weeks. The actual LSATs referred to below are the LSAT exams published by LSAC and available at *www.lsac.org* or at a bookstore. It is not necessary to do all sections of an assigned test at the same time, except when a full mock test is assigned. After completing a test section, review both your timing and testing strategy. For a two-month study plan, go through the four-week plan twice.

Table 3. Four-Week Study Plan

	BARRON'S CHAPTERS	PRACTICE TESTS
FIRST WEEK		
Days 1 and 2	Read the Table of Contents, Introduction, and General Strategies chapter	Do a full diagnostic test, timed. Use an actual LSAT.
Days 3 and 4	Read the Logical Reasoning chapter	Do a practice LR section, untimed, using an actual LSAT.
Days 5, 6, and 7	Read the Reading Comprehension chapter	Do a practice RC section, untimed, using an actual LSAT.
SECOND WEEK		
Days 1, 2, and 3	Read the Analytical Reasoning chapter	Do a practice AR section, untimed, using an actual LSAT.
Days 4 and 5	Review the Introduction	Do a full diagnostic test, timed. Use an actual LSAT.
Days 6 and 7	Review the General Strategies chapter	Review the diagnostic test for strategy.
THIRD WEEK		
Days 1 and 2	Review the Logical Reasoning chapter	Do a practice LR section, timed, using an actual LSAT.
Days 3 and 4	Review the Reading Comprehension chapter	Do a practice RC section, timed, using an actual LSAT.
Days 5, 6, and 7	Review the Analytical Reasoning chapter	Do a practice AR section, timed, using an actual LSAT.
FOURTH WEEK		
Day 1	Do a final review of the Introduction and Logical Reasoning chapter	Do the Barron's Practice Test, sections 1 and 2, timed. Review.
Days 2 and 3	Do a final review of the Reading Comprehension and Analytical Reasoning chapters	Do the Barron's Practice Test, sections 3 and 4, timed. Review.
Days 4 and 5	Review as needed	Do untimed practice on all sections of an actual LSAT.
Days 6 and 7	Review as needed	Do a full mock test, timed. Use an actual LSAT. Review.

General Strategies 1

This chapter introduces important strategies that apply to the entire LSAT. The later chapters review in-depth strategies specific to each section.

YOUR PLAN OF ATTACK

There are two tasks that you must accomplish to get a top score on the LSAT:

1. Master timing strategy.
2. Learn the patterns for each type of test section and master the strategies for getting to the correct answer.

Timing strategy is extremely important for improving your score. Timing strategy is covered below and is reviewed at the beginning of each chapter. Many people underestimate the importance of good timing. Timing strategy involves learning how to use your time as effectively as possible.

In addition to timing, the essence of improving on the LSAT is learning the behind-the-scenes agendas and patterns for each of the three types of LSAT sections and then learning the powerful strategies that help you get to the correct answer more quickly and more accurately. This introduction teaches important strategies that apply to the entire LSAT. Each chapter of this book teaches you the specific strategies that you need to master each type of LSAT question.

Mastering Strategy

All LSAT questions require strategy. LSAT questions do not test knowledge of the real world, law, or any other academic subject. If you miss a question, there is a strategy that you could have used to answer that question correctly. Carefully review every question that you get wrong to make sure you understand the patterns in the question and the strategies you could have used.

Many people, when they review a question, feel that they made a careless error. In fact, most errors that seem "careless" are *not* the result of being "sloppy" but rather are the result of (1) not using time well, such as rushing or quitting too soon; (2) missing an important distinction; or (3) having misunderstood the question stem. Look beneath the surface to determine the cause of your error.

How to Practice

There are several ways to practice LSAT questions. The main way is to practice untimed. Untimed practice lets you experiment with strategies. It allows you to push your abilities by working on a question for ten or fifteen minutes, or more. Untimed practice is the best way to analyze the test and build your strengths.

As you become more skilled, you will also do occasional timed sections. After you have studied timing strategy, do a timed section just for the purpose of trying out your new timing approach. Later on, you can do timed sections to see how you are scoring and to evaluate your timing strategy. Eventually, you can challenge yourself by doing several timed sections at a sitting, or by doing a full, timed test. You may also wish to build your stamina by testing under distracting conditions or with a reduced time limit.

As you get closer to your test, plan on at least one full, timed test. Even up to your test day, though, continue to do untimed practice to build your skills.

LSAC has many previous actual LSATs available for sale. These are extremely valuable to study. Be aware, however, that tests more than four or five years old may have slightly different patterns than the current test.

TIMING STRATEGY

What does "timing strategy" mean? You may say, "I need to learn how to go faster to get to all the questions. That's the only way I can get more points." Consider this view carefully to see whether it is valid.

Everyone develops certain strategies for taking tests over the years, and these strategies operate on a subconscious level. As you take a test, you continually make decisions about how to use your time without being aware of these decisions. For example, when a test section begins, what do you do first? Most people begin with the first question. That may not be the best way to start a section, but it is an assumption that you may have developed from your past test-taking experience. This, and other assumptions, can be analyzed carefully to determine what is actually the best approach on the LSAT.

How many questions do you hope to work on? Should you be pushing yourself to work faster or letting yourself relax and work more carefully? When you finish one question, on which question should you work next? If you are having trouble with a question, should you guess and move on now or spend more time on it? How much time is acceptable to spend on a question? If you get stuck on a question and cannot think of anything else to do with it, should you guess and move on or do something else?

If you were to take the LSAT right now, you would have to make the above decisions, but your decisions would probably not be the best ones for the LSAT. Study the strategies below so that you can test and adjust your assumptions about timing strategy.

Step 1: Test Layout

The first step in developing a good timing strategy is to know the "geography" of each test section—how many questions there are and how many problem sets, as well as how much time you have for the entire section.

Step 2: Keeping Track of Time

You will need to keep track of time during the test. You are allowed to bring one watch into the testing room but it cannot be digital. In other words, it can only be a watch with hands (analog) and it *cannot* have any functions other than keeping time, such as a calculator or stopwatch.

Your watch should be large enough so that you can see the hands clearly and can easily pull out the stem. It is not necessary for the watch to have a second hand because you will only use the minute hand for timing.

How to Use Your LSAT Watch

During each test section, you need to know when the thirty-five minutes for the section is almost up. Because your watch will be used for keeping time for each question, rely on the monitor to give a five-minute warning. At this time, fill in the bubbles for any questions that you have left blank up to this point—without actually looking at the questions to which the bubbles correspond—and then continue to work on questions until the monitor calls time. If there is a wall clock in the test room, you can also use that to know how much time is left on the section. However, if the clock is behind you, the monitor may not allow you to turn around frequently.

As you begin each question, set the two hands of the watch to 12 o'clock. The minute hand will act as a stopwatch, showing how many minutes have elapsed. The minute hand will never go further than five minutes. Ignore the hour hand, as it will stay on 12. You only need to keep track of the time that you spend on an individual question. It is not necessary to keep track of the time setting up an RC or AR passage. For most questions, you will arrive at an answer within a minute or two and will not need to refer to your watch. You will simply enter your answer, go on to your next question, and reset the watch to 12. However, on a few critical questions, you may need to spend extra time, and then it is important to know how much time you have already used.

On most questions, you will not need to know how much time you spent. However, because you cannot know in advance for which questions you will need to know the time, you must reset your watch at the beginning of every question. Once you are used to resetting the watch, it takes only a second to do so. Although this process may use a minute of a section, there is no alternative. If you do not know the time you have spent on a critical question, you will either cut your time short and miss a question that you otherwise could have gotten, or you will spend too much time on the question.

Some people can keep track of time in their head but this comes at a price. When part of the brain is keeping track of time, you are partly distracted from the problem-solving process. In addition, there is a tendency to rush. Free up your problem-solving abilities by using an external device (your watch) to keep track of time. If you find this distracting at first, stick with it! Most people, even those who at first become very anxious by keeping track of time, find that with some practice, the watch gives them a sense of control over time and reduces anxiety.

When you practice, whether timed or untimed, keep track of time for each question and write the time down. On the actual exam, you do *not* write the time down. By doing this when you practice, though, you can review your results to see whether you spent enough time on certain questions or if you tended to rush.

Step 3: Understanding Timing

The test-taking assumptions that you have developed over the years make up a mental test-taking model that is counterproductive on the LSAT. To help you develop a more effective mental framework, consider the following hypothetical model. This model is for instructional purposes. Do *not* take this model literally!

During an LSAT there are many factors that will determine how you will do on each question. These include how much practicing you have done, how well you have learned testing strategies, how well you slept the night before, how alert or tired various systems of your body are, and how many or few distractions are in your mind. Imagine that, if you were going to take the LSAT tomorrow, you had an all-knowing perspective, an omniscient viewpoint, and could determine exactly how long it would take to get the correct answer for each question. An omniscient viewpoint might tell you, for example, that for question 17 you would get the right answer after 4 minutes and 17 seconds and not a second before. (This is hypothetical! In real life you clearly cannot know this.)

With this knowledge, see if you could plan the perfect timing strategy. The purpose of this exercise—given that you clearly cannot do this on a real test—is to understand the elements that lead to your best score. To keep things simple, suppose a test section had ten questions and you had fifteen minutes to complete it, and suppose that you could determine the following times (in minutes and seconds) needed to get each question right.

Table 1.1. Hypothetical Test Section

QUESTION	TIME	QUESTION	TIME
1	4:03	6	0:29
2	0:47	7	2:26
3	7:38	8	1:40
4	1:12	9	2:30
5	3:55	10	3:15

Which question would you do first? Would you start with question 1 or would you start somewhere else?

Which question would you do second? Third?

Do you see that you should do the quickest question first? That is question 6 at 0 minutes and 29 seconds. Because every question is worth one point, regardless of how difficult it is, to get the most points, just choose the quickest questions.

Following this logic, the second question is question 2 at 0 minutes and 47 seconds, then question 4, and so on. Here is a chart of the best timing strategy:

Table 1.2. Best Strategy for the Hypothetical Test

QUESTION	TIME USED	TIME LEFT
6	0:29	14:31
2	0:47	13:44
4	1:12	12:32
8	1:40	10:52
7	2:26	8:26
9	2:30	5:56
10	3:15	2:41
5	3:55 not enough time	

This would give you seven correct answers and you would guess cold on the remaining three questions. Notice that after question 10, there is not enough time left to get the next easiest question, question 5.

Suppose you need to get eight questions right in order to get the score you want. The above result is one short. How could you tweak it? Consider this carefully. What different way could you use your time to get one more correct?

If you try to save time on certain questions by going faster, you will get those questions wrong. For example, if, on question 9, you only spend 2 minutes, you will not get it correct. According to the omniscient viewpoint, question 9 requires a full 2:30. Do you see that there is no way to get more points?

Most of the elements of this hypothetical model *cannot* be applied to the actual test. You obviously will not know how long it will take you to do a question, nor can you compare all the questions and figure out definitively which one will take the least time. However, this exercise brings out several important points that you can use to your advantage. This strategy can be *simulated* in two steps: (1) choose the best (quickest) question to work on next, and (2) give each question the full time that it needs.

It *is* possible to simulate choosing the next quickest question. For each type of section, you will learn a specific strategy for doing so. The strategy is only an approximation. It would be too time-consuming to evaluate each question precisely. However, without a strategy for choosing, most people do the questions in order. They work on some difficult questions and leave some easy questions undone.

To approximate choosing the next quickest question, you need a strategy for quickly assessing questions. The strategy varies with the type of section. In RC and AR, you can choose by passage. In LR, you have to choose on a question-by-question basis. Because choosing questions is an approximation, you may find that you have chosen some hard questions. This is inevitable. It does not mean that your system for choosing is wrong.

It is also possible to approximate giving each question the time that it needs. Without a strategy for doing so, most people quit on hard questions too soon, leaving a trail of ten or fifteen wrong answers in their wake. Throughout this book, you will learn strategies for giving questions the time that they need.

Another lesson of the omniscient viewpoint model is that you do not need to decide how many questions you are going to attempt. If you set a goal, you will inevitably rush to meet it. Let the test tell you how far you can get. In the preceding example, the test told you that you could do seven questions and get all of them correct. If you tried to do eight questions, you would have gotten only six correct, at most. If you choose what to work on next and give each question the time that it needs, you can be confident that you are using your time in the best way.

The strategy of choosing what to work on and giving it the time that it needs is effective even for people aiming for scores in the upper 170s. This strategy does not *require* you to skip certain questions. It simply allows you to do so if necessary. The strategy of giving each question the time that it needs helps ensure that you do not lose even one point through a careless error.

Strategy for RC and AR Sections

There are some general strategies for choosing what to work on that are successful for both RC and AR, in which each passage is followed by multiple questions. These strategies are expanded upon in the RC and AR chapters. (For choosing what to work on in LR sections, see Chapter 2.) Scan through the test section before you begin working on it to identify which passages seem to be the most difficult. This can be done in 20 seconds or less. These are the passages you will do last, if at all. Choose whole passages, not individual questions. Within a passage there are some easy questions and some hard questions. However, it would be far too difficult and time-consuming to pick only the easy questions from all of the passages. Doing so would force you to work on even the hardest passages. Choosing passages that are easier and then working on all of the questions in that passage seems to work better for most people. In both RC and AR, there is a general tendency for the first passage to be easier and the last harder, but there are many exceptions.

Once you have ranked the four sets in terms of difficulty, start with the easiest set, and work every question in it before going on to the next easiest set. As you continue, it is important not to put an expectation on how many questions you will be able to do. Let the test tell you how far you can get.

As you approach the end of the time for a section, avoid the pressure to rush. If you start a new set with limited time left, it is important to choose the easiest questions within that set. A common error is to try to get to all of the questions in the set before time is called. Inevitably, if you do this, you will get most of the questions wrong. There are no extra points awarded for finishing a set! Continue to work carefully and to give each question the time that it needs. Be prepared to leave a set unfinished. Of course you will put cold guesses down for any question that you do not actually work.

Strategy for All Sections

What about giving each question the time that it needs? (This applies to LR, as well as RC and AR.) In our example of the omniscient viewpoint, you knew exactly what that time was. In reality, you do not. Obviously, spending ten minutes on a question is too long, even if you get it right. Spending only one minute is too short. Many questions cannot be answered in one minute. How long is acceptable to spend on a question?

Many people get an internal warning when they have spent more than a minute and a half on a question. This is probably based on college exams. For the LSAT, a cutoff of a minute and a half or two minutes is too short. The exact amount of time that will optimize your score varies among people. However, experience suggests that you should allow at least three minutes on hard questions and sometimes four or five. You will only have to do this on a handful of questions, but those are the very questions that will increase your score.

Assuming you are willing to spend some extra time on a question, how do you know when you have given a question the time that it needs? If you are getting close to four or five minutes and still have no inkling, guess and move on. However, if you guess and move on at two or three minutes, you will cheat yourself out of points. If necessary, rest your eyes for a few seconds, take a breath, and then do what it takes to be certain of your answer.

If you are spending three or four minutes on questions but still not getting them correct, you need to learn more patterns and strategies. Do this by reviewing the chapters and working untimed on practice questions.

Cold Guesses

There is no penalty for wrong answers on the LSAT, so put an answer down for all questions, including the ones on which you do not have time to work. On all sections of the test, stop when the monitor gives a five-minute warning and fill in all remaining bubbles. When you fill in bubbles, do not spend time looking at the questions. Some people are tempted to spend a few seconds trying to eliminate some answers on the questions for which they are putting a cold guess. This is not a good use of time. Either give a question the time that it needs to get it right or else fill in the bubble without looking at the question.

When filling in bubbles, choose one letter and stick with it. The odds for any of the five answer choices are virtually the same, although on some sections there may be a minuscule statistical advantage to D or E. Do not try to second-guess patterns of answers on the bubble sheet, such as whether there seem to be too few Cs, for example. Also, do not use a different letter for each answer in hopes of "shot gunning" your way to more answers. Stick with one letter.

After filling in the bubbles, there will be time left. Continue choosing questions and working on them until time is called. Working under such time pressure may seem hopeless but one more point can increase your scaled score, so make use of the last few seconds. Be ready to fill in the bubble for the final question the instant that the monitor announces the end of the section.

Perfect Timing Strategy Versus Perfect Testing Strategy

If you choose the next easiest passage to work on and give each question the time that it needs, you might not get the score you were hoping for but you will get the best score that is possible for you that day. Your goal is to become 100 percent efficient, meaning that you get every question that you work on correct. This is, of course, an ideal toward which you can aim, even though in reality you might not achieve it. It is very important to realize that you cannot increase your score by going faster or trying to get to more questions. If you save time on a question but get it wrong, you have wasted all the time you spent on it.

Suppose that you achieve close to 100 percent accuracy in timing but are only scoring a 155 and you want to score 165. Going faster will not gain extra points but learning the patterns of the test more deeply and practicing the strategies for getting correct answers will improve your performance and increase your score.

Step 4: Evaluating Your Timing

To evaluate your timing, look at the questions on which you actually worked, as opposed to questions on which you guessed cold. If you answered any of the questions on which you worked incorrectly, check how much time you spent on the question. If you spent fewer than three or four minutes, you may have stopped too soon. If you got three, four, five, or more questions wrong (on which you worked), you may have been able to get more questions right by working on fewer questions and taking more time on the remaining questions.

TIMING VARIABLES THAT INCREASE YOUR SCORE

1. Put cold guesses for unworked questions.
2. Choose what to work on instead of doing questions in order.
3. Sacrifice some questions to spend more time on a few other questions.

Write down the time you spend on each question for both untimed and timed practice. Look at each question you got wrong. How much time did you spend on it? If you spent only one to three minutes, you are stopping too soon. For questions that you answer incorrectly, consider what strategy you could have used to get the question right. The more comfortable you are with your strategies, the more likely you will allow yourself the extra time to get an answer correct.

On your official LSAT you *should* keep track of time but you should *not* write down times. When you do a practice test, you *should* write down your times for *each* question so you can evaluate your timing strategy.

Applying Timing Strategy

A good timing strategy for the LSAT is very different from a timing strategy in an academic class. On the LSAT, you are *not* trying to beat the clock. The difference between getting your average score and getting your best score depends on how you perform on one, two, or three more difficult questions on each section. Getting those questions right requires taking extra time with them. How do you know which questions those will be? You can recognize them because they will feel difficult; you will feel frustrated with them; you will feel as though you do not know how to answer the question; and you will feel pressured to move on to another, easier question. These are the signs that the very question you are working on is the one that can push your score up!

When you run into such a question, check your watch. If you have only spent a minute or two, take more time. If you cannot answer the question after four minutes, make your best guess. There is no guarantee that by working on a tough question you will get it right. However, if you work on five such questions, you may get two or three right, which is enough to increase your scaled score. Working longer on some difficult questions may mean cutting four or five others. However, you will get one point by guessing cold on the questions you cut.

As paradoxical as it may seem, many test takers learn to forget about time for the three to five minutes that they might need on some questions. This allows them to feel more relaxed and to think more clearly. This approach has been described as creating a "timeless five-minute bubble" around each question. While you are in the bubble, you do not need to think about time. When you are finished with the question you are working on, you can move on to the next question and create a timeless bubble around it. Put in terms of neuropsychology, concern about time tends to lock the brain into detail thinking mode and, in this mode, it is difficult for the brain to effectively problem solve. Learning to work from a global (big-picture) perspective allows the brain to set aside thinking about time and problem solve creatively.

If Your Watch Is Not Allowed

Monitors have the final say in what is allowed in the testing room. There is a small chance that, even though your watch meets the requirements, a monitor may not allow it. If a polite discussion does not change the monitor's mind, use a backup plan. Your backup plan is to use the clock in the testing room to keep track of time for each question. This can be hard if the clock is behind you. Explain to the monitor what you will be doing so he or she knows you are not cheating.

To keep track of time for each question, write down the time when you start working on the question. To figure how much time you have spent, you have to look at the clock and compare the current time to the starting time.

Summary of Your Timing Strategy

1. Set your watch to 12 o'clock to keep track of time for the whole section.
2. For RC and AR sections, in about twenty seconds scan the whole section and rank the passages from easiest to hardest. For LR, apply the timing strategy taught in Chapter 2.
3. For RC and AR, go to the easiest passage first. Do all of the questions in that passage—even the ones that are difficult—before going on to the next passage. Skip the passages you had agreed to cut.
4. For LR, go to the first question that you choose to work on and give it the full time that it needs.
5. Each time you begin a question, set your watch to 12 o'clock. As you are working on the question, if you start feeling that it is taking too long, glance at the clock. If you have spent less than four minutes, take more time with the question. If you believe you have done everything possible, you can guess and move on, even if it is less than four minutes. However, if in doubt, always err on the side of spending more time. At five minutes, if you are not close to an answer, guess and move on.
6. You do not need to keep track of time used for reading or setting up a passage. You only keep track of time while you are working on a specific question.
7. For RC and AR, if there is enough time to start a new passage but not enough to finish it, do not read the setup. Skim the questions and look for any that can be answered with only a quick reference to the setup.

8. When the monitor gives the five-minute warning, fill in bubbles for everything on which you have not worked, without spending time trying to work the questions. You will get one in five right by chance.

9. Use the remaining time to keep working till the end. Even one more right answer could increase your score.

⊙⎯⚷ LSAT STRATEGY

Why Is Strategy Important?

Mastering the LSAT is primarily a matter of strategy. Strategy involves learning how the LSAT is put together—the hidden patterns and agendas—and learning tools for getting even the most difficult questions correct. The LSAT does not test factual knowledge in any area. All questions are answerable solely based on understanding what the LSAT writers are looking for and on having the tools to critically compare and contrast answer choices that seem potentially correct.

LEARNING TO WORK QUICKLY WITH STRATEGIES

At first, new strategies can seem to take a lot of time. By giving yourself plenty of time to experiment with new strategies now, they will become second nature by the time you take your test, and you will be able to apply them quickly.

The Fundamental Agenda of the LSAT

Most LSAT takers report that they can narrow answers down to two possibilities and then have difficulty finding the correct answer. Many test takers assume that the test writers think one answer is somehow better, more clever, or more elegant than the other answer. It may seem that the test writers simply like their answer better. None of these impressions is accurate. In reality, the LSAT is designed so that one answer is correct and the other answer that you are considering is dead wrong. A wrong answer is wrong because it has a fatal flaw. A correct answer is correct because it can be *proven* to be correct.

The fundamental agenda of the LSAT is that a correct answer must be defendable—in court, if necessary—by specific words in the passage. If a person were to sue LSAC over a credited answer, the writers of the LSAT would be able to point to specific words in the passage to prove that their answer was indeed correct. Similarly, the writers of the LSAT could point to the fatal flaw in your answer choice. As you begin to study the LSAT, you may not at first spot the information that defends a certain answer and you may not spot the fatal flaw in the wrong answers. Once you become more familiar with the test, you will find that the defenses and the fatal flaws are easier and easier to spot. The primary goal of this book is to help you learn exactly this, both through the instruction in the chapters and through the thorough explanations of each test question.

The exact nature of defenses and fatal flaws varies among the three section types. Each chapter teaches the strategies you need for that section of the LSAT.

Below are important strategies that apply to the LSAT in general. Detailed strategies for each section type are covered in the chapter for each section.

Do All the Questions in a Set

When working on a passage with multiple questions, in RC and AR, do all of the questions in the set, even if some are difficult. Even in easier passages, some questions are hard. If one question in a passage stumps you, go on to others in that passage. After you have worked the other questions, it may be easier to answer the harder one. It is not necessary to do questions within the passage in order. Do not go on to the next passage until you have worked on every question in the current passage. Do not plan to come back to a passage later to finish it.

When to Guess

For all section types, if, at five minutes, you are not close to an answer, put down your best guess. Do not leave it blank. In guessing, be careful not to choose an answer just because it "seems" good. You will probably be falling for a distractor.

What is a distractor? The test writers build at least one wrong answer choice into most questions that is designed to mislead you. This distractor may look better than the real answer for various reasons. It may just make sense. It may use wording from the passage that seems familiar. It may contain numbers or patterns that seem related to the passage. It may draw on emotionally charged issues (e.g., *C. Everyone should have affordable legal representation*).

Unless you have a clear reason to choose one answer over another when you are down to two, it is safer to use a rule of thumb. A good rule is to choose the answer that is lowest on the page. Then you have a true 50:50 chance of being right. If you look for an answer that "feels" better, you will pick the distractor.

It should be very rare that you have to guess. Only guess if (1) you have used your full four to five minutes, or (2) you have exhausted all of your strategies. Never guess just because the question is hard and you want to save time. You need to give each question the full amount of time that it requires.

Use Your Eyes, Not Your Memory

Most test takers have a strong habit of reading the setup and a question and trying to work out the answer in their head, using their memory of what they read and their memory of what the question is asking. Your memory is not accurate enough to do a good job of this, especially during a long test.

Train yourself to continually look back at the printed information to get the facts you need. This takes a burden off of the processing functions of your memory. Sometimes people complain that they have to continually go back and forth between the questions and the passage, reminding themselves of what they have already read. In fact, this is the *best* way to process information accurately.

The minute you finish reading something and turn your eyes away, the memory of what you read begins to change. Details become blurred and the brain starts interpreting what it remembers. You can notice that you sometimes miss a question because you remembered information from the passage inaccurately.

After reading a question and considering the first answer choice, it is possible that you no longer remember accurately what the question was asking, especially if it is a complex question. Get in the habit of going back and briefly looking at the **question stem** (the statement of the question, not including the answer choices) again before going on to the next answer choice. The habit of relying on memory is a strong one and a difficult one to change. You may feel that answering the question from memory is faster or easier than going back and rereading again. It may be faster but it is also less accurate.

When reviewing a question you got wrong, look for signs that you remembered things inaccurately or did not go back and look for the facts. Notice if you misconstrued the question or the answer choice. These indicate a reliance on memory instead of real facts.

Orienting

Each LSAT question is based on certain information—either a long passage (RC), a short paragraph (LR), or a game setup (AR). It is important to orient yourself to this information. For each LSAT section there are specific ways to orient. Do not simply read the information superficially and then try to answer the questions. At the same time, a good orientation often means that you have not bogged down in reading too much detail. Orienting means letting the information "sink in."

Similarly, when you read a question stem, take time to orient to it. Ask yourself if you understand the question. Identify any confusion that you may have about the question. Consider what your strategy is going to be. Many errors are the result of not having oriented well to the passage and/or the question stem. Look for this error in your practicing and take more time to orient.

Use Visual Aids

This strategy is a corollary of "Use your eyes, not your memory." Memory is not very effective at keeping distinct categories separate, whereas a picture can compare and contrast two categories clearly. Much LSAT strategy depends on keeping two categories distinct, so using visual aids is a critical tool.

EXAMPLE

Consider the following confusing information about two vehicles owned by Maria. Her truck is red. She also has a Subaru. The Toyota has a camper top. Maria could sleep in the back of the Subaru if she sleeps sideways. The four-wheel drive is great for camping in the desert. The silver vehicle is cooler in the desert than the red one, even if it only has all-wheel drive. What Maria likes most about her oldest vehicle is that when she sleeps in it in the desert, which she does without being sideways, it has an air conditioner in case she needs it.

Answer this question without looking back. Does the four-wheel drive vehicle have air-conditioning? Even if you go back and review the words in the above paragraph, you will probably have to do a lot of mental work to keep the two categories—truck versus car—straight. Now let's look at how much clearer it is to organize this same information visually and graphically.

Use two columns to compare and contrast the two vehicles. A contrast between two categories is a fundamental pattern in the LSAT. The first sentence says the truck is red, so "truck" and "red" go in the same column.

truck	
red	

The next sentence shows that in contrast to "truck" and "red" there is "Subaru." This goes in the contrasting column. Notice that each line so far represents a certain quality. The first line represents body style. The line for Subaru represents make. This helps show what is known about each category. So far the body style and color of Subaru are not known.

truck	
red	
	Subaru

The next fact is "The Toyota has a camper top." Because "Toyota" cannot be "Subaru," this information goes in the first column.

truck	
red	
Toyota	Subaru
camper top	

The next fact tells us that it is possible to sleep in the Subaru, but only sideways.

truck	
red	
Toyota	Subaru
camper top	
	sleep only sideways

"The four-wheel drive is great for camping in the desert." This information is not related to anything else that is already known so far. Scan the rest of the facts for clues. The next sentence says that the silver vehicle is all-wheel drive. Because silver is not red, the sentence must refer to the second column. Because all-wheel drive is not four-wheel drive, four-wheel drive goes in the first column.

truck	
red	silver
Toyota	Subaru
camper top	
	sleep only sideways
four-wheel drive	all-wheel drive
great for camping in desert	cooler in desert

Does the last sentence provide anything new? "What Maria likes most about her oldest vehicle is that when she sleeps in it in the desert, which she does without being sideways, it has an air conditioner in case she needs it." Fill in the blank rows.

truck	
red	silver
Toyota	Subaru
camper top	
	sleep only sideways
four-wheel drive	all-wheel drive
great for camping in desert	cooler in desert

Using two-column visual organizer allows you to sort the information more reliably than doing it by memory. At the same time, a visual organizer allows you to compare and contrast information quickly and effortlessly. Can you now answer the question "Does the four-wheel drive vehicle have air conditioning?"

The visual aid also shows us what is not known. This is particularly helpful because memory tends to fill in blanks based on assumptions. Is the Subaru a sedan? You might have assumed so. You might have assumed it was not. The truth is that this information is unknown. The space in the second column that represents body type is blank. What else is unknown about the Subaru? The Toyota?

Whenever information needs to be compared or contrasted, use a visual aid, making use of the limited scratch space in your test booklet. Making columns is one of the most powerful organizing tools, but you can experiment with other ways of visually organizing information, such as using sketches and making circles to represent sets. If you make an error because you did not have the information organized well enough, do the problem again using visual aids.

Big-Picture Thinking Versus Detail Thinking

These are two distinct mental modes of processing information—detail thinking and big-picture thinking. These modes correspond roughly to left-brain and right-brain processing, respectively. Detail thinking is linear. It focuses narrowly on the problem and forges straight ahead, using calculations. Big-picture thinking is global and holistic. It does not focus on a goal but rather tries to see as much as possible. It steps back from the situation and looks at it freshly. For many people, the brain is not able to operate in these two modes at the same time.

Both of these processing styles are necessary for the LSAT. In fact, part of what the LSAT is testing is your ability to use these two styles at the appropriate times. Problem solving requires the ability to use both. Because the two modes typically cannot be used together, problem solving requires learning when to use each and how to switch between them.

Most people have a preference for one of these styles over the other. Even if you are naturally an intuitive thinker, you may find that because the LSAT involves logic, time pressure, and psychological pressure, you automatically switch into detail thinking. This may prevent you from using your greatest asset—the ability to do big-picture thinking.

Try to discover which of these modes comes most naturally to you. Notice when you are using big-picture thinking and when you are using detail thinking. Notice how you switch, or have difficulty switching, from one to the other.

Are You Stuck in Detail Mode?

One sign that you are stuck in detail mode is that you have failed to see the obvious. Consider this problem: Two pizzas are to be divided among seven people, while leaving a third of the total pizza for the next day. On the next day the remainder of the pizza is divided among five people but only after a quarter of the original amount is thrown away. How much is left? Suppose a test taker comes up with the answer of 2.17 pizzas. This person's detail thinking may have followed all of the details and come up with an answer. A big-picture perspective, however, indicates that there were only two pizzas to start with, so there cannot possibly be 2.17 pizzas left! There must have been a calculation error at some stage. Big-picture thinking is a reality check on detail thinking.

Are You Stuck in Big-Picture Mode?

It is also possible to be stuck in big-picture mode. One sign of this is not having the focus to deal with details. The person stuck in big-picture mode has a general sense of the passage but would rather guess on a challenging question and move on than deal with having to crunch numbers, organize information, and problem solve. Many of the testing strategies presented in this introduction are good tools for helping you dig more deeply into the details.

The Big-Picture Sandwich

How can you coordinate these two modes? Do not expect to use them at the same time. Most people find that this is not possible. You can, however, switch between them. One powerful tool for doing this is the big-picture sandwich. Start each problem from a big-picture perspective. Understand what you are dealing with and organize your plan of attack. Then switch to detail thinking to analyze the data. Finally, before leaving the problem, switch back to big-picture thinking to make sure your answer makes sense. During the process of solving the problem, you may also need to switch back and forth several times. Big-picture mode allows you to monitor how confident you are in the answer. If your confidence is low, you are not done.

Confidence Level

When you decide on a correct answer, you always have some sense of how confident you are in your answer, even if you are not consciously aware of that sense. As you come back to the big picture at the end of a question, monitor your confidence level. If you are not confident in your answer, you are not yet done with the question! One of the most common causes of wrong answers is ignoring your lack of confidence in the answer and moving on. To look at it the other way around, one of the most powerful tools you can use to pick up a point that you would otherwise have lost is to notice that your confidence level is low and to continue working on the problem.

Sometimes your confidence in your answer is low but you have eliminated all of the other answers. If you cannot defend your answer with confidence, that answer cannot be correct. In such cases, you have most likely already eliminated the correct answer and are left with two answers, neither of which is correct. By starting from scratch, you can win back an extra point.

Your Plan of Attack

On a typical question you will orient yourself to the information and then you will read the question stem and orient yourself to it. At this point, rather than simply diving into the answer choices, take a moment to strategize. Consider what your plan of attack is going to be. In some cases you need to go back to the passage to review information. In other cases you need to refresh your memory as to the main idea of a passage. Some problems require you to sketch out logical arguments. In some cases you will evaluate the answer choices in order and in other cases you will not. Taking a moment to consider your plan of attack is an orienting step. Do this after you have oriented to the question stem but before you start going through answer choices.

The Generic Way to Answer a Question

Use a systematic approach on every question. Many people simply read through a question quickly and then look at the first answer choice. This is not necessarily the best way to problem solve. Here is how the process can be broken down and made more systematic. The systematic process described below applies to the RC and LR sections of the test. The AR section has its own systematic approach, described in depth in Chapter 4.

Step 1. Orient to the Question Stem

After you have oriented yourself to the passage, read the question stem carefully, without yet looking at the answer choices, and orient to it. Is there anything confusing or ambiguous about it? Is it clear what the question is looking for? It is sometimes helpful to take a moment to mentally picture the situation that the question deals with. Many people feel that they should get through the question quickly in order to get to the "important" part—the answer choices. In fact, taking the time to be well oriented to the question can help you avoid many errors.

Step 2. Plan of Attack

Consider how to start working on the question. Do not simply start reading choice A. There is often a better way to start. Sometimes it is best to go back to the setup and clarify concepts and facts. Often it is helpful to create a sketch, or organize the information graphically. Sometimes there is specific information stated in the passage that will determine the answer. Find this first before looking at the answer choices.

Step 3. First Pass Through the Answers—Process of Elimination

After completing Step 2, make a first pass through the answer choices, eliminating only those answers that are clearly out. You are learning strategies that will allow you to evaluate answers in depth, but do not use those in-depth strategies during this pass. In-depth strategies require extra time. You might, for example, spend a lot of time carefully evaluating answer choices A through

D, only to find that answer choice E is obviously the right one. The time spent on A, B, C, and D would have been wasted. The first pass gives you a quick overview of the answer choices. Save in-depth analysis for the second pass.

Be conservative about eliminating answer choices at this point. Only eliminate answer choices that are clearly out. If there is any uncertainty, leave the answer in until the second pass. Answers can often be categorized as going in the right direction or the wrong direction. For example, if a question asks what would be true about Einstein, then the answer choice "He never came up with any original ideas" goes in the wrong direction. The statement "He was very smart" would go in the right direction but still might not be the correct answer because of other factors. Answers that go in the wrong direction are clearly out.

Step 4. Second Pass with In-Depth Analysis

For the remaining answer choices, use your strategies to determine the correct answer. There may only be two choices left at this point or there may be more. For each type of LSAT section there are many specific strategies that you can use to compare and contrast two answer choices. For AR questions, you will learn a complete system of logic that allows you to accurately find the correct answer. For RC and LR, the most powerful way to apply your strategies is through the **adversarial approach**, described below.

Use the two-pass approach on all RC and LR questions. For instructional purposes, the explanations of RC and LR questions in this book do not usually go through a two-step process but rather focus on the essential problem-solving strategies that you would use in either the first or second pass.

Marking Answer Choices

As you work through the answer choices in your two passes, use marks to indicate which answer choices are out, which ones are in but are weak options, and which answer choices are likely. Draw a line through the letter of answer choices that are out, use plusses or double plusses, and question marks.

Once you have determined a correct answer, circle it, as with answer choice E, and then write the letter of the correct answer next to the question number. This helps you be accurate as you transfer answers to the bubble sheet. See pages 159–161 for a more in-depth explanation and a diagram of this process.

The Adversarial Approach—The Secret Weapon for Finding the One Correct Answer

There are probably five, ten, fifteen, or more questions that you are getting wrong now but which you can get right with good strategy. These are the questions that will raise your score. These questions probably all have one thing in common. You get down to two possible answers but then choose the wrong one.

The adversarial approach is the most powerful tool for finding which of two answers is correct, particularly on the RC and LR sections. Here is how the strategy works.

When there are two answers left, most people like one answer better than the other and, at first, simply pick the answer that they like. When it becomes clear that they are often wrong, test takers begin to look more carefully at the two answers, comparing them and trying a little harder to evaluate them. When you find yourself doing this, notice that there is still a bias toward the answer that you liked in the first place. This bias often prevents you from being objective, so, despite your effort, you still get many wrong answers.

Even when you want to be more objective, it is difficult to do so. The power of our biases cannot easily be overcome. It takes a specific, active strategy to achieve objectivity. The strategy for this—the adversarial approach—is drawn from the American legal system.

In some legal systems, one attorney argues both sides of a case before the judge. It is that attorney's responsibility to understand both sides, evaluate them, and present a balanced perspective. In America, an adversarial system is used. Each side is represented by its own attorney. Each attorney focuses only on his or her perspective—either attacking or defending a position. By eliminating the constraint of being balanced, the system allows each side to aggressively pursue one point of view. It is then the judge's responsibility to synthesize both sides. In theory, the adversarial system results in a clearer picture of each side of the issue.

How does this apply to RC and LR? Suppose that you have eliminated choices B, C, and E. Choice A seems strong to you. Choice D seems unlikely. You can now apply the four steps of the adversarial approach. They do not have to be applied in a specific order.

(STEP 1) Attack the answer you like.

(STEP 2) Defend the answer you do not like.

(STEP 3) Defend the answer you like.

(STEP 4) Attack the answer you do not like.

Step 1 requires you to attack choice A, but choice A is the answer choice that you like. Similarly, Step 2 requires you to defend choice D, but you do not really believe that choice D is correct. Steps 1 and 2 are the most counterintuitive, but this also makes them the most powerful. If you can conscientiously attack the answer choice that you like and conscientiously defend the answer choice that you do not like, you will see the aspects of the issue that you missed before. It may or may not turn out that you were correct in the first place.

In Steps 3 and 4 you justify your original bias, which may turn out to be correct. However, you now do so in more depth. As you try to prove that choice A is correct, you may discover that it is difficult to do so. As you try to prove that choice D is incorrect, you may discover some merits to it. These steps, then, are also valuable. However, the most powerful aspect of the adversarial approach is in reversing your mental bias so that you can see what before was hidden by your blind spots.

It is not easy to reverse your bias. There is a strong tendency to slip back into defending the choice that you like and attacking the choice that you do not like. It may help to imagine that you are an attorney who will be paid a million dollars if you can prove that someone is innocent. You may deeply believe that the person is guilty but you have a strong incentive to prove him or her innocent. You may have to dig very deeply to find any basis for a defense but that is exactly what your job is.

One unexpected obstacle to effectively using the adversarial approach is the possibility of falling into a neutral position. Neutrality may sound "fair" but in this case it is not effective. If you try to see both the pros and cons of an answer choice, you will miss the extremes. To pursue the analogy above, you must leave "fairness" to the judge, whose role you will take on only after you have presented the extremes. Your first job is to be extreme.

By focusing all your attention on finding the defense for an answer, you see elements that you could not have seen before. The same holds true for the attack. By doing all four steps, you have the best chance of seeing all the points. As you apply this approach, you are not yet in the judge's position of weighing the pros and cons. That will come at the end. The most common error in applying the adversarial approach is falling back into the judge's position too soon, and therefore failing to attack from the extreme standpoint and defend from the extreme standpoint. If you continue to get wrong answers, work harder at attacking and defending from the extremes.

Ambiguity

Sometimes the wording in a question or answer choice is confusing. The wording may have two different interpretations.

EXAMPLE

You are responsible for collecting research information from three hospitals, two clinics, and five universities. Each institution must have its own unique data collection form.

Do you see the ambiguity? Are there three institutions or ten? It is important to identify ambiguity or confusion if it exists. Many people are resistant to feeling confused. They may hope they will catch on later. In fact, it is very helpful to notice confusing wording, identify why it is confusing, and then find a way to resolve the confusion.

In the above example, does creating a unique form for each institution require making ten forms or three forms? The word *institution* is ambiguous. "Hospital" could an example of one institution. Alternatively, the sentence could mean that Hospital A is one institution and Hospital B is another. How is the test taker supposed to know the correct interpretation?

The LSAT cannot contain a question that is truly ambiguous. There must be some evidence that shows which interpretation is intended. To deal with an ambiguity, first identify the two interpretations. Then ask which interpretation would be defendable based on the information given in the test.

Consider the rest of this passage.

EXAMPLE

Data must be collected within a week of the time it is compiled and must be delivered directly to the office of the research coordinator. Each of the ten institutions is responsible for double-checking the accuracy of its form. You are responsible for getting the signature of the head of staff at each hospital and clinic, but the universities do not need to have their forms signed.

The phrase "each of the ten institutions" defines how the word *institution* is being used.

The Default Multiple-Choice Question

A common cause of errors is misinterpreting the question stem. You may have understood the question stem when you started working on the question, but as you proceed, your brain can easily drift from what the question stem actually said to what can be called the default multiple-choice question.

> Find the correct answer to the following:
> (A) The moon is made of green cheese.
> (B) Three plus five is nine.
> (C) Earth revolves around the Sun.
> (D) Spinach is delicious.
> (E) All lawyers make more money than any doctors.

Most likely you chose answer choice C. What question were you answering? The default multiple-choice question is "Which answer choice is true in the real world?" Sometimes an LSAT question asks this but often LSAT questions are *not* asking the default question. As you orient to a question stem, ask yourself whether it is asking for a fact that is true or for something else. If it is asking for something else, be on guard not to slip into the default question.

Working Backward from Answer Choices

This is similar to the adversarial approach but not quite as rigorous. Test an answer choice by temporarily assuming it is correct. Would that result in any contradictions? Would the answer fit the information in the passage? Testing an answer choice can help you see things about it that you would not see otherwise.

Answers That Seem Too Easy

Some people eliminate an answer choice because it seems too easy or obvious. However, if the answer choice is defendable, it must be the correct answer. There *are* easy questions on the test.

The Voices in a Passage

RC and LR passages reflect the attitude and opinions of the author of the passage but they may also refer to the attitudes of other parties. The emotional and logical stance of a person is referred to as the person's voice. For example, if an author is excited about a new theory and feels that all of the evidence supports that theory, there will be wording in the passage that reflects these emotions and beliefs on the part of the author. If the author then quotes from a scientist who feels negatively about the new theory, then the scientist's voice is different from the author's. Some RC and LR questions require you to distinguish the voices in a passage.

Put Cold-Guess Answers for Any Question That You Do Not Work

As described earlier under Timing, there is no penalty for wrong answers, so fill in a bubble for each question, including ones that you do not have time to work.

Filling in Bubbles

When you fill in bubbles for questions that you *have* worked on, you can use one of several approaches. The approach you choose should be the one that prevents you from mistakenly filling in a wrong bubble.

Some people have to fill in the bubble immediately after getting an answer. This lowers the chances that you will fill in the wrong bubble because you only have to keep one letter in mind. On the other hand, it is more time-consuming because you have to go back and forth between the test booklet and the answer sheet many times.

On the other extreme, some people transfer all of their answers to the bubble sheet toward the end of the time for the section. This has the advantage of only going from the test booklet to the answer sheet once. It has the disadvantage that transferring so many answers at a time may lead to inaccuracy.

A middle ground is to do a certain number of questions, such as those on one or two pages, and then transfer answers. If you find yourself filling in the wrong bubble, transfer your answers more frequently.

If, on your actual LSAT, you find that you have transferred a block of answers incorrectly—in other words, all of your answers are one or two lines off of where they should be—you have some options. If there are only a small number of answers involved, you may need to take the time to thoroughly erase your original answers and reenter them on the correct line. If you need to do this, it will be important that you have written the letter of the correct answer next to the question number in your test booklet.

If there are so many answers off that taking the time to correct them would hurt your score, you can ask to have your answer sheet hand scored. If possible, make a note on the answer sheet to indicate where the numbers got off and where you got back on the correct numbers. As soon as the section is over, raise your hand to inform the monitor. The monitor may not respond to you until the end of that half of the test day, namely, at the break or at the end of the day. Let the monitor know what happened and that you would like to have your answer sheet hand scored. There have been cases in which the monitor has allowed a test taker to correct the bubbling right then, though you should not expect this. If your bubbling error is so severe that the sheet cannot be adequately hand scored, it may significantly lower your score. You may then need to retake the test, and you should inform the schools to which you are applying about the reason for your low score.

Always Look at All of the Answers

One of the most common causes of wrong answers is choosing an answer that looks good without having considered all of the answers. Even if you are confident in an answer, you should at least quickly look at the remaining answers. Otherwise, you may fall for a distractor. This is one of the most important strategies for avoiding errors. Train yourself to do this on every single question.

Questions with EXCEPT and LEAST

Questions that use the words "EXCEPT" or "LEAST" are logically complex. Consider the question "All of the following are brown EXCEPT . . ." Your attention will focus on the quality of being brown but the correct answer is something that is not brown. It is easy to get confused and choose something brown. When an LSAT question asks for an exception—for the opposite of what the test taker would normally look for—the word EXCEPT or LEAST is capitalized to draw your attention to it.

Orient to exception questions by reminding yourself that you are looking for four of whatever is expected, such as four brown things in the example above, and that these four are the wrong answers. The correct answer will be whatever is remaining when you identify the four (incorrect) brown answers. You can hold out four fingers to remind yourself. Use this strategy in conjunction with going back and skimming the question stem before looking at each answer choice. Notice if you have a tendency to stumble on exception questions.

Consider a question that asks "All of the following are good EXCEPT . . ." You might think that the correct answer must be something that is bad but this is not necessarily true. Four of the answer choices are good but the remaining choice may be neutral. The exception is not necessarily the opposite of the quality that defines the four other answer choices. It may just be the absence of that quality.

Stamina

The LSAT is a very long test. There is no question that you will get tired and that your brain will not be at its optimum at all times during the test. There are some simple things that you can do to maximize your endurance during the test.

Intense brain activity consumes oxygen. Combined with sitting still for hours, your brain will become oxygen-deprived. When you feel tired and your thinking is foggy, you can stretch and flex your arms and legs and yawn and breathe deeply. During the test you need to be moderately unobtrusive about this but frequent mild stretching and deep breathing will help you think more clearly.

Your eyes will also become overworked in the test. The eyes are involved not only in seeing what is on the page but in mental processing as well. When you have trouble focusing your attention, try closing your eyes, blinking them rapidly, or covering them with the cupped palms of your hand. Shifting your focus to a point in the far distance also can relax the eye muscles.

When you are tired, you may be more bothered by distractions. You should assume that you will have distractions during your test day and be prepared for them. It may help you practice for distractions by occasionally working on questions in a noisy or distracting environment.

An often unrecognized symptom of physical and neurological fatigue is an emotional one. Some people, partway through the test, start to feel discouraged. They may find themselves thinking "I don't care about this any more. I'm probably not supposed to go to law school anyway, so just please let this be over so I can go home and eat chocolate." If you start to have negative, discouraged thoughts, recognize it as a sign of fatigue. Stretch, flex, breathe deeply, blink your eyes, and keep going. It may help to tell yourself, "Of course, I'm supposed to go to law school. Get with it!"

During the week before your test, simulate the schedule of the test day. Keep a note card with approximate times of day that each section will start and finish, along with break times. No matter what you are doing—working, shopping, going to class, or actually working on the test—during the time that will be devoted to a test section on your actual test day, do not eat, drink, or use the bathroom. If you find that you have trouble following that schedule, such as needing to use the bathroom, getting hungry, or having low blood sugar, adjust your eating and drinking patterns.

Identify any areas of anxiety that you have, such as a fear of not finding the test center, of not waking up on time, or of not getting the score you need, and come up with a backup plan for each concern. Dealing with these concerns in advance may help you get a good night's sleep before your test.

Analyzing Your Testing Strategy

After completing a section, either timed or untimed, go over each wrong answer to determine which strategies you could have used to avoid the error. On the following pages is a list of possible errors to which you can refer, along with a worksheet for keeping track of your errors.

If you get a question wrong, look at it carefully. Although some errors may strike you as "careless," errors are usually not because of carelessness. They are the result of incorrect timing or testing strategy. Every error gives you a chance to learn how to approach the test more effectively. Use the checklist on page 42 to review the causes of errors. As you review an error, go back to the chapters in this book and look for the information that would help avoid that particular error.

⛭ LIST OF REASONS FOR ERRORS

1. **Did not use big picture.** Got lost in details. Did not step back to see the big picture. Missed obvious information because focus was too narrow.
2. **Time pressure.** Not careful enough because of feeling rushed to get on to other questions. Tried to do too many questions.
3. **Could not organize information.** Confused by complex details, facts, and concepts. Lacked tools to organize the information. Got lost partway through. Did not use visual aids—drawing, charts, columns—when needed. Did not create a systematic road map of how to solve the problem.
4. **Eliminated the correct answer.** Crossed out the correct answer.
5. **Misread question or facts.** Misinterpreted part of the question or information. Did not apply strategy for ambiguous questions. Did not orient to the question. Read something into the problem or made an unwarranted assumption.
6. **Spent less than three minutes.** Chose a wrong answer on a question that could have been gotten right with more time. Did not keep track of time. Felt hesitant to spend four or five minutes.
7. **Remembered something inaccurately.** Did not double-check the facts. Used memory instead of eyes. Rushed.

8. **Thought you had it right.** Did not take an extra moment to see if you missed anything. Did not challenge your answer or defend other answer choices.

9. **Did not read all answer choices.** Chose an answer without using the other answers as a double check. Tried to save time by not reading all answer choices.

10. **Did not check your confidence level.** Did not notice that you were not confident about the answer. Unsure of answer but did not want to take more time. Did not use double checking or big picture to increase confidence. Chose an answer you did not like because all of the others seemed wrong. Did not go back and start from scratch with all answer choices.

11. **Did not know what strategies to use on question.** Did not step back to see the big picture. Did not use diagram to organize the information. Did not use the adversarial approach. Did not work backward from answer choices. Did not use imagination or intuition to get new insights into the problem. Did not check whether some answers were too big or too small.

12. **Got uncomfortable or anxious and quit question too soon.** Let physical/ psychological discomfort level dictate your timing strategy instead of controlling time yourself. Did not use the tension between two answers to help you analyze more deeply (adversarial approach.)

13. **Fell for a distracter.** Chose an answer that felt right or that seemed good for a vague reason. Did not use the adversarial approach. Did not give the question enough time. When guessing, tried to justify one answer instead of using a random rule of thumb.

14. **Picked right answer but put wrong letter.** Do not yet have perfect strategy for transferring answers to the bubble sheet.

15. **Got down to two answers and picked wrong one.** Did not use the adversarial approach. Tried the adversarial approach but did not argue all the way to the end. Not able to turn energy of frustration into energy for analysis. Did not give the question a full four to five minutes. Did not use estimation. Did not focus on what the difference was between the two answer choices.

16. **Did not use process of elimination.** Could have gotten closer to an answer by eliminating the wrong answer choices.

17. **Mistake on game setup.** Misinterpreted or missed game conditions, other than if/thens.

18. **If/Then errors.** Incorrectly interpreted if/then conditions.
19. **Made logic errors on AR.** Was not accurate in diagramming options.
20. **Could not resolve an ambiguity.** Did not identify the two (or more) possible interpretations and ask which interpretation was defendable.
21. **Did not get the main idea.** Did not analyze the setup clearly enough for the big picture. Did not find the main dichotomies. Got too bogged down in detail. Not enough practice scanning for structure. Thrown off by a difficult topic.
22. **Missed author's tone question.** Did not see answers in terms of continuum.
23. **Other.** Describe.

Analysis of Wrong Answers

Use a worksheet like this to evaluate your wrong answers every time you do a test section. For each question you got wrong, put down the time you spent on it and the reasons you got it wrong. Choose your reason from the master list of reasons. If you choose "other," explain. For each error, review the strategy for avoiding that error. You do not need to include questions on which you guessed cold.

Note: This page may be photocopied.

🔑 ANALYSIS OF ERRORS

Example: Q #15   Time: 3:30   Reason: Eliminated correct answer.
                                                    Time pressure

Test # _____ Section: _____

Q # _____   Time: _____   Reason: _____

Q # _____   Time: _____   Reason: _____

Q # _____   Time: _____   Reason: _____

Q # _____   Time: _____   Reason: _____

Q # _____   Time: _____   Reason: _____

Q # _____   Time: _____   Reason: _____

Q # _____   Time: _____   Reason: _____

Q # _____   Time: _____   Reason: _____

Q # _____   Time: _____   Reason: _____

Q # _____   Time: _____   Reason: _____

Q # _____   Time: _____   Reason: _____

Q # _____   Time: _____   Reason: _____

Q # _____   Time: _____   Reason: _____

Q # _____   Time: _____   Reason: _____

Q # _____   Time: _____   Reason: _____

Q # _____   Time: _____   Reason: _____

Q # _____   Time: _____   Reason: _____

Q # _____   Time: _____   Reason: _____

Q # _____   Time: _____   Reason: _____

Q # _____   Time: _____   Reason: _____

Logical Reasoning | 2

^^^^^^^^^^^^^^^^^^^^^^^^^^^^^^^^^^^^

T he Logical Reasoning (LR) chapter teaches you the skills that you need to quickly and accurately answer LR questions. You will learn all of the elements listed above. This chapter includes breakdowns of sample LR passages and questions with complete explanations, so that you can put into practice the information that you learn in the chapter. At the end of the chapter is a practice LR section with complete explanations of answers.

Some tables in this chapter have complex breakdowns of important LR patterns. These tables are reference tools. It is not necessary to memorize them. Glance through them now. Return to them as you work on questions.

Read through the chapter carefully now. Then, as you work on questions, come back to the chapter to review the applicable strategies and patterns.

INTRODUCTION TO LOGICAL REASONING

There are two scored LR sections on every LSAT. If you get a third LR section, one of the three is an unscored, experimental section. There is no way to know which of the three is unscored. Do your best on all three. An LR section typically consists of twenty-five or twenty-six **passages**. Older practice tests may have sections with twenty-four.

Each passage begins with the **setup**, usually a short paragraph or a short dialogue between two people. The setup is followed by one **question stem**—a sentence that states the question. This is followed by five **answer choices**, labeled A through E (See Figure 2.1). Older tests may have setups followed by two question stems.

Setup --> Frank: Anyone who does not like fruit must not like people either.
Shannon: You are wrong. I like fruit but I do not like people.
Therefore, people who do not like fruit, do like people.

Question
Stem --> Frank's and Shannon's statements provide the most support for the claim that they disagree over the truth of which one of the following?

Answer
choices --> (A) People who do not like people also do not like fruit.
(B) People who do not like people do like fruit.
(C) People who like people also like fruit.
(D) People who like fruit may like people.
(E) People who do not like fruit like people.

Figure 2.1. Anatomy of an LR passage

The subject matter for the setup comes from a wide range of areas. Certain unusual topic areas appear with an unexpected frequency, such as "traffic" and "city council/municipal issues." A list of major topic headings is found in Table 2.1:

Table 2.1. Major Topics That Appear in LR Setups
and Their Relative Frequency

	Percent of LR Setups in Which Each Topic Appears
Physical Science (animals, anthropology, archaeology, astronomy, biology, ecology, garden/botany, geology, paleontology, physics/chemistry, weather)	21
Health (diet, food, health, medicine)	16
Social Science (ethics, history, philosophy, political science, psychology, sociology)	15
Business/Government (business, city council/municipal issues, employees) NOTE: city council/municipal = 5%; other business/government topics = 9%	14
Arts (art, literature, music, performing arts)	7
Transportation (aircraft, traffic, transportation)	7
Technology (technology)	5
Legal (legal)	4
Education (education)	4
Journalism (journalism, media)	3

To master LR, you need to learn four skills:

1. Understand the structure of logical arguments.
2. Understand the types of questions that the stems ask.
3. Understand the types of arguments that LR tests.
4. Master the strategies for determining exactly why one answer is correct and the other answers are incorrect.

🔑 TIMING STRATEGY

A strong LR timing strategy helps you (1) gain points by working efficiently, (2) avoid errors caused by working too quickly, and (3) reduce anxiety.

Adapting Timing Strategy to the Logical Reasoning

Review the general timing strategy described in the General Strategies chapter (Chapter 1). The timing strategy for LR is a little more complex than for RC and AR. Because LR is not divided into four passages, you cannot simply choose certain passages. Instead you must choose on which of the twenty-five or twenty-six questions to work.

To control your time on the LR, make two passes through the section. When timing begins, start on the first page and go through to the end of the section *choosing only a modest number of questions on which to work* (deciding the exact number is described below). You will pick a small number of the easiest questions and you will skip the rest. By the time you have finished this first pass, you have seen every page of the section, done the easiest questions, and left the hardest. Then, on your second pass through the section, go back to the first page of the section and pick the next easiest of the remaining questions, going page by page until the five-minute warning. At that time, you will put a cold guess down (choose one letter and fill in the bubble for that letter) for every question that is left and then continue working on a problem until time is called.

When you choose which question to work on or to skip, do so at a glance, using only a few seconds. When you fill in cold guesses for questions on which you have not worked, do not take time to look at the question or to try to eliminate answers. For each question, either work it thoroughly or fill in a bubble randomly.

How many questions should you work on in your first pass? How do you choose which questions to work on? Consider Sheila, a fictitious but otherwise typical prelaw student. Sheila usually scores from ten to fifteen questions correct on a timed LR section. She has never gotten fewer than ten questions correct under timed conditions. Sheila sets a **target** of eight questions for her first pass. Sheila's target is low enough that even on the most difficult LR section, and even when she is having a bad day, she can still get her target of eight questions. This allows her to work in a relaxed and careful way during her first pass.

When the timing for an LR section begins, Sheila starts with the first page. Because there are usually eight pages on the LR section, Sheila plans to work on an average of one question per page during her first pass. Sheila quickly scans the first page and chooses one question that seems relatively easy.

There is no guarantee that Sheila has in fact chosen the easiest question. She chooses at a glance and it is possible that the question may be harder than she thought. With practice, Sheila will be more accurate at finding easy questions.

When Sheila finishes with her first question, she turns the page and is looking at pages 2 and 3. She picks the two easiest questions on these pages. They may be on the same page. She keeps up her average pace of one question per page. Sheila knows that the first five questions of an LR section are typically easier than questions at the end. She may choose some extra questions from the first three pages. She also knows that the last five questions are usually the hardest. She may not choose any from the last five. By her eighth question, she has looked at every page of the section. She knows she has made an effort to work the easiest questions and avoid the hardest ones.

After her first pass, Sheila has time remaining, because she chose a low enough target number. She goes back to the first page, choosing the next easiest question, and continues page to page choosing the best question to work on. When the monitor gives the five-minute warning, Sheila fills in choice D on the bubble sheet for each question that she has not answered. Then she goes back to the test and keeps working. Using the last minutes well may raise her score.

When Sheila starts her second pass, she does not have any preconceived idea of how many more questions she will do. If the section is difficult and/or if she is having a slow day, she may only get to a few more questions. If the section is easy and/or she is having a great day, she may get to many more questions. Sheila lets the test and the testing conditions tell her how far she can get. If she rushes to get more questions, she gets many wrong and lowers her score.

If, as Sheila practices, she improves and is always getting at least fifteen questions right, she will change her target. Making her target twelve, instead of eight, allows her to choose one question from one page and two from the next, one from the third, and two from the fourth, and so on. It is not important exactly how many she does per page. She simply needs a simple plan for working on twelve questions during her first round.

Sheila may eventually be able to answer twenty or more questions correctly. Choosing twenty questions during her first pass is cumbersome. Instead, she changes her strategy. She will *cut* one question per page during the first pass, for a total of about eight questions. This guarantees that she can work in a relaxed way during the first pass. During her second pass, she goes back to the eight questions that she cut and chooses one more on which to work. Once she has carefully solved that question, she chooses another.

People who are untrained in timing typically start at the beginning and work every question in order until time is called. They are working on many difficult problems and leaving many easy ones. In theory, by making two passes, you choose the easiest, and leave the hardest, questions. In practice, you may end up working some hard questions and leaving some easy ones, but you will have greatly improved your efficiency.

Even though, statistically, the questions start out easier and become harder, it is not a good idea to simply start at the beginning and work questions in order. There are many difficult questions toward the beginning and many easy questions later. Get your best score by choosing for yourself.

How Much Time Should You Spend on Each Question?

Another difference between Sheila and untrained test takers is that untrained test takers rarely spend more than a minute and a half on a question. They rush to get to all of the questions and, as a result, get many questions wrong. Sheila has learned that, even though the average time she spends on a question is about a minute, she can increase her score by spending more time on a handful of more difficult questions, thus getting them right.

How you make decisions about the amount of time you spend on a question is probably the most important part of your timing strategy. Carefully review the general instructions on timing strategy in the "General Strategies" chapter (Chapter 1). Beware of the "average time per question" trap! Many people calculate that, for thirty-five minutes and twenty-five questions, there is a minute and a half per question, and they then allow themselves only that much time. This approach is based on several erroneous assumptions. One such assumption is that you are going to attempt every question in the section. For over 90 percent of LSAT takers, that is not the best strategy. Another assumption is that each question should be given the same amount of time. In reality, many questions take less than a minute and a half, so there is extra time left over for those questions that do take longer.

To implement a successful timing strategy, you have to know how much time you have spent on a question. This requires that you use a watch. Review the guidelines for using a watch given in the "General Strategies" chapter (Chapter 1). Also, review the guidelines for evaluating your timing strategy.

SUMMARY OF TIMING STRATEGY FOR LR

1. Scanning the first page of the section, choose an easy question and work on it. Most questions take about a minute but on some questions, you will take up to three or four minutes if necessary. Do not exceed five minutes.

2. Use your watch to keep track of time on each question by setting the hands to noon when you start each question.

3. Depending on your target number, choose another question on the first page or go on to the next page.

4. If you are looking at two facing pages, it is all right to choose more questions from one page than the other. It is all right to choose slightly more from among the first five questions and fewer or none from among the last five.

5. Continue working your target number of questions until you have gotten through the last page of the section.

6. If there is time left, go back to the beginning and choose one easy question. Continue this process as long as there is time left.

7. At the five-minute warning, fill in bubbles for questions not already answered.

8. Continue working on a question until time is called.

THE STRUCTURE OF AN ARGUMENT

The LR section tests your ability to understand and manipulate logical arguments. LR questions are *not* a test of your world knowledge, your ethics, your values, or your opinions about issues.

Before you study the types of LR arguments, it is important to understand the basic elements of any logical argument. Consider the following exchange:

> *George: All white cats are deaf, right?*
> *You: Sure, I guess so.*
> *George: And Little Binky is white, right?*
> *You: Yes, Little Binky is white.*
> *George: Aha! Then Little Binky is deaf.*
> *You: OK. You win.*

An arguer is trying to convince you of something that you do not already believe to be true. The arguer starts with facts that you already believe to be true (*all white cats are deaf* and *Little Binky is white*) and then establishes that if those facts are true, something else—something that you had not previously thought of—must, by virtue of the principles of logic, also be true (*Little Binky is deaf*).

Every logical argument must include both facts that are accepted as true by all parties and some new fact that is derived from the established facts.

Premises

The established facts that all parties must agree are true are called **premises**. In the argument above, the premises (P1 and P2) are:

P1: *All white cats are deaf.*
P2: *Little Binky is white.*

When George presents these premises and asks "Right?" you have to say, "Right." If you question a fact, for example by saying, "Wait. Who told you all white cats are deaf?" there is no longer a basis for an argument. This is an important principle. When a question stem says, for example, "Which one of the following, if true . . ." the stem is indicating that the answer choices are to be considered as premises. You cannot question them. It can be very tempting to cross out an answer choice that says something like "It is good for children to eat lots of candy" or "People should never say hello to a lonely person." However, when the answer choices are premises, you cannot evaluate whether they are true or not. You must accept them as true and consider how they affect the argument.

Likewise, if a question stem reads, "If the above are true, . . ." the stem indicates that the statements in the setup are to be considered as true premises. You cannot decide that some of the statements are not true.

Conclusions

When George applies logic to the two premises on which you and he both agree and comes up with a new fact, he is creating a **conclusion**. In the argument above, the conclusion (C) is:

C: *Little Binky is deaf.*

Many LR questions ask what can be concluded. To be concluded, a statement must follow from the premises and from valid principles of logic.

Assumptions

For LR, an **assumption** is a premise that is necessary to make an argument work but which is not stated. Test out the following possibilities. Which one is an assumption in George's argument?

> A. *All white cats are in fact deaf.*
> B. *You have seen Little Binky.*
> C. *Little Binky belongs to George.*
> D. *Little Binky is in fact deaf.*
> E. *Little Binky is a cat.*

Choice A is not an assumption. The fact that all white cats are deaf is a stated premise, not an unstated one. Choice B is irrelevant. It does not matter whether you have seen Little Binky or not, as long as you agree that Little Binky is white. Test choice C. Suppose Little Binky does *not* belong to George but rather belongs to Jacki. Does this destroy the argument? No. Therefore, choice C is not an unstated fact that is necessary to the argument.

Choice D is a stated premise. Test choice E. Suppose Little Binky were not a cat but a rhinoceros. What happens to the argument? It falls apart completely. The argument depends on Little Binky being a cat, a fact which was not stated. Choice E is an assumption in George's argument. When a real assumption is negated (e.g., making Binky *not* a cat), the argument is destroyed.

When an LR question stem asks "Which one of the following is an assumption in the above argument?" the word *assumption* is being used with the technical meaning described above. Note that this technical meaning is different from the meaning of *assumption* as used in casual conversation.

Inference

The term **inference** is also used in a technical sense in LR. Inference refers to a process, specifically the process of moving through premises and assumptions to a conclusion. In other words, the process of making a logical argument is *inference*.

The word *inference* also refers to the end product of the inference process, namely the conclusion. To infer means to arrive at the conclusion. Therefore, when an LR question stem asks "Which one of the following can be inferred?" it is asking what can be concluded. Do *not* apply the casual meaning of the word *infer* when working LR questions. In a casual sense, infer could mean "What might you read into this?" or "What else might be true?" In LR, the word *infer* must refer only to what can be concluded through valid logic based on given premises. An inference is a statement that can be defended as being true. An inference need not be the *main* conclusion of an argument—only *a* conclusion.

Valid Logic

There is a small but critical step between George's establishment of the premises and his presentation of the conclusion. George applied logic to the premises. Specifically, George used the principle that if all members of a set have characteristic C and if individual M is a member of that set, then individual M also has characteristic C.

There are many forms of valid logic. Consider the argument:

> Staci: I played a wide variety of sounds while Little Binky was playing
> in the living room and Little Binky did not respond to any of them.
> Therefore, there is a significant chance that Little Binky is deaf.

The conclusion is similar to George's but follows different logic. Staci's logic is based on the definition of deafness and on experimental results.

When you evaluate a logical argument, consider not just the conclusion of the argument but also the premises upon which it is based and the type of logic that is used to move from the premises to the conclusion. Two arguments may reach identical conclusions and yet proceed in completely different ways.

Flawed Logic

The LR section also tests your ability to identify when an argument is *not* valid and why. Many LR questions present flawed arguments. There are two ways that an argument can be flawed. The argument may use a valid type of logic but apply it incorrectly. Alternately, the argument may use logic that is inherently flawed.

Consider George's argument about Little Binky. Without the assumption that Little Binky is a cat, George's argument is flawed because he does not establish that Binky is a member of the set of white cats. His logical principles are still valid, but he would not be applying them appropriately.

In the following argument, the logic itself is flawed:

> Jason: My cat was named Little Binky and was deaf, so your Little
> Binky is also deaf.

Jason's underlying logic is that if two individuals have the same name, they must have the same characteristics. This is not a valid logical principle.

TYPES OF ARGUMENTS

This section breaks down the types of valid and flawed logic. You will learn diagramming tools and common logic concepts—such as cause and effect and analogy—that are tested in LR questions.

Valid Arguments

There are two broad categories of logical arguments—deductive and inductive. You need to use different tools for working with these different categories.

Deductive Arguments

For the LSAT, deductive arguments are arguments that present absolute rules:

> *If you go to the store, you will be late for school.*
> *All baseball players have red sports cars.*

Do you see how the above arguments are absolute? If you go to the store, there are no options. You *will* be late. If someone meets the condition of being a baseball player, that person *does* have a red sports car. Deductive arguments are meant to be taken as inviolable rules.

Deductive arguments deal with an idealized universe in which certain relationships are true with absolute certainty. Deductive logic is almost mathematical. Deduction is not concerned with your opinion, with alternate options, or with what is fair. Deductive arguments require you to understand and apply absolute rules in a logically precise way.

Compare the previous arguments with these nondeductive statements:

> *If you go to the store, you might have a hard time catching the bus to school.*
> *A lot of baseball players seem to like fancy cars.*

These nondeductive statements do not make an absolute prediction. You may or may not make it to school on time if you go to the store. A baseball player may or may not have a fancy car. These statements are about the real world, not about the idealized world of absolute rules to which deductive arguments refer. Even though the above examples are fairly obvious, it can sometimes be difficult to distinguish a deductive argument from a nondeductive (inductive) one. Consider:

> *My friends and I go to the lake on the Fourth of July. We play tennis*
> *or volleyball but we never play football.*

This sounds like a conversational, real-world inductive setup. In fact, though, it presents absolute rules, which can be expressed in a condensed notation:

> Rule 1: *If "Fourth of July," then "lake"* and
> Rule 2: *If "Fourth of July," then "tennis or volleyball and*
>   *not football."*

To work with deductive arguments you often need to diagram or symbolize them. The two main types of deductive arguments require two different diagramming systems. The two types are **set** arguments and **if/then** arguments.

Set Arguments

Set arguments establish groups, or sets, of people or objects and then state certain characteristics of members of the set. In the argument *All baseball players have red sports cars,* the set is *baseball players* and all members of that set have the characteristic of owning a red sports car.

A set argument can be diagrammed by drawing a circle to represent the set, as shown in Figure 2.2. The arrow points to the characteristic that is true for all members of the set. The rectangle around the diagram represents the boundaries of the logical "universe." In other words, the diagram can be interpreted as saying that baseball players are a subset of the universe. You do not need to draw the rectangle in your diagrams but the rectangle is useful for learning purposes.

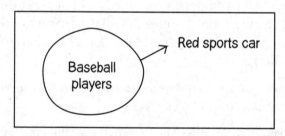

Figure 2.2. Circle diagram representing a set argument

Set arguments may show complex relationships between two or more sets:

> *Any small business is an entrepreneurial venture. All entrepreneurial ventures are risky. John's business is a small business. Therefore, John's business is risky.*

In this example, *small business* is a set and so is *entrepreneurial venture*. What is the relationship of these two sets?

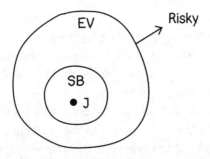

Figure 2.3. Small business (SB) is a subset of entrepreneurial venture (EV). John (J) is a member of SB and therefore of EV.

Small business is a subset of entrepreneurial venture. In Figure 2.3, the circle representing small business falls completely within the circle representing entrepreneurial venture. John's business falls in the category *small business* and is represented by a dot in the SB circle. Thus, John's business has the characteristic *risky*. Consider:

> *Any small business is an entrepreneurial venture. All entrepreneurial ventures are risky. Greta's business is risky.*

How would you diagram this? The two circles are the same as in Figure 2.3. Where would you put the dot for Greta's business? What do you know about Greta's business? Because it is risky, it is *possible* that it is a small business, in which case Greta's business can be placed within the small business circle. However, it is also possible that Greta's business is not a small business.

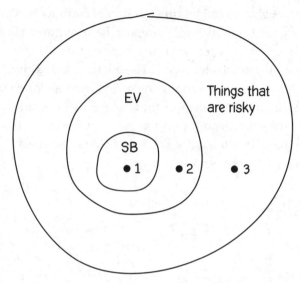

Figure 2.4. Circle diagram representing Greta's business. Dots 1, 2, and 3 represent the three possible locations for Greta's business.

In Figure 2.4, the circles for small businesses and entrepreneurial ventures are shown as a subset of all things that are risky. Dot 1 represents the case in which Greta's business is a small business. Dot 2 represents the case in which Greta's business is not a small business but is an entrepreneurial venture. Dot 3 represents another possibility—that Greta's business is neither a small business nor an entrepreneurial venture. It is simply something else that is risky.

In actuality, the argument does not provide enough information to determine where Greta's business should be placed. It is important to know that you do *not* know where Greta's business goes. An LR question might ask the following:

EXAMPLE

Which one of the following statements can be inferred about Greta's business?

(A) It is a small business.

(B) It is an entrepreneurial venture but not a small business.

(C) It is not an entrepreneurial venture.

(D) It is a small business but not an entrepreneurial venture.

(E) It might be a small business.

Choices A through C could be true but do not have to be. Choice D cannot be true. All small businesses are entrepreneurial ventures. Choice E might strike you as being a nonanswer. Anything *might* be a small business. However, choice E is the only defendable answer. The question tests your ability to distinguish what is known, what is not known, and what might be true.

With any set argument, remember that, whereas all members of a set may have a certain characteristic, it is possible that other elements in the universe may also have that characteristic. Just because Greta's business is not a member of EV does *not* mean that it is not risky.

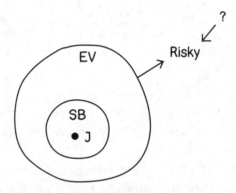

Figure 2.5. Remember that there can be other elements in the universe (shown by the question mark) that have the same characteristics as a set.

Set arguments are not very common on the LR but are easy to diagram. Diagram a set argument in a question that asks you to find a parallel argument with the same structure.

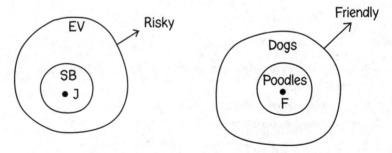

Figure 2.6. Parallel set arguments with different content but the same structure.

In Figure 2.6, the diagram on the right represents the statement *All dogs are friendly. All poodles are dogs. Fido is a poodle. Therefore, Fido is friendly.* The structure of the two arguments is the same, though the content is different.

If/Then Arguments

If/then arguments are the second type of deductive argument used in LR questions. If/thens are used in many LR questions, as well as in the Analytical Reasoning section, so it is important to study them carefully. If/then arguments are not diagrammed with circles but rather by symbolizing the if/then statements, for example, *If A, then B.*

The anatomy of an if/then argument. An if/then argument states an absolute rule about the universe. *If it rains, the sidewalk will be wet.* The if/then argument relates two events:

1. raining, and
2. the sidewalk being wet

One of the two events is the **determining factor**. The other is the **result** that must occur if the determining factor takes place. The determining factor usually occurs first in time and the result usually occurs later in time. In the above example, the determining factor is *raining* and the result is *the sidewalk being wet.* Remember that this is an absolute rule. If the determining factor occurs, the result *must* occur.

The if/then argument above can be symbolized as:

If rain → *wet*

The left side of this expression—*If rain*—expresses the determining factor. The right side expresses the result. This is a natural way to write the if/then because, reading from left to right, the event on the left happens first and the event on the right happens second. This left-to-right order is referred to here as the **standard** form. The arrow represents the word *then*. The words *rain* and *wet* are condensed versions of the more complex statements *it rains* and *the sidewalk will be wet.* It is more efficient to use a condensed shorthand rather than the entire statement.

A complete if/then argument gives you an if/then rule and then tests you to see if you can apply the rule. For example:

> **The rule:** *If it rains, the sidewalk will be wet.*
> **The test:** *It is raining. What must be true?*
> **The answer:** *The sidewalk will be wet.*

Symbolically, a complete if/then argument might look like this:

> *If rain* → *wet*
> *Rain*
> ∴ *wet*

The symbol ∴ stands for the word *therefore*. The above shows the three steps separately but such a statement is usually written as two lines, with the second and third steps combined:

> *If rain* → *wet*
> *Rain* ∴ *wet*

The first line is the rule. The second line starts with the test case—*there is rain*—and ends with the result—*wet*. The complete if/then argument can be read as *If it rains, the sidewalk will be wet. It is raining. Therefore, the sidewalk will be wet.*

Valid and invalid variations on an if/then. The previous argument is clearly valid. Given the rule that if it is raining, then the sidewalk will get wet, and given the fact that it is raining, the sidewalk will get wet. However, what if the test case is not so simple? Try the examples below:

> **The rule:** *If it rains, the sidewalk will be wet.*
> **The test:** *It is <u>not</u> raining. What must be true?*
> **The answer:** *?*

Or

> **The rule:** *If it rains, the sidewalk will be wet.*
> **The test:** *The sidewalk is wet. What must be true?*
> **The answer:** *?*

Or

> **The rule:** *If it rains, the sidewalk will be wet.*
> **The test:** *The sidewalk is <u>not</u> wet. What must be true?*
> **The answer:** *?*

Do you feel confident in your answers? It is extremely important to be able to distinguish which variations on an if/then statement are valid and which are invalid. Both the LR and the Analytical Reasoning sections test you on this.

Consider the above examples, using symbols. The first example says:

> **If rain** → **wet**
> *–rain* ∴ ?

Note the negative sign in front of the word *rain*, indicating *not rain*. You may be tempted to say "*–rain ∴ –wet.*" Is this valid? In this universe in which rain must result in the sidewalk being wet, is it true that if it does not rain, the sidewalk will not be wet? It is *not* true. There can be other factors that cause the sidewalk to be wet. Perhaps the sprinkler was on.

What about the next statement?

> *Wet ∴ ?*

It is tempting to say that if the sidewalk is wet, it must have previously rained. However, this is not valid, for the same reason. If the sidewalk is wet, it could have been because of a different cause, such as the sprinkler.

Finally, there is the third statement:

> *–Wet ∴ ?*

If the sidewalk is not wet, is it true that it did not rain? In this case the answer is yes. If the sidewalk is not wet, it could not have rained because if it had rained, the sidewalk would be wet. This final variation on the original if/ then statement *If rain → wet* is a valid variation and in fact is the only valid variation.

The variations that you just read about can be represented generically as:

1. *If A → B*

    A ∴ B (Valid)

2. *If A → B*

    –A ∴ –B (Invalid)

3. *If A → B*

    B ∴ A (Invalid)

4. *If A → B*

    –B ∴ –A (Valid)

Look carefully at these four variations. In the first one, the second line simply repeats the first line, and is thus valid. In the second variation, both sides of the first line are negated in the second line. The *A* in the first line becomes *not A* (*–A*) in the second line, and similarly for the *B*. This is not valid logic. It may sound reasonable to say that if rain makes the sidewalk wet, then not raining makes the sidewalk dry but this is not valid and the LSAT tries to trap you into this error.

In the third example, the two sides of the original are switched in the second statement. The *B* is moved to the left side and the *A* to the right side. This is also an invalid variation. *If the sidewalk is wet, it must have rained, right?* Wrong. Do not fall into the trap.

So far the variations have either negated the elements or switched them from left to right. The final variation does both. In moving from the first line to the second line, it switches the elements from left to right and it also negates each of them: –*B* ∴ –*A*. This is a valid argument. To summarize, when you start with an if/then statement in standard form, negating both sides is not valid. Switching the sides is not valid. However, doing both does result in a valid statement:

If A → B
–*B* ∴ –*A*

This variation is called the **contrapositive**. Every if/then statement has a contrapositive and the contrapositive is also a valid statement. The contrapositive reverses the two sides of the standard if/then and negates them. Consider:

If you don't eat, then you will be hungry.

Or written symbolically:

If –eat → hungry.

Create the contrapositive. *Hungry* must go on the left and *eat* must go on the right. Negating *hungry* results in

–hungry ∴

but how do you negate *–eat*? It already has a negative in front of it. To negate a statement that originally is negative, turn it into a positive:

–hungry ∴ *eat*

If you are not hungry, you must have eaten because if you had not eaten, you would be hungry.

If you have trouble remembering which variations are valid and which are invalid, try using a real-world if/then statement, such as *If you do not take the LSAT, you will not get into law school.* If you test out the variations on this statement, you should find that it is intuitively obvious whether they are true or not. For example, if you do not remember whether negating both sides is valid or not, test the statement *If you do take the LSAT, you will get into law school.* This is intuitively untrue and so you have proven to yourself that negating both sides does not create a valid statement.

Creating a standard if/then. The LSAT presents if/then statements in words, not in symbols. Sometimes the wording is easy to understand, such as *Anyone who takes physics in the fall must take organic chemistry in the spring.* However, in other cases the wording is very complex and difficult to understand, for example, *The empire will crumble only if the educated become complacent,* or *The Tigers will win the tournament unless the Coyotes replace their team captain.* For the untrained test taker such wording can be intimidating, if not impossible, to analyze. However, you can use a simple, three-step process to easily break down any if/then statement. Apply the following three steps to the statement *The empire will crumble only if the educated become complacent.*

STEP 1 **Identify the two elements that are being related.** The two elements, in abbreviated form, are *empire crumble* and *educated complacent.*

STEP 2 **Determine which one happens first (or is the determining factor) and which one happens second (the result). Create an if/then statement with the determining factor on the left and the result on the right, leaving a little space before each.** The complacency of the educated seems to be the cause and the crumbling of the empire seems to be the result:

> *If (blank) educated complacent* → *(blank) empire crumble*

STEP 3 **Determine whether it is the presence or the absence of the determining factor that is important. Complete the if/then by entering any needed negative signs.** At this point you must determine whether the statement is saying that the fact of the educated becoming complacent guarantees that the empire will crumble or that as long as the educated do not become complacent (the absence of *educated complacent*) the empire will not crumble. If the answer is not clear, use the example of the LSAT and law school by creating parallel language. In other words, create a true statement about the LSAT and law school using the wording *only if.* You would have to say something like *You will get into law school only if you take the LSAT.* Does this imply that if you take the LSAT, you will get into law school? No. Therefore, it is the absence of the LSAT and the absence of *educated complacent* that determines *not law school* and *not empire crumble:*

> *If –educated complacent* → *–empire crumble*
> (compare with *If –LSAT* → *–law school*)

We have taken the statement from Step 2 and entered in negative signs. The result is a valid if/then statement in standard form. Create the contrapositive:

Empire crumble ∴ *educated complacent*
(compare with *law school* ∴ *LSAT*)

The empire crumbled, therefore the educated must have become complacent. You got into law school. Therefore, you must have taken the LSAT.

Special if/then wording. In the example above you analyzed an if/then statement that used the wording *only if*. There are two other wording variations with which you should be familiar—the wording *unless* and the wording *if and only if*. Try to memorize the interpretation of these wording variations. However, if you do forget how to interpret them or become confused about their interpretation, you can (1) apply the three steps and (2) use a parallel example, such as the law school and LSAT example, to figure out the meaning.

The word *unless* is easy to interpret. Simply translate *unless* into *if not*:

*You will not get into law school **unless** you take the LSAT.*
*You will not get into law school **if** you do **not** take the LSAT.*

The word *unless* indicates that it is the absence of the determining factor that predicts the result. The absence of taking the LSAT guarantees that you will not be accepted. This strategy will work for all instances of *unless*. The *unless* statement above does not predict what happens if you *do* take the LSAT.

The expression *only if* also indicates the absence of the determining factor. However, an *only if* statement has a different construction from an *if not* or *unless* statement. Compare:

*You will **not get into** law school **if** you do **not take** the LSAT.*
*You will **not get into** law school **unless** you **take** the LSAT.*
*You will **get into** law school **only if** you **take** the LSAT.*

All of the statements say *The absence of LSAT leads to the absence of law school* but use different forms:

If absence of A, then absence of B.
Unless presence of A, absence of B.
Only if presence of A, presence of B.

Do not worry if the wording variations seem confusing. Use the three-step approach and the example of LSAT and law school to understand any complexly worded if/then statement. For *only if* statements, you can also use an easy strategy. When you read a statement such as *Only if you eat your dinner will you get dessert*, think of it as being followed by the statement "Otherwise, not."

> *Only if you eat your dinner will you get dessert. Otherwise (if you do not eat your dinner), not (you will not get dessert).*

This is the same as saying

> *If not eat dinner → not dessert,*

which is the correct interpretation.

In terms of *A* and *B*, the statement *Only if A, then B* is equivalent to

> *Only if A, then B. Otherwise (if not A), then not (not B),*

which is equivalent to

> *If –A → –B.*

The logic becomes a little more challenging if the *only if* statement itself already contains a negative. Consider *Only if you do not fail the exam will you graduate*. Break this down using the "otherwise" method:

> *Only if you do not fail the exam will you graduate. Otherwise (fail the exam), not (not graduate).*
> *If fail the exam, then not graduate.*

Notice that the *otherwise* phrase negates the negative expression *not fail* and turns it into the positive, *fail*. In this complex logic, it is the absence of *not failing* that is the determining factor. Using the *otherwise* method is easier if you put the *only if* part of the sentence first.

The third wording variation for if/thens is *if and only if*. Consider the statement *If, and only if, you are accepted to law school will you start law classes in the fall*. This statement includes an *only if* but also includes an *if*. It is equivalent to saying:

> *Only if you are accepted to law school will you start law classes in the fall*

AND

> *Getting accepted to law school DOES guarantee that you will start law classes in the fall.*

In other words, *If you do not get accepted, you will not start* AND *If you do get accepted, you will start.*

Thus, an *if and only if* statement actually consists of two distinct if/then statements. In symbols, an *if and only if* statement reads:

$$If -A \rightarrow -B$$

AND

$$If A \rightarrow B$$

These two statements cover all the possibilities. If A occurs, you know what happens. If A does not occur, you know what happens.

Compare the three wording variations in Table 2.2.

Table 2.2. Special If/Then Wording

	Wording	**Symbols**	**Logic**
unless	Unless A, then not B	If $-A \rightarrow -B$	Absence of determining factor predicts absence of result.
Only if	Only if A, then B	If $-A \rightarrow -B$	Absence of determining factor predicts absence of result.
If and only if	If, and only if, A, then B	If $-A \rightarrow -B$ If $A \rightarrow B$	Absence of determining factor predicts absence of result. Presence of determining factor predicts presence of result.

If/then logic can quickly become overwhelming and confusing. If you find yourself becoming lost in the words, go back to the three steps and identify:

1. What are the two factors?
2. Which one is the determining factor?
3. Is it the presence or the absence of the determining factor that predicts the result?

Also, you can use the relationship between taking the LSAT and law school to figure out *unless* and *only if* statements and you can use the relationship between being accepted to law school and starting classes in the fall to figure out *if and only if* statements.

Triggers. The determining factor was defined earlier as the one element (of the two elements that are being related in the if/then) that determines the result. In the LSAT and law school example, LSAT is the determining factor. In order for you to put this determining factor to use, though, you have to know whether it is the presence of the LSAT or absence of the LSAT that leads to a result. Because it is the absence of the LSAT that leads to the absence of being accepted to law school, we can call the absence of the LSAT (*–LSAT* or *not LSAT*) a **trigger**. A **trigger** is an expression in an if/then statement that guarantees a certain result. In the statement

If *–LSAT* → *–law school*

the term *not LSAT (–LSAT)* is a trigger. It guarantees the result *not law school.* Now consider the contrapositive:

law school ∴ *LSAT*

ABOUT IF/THEN NOTATION

The therefore sign (∴) may be used instead of the then sign (→) when the element on the left occurs after the element on the right. The statement

B ∴ A can be read as B, therefore A must have previously taken place.

In this statement, *law school* is a trigger. If you are accepted to law school, it is guaranteed that you have taken the LSAT. For any if/then statement, if you write out both the statement and the contrapositive, the elements on the left side are always triggers and the elements on the right side are *not* triggers (Table 2.3).

Table 2.3. Triggers and Non-Triggers

Triggers	NOT Triggers
Not LSAT	LSAT
Law school	Not law school

If you feel comfortable with the following shortcut, you can determine the triggers just from the standard if/then statement, without writing out the contrapositive. The element on the left is a trigger. The negation of the element on the right is a trigger. (Remember that the negation of a negative is a positive.) The element on the right is not a trigger and the negation of the element on the left is not a trigger. In the statement and contrapositive below, the triggers are shown in bold:

$$If\ A \rightarrow B$$
$$-B \therefore -A$$

Triggers: $A, -B$

Non-triggers: $-A, B$

Use triggers to your advantage. Consider a passage that begins:

> Anyone who eats cheese regularly does not have a calcium deficiency. John does not eat cheese regularly.

The first sentence gives you the rule. The second sentence gives you additional information. You may need to determine what, if anything, can be validly concluded about John, given that he does not eat cheese regularly. The standard statement and the contrapositive are:

> If **cheese** → –calcium deficiency
> **Calcium deficiency** ∴ –cheese

The two triggers (bolded) are on the left: *cheese* and *calcium deficiency*. Is the information given about John a trigger? No. Not eating cheese does not match either of the triggers. This tells you that there is no further conclusion you can derive about John. Now consider the variation:

> Anyone who eats cheese regularly does not have a calcium deficiency. John does not have a calcium deficiency.

This new statement about John (*not calcium deficiency*) is still not a trigger. You still cannot conclude anything else about John. Next consider:

> Anyone who eats cheese regularly does not have a calcium deficiency. John has a calcium deficiency.

Calcium deficiency is one of the triggers. It predicts that John has not eaten cheese regularly. Consider the following:

> Anyone who eats cheese regularly does not have a calcium deficiency. John eats cheese regularly.

Eats cheese is a trigger. You can conclude that John does not have a calcium deficiency. To summarize, the elements on the left of the if/then and the left of the contrapositive are triggers. If you are given a trigger, you can come to a new conclusion. The elements on the right are not triggers. You cannot conclude anything new from them.

PRACTICE EXERCISE 1

For each if/then statement below, identify the two elements that are triggers. The answers are below.

1. If rain → wet

2. If clean plate → dessert

3. If –homework → fail

4. If –work → –money

5. If A → B

For an *if and only if* statement—which contains two distinct *if/thens*—all of the elements and their negations are triggers:

> If A → B
> If $-A$ → $-B$

Do you see why *A, not A, not B*, and *B* are all triggers when both of the statements above are given?

A trigger can predict forward or backward in time. If you are accepted to law school, you must have previously taken the LSAT.

Answers to Practice Exercise 1:

1. rain, –wet

2. clean plate, –dessert

3. –homework, –fail

4. –work, money

5. A, $-B$

Necessary conditions versus sufficient conditions. You will see the terms **necessary conditions** and **sufficient conditions** on some LR questions. In questions that ask you to identify a logical flaw, an answer choice may say:

> *takes a condition necessary for X to be a condition sufficient for X*

or

> *treats a condition sufficient for X as a condition necessary for X*

Consider the statement *If you eat ice cream, you will gain weight.* Eating ice cream is sufficient to guarantee that you will gain weight. However, is eating ice cream necessary for you to gain weight? No. You could gain weight in other ways. Consider the general statement:

> If A → B

The element *A* is sufficient to guarantee that *B* will take place. However, the element *A* is not necessary for *B* to take place, because other factors could cause *B*. Consider the example *If it rains, the sidewalk will get wet:*

> If rain $\rightarrow$ wet

Rain is sufficient to make the sidewalk wet. However, it is not necessary for it to rain for the sidewalk to be wet. The sprinkler may have run. A sufficient condition is a condition, the presence of which guarantees a result.

If the *absence* of the determining factor guarantees the result, then the determining factor is a *necessary* condition. The result cannot happen without that determining factor. Can you get into law school without the LSAT? No. Taking the LSAT is a necessary condition for *getting accepted to law school* to occur. However, taking the LSAT is not sufficient for getting into law school:

> If –LSAT $\rightarrow$ –law school
> If –A $\rightarrow$ –B

LSAT is necessary for *law school* and *A* is necessary for *B*.

If the terms *necessary* and *sufficient conditions* are a bit confusing for you, use the concept of whether it is the presence or the absence of the determining factor that guarantees a result. If the absence of *X* guarantees the absence of *Y*, then *X* is necessary for *Y*. If the presence of *Q* guarantees the presence of *Z*, then *Q* is sufficient to produce *Z*.

If Aurelia says, "I took the LSAT, so I'm going to get into law school," what logical flaw has she made? She has *taken a condition necessary for getting accepted to be a condition sufficient for getting accepted.* Without the LSAT, she cannot get accepted, but she has mistaken this for a different condition that says that the LSAT alone is sufficient for getting accepted.

Necessary and sufficient conditions can also work backward in time. If Aurelia says, "Jocelyn didn't get into law school, so she must not have taken the LSAT," she is confusing the necessary condition—taking the LSAT—for a sufficient condition. She is looking at the result—not getting into law school—and then looking back in time and assuming that taking the LSAT would have been sufficient for (it would have guaranteed) getting in.

If an if/then statement gives you a sufficient condition, then the contrapositive of that statement is a necessary condition, and vice versa. Consider the statement:

> If rain $\rightarrow$ wet

The element *rain* is sufficient to guarantee the occurrence of *wet*. By writing the contrapositive

> –wet $\therefore$ –rain

you can see that without wet, *rain* could not have occurred. In other words, *wet* is necessary for *rain* to have previously taken place. The absence of *wet* guarantees the absence of *rain*.

If the original statement gives a necessary condition

> If –LSAT → –law school,

then the contrapositive

> law school ∴ LSAT

indicates that getting into law school is sufficient to prove that you had previously taken the LSAT. The presence of *law school* guarantees the previous presence of *LSAT*.

In some situations a certain element may both be necessary and sufficient. If you have a ticket for a movie, you will get in. If you do not, you will not. Having a ticket is necessary and having a ticket is also sufficient. (Remember that if/then logic is deductive and deals with an idealized, absolute universe. In the real world there may be other factors that would keep you from getting into the movie.) The movie scenario can be expressed by an *if and only if* statement: *You will get into the movie if, and only if, you have a ticket.*

Table 2.4 summarizes the characteristics of necessary and sufficient conditions.

Table 2.4. Necessary and Sufficient Conditions

	Sufficient or Necessary	Presence or Absence	Basic Wording	Alternate Wording
If A → B	A is sufficient for guaranteeing that B will occur.	The presence of A is the determining factor.	If A occurs, B will occur.	
If –A → –B	A is necessary for B to occur.	The absence of A is the determining factor.	If A does not occur, B cannot occur.	B does not occur unless A occurs. B occurs only if A occurs.
If A → B **If –A → –B**	A is necessary for B to occur and A is sufficient for guaranteeing that B will occur.	Both the presence and absence of A are determining factors.	If A occurs, B will occur and if A does not occur, B will not occur.	B occurs if, and only if, A occurs.

If/then arguments that test a rule. Some arguments present a rule and then test your understanding of the rule by giving you a case and asking you to come to a conclusion. Consider the following argument:

> *Every current employee who has worked at AAA Storm Door for at least three years gets two weeks of vacation. Jurgen started working at AAA Storm Door in 2009 and has worked there without interruption since that time.*

The if/then statement in the first sentence can be symbolized as:

> *If 3 years → 2 weeks of vacation*

What do you know about Jurgen? Because the year 2009 is more than three years ago and he has worked at AAA Storm Door continually since then, he must meet the criterion *has worked at AAA Storm Door for at least three years.* The argument now reads:

> **Rule:** *If 3 years → 2 weeks of vacation*
> **Case:** *Jurgen = 3 years*
> **Conclusion:** *Jurgen = 2 weeks of vacation*

The argument presents a rule, *If A → B,* and then gives you a test case: *A.* Your task is to determine what can be concluded. In order to derive a valid conclusion, you must know what the triggers are for the argument. Consider:

> *Nura told us that if she is accepted to the study abroad program, she will go to Qatar for next semester. Unfortunately, Nura was not accepted to the study abroad program.*

What can be concluded? Symbolize the if/then statement and write down the two triggers. Then read the explanation below.

For the above argument, the first sentence gives the if/then statement (the rule) and can be symbolized in standard form as:

> *If accepted → Qatar*

The triggers are (1) the element on the left side of the standard form (*accepted*) and (2) the negation of the element on the right side (*–Qatar*). The test case that you are given is that Nura is not accepted. *Not accepted* is *not* one of the triggers. There is nothing that follows from the fact that Nura is not accepted.

Combining if/thens to create an argument. Some arguments present two if/then statements and test your understanding of the relationship between them. You have probably seen arguments such as:

If Jason goes to the party, Mariah will go.
If Mariah goes to the party, Sara will go.
∴ If Jason goes to the party, Sara will go.

A deductive argument that includes two premises and then draws a conclusion based on the premises is called a **syllogism**. You should be prepared to draw conclusions from syllogisms and to evaluate whether or not they are valid.

In the argument above, the two if/then statements have a common element. Mariah appears in both. For a syllogism to be valid, there must be a common element between the if/thens:

If A → B
If B → C
∴ If A → C

Is there a common element in the following if/then statements?

If Eduardo orders spaghetti, Jessica orders lasagna. If Olivia orders salad, Jessica orders lasagna.

The statements can be symbolized as:

If A → B
If C → B

The common element is *B*, Jessica orders lasagna. However, the argument does not function as a valid syllogism. If *A* occurs, you know that *B* occurs, but what follows from *B* occurring? Nothing. In order to make a valid syllogism, you would need to have another if/then rule in which *B* is a trigger for some other event, *C*. In the statement If *C* → *B*, *B* is not a trigger. You can think of each element as a stepping stone across a stream. You need to step from *A* to *B* and then from *B* to *C*. In the above argument you can step from *A* to *B* but then cannot step anywhere from *B*. You can step from *C* to *B* but this does not help you get across the stream (Figure 2.7).

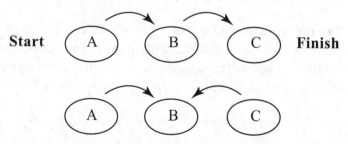

Figure 2.7. The top diagram shows *If A then B, If B then C.*
The bottom diagram shows *If A then B, If C then B.*

Now consider the following argument:

> *If Eduardo orders spaghetti, Jessica orders lasagna. If Olivia orders*
> *salad, Jessica does not order lasagna.*

The two statements can be symbolized as:

$$If \ A \rightarrow B$$
$$If \ C \rightarrow -B$$

This looks very much like the previous example, which was not a valid syllogism. Look carefully. What is the common element? There are two occurrences of *B* but one is positive and one is negative. Rewrite the second if/then so that it is positive. Do this by writing the contrapositive:

$$B \therefore -C$$

If *A* occurs, you know that *B* occurs. If *B* occurs, you know that *not C* occurs. Now there is a valid syllogism:

$$If \ A \rightarrow B$$
$$B \therefore -C$$
$$\therefore If \ A \rightarrow -C$$

Note that the *therefore* symbol is used in two different ways. In the second line, it represents the fact that *B* happened second and therefore –*C* must have occurred previously. In the third line it represents a conclusion.

Just as a single if/then statement may present a rule and then give you a test case, a syllogism can present rules and then give you a test case. Consider the argument in the following exercise:

PRACTICE EXERCISE 2

If Jill goes to school in Montana, Kerri goes to school in Nebraska. If Lou goes to school in Pennsylvania, Jill goes to school in Montana. If Hank goes to school in Ohio, Kerri does not go to school in Nebraska. If Lou does not go to school in Pennsylvania, Jill does not go to school in Montana.

List all of the statements that must be true if Kerri does not go to school in Nebraska. Use your tools to work out all of the if/then relationships. Then check your answers against the explanation at the end of this section.

PRACTICE EXERCISE 3

For each of the statements below, follow the three steps for evaluating if/thens.

1. List the two events that are being related.

2. Identify which event is the determining factor.

3. Determine whether it is the presence or absence of the determining factor that determines the result.

Write out an if/then statement in standard form, first as a complete sentence and then using symbols. Then write the contrapositive. Finally, write down the two triggers. The answers and explanations are given at the end of this section.

1. Mushrooms pop up overnight whenever it rains.

2. Trees that are not fertilized annually will not grow properly.

3. If you do well on the test, you must have studied for three hours.

4. Unless you finish your dinner, you cannot have dessert.

5. The shuttle launch will take place Saturday only if it does not rain.

6. Acme Corporation will file for bankruptcy if, and only if, they are not approved for a loan.

PRACTICE EXERCISE 4

For each of the following statements, tell whether each conclusion is valid or invalid. The answers are at the end of this section.

1. Kurt does not take a vacation unless Fiona takes a vacation. Fiona takes a vacation. Therefore, Kurt takes a vacation.

2. Kurt does not take a vacation unless Fiona takes a vacation. Kurt does not take a vacation. Therefore, Fiona takes a vacation.

3. Taylor signs up for Philosophy only if Reggie signs up for Linguistics. Reggie signs up for Linguistics. Therefore, Taylor signs up for Philosophy.

4. Taylor signs up for Philosophy only if Reggie signs up for Linguistics. Reggie does not sign up for Linguistics. Therefore, Taylor does not sign up for Philosophy.

5. If Ken goes to the baseball game, Sandra goes to the hockey game. If Greg goes to the football game, Sandra does not go to the hockey game. Ken goes to the baseball game. Therefore, Greg does not go to the football game.

Answers to Practice Exercises 2–4:

Practice Exercise 2

Symbolize the statements in standard form:

$$If J = M \rightarrow K = N$$
$$If L = P \rightarrow J = M$$
$$If H = O \rightarrow K = -N$$
$$If L = -P \rightarrow J = -M$$

The test case is that Kerri does not go to school in Nebraska. Look for $K = -N$ as a trigger (on the left side). It does not occur on the left side in the standard forms, so rewrite one of the statements with K as a contrapositive. Rewriting the first if/then would give $K = -N \therefore J = -M$. Rewriting the third if/then would give K in N, rather than K not in N.

The only trigger with K not in N, then, results in J not in M. Add this to the list of true statements that follow from K not in N. Now find what must be true if J is not in M. $J = -M$ does not appear as a trigger in the left side of any of the standard if/thens. Check the contrapositives. Look to see if the negation of $J = -M$, namely $J = M$, occurs on the right side of any of the standard forms. It is in the second if/then statement. The contrapositive of the second statement is $J = -M \therefore L = -P$.

Add $L = -P$ to the list of true statements. Now look for instances of $L = -P$ as a trigger. It occurs on the left side of the last standard if/then statement, with the result that $J = -M$, which is already listed as a true statement. Double-check to see if the negation of $L = -P$, namely $L = P$, occurs on the right side of any of the standard if/then statements. It does not, so all of the results of K not in N have been found.

True statements:

$$J = -M$$
$$L = -P$$

Practice Exercise 3

1. *Mushrooms pop up overnight whenever it rains.*
   (STEP 1) Mushrooms pop up. Rain.
   (STEP 2) The determining factor is rain.
   (STEP 3) It is the presence of rain that determines mushrooms popping up.
   If it rains, mushrooms pop up. If R $\rightarrow$ mushrooms.
   Contrapositive: –mushrooms $\therefore$ –R
   Triggers: R, –mushrooms

2. *Trees that are not fertilized annually will not grow properly.*

(STEP 1) Fertilize. Grow properly.

(STEP 2) The determining factor is fertilize.

(STEP 3) It is the absence of fertilize that determines not grow properly.

If trees are not fertilized annually, they will not grow properly. If –fertilize → –grow.

Contrapositive: grow ∴ fertilize

Triggers: –fertilize, grow

3. *If you do well on the test, you must have studied for three hours.*

(STEP 1) Do well. Studied.

(STEP 2) The determining factor is studied.

(STEP 3) It is the absence of studied that determines the absence of doing well.

If you do not study for three hours, you will not do well on the test. If –study → –do well.

Contrapositive: do well ∴ studied

Triggers: –study, do well

NOTE: It may not have been obvious to you that it is the absence of studying that results in not doing well. You can avoid making an error by double-checking the contrapositive. When the standard form for this example is written as the absence of studying causing not doing well, the contrapositive conforms exactly to the original statement.

4. *Unless you finish your dinner, you cannot have dessert.*

(STEP 1) Finish dinner. Get dessert.

(STEP 2) The determining factor is finishing dinner.

(STEP 3) It is the absence of finishing dinner that determines not getting dessert.

If you do not finish your dinner, you do not get dessert. If –finish → –dessert.

Contrapositive: dessert ∴ finish dinner

Triggers: –finish, dessert

NOTE: Convert the word *unless* to the expression *if not*. It will then be clear that it is the absence of finishing that is the determining factor.

5. *The shuttle launch will take place Saturday only if it does not rain.*

(STEP 1) Launch. Rain.

(STEP 2) The determining factor is rain.

(STEP 3) It is the absence of *not rain* that determines the absence of launch.

If it rains, the shuttle launch will not take place on Saturday. If R →
–launch.

Contrapositive: launch ∴ –R

Triggers: R, launch

NOTE: This is an example of a complex *only if* in which the original
statement contains a negative. Apply the *otherwise* strategy. *Only if it does
not rain will the shuttle launch take place on Saturday. Otherwise (does rain),
not (not launch).*

6. *Acme Corporation will file for bankruptcy if, and only if, they are not approved
for a loan.*

An *if and only if* statement should be broken into two parts. Both are
true. In this example, the first part is *Acme Corporation will file for bankruptcy if they are not approved for a loan.*

(STEP 1) Bankruptcy. Approved.

(STEP 2) The determining factor is *approved.*

(STEP 3) It is the absence of *approved* that determines *bankruptcy.*

If they are not approved for a loan, the corporation will file for bankruptcy.
If –approved → bankruptcy.

Contrapositive: –bankruptcy ∴ approved

Triggers: –approved, –bankruptcy

The second part of the statement is *Acme Corporation will file for bankruptcy only if they are not approved for a loan.*

(STEP 1) Bankruptcy. Approved.

(STEP 2) The determining factor is *approved.*

(STEP 3) It is the absence of *not approved* (= the presence of *approved*) that
determines the absence of *bankruptcy.*

If they are approved for a loan, the corporation will not file for bankruptcy. If approved → –bankruptcy.

Contrapositive: bankruptcy ∴ –approved

Triggers: approved, bankruptcy

Note: Use the *otherwise* method. *Only if they are not approved for a loan
will Acme Corporation file for bankruptcy. Otherwise (are approved), not (not
bankruptcy).*

Practice Exercise 4

1. *Kurt does not take a vacation unless Fiona takes a vacation. Fiona takes a
vacation. Therefore, Kurt takes a vacation.*

Solution: If –Fiona → –Kurt. The only triggers are –Fiona and Kurt. The
presence of Fiona is not a trigger, so the conclusion is invalid.

2. *Kurt does not take a vacation unless Fiona takes a vacation. Kurt does not take a vacation. Therefore, Fiona takes a vacation.*
Solution: As in number 1, the absence of Kurt is not a trigger, so the conclusion is invalid.

3. *Taylor signs up for Philosophy only if Reggie signs up for Linguistics. Reggie signs up for Linguistics. Therefore, Taylor signs up for Philosophy.*
Solution: If –R = Linguistics → –T = Philosophy. The only triggers are Reggie not signing up for Linguistics and Taylor signing up for Philosophy. The presence of Reggie signing up for Linguistics is not a trigger. The logic is invalid.

4. *Taylor signs up for Philosophy only if Reggie signs up for Linguistics. Reggie does not sign up for Linguistics. Therefore, Taylor does not sign up for Philosophy.*
Solution: The standard form of the if/then is *If –Reggie = Linguistics → –Taylor = Philosophy.* As in number 3, Reggie not signing up for Linguistics is a trigger and it predicts that Taylor will not sign up for Philosophy. The logic is valid.

5. *If Ken goes to the baseball game, Sandra goes to the hockey game. If Greg goes to the football game, Sandra does not go to the hockey game. Ken goes to the baseball game. Therefore, Greg does not go to the football game.*
Solution: The logic is valid. It can be derived from:
If Ken = baseball → Sandra = hockey
and
Sandra = hockey ∴ Greg not = football, which is the contrapositive of *If Greg = football → Sandra not = hockey.*

Induction

On the LSAT, an **inductive** argument can be defined as any argument that is not deductive. Whereas deductive arguments are built on absolute rules, inductive arguments are not limited to absolute rules. An inductive argument may contain rules but usually also contains information that is not absolute. Rather than being based on *must* statements, inductive reasoning may include *should* or *might* statements. Where deductive arguments refer to an absolute universe, inductive arguments refer to "real-world" situations. Compare:

> **Deductive argument:** *If a species is endangered, it cannot be hunted.*
> **Inductive argument:** *If a species becomes so rare as to be endangered, it would be helpful if society agreed to stop or limit the hunting of that species.*

The inductive argument above sounds more like a real-world discussion than a logical proposition. This is true for most inductive arguments. Beware, however, of arguments that sound like real-world discussions but which in fact contain absolute rules.

> No one wants to see a species become extinct. Today, species are becoming extinct at an alarming rate. Any species that becomes so rare as to be on the endangered species list must be protected by law from being hunted. In addition, any animal that is illegal to hunt is worthy of respect. The Mexican gray wolf is on the endangered species list. Therefore, the Mexican gray wolf is worthy of respect.

Do you see that the above argument, even though it sounds like a real-world discussion, actually presents absolute rules?

Rather than worrying about the term *inductive,* think of LR arguments as either deductive or not deductive. If an argument is deductive, you must be careful to identify the absolute rules and interpret them correctly. You may need to diagram a deductive argument, either using sets or if/then statements. If an argument is not deductive, you do not need to apply these steps.

Major Types of Valid Inductive Logic

There are six common types of inductive logic that you should be familiar with on the LR. They are:

1. Analogy
2. Cause and effect
3. Elimination of other options
4. Generalization
5. Statistical arguments
6. Tautology

Analogy. An argument by **analogy** arrives at a conclusion about situation A by establishing that situation A is similar in some respects (is analogous) to situation B and therefore situation A must be similar in another respect to situation B.

> *Dogs are very similar to wolves in their genetic makeup and in their temperament. Wolves are healthiest when they eat freshly killed meat. Therefore, we can assume that the best diet for dogs would consist primarily of freshly killed meat.*

Table 2.5 below shows the analogy between wolves and dogs that is established by two known similarities. When a new fact is introduced about wolves, a conclusion about dogs is drawn based on the analogy.

Table 2.5. Analogy Between Wolves and Dogs

	Wolves	**Dogs**
Similarity	**Fact:** genetics	**Fact:** genetics
Similarity	**Fact:** temperament	**Fact:** temperament
Similarity	**Fact:** freshly killed meat is healthy	**Conclusion by analogy:** freshly killed meat is healthy

Cause and effect. Cause-and-effect arguments are based on the logic that if event A often occurs before event B, event A might be the cause of event B.

Many people who smoke cigarettes later develop lung cancer. Therefore, smoking cigarettes contributes to the development of lung cancer.

The argument above establishes that (1) smoking cigarettes takes place before the development of lung cancer and (2) there is a significant **correlation** between smoking and developing lung cancer.

Cause-and-effect arguments are based on a **correlation** between two events. There is a correlation between two events if one event regularly occurs after the other or if the two events regularly occur at the same time. A correlation may indicate a **causal relationship** between the two events. A cause-and-effect argument makes the claim that the correlation proves a causal relationship.

Elimination of other options. An argument by **elimination** identifies all possible options and proves that one option is the correct one by showing that the other options must be eliminated.

The Turkey Trot Restaurant offers a choice of mashed potatoes, wild rice, or mixed vegetables with their entrees. However, the restaurant has run out of both mashed potatoes and wild rice. Therefore, the restaurant will serve mixed vegetables with their entrees.

Generalization. An argument by **generalization** relates information about specific examples to information about a general category.

> *I have had five pit bulls over the years and every one of them was friendly and loyal. It must be that all pit bulls are friendly and loyal.*

The argument establishes that something is true of many members of a group and then concludes that the same thing must be true about all members of a group.

Conversely, an argument by generalization can start with a fact that is true about a group in general and conclude that the same fact must be true for a particular member of the group.

> *It is a well-known fact that people from warm climates are typically gregarious. The ambassador is from a warm climate. We can therefore expect the ambassador to be gregarious.*

Statistical arguments. A **statistical** argument is an argument that bases its conclusion on statistical evidence.

> *Over 40 percent of the sedans produced by Company X last year had serious problems with their brakes. Therefore, it is likely that your sedan, which was produced by Company X last year, will have brake problems.*

A variation on statistical arguments involves surveys. These arguments sample a representative subgroup.

> *In a telephone survey, over 85 of 100 homeowners in the metropolitan area said they would vote for Senator Jackson in the upcoming election. Therefore, it is probable that Senator Jackson will get most of the metropolitan homeowner vote.*

Tautology. A **tautology** is an argument that is true by definition.

> *All bachelors are unmarried men.*

A tautology is valid. A bachelor is by definition a man who is not married.

Additional Tools for Inductive Logic

In addition to the specific types of inductive argument presented above, there are a number of tools that inductive logic can use to support conclusions.

Application of a moral principle. A conclusion can be supported by citing a moral principle. For example, *It is better to choose a plan that benefits many people a small amount than a plan that benefits a few people greatly. Therefore, the city should choose the plan that reduces the sales tax slightly rather than the plan that creates a lottery.*

Argument by facts. A conclusion can be supported simply through relevant facts. *Everyone needs calcium and sesame seeds have calcium. Therefore, if people want to get more calcium, they can eat sesame seeds.*

Citing an authority. Quoting the opinion of an authority in a relevant field is a tool for supporting a premise. *Albert Einstein said that studying physics can help people improve their memory.*

Comparison and contrast. Establishing similarities or differences between two phenomena can help establish or disprove qualities that the two phenomena share, strengthening or weakening an analogy. *Even though Weimaraners and Dachshunds are members of the same species, they have very different temperaments. The fact that Weimaraners are long-lived does not mean that Dachshunds are long-lived.*

Predict the future from an established pattern. This tool uses an established pattern of events to predict that another event will occur in the future. It is a type of generalization. *Every year for the past ten years it has rained on the Fourth of July. Therefore, we are canceling the outdoor picnic that is scheduled for the Fourth of July this year because it is almost certain to rain.*

What is true for a group must be true for each member of the group. This type of logic argues that if a group as a whole has a certain characteristic, the members of the group also have that characteristic. *Dogs are smarter than sheep. Therefore, my dog is smarter than your sheep.*

Flawed Arguments

So far this chapter has discussed types of valid arguments. The LR section also tests your ability to identify types of flawed arguments. Some flawed arguments are simply the result of incorrectly applying a valid type of logic. Other flawed arguments are based on reasoning that is inherently flawed. In the sections below you will first learn the most common types of flawed arguments. Then you will review the less common types.

Most Common Flawed Arguments

There are over fifty types of flawed arguments that have appeared on recent actual LSATs. The most common ones are listed here. There are many possible flawed argument types. By carefully studying all of the types listed here, you will be prepared for whichever types are used on your test.

Confusing Necessary and Sufficient Conditions

This is one of the three most frequently used types of flawed arguments. In your review of if/then arguments you learned that a sufficient condition is one that guarantees a result. *Raining guarantees that the sidewalk will be wet.* A necessary condition is a condition without which something cannot happen. *Taking the LSAT is necessary for you to get accepted to law school (if you do not take the LSAT, you will not get into law school).*

Table 2.6. Necessary and Sufficient Conditions

	Condition	**Result**
Sufficient condition	Rain	Wet
Necessary condition	Taking LSAT (without this condition) $\rightarrow$	Getting into law school (not this result)

Confusing necessary and sufficient conditions can mean either (1) starting with a necessary condition and mistakenly thinking it is sufficient, or (2) starting with a sufficient condition and mistakenly thinking it is necessary. Consider:

> *I took the LSAT. Why didn't I get accepted to law school?*

Even though taking the LSAT is necessary for getting accepted, it is not enough (sufficient) to guarantee acceptance. The arguer above has taken a necessary condition as sufficient.

The arguer below mistakenly takes a sufficient condition to be necessary:

> *My professor said that if I missed any more classes, I would fail the course. I didn't miss any more classes. Therefore, the professor should not have failed me.*

Missing classes was sufficient for failing the course but it was not a necessary condition for failing. Failing could occur without missing any more classes.

Inferring That What Is True of the Parts Must Be True of the Whole

This is another one of the three most common flawed arguments.

> *None of the berries on this plant would make me sick, so if I eat all of the berries, I will not get sick.*

> *The living room and kitchen are decorated in a Mediterranean motif, so we can assume that the entire house is designed in a Mediterranean motif.*

This flawed reasoning mistakenly attributes properties that are true of part of something (each berry is non-toxic) to be true of the entire thing (if I eat all of the berries, the combination will not be toxic). In a variation, this type of flaw attributes characteristics of members of a group to the group as a whole.

False Cause

False cause is the third of the three most common types of flawed argument. A valid cause-and-effect argument correctly infers that a certain event that often comes before another event is a cause of the second event. In many cases, however, the simple fact that one event comes first and another comes later—or that two events often occur together—does not mean there is a causal relationship. False cause arguments see a correlation between two events and incorrectly assume a cause-and-effect relationship. In some cases, the fact of two events occurring together is a coincidence. In other cases, it may be that they are both caused by a third factor.

> *People with lung cancer often have discolored teeth. Therefore, discoloration of the teeth must lead to lung cancer.*

The argument is flawed because it fails to consider the possibility that smoking leads to both discolored teeth and lung cancer.

In another type of false cause argument, event A and event B frequently occur together and the argument concludes that A causes B, when in fact it is equally possible that B causes A.

> *Whenever Viet drives fast, he feels the urge to use the bathroom. Driving at high speeds must cause him to have to empty his bladder.*

The argument is flawed because it fails to consider that having a full bladder may cause Viet to start driving at high speeds.

Ambiguity

In the LR section, **ambiguity** refers to a word that is used in two contexts with two different meanings.

> *Martha claims to have a lot of energy. She runs, plays tennis, bicycles, and dances. Ed claims to have a lot of energy but all he does is lift weights, which requires only the most minimal of movement.*

Martha and Ed are using the word *energy* in two different ways. For Martha, energy refers to movement. For Ed, energy refers to muscle power.

A special instance of ambiguity is with the use of pronouns.

> *Union member: We will benefit if the company matches the retirement*
> *contributions of the workers.*

> *Manager: On the contrary. We will not benefit at all if we have to pay*
> *the additional amount.*

The word *we* is being used to refer to two different groups. In the first case it refers to the workers. In the second case it refers to management. Pronouns are inherently ambiguous. They refer to different people depending on the context.

Circular Reasoning

A **circular** argument is one in which the conclusion is a restatement of one of the premises. In other words, the arguer has slipped in a premise that states the very conclusion that the arguer hopes to prove.

> *People who do not eat meat do not die as soon as people who do eat*
> *meat. Such people also have fewer diseases. Therefore, vegetarians live*
> *longer and healthier lives than meat eaters.*

The premises contain all of the information that the arguer puts in the conclusion. The argument is circular. It ends up where it started.

Unrepresentative Sample

An argument based on an **unrepresentative sample** relies on data from individuals who may not be representative of the group about which the argument is trying to draw a conclusion.

> *I asked a dozen people at the mall if they planned to buy the latest*
> *teen fashion and none of them did. Therefore, the latest teen fashion is*
> *unlikely to sell well.*

The argument is flawed because the people who were questioned may not have been representative of the teenagers who are the market for the latest fashion.

Assuming There Are No Other Options

An argument may falsely assume that there are only certain options in a situation, when in fact there may be other options that the argument fails to consider.

> *Jefferson and Ortega are both running for mayor but Ortega's support has all but disappeared. Therefore, Jefferson will be the next mayor.*

The argument fails to consider that there may be other candidates for mayor.

Argument Against the Person

Known in formal logic as an ad hominem (Latin: to the person) argument, this type of flawed reasoning attacks the character of the person whom the arguer is trying to rebut, instead of addressing the person's argument. To be a flawed argument, the attack on the person's character must be irrelevant to the argument.

> *Fred says that we should all tighten our belts during this time of recession, but Fred has been convicted three times of driving while impaired, so I hardly think we should listen to his advice.*

Unreliable Source

An argument that uses an **unreliable source** draws its premises from a source that for some reason is questionable, perhaps because the source is biased or perhaps because the source is uninformed.

> *According to John, his opponent does not have the necessary skills to serve as chair of the board of directors. Therefore, I will vote for John.*

Applying a Generalization to an Inappropriate Case

This flawed argument applies a generalization to a situation that the generalization was not meant to cover.

> *One should be polite to one's elders. Olivia was in the wrong, then, when she spoke harshly to the older man who tried to grab her purse.*

The generalization of being polite to one's elders was not meant to apply to people who are trying to commit a crime.

False Appeal to Authority

An argument that falsely appeals to authority is one in which an authority is cited to support a conclusion but the authority is not an expert in the field with which the argument deals.

> *Albert Einstein recommended that we wash our hair every day.*

Albert Einstein was an authority on physics, not on hair care.

Distorting a View to Make It Vulnerable to Criticism

In this type of flawed argument, the arguer distorts the view of another person in such a way that the other person's view can be more easily attacked.

> *Ferguson: There are so many unwanted pets suffering on the streets that the city ought to set up a new shelter to accommodate these pets until homes can be found for them.*

> *Petrick: If the city were to take in every stray dog, cat, ferret, and python, the costs of food, shelter, and medical attention would be crippling to our budget.*

Petrick distorts Ferguson's argument. Ferguson argues for a shelter to accommodate some of the stray pets. Petrick portrays Ferguson's argument as calling for a shelter for all such pets, an argument that is easier to attack.

Disproving a Claim That Was Not Made

In this flawed argument, the arguer attacks a certain claim but the claim that is attacked was in fact never made by the person whom the arguer is trying to rebut.

> *Ferguson: There are so many unwanted pets suffering on the streets that the city ought to set up a new shelter to accommodate these pets until homes can be found for them.*

> *Petrick: It is not true that the city has enough money left over from last year's budget to create a new shelter. In fact, there was a shortage last year.*

Ferguson did not claim that there was money left over from last year's budget.

Concluding That Something Is True Because Most People Believe It to Be True

This type of reasoning is clearly not valid.

> *Everyone feels that Pacheco will win the election. Therefore, Pacheco's only opponent should save money by withdrawing now.*

The argument assumes that Pacheco will win, based on the beliefs of most people.

Accepting a Fact as True Because It Has Not Been Proven to Be Incorrect

In this type of flawed argument the arguer shows that there is no evidence against a certain proposition and concludes that therefore the proposition must be true.

> *No one has yet proven definitively that time travel is impossible. Therefore, scientists should accept that time travel is a reality and should begin work on developing the technology to achieve it.*

The argument is flawed because it fails to consider the possibility that even though there is no proof that time travel is impossible, it may turn out to be.

Rejecting a View Because It Has Not Been Proven

This type of flawed argument is the inverse of the previous one. Here a view is thrown out because it has not been proven definitively to be true.

> *Despite years of attempts, no one has yet proven the existence of the purported yeti. Therefore, scientists should admit that the Abominable Snowman is a myth.*

The argument is flawed because it fails to consider that even though there is no proof of the yeti's existence, the yeti may still prove to be real.

Inferring That Because Something Is Possible, It Must Occur

Consider the following:

> *Spending twenty minutes a day under a sun lamp in the winter sometimes cures seasonal depression. Therefore, if Ferenc spends twenty minutes a day under a sun lamp this winter, his usual seasonal depression will not occur.*

The argument is flawed because it fails to consider that, even though the treatment can cure depression, it is not guaranteed to cure depression.

Inferring That Because Something Is Unlikely to Occur, It Will Not Occur

This is the inverse of the previous type of flawed argument.

> There are hardly ever any accidents on Route 147. Sandy is driving Route 147 tonight, so she will not have an accident.

The fact that accidents are unlikely does not warrant the conclusion that an accident cannot happen.

Assuming That Because a Conclusion Is False, All of the Premises Are False

This type of flawed reasoning fails to consider the possibility that even though a conclusion is not valid, some of the premises in the argument may be correct.

> Jason argues that the moon is a celestial body and that some celestial bodies host life. Jason has concluded that the moon hosts life, which is clearly incorrect. Therefore, we must conclude that the moon is not a celestial body.

The fact that the conclusion of Jason's argument is incorrect does not imply that the premises of his argument are incorrect.

Less Common Flawed Arguments

There are many types of flawed arguments that only appear on the LSAT occasionally. Even though any given type occurs rarely, every LR section has less common flawed arguments. Become familiar with all of the types listed below.

Accepting a Claim Because an Opposing Claim Was Not Well Defended

> Forbes claims that most people prefer coffee to tea but Forbes's argument is inconclusive. Therefore, most people prefer tea to coffee.

Analogy

Although argument by analogy is valid, it is easy for an analogy to be incorrect. Simply because two things are similar in one way does not mean that they are similar in all ways. The following is an example of a false analogy:

> Both church services and baseball games take place on Sunday. Eating ice cream in church on Sunday is considered inappropriate, so John should not eat ice cream at Sunday's baseball game either.

Assuming There Are No Additional Necessary Factors

This flawed argument states that A is necessary for B to occur and that A occurs and thus B occurs. If fails to consider that A is not sufficient for B to occur and that there may be other factors that must occur along with A in order to guarantee the occurrence of B.

> *For a seed to sprout, it must have water. I have regularly watered the seeds I am trying to grow, so the seeds will sprout.*

Biased Language Used Against Opponents

This argument uses language that reflects poorly on people who may disagree with the arguer.

> *Statistics clearly show that most people want LaVail to win the election. The supporters of Sterling, then, must be either ignorant, stubborn, or both.*

Contradictory Premises

An argument that contains premises that are mutually contradictory is flawed.

> *Inez plays tennis every Saturday. Tomorrow is Saturday and Inez sometimes does not play tennis on Saturday. Therefore, there is a chance that Inez will not play tennis tomorrow.*

Failure to Apply a Generalization to All Cases

In this type of flawed reasoning the arguer cites a generalization but does not apply it to all applicable cases.

> *It is widely believed that people with red hair have fiery tempers. Edward has red hair, but there is no reason to believe that he has a fiery temper.*

Fails to Consider

This category includes several types of flawed reasoning. In all of these types the arguer fails to consider a certain possibility and thus the arguer's conclusion is flawed.

Fails to consider whether a specific situation meets a definition. Consider the example:

> *Most people believe that entertainment without any redeeming value is a waste of time. Therefore, most people believe that watching television reality shows is not a productive use of a person's time.*

The argument fails to consider whether *watching television reality shows* meets the definition of *entertainment without any redeeming value.*

Fails to consider that there may be an exception to a rule and that the exception would negate a recommendation.

> *Drug X grows new hair on bald heads in 90 percent of bald men. Therefore, any man who is bald and who wishes to grow new hair should take drug X.*

The argument is flawed because it fails to consider that there may be some men who can grow new hair only if they do *not* take drug X.

Fails to consider that if A causes B, something else other than A can cause B.

> *Drug X and drug Y both reliably grow new hair on bald heads. Henry is bald and wants to grow new hair. If he does not take drug X or drug Y, he will not grow new hair.*

The argument is flawed because the arguer fails to consider that there may be other ways in which Henry can grow new hair.

Fails to Establish

Similar to *fails to consider*, this category also includes a number of variations.

Fails to establish that an alternate approach is viable. In this flawed argument the arguer proposes an alternate approach but does not establish that the approach would work.

> *The Johnson firm has studied the feasibility of building a bridge across the river in the middle of town and has found that the project would be costly. Therefore, the city should plan to establish a ferry service to carry people and cars across the river.*

The argument is flawed because the arguer does not establish that the ferry service would be viable.

Fails to establish that the evidence presented is relevant to the conclusion.

> *We clearly need a ferry service to shuttle people and cars across the river in the middle of town. Both Eudora and Plainsville have had ferry service across the rivers in their towns for many years.*

The argument is flawed because the arguer fails to show that the information about the ferries in the other towns is relevant to the conclusion that the arguer's town should have a ferry. This flaw is not the same as citing irrelevant evidence because the evidence in this argument may or may not be relevant. The arguer has simply failed to establish that the evidence is relevant.

False Appeal to Fear

In this flaw the arguer tries to persuade the listener by appealing to fear rather than through logic.

> *Vote for Sanders for mayor. I hate to think of the terrible consequences that will follow if Sander's opponent wins the election.*

False Assumptions About Groups

This type of flawed argument assumes that every member of a group has a certain quality that most members of the group have. Alternately, this flawed argument attributes the characteristics of one group to another group that does not necessarily have those characteristics.

> 1. *It is well known that Labrador retrievers are gentle with children. For that reason, it is not possible that my Labrador retriever attacked your child, as you claim.*
> 2. *Surely fish must be among the cruelest of animals. They show no affection whatsoever for their young, abandoning them completely or, even worse, eating them.*

The second argument is flawed because it attributes certain emotions about offspring to animals that do not necessarily hold those emotions.

Hasty Generalization

This flawed argument takes a narrow premise and makes a generalization that is overly broad.

> *Marek did not eat any meat for breakfast today and he feels unusually good. Therefore, vegetarians must live long, healthy lives.*

Invalid Inferences

There are a number of types of flawed arguments in which the arguer infers (concludes) something incorrectly.

Infers from most similar situations to the current situation. This flawed argument concludes that because most similar situations have a certain characteristic, the current situation has the same characteristic.

At most baseball games, hot dogs are sold. Therefore, if Lon goes to the baseball game tomorrow, he will be able to buy a hot dog.

Infers from behavior to intention. This argument considers a behavior and makes an invalid conclusion about the intention behind the behavior.

The citizens of Riverdale voted overwhelmingly for the new mayor, who promptly raised the city's sales tax. It must be that the citizens wanted to pay higher taxes.

Infers from a person holding a belief to the person holding an implication of that belief. This flawed argument makes the unwarranted conclusion that if a person holds a certain belief, the person also believes an implication of that belief.

> *Ernesto believes that children should not be spanked. It is clear that if a child is never spanked, he or she will grow up to be spoiled. Apparently, Ernesto believes that children should grow up to be spoiled.*

Irrelevant Considerations

An argument is flawed if the premises on which it relies are irrelevant to the conclusion.

> *Drug Z has had a successful record of curing depression in young adults and particularly in men. Robert is an overweight middle-aged man. He should try drug Z. It might help him.*

Drug Z is only known to cure depression in young people. Robert is not young and has not been shown to be depressed. The information about drug Z is irrelevant to the conclusion that Robert should try it.

Treats One Element as Something Else

There are a number of flawed arguments that misinterpret one element of the argument.

Treats a rebuttal of an argument as proof that the argument is false.

> *John cited a report that claimed that 60 percent of town residents favored a property tax increase in order to fund the proposed new high school as proof that the high school should be built. John's citation was incorrect. In fact, the report claimed that 40 percent of town residents favored the property tax increase. Therefore, the new high school should not be built.*

The arguer rebuts the original argument by pointing out a factual error. However, it is not valid to then infer that the conclusion of the original argument was flawed. There may be other reasons why the high school should be built.

Treats a proof as merely a reinforcement of an argument.

It is true that all members of this year's graduating class have gotten job offers and that Una is a member of this year's graduating class. However, that does not prove that she received a job offer. It simply makes it likely that she did.

The arguer refuses to admit that the premises prove the conclusion and instead tries to persuade the listener merely that the conclusion could be true.

Treats supporting information as information that proves the conclusion. This is the reverse of the previous flaw. The arguer tries to make supporting information seem sufficient to prove the conclusion.

Many of the members of this year's graduating class have received job offers. More women than men have received job offers. Una is a woman and is a member of this year's graduating class. Therefore, Una must have received a job offer.

Treats an unjustified assertion as an intentionally false assertion.

Francesca claimed in her argument before the Senate subcommittee that the Mexican gray wolf was not an endangered species. In fact, it is an endangered species. Clearly, Francesca attempted to mislead the members of the subcommittee.

The argument fails to consider that Francesca's error was unintentional.

Treats the existence of an effect as proof of intention to produce the effect.

As a result of Norman's decision to invest his company's retirement plans with Acme Investments, 40 percent of the value of the funds was lost and several employees were forced to postpone their retirement. Because intentionally losing employees' money is a crime, Norman should be charged with a crime.

The argument establishes that Norman's action had a certain result but errs in asserting that Norman intended for that result to happen.

Treats a hypothesis as a fact. In this flawed argument a hypothesis is presented as an unsupported possibility but is then taken to be a fact.

Although there is no evidence for it, one possible explanation for Thompson's sudden departure from the law firm is that he was embezzling money from the firm. Therefore, an audit should be done immediately and Thompson should be required to pay any missing sums.

The arguer first admits that there is no evidence to support a hypothesis that Thompson embezzled but the conclusion assumes that Thompson did embezzle.

Treats a main factor as a necessary condition. This flawed argument misconstrues a factor that is important for a certain result as a factor without which the result cannot happen.

> *A strong personal statement is an important factor in the admissions committee's decisions for accepting students into law school. Mario does not have a strong personal statement. Therefore, Mario will not be accepted.*

The personal statement is defined as an important factor but the arguer misinterprets the definition as stating that the personal statement is a necessary factor.

Refuting Arguments

Many LR questions involve an argument that attempts to refute a previous argument. Some more complex arguments may involve refuting a previous argument that attempted to refute an even earlier argument. You may be asked to identify the type of reasoning that the second arguer uses to refute the first argument or to identify reasoning that would weaken the first argument.

A refutation can involve simply pointing out a logical flaw in the first argument. The flaws may be any of the types of flawed arguments that you reviewed above. A refutation is *not* a type of flawed argument. Rather, refutations are valid arguments that point out flaws or drawbacks in the argument that the refutation is trying to attack. Below are specific tools for refuting arguments.

Challenge an Argument by Providing Additional Evidence

The arguer brings in new information that then changes the conclusion without having to challenge the original information or the original logic.

> *Ned: Emissions from the Jones factory are well below the national standards, so there is no reason to believe the emissions are the cause of the increase in asthma among our children.*

> *Tamara: The increase in asthma is much greater among children who live downwind of the Jones factory than it is among children who live upwind of the factory. If Ned is looking for evidence to link the emissions to asthma, there it is.*

Challenge an Argument by Presenting an Alternate Explanation

> *Paula: Last winter there was twice as much rain as in any of the previous twenty years. Undoubtedly the rain must have weakened the foundations of the dam and that must be what caused the dam to break.*

Rajesh: Last winter there were two serious earthquakes centered within miles of the dam. It is more likely that the earthquakes were the cause of the dam's failure.

Rajesh's argument provides a different cause for the effect that Paula discusses, thus weakening Paula's argument.

Challenge an Argument by Showing That Its Conclusion Would Lead to Undesirable Results

The arguer acknowledges the strengths of the original argument but points out an undesirable result that the original arguer did not address.

Granted the penalty on factory emissions proposed by city hall would significantly decrease pollution and increase the health of our residents. However, the penalty would also cause many factories to move to more lenient locations, with the result that many of our residents would lose their livelihoods.

A related rebuttal points out that the conclusion of the original argument would lead to a logical absurdity.

The city has proposed a policy that no one can water their yards more than three times a week. According to the proposal, residents can request a waiver but only if they can show that the plants in their yard have died from lack of water. This policy is absurd. The point of watering is to keep your plants alive.

Challenge a Generalization

This type of rebuttal attempts to show that a generalization made in an argument does not apply or is not valid.

Frank claims that no one needs three weeks of vacation a year but studies have shown that most people work better if they do have three weeks of vacation. (Challenges by showing that the generalization is false.)

It's true that most books say that parakeets are friendly but my parakeet is clearly unfriendly. (Challenges by showing an exception to the generalization.)

Establish a Generalization and Use It Against an Argument

This tool sets up a generalization that can then be used to rebut another argument.

Everyone on my block is opposed to the new trash collection schedule. Nearly everyone on the adjacent block is opposed to it. Clearly the vast majority of people in our neighborhood are opposed to the new schedule, so the city should drop the proposed change despite the advantages the city cited.

Challenge by Analogy

This attacks an argument by showing that an analogous argument is flawed.

The mayor says that if we all tighten our belts, we'll be back in prosperous times within six months. That is exactly what the previous mayor convinced us to do, and it was three years before prosperous times returned.

Challenge the Validity of an Analogy

This type of rebuttal points out that two phenomena that are supposedly similar are in fact not similar in an important way.

Mr. Anderson claims that our city would benefit from a new convention center just as our neighboring city Oakville did. What Mr. Anderson did not mention was that Oakville has five times the population of our city. Our small city could never support such a center.

Undermines an Apparent Counterexample to a General Claim

In this type of rebuttal, the first arguer cites a claim made by another party—either the second arguer or another party not present in the argument—and then attacks the claim by citing a counterexample to the stated claim. The second arguer rebuts the first arguer by showing that the counterexample does not apply.

Valeria: University policy states that plagiarism is a serious offense punishable by expulsion. However, the university president herself, in her recently published book on academic principles, borrowed extensively from better-known authors. The university president has not been expelled so the policy should be abandoned.

Zack: Plagiarism is the use of previously published material without attribution or permission from the author. The university president has written permission from all of the authors whom she quoted and attributes her quotes to them. Therefore, the university president did not commit plagiarism.

Valeria attacks the policy on plagiarism by attempting to show that the university president was not subjected to the university policy. Zack challenges Valeria's argument by showing that the university president's case does not constitute an exception to the university policy.

QUESTION TYPES

This section teaches you to recognize and understand the types of question stems that LR items use. There are five categories of question types that account for over 75 percent of all LR questions. There are an additional ten question types that are less frequent but that are important for you to understand.

MOST COMMON QUESTION TYPES

The effect of a new premise (strengthen, weaken, or resolve a paradox)—29% of LR questions

Assumption—13% of LR questions

Identify a conclusion—13% of LR questions

Identify the flaw—13% of LR questions

Parallel reasoning—7% of LR questions

LESS COMMON QUESTION TYPES

Application of a principle

Committed to disagree/agree

Complete the sentence/argument

Consistent with both arguments

Identify an element of an argument

Match a principle to a concrete example

Must be true

Relevant information

Role of a claim

Type of reasoning

Most Common Question Types

The following five categories of questions are listed in the order of how frequently they occur. Most of the categories encompass several distinct question types or variations.

The Effect of a New Premise

This is the most common category of LR question. In nearly 30 percent of LR questions, the answer choices are new premises and you must find the one that—depending on the specific question stem—strengthens the conclusion, strengthens the conclusion by applying a principle, weakens the conclusion, or resolves a paradox presented in the argument.

The premises in the answer choices *must* be accepted as true. You cannot throw out an answer choice simply because you do not think it is true or consistent with the passage. Assume each answer choice is a true statement and then test whether it accomplishes the goal stated in the stem (strengthens, weakens, or resolves the paradox). This advice may sound straightforward but most test takers initially find themselves falling into the trap of throwing out an answer choice because it seems untrue. On most multiple-choice questions on exams that you have taken, you have to evaluate whether an answer choice is true or false, so you must train yourself *not* to do this on questions that test the effect of new premises.

Because all *effect of a new premise* questions require you to assume that the answer choices are true, the question stems nearly always use wording such as *Which one of the following, if true; which one of the following, if valid;* or *which one of the following, if assumed*. Be particularly careful when you see the wording *if assumed*. Such a question is *not* an *assumption* question.

To solve an *effect of a new premise* question, first identify the structure of the original argument. Identify the premises. Identify the conclusion. Identify the type of reasoning that the arguer uses. These may sound like simple steps but in fact it can be difficult to identify these elements of the argument. Take the time to carefully identify the elements of the argument and write them down in the scratch area of your test.

Strengthen a Conclusion

Nearly half of the *effect of a new premise* questions ask you to find the new premise that **strengthens** the argument. To solve a *strengthen* question, identify the structure of the argument and test the answer choices to see which one makes the argument more convincing. Such arguments typically involve cause-and-effect arguments, matching of terms, or matching of two events. These are explained below.

Strengthen questions based on cause-and-effect arguments. The majority of *strengthen* questions involve cause-and-effect arguments, in which two or more factors have a correlation and the conclusion states that one factor causes another.

Consider an argument that states that many people who snore also suffer from insufficient sleep. The statement establishes a correlation between snoring and lack of sleep. The argument may then conclude that snoring causes people to lose sleep. A cause-and-effect argument typically starts with a correlation and then concludes that one factor causes the other. A correlation between two events is not enough to prove that event A caused event B. It is possible that event B caused event A, that another factor caused both A and B, or that B was caused by a factor that has no relationship to A. Consider the ways in which the following statements strengthen the conclusion that snoring causes loss of sleep. In terms of A and B, in which A is snoring and B is sleeping, the original argument says

A leads to not B. Therefore, A causes not B.

1. *Before John started snoring, he slept well.*

This premise shows that lack of snoring is correlated to sleeping well or *not A leads to B*. Combined with the original premise, the argument now reads

A leads to not B. Not A leads to B. Therefore, A causes not B.

The method of strengthening, then, is based on the logic that if a certain event causes a second event, then if the first event does not occur, the second event should not occur either.

2. *John is not kept awake by noisy neighbors.*

This premise eliminates an alternative explanation for John's lack of sleep. Eliminating alternative explanations strengthens the case that it was snoring that prevented John from sleeping, not some other factor.

3. *When John's snoring worsened, he began to sleep even less.*

The logic in this premise is that if a little of A causes a little of B, then a lot of A should cause a lot of B.

4. *John's lack of sleep does not cause him to snore.*

This premise strengthens the argument by eliminating the possibility that it is B that causes A.

5. *Snoring is known to disrupt deep sleep brain rhythms and cause the sleeper to briefly wake up.*

This premise strengthens the argument by providing an explanation for the mechanism by which A causes B.

The examples above include the most common methods for strengthening a cause-and-effect argument. They are listed below.

THE MOST COMMON METHODS FOR STRENGTHENING A CAUSE-AND-EFFECT ARGUMENT (A CAUSES B)

1. The absence of A causes the absence of B.
2. Eliminate other possible causes of B.
3. More of A causes more of B.
4. B does not cause A.
5. Provide an explanation for the mechanism by which A causes B.

PRACTICE EXERCISE 5

Create five premises that strengthen the following cause-and-effect argument, using each of the methods above.

Many people who jog regularly have fast metabolisms. Therefore, jogging must cause people's metabolisms to speed up.

The arguments above, relating snoring and lack of sleep and relating jogging and metabolism, are relatively simple, with one A factor and one B factor. Other cause-and-effect arguments in a *strengthen* question may be more complex. Below are examples of variations on cause-and-effect arguments, along with the methods for strengthening the arguments.

1. **Argument:** *Snoring is not associated with lack of sleep. Therefore, people who do not sleep well probably have an underlying medical problem other than snoring.*

   A is not associated with B. Therefore, a different factor, C, is the cause of B.

   Strengthening premise: *People who snore usually sleep longer than people who do not snore.*

   The premise strengthens by presenting more evidence that A does not cause B.

2. **Argument:** *Snoring physically disrupts the sleep cycle but in fact most people who snore sleep better than the general population. Therefore, people who snore are probably genetically predisposed to sleep well.*

   There are reasons why A does not cause B but in fact A is associated with B in this case, so there likely are genetic factors that override A's usual effect on B.

Strengthening premise: *People who snore usually report that at least one of their parents slept well.*

The premise strengthens the argument by showing that a blood relative has the trait identified as genetic.

3. **Argument:** *People who sleep only during the day often snore. These same people often do not sleep well. This indicates that there is something about sleeping during the day that leads to not sleeping well.*

   A and B are found together. A, B, and C are also found together. Therefore, A must cause C.

   Strengthening premise: *People who sleep only during the day but do not snore and otherwise sleep in conditions similar to people who sleep only during the day who do snore, sleep well.*

   The premise strengthens the argument by showing that when A occurs without B but all other conditions are equal, C does not take place. This eliminates B as a cause of C and strengthens A as the cause.

4. **Argument:** *Many people injure themselves exercising. However, proper exercise can help people avoid injuries, so it is not necessary to avoid exercising in order to avoid injuries.*

   A factor that might seem to cause a negative result actually occurs along with a positive result, so it is not necessary to avoid the seemingly negative factor.

   Strengthening premise: *Proper exercise strengthens tendons that otherwise might tear under strain induced by exercise.*

   The premise strengthens by showing the mechanism by which a seemingly negative factor actually accomplishes a positive result.

5. **Argument:** *Snoring leads to lack of sleep. Snoring also leads to general medical complaints. Therefore, snoring accounts for an increase in the number of visits to physicians.*

   A causes B. A also causes C. Therefore, A causes a consequence (visits to physicians) of both B and C.

   Strengthening premise: *Many people consider lack of sleep to be a condition that they should discuss with their physician.*

   The premise strengthens the argument by showing how B leads to the same consequence to which C leads.

6. **Argument:** *Snoring leads to loss of sleep, which is unhealthy. Sleeping on your side can prevent snoring. Therefore, if you tend to snore, you should make a resolution to sleep on your side whenever you get into bed.*

   A (sleeping on one's side) is desirable. Therefore, one should resolve to do A.

Strengthening premise: *Resolving to take an action during sleep is often effective in actually performing the action.*

The premise strengthens by stating that a resolution actually leads to the desired action.

SUMMARY OF STRATEGIES FOR MORE COMPLEX STRENGTHENING BASED ON CAUSE AND EFFECT

1. Provide further evidence for one of the premises.
2. Strengthen a genetic argument by establishing that a blood relative has the trait in question.
3. State additional relationships between the events in such a way as to strengthen the argument.
4. Explain the mechanism by which a seemingly negative event is actually positive.
5. State that a prelude to an event, as suggested by the argument, actually leads to the event.

Strengthen questions based on matching terms. In these questions there are two distinct terms that are used to establish a correlation. To strengthen the argument, find a premise that shows that the terms refer to the same phenomenon.

1. **Argument:** *In the past, American politicians lacked an in-depth understanding of both the history and political philosophies of European countries. Fortunately, this is no longer the case today. As a result, American politicians make better judgments about foreign policy issues.*

   Strengthening premise: *An understanding of the history and political philosophy of a country leads to making better judgments in foreign policy decisions.*

   The original argument uses two distinct phrases—*in-depth understanding of history and political philosophy* and *make better judgments.* The argument implies that the one leads to the other but does not state it. The new premise strengthens the argument by stating that the two terms are related.

   Strengthen questions based on matching events. This type of question is similar to the matching of two terms but instead of matching specific terms, the argument attempts to match broader events.

2. **Argument:** *Maria has refused to attend every sporting event to which we have invited her. Her husband, Greg, dislikes most sporting events, so clearly Greg is convincing Maria not to attend.*

The argument tries to tie Maria's behavior to Greg's behavior.

Strengthening premise:*The only sporting events that Maria has refused to attend have been in a field of sports that Greg dislikes.*

The new premise makes a closer connection between Greg's dislikes and Maria's behavior.

Strengthen questions based on miscellaneous types of logic. Some *strengthen* questions are not based on either cause and effect or matching two events or terms.

1. **Argument:** *Acme Corporation will be hiring college students for summer jobs. In the past, Acme has only hired students with high grade point averages. If you want to get a job at Acme, it is important to keep your grades up.*

   Strengthening premise: *Acme has stated that the only criterion needed for a college student to get a job is a high grade point average.*

   The original argument implies that grade point average is important for getting a job. The new premise documents that a high grade point average is the only criterion needed for getting a job.

2. **Argument:** *The black locust is a faster-growing tree than the pinyon pine. Therefore, the black locust makes a better shade tree.*

   Strengthening premise: *A tree that grows faster develops a thicker canopy than a slower-growing tree, thus blocking out more sunlight.*

   The original argument implies that there is a relationship between rate of growth and shading properties. The new premise specifies this relationship.

3. **Argument:** *In the past ten years many universities have eliminated general studies degrees. At the same time, there has been an increase in the number of universities offering computer science degrees. Therefore, the number of students earning degrees in computer science must now be larger than the number of students earning degrees in general studies.*

   Strengthening premise: *In general there are many more students enrolled in any computer science degree program than there are students enrolled in any general studies degree program.*

   The original argument compares the number of degree programs in one area with the number of degree programs in a different area. However, the original argument's conclusion refers to the number of students. The new premise makes a connection between the number of students and the type of program.

In this type of question you must distinguish the number of categories from the number of members of a category. Table 2.7 illustrates two scenarios. In both scenarios there are more computer science programs (500) than general studies programs (300). In scenario 1, there are fewer students enrolled on average in a general studies program (50) compared to the average number of students enrolled in a computer science program (200). As a result, the total number of students enrolled in all computer science programs is larger than the total number of students enrolled in all general studies programs.

In scenario 2, the average number of students in a general studies program is 200, whereas the average number of students in a computer science program is 50. As a result, there are fewer total students enrolled in all computer science programs, even though there are many more computer science programs than general studies programs.

Table 2.7. Distinguish Number of Categories from Number of Members of a Category.

	# of Students per Program	# of Programs	# of Students
Scenario 1 General studies	50	300	15,000
Scenario 1 Computer science	200	500	100,000
Scenario 2 General studies	200	300	60,000
Scenario 2 Computer science	50	500	25,000

4. **Argument:** *The New Daily Times movie critic gave the same star rating to both the latest vampire movie and the new documentary on the Mexican gray wolf. Therefore, the two movies must have the same value to society.*

   Strengthening premise: *The New Daily Times movie critic assigns star ratings based on a movie's value to society.*

   The original argument implies that there is a relationship between the star rating and the social value of a movie. The new premise documents the relationship.

There can be many variations in *strengthen* questions. In addition to studying the examples above, carefully review the *strengthen* questions that you encounter in your practice exams.

SUMMARY OF STRATEGIES FOR MISCELLANEOUS STRENGTHENING QUESTIONS

1. Establish that a criterion given as important in the original argument is actually the sole criterion.
2. Explain the mechanism by which a phenomenon given in the original argument occurs.
3. Support the argument's conclusion about the number of members in distinct groups.
4. Document that a relationship that is implied but not specified in the argument actually holds true.

Wording variations for strengthen arguments. The basic wording for a *strengthen* question stem is:

Which one of the following, if true, most strengthens the argument?

To recognize a *strengthen* question stem, first look for wording such as *which one of the following, if true*. Then, look for wording that indicates that the argument or conclusion above is to be strengthened, supported, justified, or correctly drawn.

Strengthen by Applying a Principle

The second type of *effect of a new premise* question type also involves strengthening the argument, but in this case, your task is to identify the principle that strengthens the original argument. The number of *strengthen by applying a principle* questions is about equal to the number of *strengthen* questions.

A principle is an abstract statement, as opposed to a concrete statement. For example, *Shanelle is a history major and she loves sushi* is a concrete statement about a specific person. On the other hand, *College students in the social sciences often prefer ethnic food* is an abstract statement, referring to categories of people and food. Abstract statements can be more difficult to understand than concrete statements.

Most questions that ask you to strengthen an argument by applying a principle are quite similar. The setup presents an argument. The argument may have a logical gap or a missing bit of information necessary to make the argument valid. The answer choices are stated in abstract terms. The correct answer matches the concrete details of the setup and strengthens the argument.

1. **Argument:** *It is true that Inez included in her thesis a statement that was virtually an exact quote from an essay by Jonathan Swift published in an anthology of essays. However, she should not be expelled for plagiarism because she got the statement from her roommate, who claimed to have made it up herself that morning.*

   Strengthening premise: *The inclusion in an academic work of previously published material without permission from the author cannot be considered plagiarism unless the person including the disputed material knows that the material was previously published.*

   The principle is an abstract one. It does not address Inez's situation specifically. However, it exactly matches her situation. In addition, the principle establishes that Inez is not guilty of plagiarism, because she thought the material was made up by her roommate.

Be careful not to confuse this type of question with a question that includes principles in the setup and then asks you to identify an answer choice that can be concluded based on the original principle. Such a question is a *conclusion* question. *Conclusion* questions are covered below.

Wording variations for arguments that strengthen by applying a principle. Basic wording for these questions is:

> Which one of the following principles, if valid, most helps to justify the argument above?

Weaken

The third type of *effect of a new premise* question is a question in which you must find a new premise that weakens the argument. *Weaken* arguments are inverses of *strengthen* arguments. The two share common elements. About 40 percent of *weaken* questions involve cause-and-effect arguments. About 20 percent involve statistical or survey arguments. About 10 percent involve analogies. The other 30 percent include miscellaneous types.

Weaken based on cause and effect. Just as in *strengthen* arguments, *weaken* arguments based on cause and effect present a correlation between events and then conclude that one event caused the other. In *weaken* arguments, look for a new premise that *weakens* the cause-and-effect relationship stated in the setup.

1. **Argument:** *One batch of jelly was made with artificial sweetener and a second batch was made with sugar. The batch made with artificial sweetener had a greater amount of spoilage. Because sugar does not have any preservative properties, it must be that the artificial sweetener actually caused spoilage.*

Weakening premise: *The jars used for the second batch were sterilized longer than the jars for the first batch.*

The new premise introduces an alternate explanation by pointing out an additional difference between the two batches. Providing an alternate plausible explanation is a significant method of weakening a cause and effect argument.

2. **Argument:** *The crack in the dam has all the markings of damage from freezing. However, the water in the dam has not frozen during the past ten years. Therefore, the cause of the crack must be minor earthquakes.*

   Weakening premise: *The only earthquakes that have occurred in the area of the dam in the last ten years have been too small to cause the type of crack that has appeared.*

   The new premise eliminates the cause suggested in the original argument.

3. **Argument:** *The recent explosion at the gravel pit occurred shortly before the increase in emergency room visits for asthma attacks among children. However, the explosion cannot be the cause of the attacks because a child would have to have been within a half mile of the explosion to be affected by it.*

   Weakening premise: *The area immediately around the gravel pit is heavily populated by families with children.*

   The new premise negates an assumption in the argument that there were few children in the vicinity of the explosion.

4. **Argument:** *In a recent experiment one group of asthma sufferers was asked to exercise vigorously for 30 minutes, whereas the control group was not asked to exercise. The group that exercised experienced fewer symptoms than the control group, so exercise must reduce asthma symptoms.*

   Weakening premise: *People who are asked to do a potentially helpful activity may experience a decrease of symptoms just from believing the activity may help them.*

   This type of question requires you to spot a flawed control group experiment. In this experiment the treatment group knew they were being treated.

5. **Argument:** *In a recent experiment one group of asthma sufferers was asked to exercise vigorously for thirty minutes, whereas a second group was asked to exercise for only five minutes. The two groups had exactly the same number of asthma attacks during the study, so the amount of exercise must not affect the frequency of asthma attacks.*

   Weakening premise: *The people in the group who exercised for thirty minutes had five times the number of asthma attacks as the people in the second group before the study began.*

   The new premise shows that the two groups were not equivalent. The premise relies on a measure of improvement (for example, from five attacks per day to one attack per day), as opposed to a simple count of the number of attacks. In Table 2.8, the number of attacks in each group is the same but the improvement (change in the number of attacks) is greater in group 1.

Table 2.8. Number of Attacks Versus Change in Attacks

	Number of Attacks	**Change in Attacks**
Group 1	1 per hour	From 5 attacks per hour to 1 attack per hour
Group 2	1 per hour	From 2 attacks per hour to 1 attack per hour

6. **Argument:** *John switched his overweight dog from commercial dog food to a special healthy dog food but despite three months on a strict diet of the healthy food, his dog has not lost any weight. Therefore, the special healthy dog food is not effective in reducing weight in dogs.*

   Weakening premise: *In most cases it takes a minimum of six months for a change in diet to have an effect on a dog's weight.*

   The new premise attacks the timeline that is assumed in the original argument.

7. **Argument:** *All of Marek's cousins like to play soccer. Marek also likes to play soccer. Therefore, the interest in playing soccer must be genetic.*

   Weakening premise: *Most of Marek's cousins attend schools that have active programs of encouraging children to participate in soccer.*

   The new premise presents an environmental (nongenetic) reason why all of Marek's cousins like to play soccer. Introducing a nongenetic cause of a behavior is a common method of weakening a genetic cause-and-effect argument.

SUMMARY OF STRATEGIES FOR WEAKENING BASED ON CAUSE AND EFFECT

1. Provide an alternate explanation.
2. Eliminate a cause suggested in the original argument.
3. Negate an assumption in the original argument.
4. Point out a flawed control group experiment.
5. Show that two groups that were assumed to be equivalent in the original argument differ in a significant way.
6. Show that the timeline on which the original argument is based is not realistic.
7. Establish a nongenetic (environmental) cause as an alternate explanation for a cause that is implied as genetic in the original argument.

Weaken based on statistical or survey arguments. In these arguments the logic is based on numerical evidence. The numerical evidence may be given as specific numbers, specific percentages, or as a statement that more people met a certain criterion than another. The evidence may come from a measurement (statistical information) or from asking people about their preferences (a survey).

1. **Argument:** *In surveys, most people do not list attending sporting events as an important priority. Despite this, some experts claim that entertainment is a top priority for people. Clearly, these experts are incorrect.*

   Weakening premise: *There are many forms of entertainment other than attending sporting events.*

   The new premise shows that the terms *sporting events* and *entertainment* do not match. This is the reverse of a *strengthen* argument that shows that two terms do match.

2. **Argument:** *The results of Josh's survey of incoming freshmen included three times as many completed surveys from freshmen who were unhappy with their courses as from freshmen who were happy with their courses. It is apparent that Josh's results are biased by his own dislike of his courses.*

   Weakening premise: *An independent study of freshmen determined that nearly four times as many freshmen were unhappy with their courses as were happy with their courses.*

   In this argument an unequal representation is taken to show a bias. The argument is weakened by showing that the unequal representation matches the actual occurrence of opinions as measured impartially.

3. **Argument:** *A new test for diabetes has a 90 percent success rate in identifying people who have diabetes, compared to the 75 percent success rate for the current test. Therefore, the current test should be replaced by the new test.*

   Weakening premise: *The current test has a 95 percent success rate in identifying people who do not have diabetes, whereas the new test has only a 60 percent success rate.*

   This method of weakening depends on understanding that a diagnostic procedure must be evaluated on four criteria: true positive results (correctly identifying people who do have diabetes), true negative results (correctly identifying people who do not have diabetes), false positive results (determining that someone has diabetes when he or she does not), and false negative results (determining that someone does not have diabetes when he or she does). Evaluating a diagnostic procedure on only one of these criteria is flawed and the argument can be weakened by showing that one of the other criteria favors the alternative diagnostic procedure.

4. **Argument:** *Your plan for reducing our company's shortfall recommends reducing vacation time but that will only save $10,000. My plan identifies ten workers who can be eliminated without reducing productivity. Because the average worker earns $20,000, my plan saves the company $200,000 and should be implemented.*

   Weakening premise: *All the workers who have been identified for elimination are interns who are working without pay.*

   The new premise shows that the group that the arguer is identifying (workers to be eliminated) does not in fact fall into the category that the arguer defined (earning $20,000).

5. **Argument:** *Of thirty-five reported small airplane crashes, only seven of the ninety-eight people involved survived. Small airplanes are clearly very dangerous. In fact, the statistics are worse than they appear because there are many unreported airplane crashes in which no one survived.*

   Weakening premise: *If an airplane crash is unreported, there is no way to know how many people did or did not survive.*

   The new premise does not necessarily destroy the original argument. The original statistics still document that small airplanes are not particularly safe. However, the new premise weakens the argument by pointing out a flaw in the argument's logic. Nothing can be known about an event that is unknown.

6. **Argument:** *Ben's Grocery has recently expanded their selection of gourmet coffees in an attempt to increase profits. The managers of Ben's apparently believe that wealthier people will buy more gourmet coffee if there is a larger selection. However, only 10 percent of Ben's customers buy gourmet coffee, whereas over 90 percent buy milk. Ben's should expand their selection of milk rather than their selection of gourmet coffee.*

   Weakening premise: *Ben's earns a much higher profit from the sale of gourmet coffee than they do from the sale of milk.*

   The new premise attacks the original conclusion mathematically, showing that a smaller number of sales of product A can lead to a higher profit if the profit per sale for product A is larger by enough of a margin than the profit per sale for product B. The logic in this attack is similar to the logic in Argument 5 on page 107, under "Weaken Based on Cause and Effect."

Table 2.9. The Fallacy of Percentages. A smaller percentage may yield a higher profit when the profit per sale is higher.

	% of All Buyers	Actual Number of Buyers	Profit per Sale	Total Profit
Gourmet coffee	10	50	$3.00	$150
Milk	90	450	$0.10	$ 45

The lesson of this example is to not be misled by percentages or by any other ratio (percentage is simply a specific type of ratio.) A higher ratio may not mean a larger result. The following argument gives a further example of the need to distinguish ratios from actual numbers.

7. **Argument:** *Three-quarters of the residents of Poplar City have BMW autos. Only one-tenth of the residents of New Madrid drive BMW autos. Clearly the total number of BMWs owned by residents of Poplar City is far greater than the number of BMWs owned by residents of New Madrid.*

   Weakening premise: *Poplar City has a population of 10,000 and New Madrid has a population of 800,000.*

   Beware of ratios (including percentages). Do not confuse ratios with actual numbers. *One out of ten* is a ratio. *Fifty BMWs* represents a number. When you see ratios in premises, look for the actual numbers in the conclusion. In the above argument, the conclusion implies that the actual number of BMWs is higher in the town that has the ratio of 3:4 versus the town with the ratio of 1:10.

Table 2.10. The Difference Between Ratio and Actual Number

	Ratio of Residents Who Have BMWs	Total Number of Residents	Total Number of BMWs
New Madrid	1:10	800,000	80,000
Poplar City	3:4	10,000	7,500

🔑 SUMMARY OF STRATEGIES FOR WEAKENING BASED ON STATISTICAL OR SURVEY ARGUMENTS

1. Show that two terms that are equated in the argument are not equivalent.
2. Establish that an unequal sampling in a survey is in fact representative.
3. Show that a diagnostic procedure that is effective in one mode of diagnosis (true positive, true negative, false positive, false negative) is not effective in another mode.
4. Show that a phenomenon that the arguer claims will lead to a benefit because of certain criteria does not actually match the criteria.
5. Point out a logical flaw in the original argument.
6. Show that a lower ratio (including percentage) results in a higher actual number, or vice versa.

Weaken based on an analogy. About 10 percent of *weaken* questions are based on analogy. An analogy states that two phenomena are similar in one way and, thus, are probably similar in a second way. To weaken such an argument, you must show that the two phenomena are not alike in some relevant way.

1. **Argument:** *Sharmain likes to play chess and she also excels at math. Hank plays chess, so he most likely excels at math as well.*

   Weakening premise: *Francesca plays chess but performs poorly at math.*

   The original argument establishes that Sharmain has two characteristics and then concludes that Hank is analogous to Sharmain through one characteristic (chess) and must therefore also have the second characteristic. The new premise establishes that there are examples of people who share the first characteristic (chess) without also sharing the second characteristic (math).

2. **Argument:** *Viet should probably add a nitrogen fertilizer to his vegetable garden. Karen added nitrogen fertilizer to her garden and it stimulated plant growth, which resulted in better fruit. If Viet fertilizes his garden with nitrogen, he will have better fruit too.*

   Weakening premise: *Viet's garden has much more nitrogen in the soil than Karen's garden had before she fertilized it, and too much nitrogen can result in poorer fruit.*

   The new premise shows that the two gardens are different in a critical way.

3. **Argument:** *The previously unidentified fossil in the local museum can now be identified as a juvenile tyrannosaurus. The proportions of the skull match nearly exactly the unique proportions of tyrannosaurus skulls. In addition, the foot bones also show characteristics that are unique to the tyrannosaurus.*

Weakening premises: *Tyrannosaurus hands typically have two clawed digits, which are not present in the fossil.*

No tyrannasauri lived in the region in which the fossil was found.

The first new premise weakens by establishing that a tyrannosaurus had qualities not present in, or different from, the fossil. The second premise weakens by showing why the fossil could not be a tyrannosaurus.

SUMMARY OF STRATEGIES FOR WEAKENING BASED ON ANALOGY ARGUMENTS

An analogy argument states that one phenomenon has certain characteristics, that a second phenomenon is similar to the first phenomenon, and that therefore the second phenomenon has the same characteristics. The primary ways of weakening an analogy argument are to (1) show that the two related phenomena are different in an important way, or (2) give a reason why the second phenomenon could not have the characteristics.

Types of Strategies:

1. Argument: Phenomenon 1 has characteristics A and B. Phenomenon 2 has characteristic A. Conclusion. Phenomenon 2 must have characteristic B. Weaken by an example of another phenomenon with characteristic A but without characteristic B.

2. Show that two phenomena that the arguments claim are analogous are different in a significant way. (Phenomenon 2 has characteristics that Phenomenon 1 does not have, or Phenomenon 2 lacks characteristics that Phenomenon 1 has.)

3. Provide a reason that supports that Phenomenon 2 cannot have the qualities that the analogy argument implies it has.

Weaken based on miscellaneous arguments. About 20 percent of *weaken* arguments have miscellaneous types of logic. Often the arguments simply present facts and make a conclusion. Below are examples of common *weaken* questions with miscellaneous logic, along with the strategies for weakening them.

1. **Argument:** *Our city could increase its water supply to meet future needs either by extending our existing wells down an additional 100 feet or by entering into a complex agreement with our nearest neighboring city that would require building miles of new pipeline. Extending our existing wells would cost far less, be completed more quickly, and involve less legal planning than an agreement with our neighboring city. Therefore, we should choose the option of lowering our existing wells.*

   Weakening premise: *Lowering the existing wells would introduce toxic minerals into the drinking water.*

   The original argument claims that choice A is better than choice B for a number of reasons. The new premise weakens the argument by establishing that choice A introduces negative effects not considered by the original argument. A variation on this type of weakening would be to show that choice B has positive qualities that were not anticipated by the original argument.

2. **Argument:** *Liam recently bought a new grill, a large supply of hot dogs, and a chef's hat and apron. Apparently, Liam is planning to grill hot dogs.*

   Weakening premise: *Liam's father is having a birthday next week and his father has expressed an interest in taking up grilling.*

   The original argument cites a series of events and states a conclusion that explains the events. The new premise provides an alternative explanation for the same events.

3. **Argument:** *According to recent theories of astrophysics, any astronomical body that is smaller than Pluto would not have a detectable gravitational effect on a star the size of our sun. No comet larger than Pluto has been detected in our solar system, so it is unlikely that a comet would ever affect the sun's gravity.*

   Weakening premise: *Astronomers have documented that a comet in a nearby part of our galaxy has had a gravitational influence on a star the size of our sun.*

   The original argument cites a theory. The new premise presents a documented fact that contradicts the conclusion of the theory. The argument below also weakens an argument by citing facts, but in this case the facts are statistical rather than observed.

4. **Argument:** *Many raw foods have antitumor properties. People who eat a lot of raw foods can reduce their risk of cancer.*

   Weakening premise: *A recent study shows that the rates of four common types of cancer are slightly higher in people who report eating raw foods as 30 percent or more of their diet than the rates of cancer of people who report eating raw foods as 10 percent or less of their diet.*

This new premise uses a statistical correlation, rather than an observed fact, to weaken the argument.

5. **Argument:** *Long-term fasting can lead to exhaustion and depression. People who want to lose weight should not resort to long-term fasting.*

   Weakening premise: *The type of fasting used by nearly all weight loss programs does not last long enough to induce exhaustion or depression.*

   The new premise weakens the original argument by showing that a premise of the original argument is irrelevant to the conclusion. The situation that the original argument is addressing, fasting for weight loss, does not match the criteria that make fasting harmful. The original premise would only be valid if the weight loss program lasted three months, for example. The original premise was correct in principle but its time frame was off.

   An original premise might also be inherently irrelevant. Consider:

   Weakening premise: *No modern weight loss program uses extended fasting of any kind.*

   In this example the original premise is not correct even in principle. It is in error and thus is irrelevant to the conclusion.

   A new premise cannot negate a premise in the setup. All premises in the setup have to be accepted as true. (*All white cats are deaf, right?*) In the above examples the new premise does not say that the original premise is false. It says, rather, that the original premise does not apply to the conclusion.

SUMMARY OF STRATEGIES FOR WEAKENING BASED ON MISCELLANEOUS ARGUMENTS

1. Show that a choice favored by the conclusion has additional negative qualities.
2. Show that a choice rejected by the conclusion has additional positive qualities.
3. Provide an alternative explanation for a series of events.
4. Attack the conclusion of a theory by citing an observed event or fact that contradicts the conclusion.
5. Provide statistical evidence that contradicts the conclusion.
6. Show that a premise is irrelevant, either because it does not match the conclusion at all or because it partially matches the conclusion but does not match the time frame or quantities involved in the conclusion.

Wording variations for weaken arguments. The basic wording for a *weaken* question stem is:

Which one of the following, if true, most weakens the argument?

Resolve a Paradox

The final category of question types involving the effect of a new premise is that of **resolving a paradox**. In *resolve a paradox* questions, the setup includes seemingly contradictory statements. The first step in solving such a question is to identify which statements constitute the paradox and what the nature of the paradox is. The paradox usually involves two premises.

The correct answer for a *resolve a paradox* question is a new premise that explains how each of the premises that constitute the paradox can be true despite the fact that the premises appear to be contradictory. Often the correct answer is something unexpected that you would not necessarily have thought of but once you consider it, it makes sense. For this reason, the best way to solve a *resolve a paradox* question is to read each answer and test whether it resolves the paradox.

Solving these questions is like solving a mystery. A piece of the puzzle that will explain everything is missing. Fortunately, the missing piece is one of the five answer choices.

Nearly any topic that is otherwise used in LR questions can be used in a *resolve a paradox* passage, though there are slightly more physical science questions than average, and fewer passages on the arts. *Resolve a paradox* questions do not have the large number of variations that *strengthen* and *weaken* questions have. Most can be solved using the same tools.

1. **Argument:** *The Flix21 movie complex responded to complaints about long waits in the ticket line by setting up three new ticket sales stations and hiring additional employees to staff the new stations. Nevertheless, on the first weekend that the new stations were in operation, the average wait in the ticket line was five minutes longer than before the new stations were implemented.*

   Resolving premise: *Flix21's ads before the weekend promised "More ticket sellers. Faster lines." As a result the number of people attending Flix21's complex greatly increased.*

   The original argument is paradoxical in that three new ticket stations should logically result in faster ticket sales and shorter waits in the ticket line. The new premise provides additional information that explains how the facts in the original argument can all be true and yet do not result in a paradox.

Wording of the question stem. About half of *resolve a paradox* question stems refer to a discrepancy, paradox, or conflict. Of these, the vast majority use the wording *apparent discrepancy*.

> Which one of the following, if true, helps explain the apparent discrepancy in the above argument?

In addition, you will also see a small number of questions with the wording *discrepancy, apparent paradox, paradox,* and *conflict*. About half of *resolve a paradox* questions use the wording *explains the facts,* without referring to a paradox.

> Which one of the following, if true, most helps to explain the facts given above?

Some such questions may hint at a paradox with wording such as *a significant difference* or *an unexpected fact*.

> Which one of the following, if true, most helps to explain the unexpected result that the dolphins that were not hand-fed grew larger?

In most cases these questions function in exactly the same way as the questions that use the wording *discrepancy, paradox,* or *conflict*. In some cases the facts in the passage may not be quite as contradictory.

The wording of the stem for all types of *resolve a paradox* questions is consistent. The wording usually includes *Which one of the following, if true* and asks which answer choice *helps to* or *most helps to* either explain or resolve.

Assumption

For purposes of the LSAT, an **assumption** is a premise that is not stated in the setup. An assumption question asks you to identify a new premise that either is necessary or sufficient to make the argument valid. Assumption questions account for a little under 15 percent of all LR questions. Just as in *effect of a new premise* questions, the answer choices consist of five premises. The answer choices must be accepted as true. You cannot eliminate an answer choice simply because you do not believe it is a true statement.

The wording for a basic *assumption* question stem takes one of two forms:

> **Necessary assumption:** Which one of the following is an assumption required by the argument?
> **Sufficient assumption:** Which one of the following, if assumed, allows the argument's conclusion to be properly drawn?

The phrase *if assumed* serves the same function as the phrase *if true* that is found in *effect of a new premise* questions. It reminds you that you must consider the premise to be true. Additionally, it lets you know that the question is an *assumption* question.

All assumption questions are based on a logical argument that makes a strong case for its conclusion but leaves out at least one important point. In other words, the argument has a gap, a missing piece of the puzzle. The correct answer identifies the missing piece. The correct answer either supplies a new bit of information that makes the argument work, or it points out an unstated premise without which the argument cannot work.

Necessary Versus Sufficient Assumptions

The two forms of question stem above represent two distinct types of *assumption* questions: **necessary** and **sufficient**. The distinction between these two types is similar to the distinction between sufficient and necessary conditions, described in this chapter's section on if/then arguments. A sufficient assumption is a premise that is enough (sufficient) to make the conclusion work. A necessary assumption is a premise that is required (necessary) to make the conclusion work. In other words, a necessary assumption is a fact that, if it were not true, would cause the conclusion to be invalid.

In part, the distinction between necessary assumptions and sufficient assumptions is one of perspective. A sufficient assumption adds something that makes the conclusion stronger. A necessary assumption, if taken away, makes the conclusion weaker (or destroys it).

There are no *assumption* question stems that combine the two types. The question stems for *assumption* questions pose either a *sufficient assumption* question or a *necessary assumption* question. When you see the word *assume* in a question stem, be prepared to identify whether the question is asking for *sufficient* or *necessary*. *Necessary assumptions* include the words *required, depends,* or *relies on.* Most include the wording *which one of the following*, but that wording is sometimes left off. Nearly all include the words *assumption* or *assume*, but those may also be left off.

Question stems for *sufficient assumptions* nearly always include the phrase *which one of the following*, along with a clause that is equivalent to *if assumed.*

To distinguish the two types of *assumption* questions, use the following summary:

> **Necessary assumptions:** *The argument depends on/relies on/requires one of the below.*
>
> **Sufficient assumptions:** *If one of the below is assumed, the conclusion will be strengthened/be properly drawn/be justified/be supported/follow logically from the premises.*

PRACTICE EXERCISE 6

Identify whether the stem represents a necessary or sufficient assumption. You can refer to the previous information. The answers are given below the exercise.

1. The scientist's argument relies on which one of the following?

2. Which one of the following is an assumption on which the scientist's argument depends?

3. Which one of the following, if assumed, enables the scientist's argument to be properly drawn?

4. The scientist's argument requires that . . .

5. The conclusion follows logically from the premises in the argument if which one of the following is assumed?

6. The conclusion drawn is most justified if which one of the following is assumed?

Answers:

1. necessary	**3.** sufficient	**5.** sufficient
2. necessary	**4.** necessary	**6.** sufficient

Necessary assumptions. In a *necessary assumption* question, there is a gap in the logic presented in the setup. The gap represents information that was not stated but must be true for the argument to work.

1. **Argument:** *Jenna loves Weimaraner dogs and has always wanted one. Until recently she has not been able to afford owning a pet, but now that she is earning enough money to support one pet, she will undoubtedly get a Weimaraner.*

   The gap in the above argument is not readily apparent. The argument seems to be valid and well supported by its premises.

   Necessary assumption: *There is not another pet that Jenna would rather own than a Weimaraner.*

   The assumption points out a gap in the argument. If there were another pet that Jenna would rather own, she would get that pet instead of a Weimaraner, given that the argument states that she can afford only one pet.

   Because a necessary assumption is required for the argument to work, the best way to test whether an answer choice is a necessary assumption is to negate the answer choice. For the above example, negate the necessary assumption:

Premise: *There is not another pet that Jenna would rather own than a Weimaraner.*

Negated premise: *There is another pet that Jenna would rather own than a Weimaraner.*

What would happen to the argument if the negated version of the assumption were true? If there is a pet that Jenna would rather own, she would get that pet instead of the Weimaraner. The conclusion—that Jenna will now get a Weimaraner—is destroyed.

Consider the possible answer choice below and test it by negating it:

Premise: *Jenna is not allergic to any dogs.*

Negated premise: *Jenna is allergic to some dogs.*

How does the negated assumption affect the conclusion? The fact that Jenna may be allergic to some dogs does not mean that she is allergic to Weimaraners, and even if she were, she may still want to own a Weimaraner. The negated premise fails to destroy the conclusion. Therefore, the original premise could not be an assumption of the argument. Only a true assumption destroys or seriously undermines the conclusion when removed from the argument (negated).

The primary strategy for solving a necessary assumption question, then, is to test the answer choices by negating them. Practice this as you work on assumption questions.

Sufficient assumptions. *Sufficient assumption* passages also have a gap in the logic of the argument. The correct answer inserts a new fact into the gap and thereby strengthens the argument. A *sufficient assumption* question is similar in this way to a *strengthen* question. You can use many of the strategies that apply to *strengthen* questions to solve *sufficient assumption* questions.

Compared to *necessary assumption* questions, *sufficient assumption* questions are more frequently based on deductive logic. Because deductive arguments are based on absolute rules, it is easier to pinpoint the missing element.

1. **Argument:** *Anyone who does not either graduate from high school or earn a high school equivalence degree will have a hard time finding a well-paying job. Victor withdrew from high school before graduating and never returned to finish his degree. Therefore, Victor will have a hard time finding a well-paying job.*

   The argument is deductive. It states that *If –graduate and –equivalence → –well-paying job.* Victor's case meets the criterion of *–graduate (not graduate).* In order to make the conclusion, it is clear that the missing piece is whether or not Victor earned a high school equivalence degree.

Sufficient assumption: *Victor did not earn a high school equivalence degree.* With this fact, the conclusion of the argument is properly drawn.

Unlike in *necessary assumption* questions, it is not necessary to negate the answer choices. Simply plugging in the answer choice as it is stated is enough to strengthen the conclusion. However, in some questions it can also be helpful to use the strategy of negating premises. If the correct answer is not clear from plugging premises into the argument, negating answer choices and testing how that affects the argument might reveal the correct answer. In fact, for many *assumption* questions—whether the question stem is stated as *necessary* or as *sufficient*—the correct answer may be both necessary and sufficient. In other words, for many *assumption* questions, the correct answer actively strengthens the argument *and* if the correct answer is negated, the argument is destroyed. In the above example, what happens if you negate the correct answer?

Premise: *Victor did not earn a high school equivalence degree.*
Negated premise: *Victor earned a high school equivalence degree.*

If Victor earned a high school equivalence degree, he does not meet the criterion of the first if/then statement and the argument falls apart. The correct answer in this case is both sufficient (it is enough to make the argument work) and necessary (without it, the argument falls apart).

Do not be overly concerned if the line between *sufficient* and *necessary assumptions* seems blurry. You can easily identify the intent of the question stem, because all *assumption* questions stems fall either into one category or the other, with no overlap. However, as you work a question, if plugging the answer choice into the argument (the strategy for *sufficient assumptions*) does not seem to help, try negating the answer choice (the strategy for *necessary assumptions*).

Conclusion

The next most common major question type is **conclusion**. *Conclusion* questions ask you to identify a conclusion of an argument. *Conclusion* questions account for a little under 15 percent of LR questions. In some *conclusion* questions you are asked to find the one main conclusion, the main point, of the argument. More often, however, a *conclusion* question asks you to find a statement that can be concluded based on the premises in the passage. In other words, it may be possible to conclude a certain fact even though that fact is not the main point of the argument and may even be peripheral to the argument as a whole. With *conclusion* questions, then, it is necessary to distinguish *main conclusion* questions from *what can be inferred* (anything that can be concluded) questions.

In a *conclusion* question, the five answer choices represent possible conclusions. This is in contrast to the question types that have been covered earlier in this chapter, in which the answer choices represented possible premises. *Conclusion* question stems never say *Which of the following, if true*, because *if true* only applies to premises. The stems may, however, say *If the above statements are true* because the above statements include premises.

What Can Be Inferred

The majority (60 percent) of *conclusion* questions ask you to identify the answer choice that can be inferred from the premises in the setup. Remember that inference is the process of moving through premises to a conclusion, applying valid logic. Do not interpret the word *infer* in the ordinary sense of something that could be true. To infer that an answer choice is logically valid means that the premises in the argument can be combined to *prove* the truth of the answer choice. An inference is identical to a conclusion.

1. **Argument:** *Cottonwood trees are fast-growing trees frequently used to create shade in a residential lot. There are a number of slower-growing trees that have the advantages of bright fall color and edible fruit, neither of which the cottonwood possesses. Most landscapers, however, avoid planting trees that they do not consider to be cost-effective for the size of the tree. Landscapers generally consider a slow-growing tree not to be cost-effective for its size.*

   Correct conclusion: *Many landscapers will continue to plant less decorative, non-fruiting trees as shade trees, even though more decorative and useful trees are available.*

   The argument presents a number of premises. It does not arrive at a conclusion. Your task is to identify the answer choice that can be proven to be true, given the premises in the argument. Below is a proof of the correct premise:

   > **Premise:** *Landscapers do not plant non-cost-effective trees.*
   > **Premise:** *Landscapers consider slow-growing trees to be non-cost-effective.*
   > **Intermediate conclusion:** *Landscapers will not plant slow-growing trees.*
   > **Premise:** *Cottonwoods are not slow-growing trees and they are good shade trees.*
   > **Premise:** *Cottonwoods are less decorative and do not fruit.*

> **Conclusion:** *Some landscapers who need to plant a shade tree will plant a less decorative, non-fruiting tree.*

What can be inferred questions are relatively straightforward to solve. Identify the premises in the passage. These are your "raw materials" for defending an answer. Test the answer choices to determine whether or not a particular answer choice can be defended using the premises in the passage and valid logic.

Must Be True

This type of *conclusion* question is a slight variation on *what can be inferred* questions. In *must be true* questions, the correct answer is forced to be true because of rigorous deductive reasoning or absolute mathematical arguments. The setup generally consists of deductive premises, typically without a stated conclusion. The question asks you to identify an answer choice that must be true, given the premises in the conclusion.

1. **Argument:** *Anyone who owns a Gabby Natty doll also owns a Tubby Tow Truck. However, anyone who owns a Tubby Tow Truck does not own a water cannon. Sandi owns a water cannon.*
   Correct conclusion: *Sandi does not own a Gabby Natty doll.*
   The deductive statements are:

   If Gabby $\rightarrow$ *Tubby*

   If Tubby $\rightarrow$ *–Water*

   Water $\therefore$ *–Tubby*

   –Tubby $\therefore$ *–Gabby*

The question stem for a *must be true* question is typically *If the statements above are true, which one of the following must be true?*

Identify the Main Conclusion

This type of *conclusion* argument is significantly different from a *what can be inferred* question. It accounts for 40 percent of *conclusion* questions. In this type it is not enough to prove that an answer choice can be proven correct. Instead, you must defend that the answer choice states the main conclusion, or main point, of the argument. This is similar to a Reading Comprehension question that asks you to identify the main point.

To answer a *main conclusion* question you must understand the premises and the conclusions that are stated in the argument. You must also identify the intent of the argument. What is the arguer trying to prove?

In some questions, the main conclusion is explicitly stated in the argument. In other questions, the main conclusion is created by combining two or more explicit statements. In a small number of questions, the main conclusion is not given in the passage, and you must infer it.

1. **Argument:** *Animal shelters in most cities have no choice but to put down hundreds of animals yearly. Shelters simply do not have the money available to maintain all of the unwanted animals for which they are responsible. However, an alternative—no-kill shelters—is likely to become prevalent in the near future. A number of cities have proven that no-kill shelters can be economically viable and have no drawbacks compared to traditional shelters.*

   Correct conclusion: *No-kill animal shelters are likely to become prevalent in the near future as an alternative to traditional animal shelters.*

   Scanning the argument, determine that the intent of the passage is to establish that no-kill shelters will become prevalent. You can defend this by showing that the other statements all support the proposal that no-kill shelters will become prevalent. The first two sentences establish that the traditional shelter has certain drawbacks and that an alternative is needed. The final sentence shows that no-kill shelters have been viable in some locations and supports the conclusion that no-kill shelters will become more prevalent. The correct answer choice is a close paraphrase of the explicitly stated conclusion.

2. **Argument:** *Economists have predicted that if gas prices drop next summer, people will drive to more distant locations on their summer vacations. However, people are more likely to stay home. Once people have experienced sharply increased gas prices, they are likely to develop habits of frugality that persist even when the price hikes that created the habits have reversed.*

   Correct conclusion: *If gas prices drop next summer, people will most likely stay home.*

   The correct conclusion in this case combines information explicitly stated in the first and second sentences of the argument. Neither sentence alone captures the full conclusion. The statement in the second sentence, *people are more likely to stay home,* by itself provides only part of the information needed to state a conclusion. In many *main conclusion* questions, you must combine information from two or more sentences to accurately state the full conclusion.

3. **Argument:** *Economists have predicted that if gas prices drop next summer, people will drive to more distant locations on their summer vacations. However, once people have experienced sharply increased gas prices, they are likely to develop habits of frugality that persist even when the price hikes that created the habits have reversed.*

   Correct conclusion: *A prediction about economic activity in the face of fluctuating prices is likely to prove incorrect.*

   This argument is a modification of the previous one. It contains all of the premises of the original but does not include the sentence that states the conclusion. The correct answer choice provides a conclusion that can be defended as being the main point, even though it is stated in general terms.

If you are unclear about what the conclusion of a passage is, examine each statement and ask yourself if that statement is meant to support another statement or concept. Statements that support another concept are premises, not the main conclusion. Two premises can be combined to create an intermediate conclusion that is then used to support the main conclusion.

> *Premise:* All fruit contains vitamin C.
> *Premise:* Pawpaws are a fruit.
> *Intermediate conclusion:* Therefore, pawpaws contain vitamin C.
> *Main conclusion:* If John needs to get more dietary vitamin C, he should eat pawpaws.

Which Conclusion Can Be Rejected?

There is a rare type of *conclusion* question that asks you to identify a conclusion that violates the premises in the argument. The correct answer choice is one that can be proven to be incorrect.

Flaw

Flaw questions make up about 13 percent of LR questions. A *flaw* question asks you to identify the logical flaw in the argument. A logical flaw is an error in reasoning. Earlier in the chapter you reviewed the categories of logical flaws that have appeared on recent LSATs. The five answer choices to a *flaw* question are often based on these categories. There can also be answer choices that are based on flawed reasoning unique to the particular setup.

For *flaw* questions, the setup contains an argument with premises and at least one conclusion. However, just as in *weaken* arguments, the argument has a gap. For *flaw* questions, the gap hints at something that is erroneous in the logic of the argument. When you read the setup for a *flaw* question, ask yourself if you "buy" the argument on an intuitive level. Does the argument sound reasonable to you? Even though you know the argument has a flaw, in some questions the flaw is so well hidden that the argument sounds viable. It is helpful in this case to acknowledge that you do not see a flaw. On the other hand, if you intuitively feel that something is wrong with the argument, try to identify what bothers you about it. If you are not able to pinpoint the error quickly, move on to analyzing the answer choices. Having focused briefly on the error, even if you cannot identify it explicitly, may help you recognize the correct answer when you see it.

Flaw questions can occur in a basic form, in which the answer choices may include any type of logical flaw, or in a specialized form, in which the stem uses the wording *fails to consider the possibility*. In the *fails to consider* form, the flaw in the argument is that there is an element that the argument has failed to consider. Your task is to identify which answer choice represents that element.

Basic "Flaw" Questions

The question stem for a basic *flaw* question can include wording such as:

> *Which one of the following most accurately describes a flaw in the argument?*
> *The reasoning in the argument is flawed in that the argument . . .*
> *The reasoning in the argument is vulnerable to which one of the following criticisms?*
> *The argument is most vulnerable to criticism on the grounds that . . .*

A more comprehensive list of wording variations is given at the end of this section. Notice that in some of the examples above, the correct answer completes the sentence. The wording *vulnerable to criticism* and its variations occurs in about half of the *flaw* questions. *Vulnerable to criticism* stems do *not* indicate a separate type of question. The wording *vulnerable to criticism* is simply an alternative way to indicate that the question is a *flaw* question.

To solve a basic *flaw* question, read through the setup to get a sense of what is missing or erroneous. Then move on to the answer choices. Scan the answer choices first to see if one answer choice seems to match your intuitive sense of the logical flaw. For easier questions, this will lead you to the answer. Harder questions, however, have one or more incorrect answer choices designed to trick you. In most *flaw* questions, then, you will have to apply a more advanced problem-solving strategy.

As you evaluate an answer choice, consider first whether it is a true statement. If it is not, then it cannot be the correct answer. Even if it is a true statement, it still might not be correct. Consider the following example:

SAMPLE PASSAGE 1

At the city's upcoming summer festival, both fruit and hot dogs will be given away. Most people like to eat fruit in the summer. Therefore, most people will choose fruit over hot dogs.

The argument is most vulnerable to criticism in that it

(A) presumes, without warrant, that people will take free food even if they are not hungry

(B) infers that because people behave a certain way in one situation, they will behave the same way in a different situation

(C) fails to consider whether people who like to eat fruit in the summer also like to eat hot dogs in the summer

(D) presumes, without warrant, that people only eat fruit in the summer

(E) fails to address the possibility that food other than fruit and hot dogs will be given away at the festival

Solution: Which answer choices are factually correct? For choice A, the passage does not address what might happen if people are not hungry. For choice B, the passage's premise that people like to eat fruit in the summer presumably refers to situations other than the summer festival, so it is true that the argument infers that people will behave the same way at the festival as they do in other situations. Choice B, then, is a true statement but is it the flaw in the argument? No. It is not a logical flaw to believe that people's food preference in other situations will be the same at the festival. Choice B is a true statement but does not represent the logical flaw in the argument.

Is choice C a true statement? The argument does "fail" to do what choice C describes. Choice C, then, is a true statement. Does choice C represent a flaw in the argument? If people who like to eat fruit also equally like to eat hot dogs, then the conclusion falls apart. Choice C does represent a flaw in the argument. Choice C is a possible correct answer.

Is choice D a true statement? There is no evidence that the argument assumes that people only eat fruit in the summer. Choice D is not a true statement and can be eliminated.

Is choice E a true statement? Yes. The argument does fail to do what choice E describes. Does choice E represent the flaw in the argument? Choice E seems to be irrelevant. Even if other food is available, people will still prefer fruit. The correct answer is choice C.

Remember that the default multiple-choice question—the question to which your brain is likely to revert—is *Which one of the following is true?* Flaw questions often try to trap you into falling for an answer choice that is true but does not represent the flaw in the argument. Beware!

Fails to Consider a Possibility

In Sample Passage 1, answer choices C and E use *fails to consider* wording. One of the categories of flawed reasoning is failing to consider a certain possibility. *Fails to consider a possibility* questions are a specialized form of *flaw* question in which all of the answer choices fall into the category of failing to consider a certain possibility. Whereas other categories of flawed reasoning point out an error in logic, the answer choices in *fails to consider* questions usually refer simply to information or possibilities that the arguer did not consider and, as a result, came to an incorrect conclusion. The difference between a logical error and an informational error (a fact that the arguer failed to consider) is illustrated below:

1. **Argument:** *Any student who does not have an official score on the LSAT will not be accepted to law school. Greg recently took the LSAT and has received his official score. Therefore, Greg will be accepted to law school.*
   Logical error: *The argument confuses a condition that is necessary for a student to get into law school with a condition that is sufficient for getting into law school.*
2. **Argument:** *Any student who does not have an official score on the LSAT will not be accepted to law school. Greg recently registered to take an official administration of the LSAT. Thus, he will have an official score on the LSAT.*
   Informational error: *The argument fails to consider that Greg might not take the exam for which he is registered.*

In the first example, confusing a necessary condition with a sufficient condition is an error in logic. In the second example, the arguer's error is in not taking into account a fact: the possibility that Greg will not actually take the exam. Most of the answer choices in *fails to consider* questions are based on facts.

SAMPLE PASSAGE 2

Martina: Striped bass are attracted to live bait. I see you just cast your fishing line and that you used live bait. You already have a fish tugging on your line, so most likely you have caught a striped bass.

Martina's reasoning is questionable in that it fails to consider the possibility that

(A)   some live bait is more effective than other live bait in attracting striped bass

(B)   some striped bass are equally attracted to lures and live bait

(C)   fish other than striped bass are more attracted to lures than to live bait

(D)   fish other than striped bass are attracted to live bait

(E)   the ability to catch fish depends on the amount of experience of the person fishing

Solution: The answer choices above are all based on facts. The logical error is that Martina has failed to consider one of these facts. All of the answer choices except D are irrelevant. Choice D is correct because it indicates that the fish on the line may be something other than a striped bass. Martina's logic is flawed because she ignored a possible fact that would have altered her conclusion.

Takes for Granted

In Sample Passage 2, Martina failed to consider a fact that could be true. Another rare type of *flaw* question involves taking for granted that something is true when in fact it might be false. It uses wording such as *The logic in the argument is questionable in that the argument takes for granted that . . .*

Wording Variations of Answer Choices

It is often difficult to recognize the type of a flawed logic to which an answer choice is referring. Sometimes the wording of an answer choice is so complex as to obscure the type of logic, so it is important for you to carefully analyze the answer choices. Review the flawed logic types that are described earlier in the chapter, if necessary.

Non-flaws

There is a category of incorrect answer choice in which the answer choice, though true, is not a logical flaw and therefore cannot be the correct answer. These **non-flaws** typically state that the argument has failed to support a premise in some way. Failing to support a premise cannot be a logical flaw because premises must be accepted as true.

Sample Passage 3

At the city's upcoming summer festival, both fruit and hot dogs will be given away. Most people like to eat fruit in the summer. Therefore, most people will choose fruit over hot dogs.

The argument is most vulnerable to criticism in that it

(A) provides no evidence to support the assertion that most people like to eat fruit in the summer

(B) does not indicate how many people will attend the festival

(C) fails to consider whether people who like to eat fruit in the summer also like to eat hot dogs in the summer

(D) fails to adequately define what constitutes fruit

(E) fails to provide support for the assertion that there will be no charge for the fruit and hot dogs at the festival

Solution: In this variation of Sample Passage 1, answer choices A, B, D, and E are all non-flaws. Each of them is a true statement. For example, the argument does not provide evidence to support the assertion that people like to eat fruit in the summer. In a real-life discussion, evidence to support a fact makes the fact more believable, but in LR it is not necessary to support a premise. Failure to do so is not a flaw in logic.

Similarly, the argument does not tell how many people will attend the festival. Telling the attendance of the festival would be information that would bolster the premise. If many people come to the festival, it is more likely that statistical correlations (such as people's preference for fruit) will hold true. However, failing to bolster a premise is not a logical flaw.

Choices D and E are also true statements that might bolster the argument. Neither is a logical flaw because it is not necessary to support or further bolster a premise. Choice C is correct because if people who like fruit also like hot dogs, the argument falls apart.

Parallel Reasoning

Parallel reasoning arguments present an argument and ask you to identify an answer choice that contains an argument that has the same (parallel) structure as the original. About 7 percent of LR passages involve parallel reasoning.

Parallel reasoning questions present five answer choices, each of which is a complete argument. For this reason, an entire parallel reasoning question can be quite long, sometimes taking up most of a column. These long passages can seem intimidating, and many people, if they are going to skip any questions at all, skip parallel reasoning questions. Some more difficult parallel reasoning questions *can* be time-consuming. However, many, even if lengthy, can be solved quickly.

In a parallel reasoning question, first identify the type of logic in the original passage. If the type of logic is one that you can readily recognize—in other words, if the logic is one of the types of logic that you have studied in this chapter—then you may be able to find the correct answer quickly.

SAMPLE PASSAGE 4

All folk music is based on recurring themes. Kerry claims that her new composition is folk music, although it is not based on recurring themes. Therefore, Kerry's new composition is not folk music.

Which one of the following is most similar in reasoning to the above argument?

(A) Classical music often draws on themes from the folk music of the composer's native country. Critics claim that Beethoven's music reflects themes from Hungarian folk music, even though Hungary was not Beethoven's native country. Therefore, Beethoven's music was not classical music.

(B) It must be true that Isaiah is not in law school. All law students spend at least twenty hours a week in the library at this time of year. Even though Isaiah has many homework assignments, he is only spending fifteen hours a week in the library at this time of year.

(C) All modern art uses abstract designs to create impressions. Li's art uses abstract designs to create impressions, even though Li has not studied modern art. Therefore, Li's art is modern art.

(D) Everyone in our building who came down with the flu last month has small children at home. Hannah came down with the flu, although she believes she did not get it from her children. Nevertheless, having small children at home must have caused her to get the flu.

(E) Michael recently choreographed a new dance and claimed that it was a folk dance. Michael's journalism professor saw the dance and claimed that it did not have any of the qualities that are necessary to make it a folk dance. Therefore, Michael's new dance is not a folk dance.

Solution: Because a parallel reasoning question requires that you match the logical structure of the original passage with the structure in an answer choice, first identify the structure of the original passage. This can be easy, moderately easy, or difficult, depending on the passage. Following is the hierarchy that correlates with the difficulty of identifying the structure of the original passage:

HIERARCHY OF DIFFICULTY IN
PARALLEL REASONING ORIGINAL PASSAGES

Easiest: deductive arguments (if/then or sets)

Moderately easy: one of the other types of logic categories described in this chapter

Difficult: an argument that is not based on deduction or any other specific category of reasoning described in this chapter

---

If the original passage is a deductive argument, you are in luck. It will be quick and easy to identify the structure. If the argument is not deductive but is recognizable as one of the other categories of logic that you have studied, you may still find that it is easy to identify the logic and match it to an answer. If none of the above hold true, then the question will probably take more time.

In Sample Passage 4, what type of reasoning does the original passage use? Is it (1) deductive, (2) a recognizable nondeductive logic category, or (3) something else? The first sentence is an absolute rule. The argument is deductive. Now analyze the logic. Is the deductive argument an if/then or a set argument? It is difficult to tell from the first sentence. Try it first as an if/then. If that does not work, you can try organizing it as a set argument.

Taking the first sentence, create a standard if/then statement. The two phenomena being related are:

1. folk music
2. recurring themes

Which is the determining factor (comes first)? *Recurring themes* seems to be what leads to folk music.

If (blank) recurring themes → (blank) folk music

The blanks indicate that we have not yet determined whether it is the presence of recurring themes or the absence of recurring themes that determines the result. It is not true that anything with recurring themes is folk music. It must be the absence of recurring themes that determines the result.

If –recurring themes → –folk music

How does this statement relate to the rest of the passage? Kerry's composition does not have recurring themes.

Rule: *If –recurring themes → –folk music*
Case: *–recurring themes*
Conclusion: *–folk music*

More concisely stated this would be:

If –recurring themes → –folk music
–recurring themes ∴ –folk music

You can write the logic in an even more generalized form simply as:

If A → B
A ∴ B

It does not matter whether A is a negative or positive statement, as long as A is the same in both the first and second line of the logic.

Now that you have isolated the structure of the logic, test the answer choices. Try testing all the answer choices in the Sample Passage.

Explanation: In choice A, the main premise (first sentence) is not an absolute statement, so choice A is not deductive and cannot be the correct answer. In choice B the first sentence does not seem to be a premise. In fact, the first sentence is the conclusion. The main premise is the second sentence, that *all law students spend at least twenty hours a week in the library.* As an if/then statement, this becomes:

If –twenty hours → –law student

The third sentence tells us:

(Isaiah) – twenty hours

because Isaiah only spends fifteen hours. The conclusion follows exactly as in the original.

(Isaiah) – twenty hours ∴ (Isaiah) – law student

Choice B is an exact match for the original. It must be the correct answer. You can quickly skim the rest of the answer choices to make sure you have not made an error. On a timed test it would not be advisable to actually work out the other answer choices because they are so long.

For learning purpose, consider choices C through E. Choice C can be diagrammed as

If –abstract → –modern
Abstract ∴ modern

This is not the same logic as the original and in fact is not valid logic. Choice C is out. Scanning choice D, you can quickly spot that it is a cause-and-effect argument. It is out. Choice E is a false appeal to authority argument. It is out.

There are three common misconceptions about parallel reasoning questions. First, a correct answer in a parallel argument question does *not* need to have subject matter that is similar to the original passage. If the original passage discusses music, be careful not to choose an answer choice simply because it also discusses music. The correct answer can be on a completely different topic.

Second, a correct answer does *not* need to have the same sentence structure as the original. Do not choose an answer choice simply because it has similar wording, phrases, or sentences. The correct answer may have completely different phrasing or sentence structure. Third, a correct answer does not have to have the logical elements in the same order as in the original. In the example above, the correct answer had the conclusion in the first sentence, whereas the original had the conclusion in the third. The order is not important.

The only thing that you must match is the logic itself. If the original passage is an if/then statement, the correct answer must have the same if/then logic. If the original passage is a cause-and-effect argument, the correct answer must be a cause-and-effect argument. Consider the following:

SAMPLE PASSAGE 5

Francesca and Nick were both tested for hand/eye coordination and spatial ability and scored in the 99th percentile. Francesca has begun taking golf lessons and is already playing exceptionally well. Nick is also interested in learning golf. It is likely that he will also play exceptionally well.

The reasoning in which one of the arguments below is most similar to the reasoning in the argument above?

(A) Anyone who plays golf well has excellent hand/eye coordination. Martin and Olivia both play golf well. It is likely that both Martin and Olivia have excellent hand/eye coordination.

(B) Patricia and Tomas both scored in the 99th percentile on the same intelligence test. Patricia studied logic puzzles for three months before taking the test. Tomas also studied logic puzzles. It is likely that studying the puzzles caused him to score high on the test.

(C) Sandra and Hugh are both realtors. Sandra's sales have equaled Hugh's for the last five years. It is likely that Hugh uses many of the same sales strategies that Sandra uses.

(D) Jennifer and Louis have both submitted proposals to the city council for the development of a new sports complex. Jennifer's proposal has the support of several architecture professors at the university. Louis's proposal does not have support from any professors, so it is likely that his proposal is not well designed.

(E) It is likely that dolphins experience sadness. Dolphins and humans have similar social needs and emotions. Humans are sometimes isolated and experience sadness.

Solution: Identify the type of logic in the original argument. Is it deductive? No. Is it a type that you have studied? Yes, it is an analogy. Two people are alike in one way. Therefore, they will be alike in another way. Scan the answer choices. Do you see one that is an analogy?

Choice A is a distracter in that it talks about golf. This does not mean that it is a wrong answer, only that you must evaluate it further. What type of logic does it use? The first sentence is an absolute statement. Choice A is a deductive, if/then argument and cannot be the correct answer.

Choice B is a distracter because it has a sentence structure that is nearly identical to the original. However, it is a cause-and-effect argument and cannot be the correct answer.

Choice C does not use any particular type of logic. It is clearly not an analogy and cannot be the correct answer. Choice D is a logical flaw that infers that Louis's project is not valid because it has not been documented as being valid.

Choice E discusses a topic that is different from the original. It also begins with its conclusion. Nevertheless, it is an analogy—dolphins and humans are alike in one way so they must be alike in a second way—and is the correct answer.

A little over half of parallel reasoning questions involve deductive arguments, generally if/then statements, although occasionally sets. The remaining are likely to be based on the most common types of reasoning.

Parallel Flaw

A special type of parallel reasoning question tells you that the original argument is flawed and asks you to identify an argument that is flawed in the same way. This type of question can be solved in virtually the same way as other parallel reasoning questions. Any answer with valid logic is wrong.

Wording Variations

The wording for parallel reasoning and parallel flaw question stems is easy to identify. The stems usually say "parallel" or "similar."

Less Common Question Types

The most common question types, covered above, account for more than 75 percent of LR questions. The remaining question types, although less common, are important and account for nearly 25 percent of LR questions. No particular type accounts for more than 3 or 4 percent—some account for much less—but as a group they represent types of questions that you must master. There are ten specific less common question types that are covered below. They are listed from the most frequent to the least frequent.

Principle

Two types of questions have to do with principles. In one type, **application of a principle**, both a principle and an application of the principle are given. In the second type, **match a concrete example to a principle**, one or the other is given, and you must match a principle with a concrete example of the principle.

Application of a Principle

In this question type the setup consists of two distinct statements, as shown below:

SAMPLE PASSAGE 6

Principle: One should donate money only if one does not expect either praise or favors in return.

Application: It was acceptable for Henry to donate money to the Red Cross, even though after he did so, he received a warm letter of thanks and a discount coupon.

Which one of the following, if true, most justifies the above application of the principle?

The principle states absolute rules that dictate whether or not a certain action is valid. In other words, the principle contains a deductive argument, usually an if/then. The application part of the setup then applies the principle to a specific situation. The application does not completely take into account all of the conditions that are required by the principle's deductive statement. Your task is to identify the missing part. *Application of a principle* questions may either ask you to identify a new premise that strengthens the argument or to identify a flaw in the argument. This type of question, then, is a specialized form of either a *strengthen* question or a *flaw* question. You can use the strategies you have learned for those two types as you work *application of a principle* questions.

Because the principle is typically a deductive, if/then statement, start by diagramming the deductive rules. For the sample passage above, what are the premises in the principle?

The two elements of the if/then statement are *expecting praise/favor* and *donating*. The determining factor (the one that comes first) is *expecting praise/favor*. It is the presence of *expecting praise/favor* that determines that you should not *donate*.

If expect praise OR If expect favor → *−donate*

Match this to the application. Did Henry expect praise? Did he expect favor? Do you see the gap in the argument? The application tells us that Henry *received* both praise and favor but this does not match *expecting* praise or favor. To justify the application of the principle, a statement is needed that shows that Henry did not *expect* to receive either the praise or the coupon.

Correct Answer Choice: Before making the donation, Henry did not expect to receive either the letter or the coupon.

Now the argument is complete. All of the conditions in the principle have been addressed.

> *If expect praise OR If expect favor → –donate*
> *Donate ∴ –expect praise AND –expect favor*

The second statement is the contrapositive of the first and therefore is a valid statement. *Henry donated, which is valid because he did not expect either praise or favor.*

Flawed application of a principle. In some *application of a principle* questions, the application contains an error. The question stem asks you to identify the flaw in the reasoning, in exactly the same way as for *flaw* questions. The stem is worded to the effect *The application of the principle is most vulnerable to criticism on the grounds that it . . .*

SAMPLE PASSAGE 7

Principle: Plagiarism is a serious breach of the trust between a student and a teacher. Any student whose work has been declared a plagiarism by an impartial committee should be expelled.

Application: The committee that evaluated Sinead's thesis contained several faculty members who had nonacademic reasons for wanting her to be expelled. Even though all the committee members agreed that her work was a plagiarism, she should not be expelled.

The above application of the principle is most vulnerable to criticism on the grounds that it

(A) fails to consider the possibility that Sinead knowingly committed plagiarism

(B) fails to provide evidence that a faculty member had nonacademic reasons for wanting Sinead expelled

(C) applies a principle that contradicts the principle stated in the passage

(D) confuses a claim that is sufficient for an event to take place with a claim that is necessary for that event to take place

(E) assumes without warrant that the committee members are able to accurately determine whether or not a statement is a plagiarism

Solution: First identify the logic in the principle and then try to spot the gap in the argument. The first sentence of the principle is merely an introduction. The second sentence contains the principle.

If declared a plagiarism by an impartial committee → expel

In order to meet the qualifications for leading to *expel*, the situation must include a committee, impartiality, and a declaration of plagiarism. Compare this with the application. There is a committee and a declaration of plagiarism. There is *not* impartiality. Therefore, Sinead's situation must be described as *not declared a plagiarism by an impartial committee*. The conclusion of the application is *not expel*. Consider the application's entire argument, then:

If declared a plagiarism by an impartial committee → expel
–declared a plagiarism by an impartial committee ∴ –expel

or

If A → B
–A ∴ –B

Do you see that this is not a valid argument? Whereas the presence of A must lead to B (plagiarism is sufficient to lead to expulsion), the absence of A does *not* necessarily lead to B (it is not necessary to have been declared a plagiarist by an impartial committee to be expelled). There may be other factors that lead to B, even when A is absent. It is not valid to conclude that Sinead should not be expelled because there may be other reasons that would lead to her expulsion.

If the real-world explanation of why the logic is flawed does not work well for you, stick with the symbolic logic. It is clear that the A/B logic above is not valid. That is all you need to know and is sometimes much easier to understand than the real-world explanation.

Now that you understand the logic, which answer choice is correct? Choice D points out that the application incorrectly turns a sufficient condition into a necessary one. Choice D is the correct answer.

Choice A is irrelevant because the conditions that lead to being expelled do not require that the person knowingly plagiarized. Choice B refers to a failure to defend a premise. This is never a logical flaw. Premises are accepted as true without proof. The argument does not do what choice C describes. Just as in choice A, choice E goes beyond the conditions that define when expulsion must take place. The principle does not require that the committee be correct, only that the committee members are impartial and declare the work a plagiarism.

Wording variations. There are only a few possible variations for the wording of the question stem in *application of a principle* questions. You can recognize an *application of a principle* question most easily by its format:

> *Principle:*
> *Application:*

Occasionally the word *application* is replaced by *conclusion*.

Match a Principle to a Concrete Example

Be careful not to confuse this type of question with the *application of a principle* question type described above. (See Table 2.11.) In a *match a principle* question the setup gives you either a principle or an application but not both. The setup is *not* labeled *Principle:* or *Application:* as in *application of a principle* questions, so you must refer to the question stem and the answer choices to determine which of these the setup represents.

Table 2.11. Distinguishing Application of a Principle Questions from Match a Principle to a Concrete Example Questions

	Setup	Answer Choices
Application of a principle	A principle and an application	Strengthen or find the flaw in the application
Match a principle to a concrete example	Either a principle or an application, but not both	Find an application that matches the initial principle, or find a principle that matches the initial application

A *match a principle to a concrete example* question either (1) gives you an initial principle and asks you to find a concrete example that correctly matches the principle, or (2) gives you a concrete example and asks you to identify a principle that matches the example. In either case the task is essentially the same. In the first case, the five answer choices are concrete examples. In the second case, the five answer choices are principles.

Principle to concrete examples. These questions start with a principle in the setup and then ask you to choose which of the five answer choices matches the principle. The principle may be deductive, with absolute rules, or not.

SAMPLE PASSAGE 8

A high-quality pair of shoes may cost many times more than the low-quality alternative. However, because high-quality shoes last longer, the person who consistently buys only high-quality shoes may spend less on shoes in a ten-year period than the person who consistently buys low-quality shoes.

Which one of the following most closely conforms to the principle illustrated in the passage above?

(A) A low-price table saw may perform just as well as a high-price table saw.

(B) Many people find that the enhanced picture quality of an expensive television screen is worth the extra cost.

(C) Buying a used car costs less up front, but the cost of replacing used cars adds up over time to more than the cost of buying a new car.

(D) A high-quality suit may cost more than a lower-quality suit, but in a business environment, a high-quality suit can make the difference between getting a job offer and not getting a job offer.

(E) People who buy low-quality kitchen appliances spend more time replacing items when the items break down prematurely than if they had bought higher-quality appliances in the first place.

Solution: In this example, the setup represents a principle. Identify the principle. *Over time, one $200 expenditure costs less than five $85 expenditures.* Which answer choice illustrates the same principle? Focus on the elements of time and expense. Over a longer time, one alternative costs less, even though over a shorter time it appeared to cost more.

Choice A does not involve time. It discusses expense but then goes on to compare quality. The original principle does not directly address quality. Choice B does not involve time. It discusses money and appreciation. Choice C discusses the short term and the long term, as well as money. It matches exactly the criteria in the principle. Choice C is most likely the answer. Quickly evaluate the remaining choices.

Choice D does not include time and adds in a different criterion—getting a job. Choice E refers to saving time, not money. Choice C is the correct answer.

Concrete example to principles. In this type of question, the setup includes a concrete example and the answer choices represent five principles. You must find the principle that matches the example. As you saw in the Sample Passage above, matching means finding the rules or criteria in the principle and proving that the example is based on the same rules or criteria.

SAMPLE PASSAGE 9

Thirty regular customers of a restaurant petitioned the manager to institute a smoking area on the outdoor patio. Two of the twenty-five waitstaff protested, claiming they would be exposed to secondhand smoke. The manager decided not to institute a smoking area.

Which of the following principles is illustrated by the situation described above?

(A) The opinion of a majority of employees takes precedence over the opinion of a minority of customers.

(B) In a disagreement between management and employees, the opinion of employees takes precedence over the opinion of the management when health issues are involved.

(C) The laws of a municipality take precedence over the requests of even a large number of customers.

(D) The opinion of even a single employee takes precedence over the opinions of a large number of customers when health issues are involved.

(E) The health of even a single employee takes precedence over the health of a large number of customers.

Solution: Because the setup is a concrete example and not a principle, it is generally not possible to identify the principle in advance. Instead, test the answer choices by comparing them with the original example.

For choice A, the setup does not refer to a majority of employees. In fact, it refers to a minority of employees. Choice A is out. Choice B is flawed in that it is not clear that there is a disagreement between management and employees. Management does not necessarily have an opinion. The disagreement is between some customers and a few employees. Choice B is out.

Choice C is irrelevant because we do not have any information on whether there are local laws governing smoking on the patio. Choice D accurately captures all of the elements of the example. Choice E is flawed because the issue does not concern the health of customers but rather the preferences of customers.

The wording of the question stem for *match a principle to a concrete example* questions is typically similar to what is used in the examples above. Read the stem to determine whether the setup is a principle or a concrete example.

Role of a Claim

Role of a claim questions are based on a complete argument set forth in the setup. The question stem then cites a statement from the argument and asks you to identify the role that that statement plays in the argument. You can recognize a *role of an argument* question by its wording. The main wordings of the stem are:

> *The claim that . . . plays which one of the following roles in the argument?*
> *Which one of the following most accurately describes the role played in the argument by the claim . . .*

The wording variations for these stems are listed at the end of this section.

The word *claim* in the question stem, along with its variations *statement* and *contention*, can refer to any information that the argument asserts to be true. You are asked to identify the role that the claim plays in the argument. There are a number of specific types of roles that are tested in LR.

Types of Roles

The answer choices in a *type of roles* question consist, naturally, of descriptions of certain types of roles, a role being the function that the statement performs. Functions fall into two categories. The first category consists of the fundamental logical elements, including premises, assumptions, and conclusions. The function of a premise, for example, is to provide evidence that leads to the conclusion. The second category of functions consists of more complex relationships involving the fundamental elements. For example, an element may be a premise in an argument that the original argument is attempting to attack.

Fundamental logical elements. The fundamental logical elements are the building blocks of an argument. They can be used alone to create a valid argument or they can be used in more complex logical roles. Review the elements and their roles listed below.

Premise: *an explicit (stated) fact that is accepted as true without the need for proof. A premise's function is to support the conclusion.*

Necessary premise: *a premise without which the conclusion would be invalid.*

Sufficient premise: *a premise that by itself is enough to guarantee that the conclusion is valid.*

Assumption: *an implicit (unstated) fact that is accepted as true without the need for proof. An assumption functions as a premise but is not stated.*

Conclusion: *a fact that is proven to be true by applying logic to accepted facts (premises, assumptions). A conclusion can also be proven by applying logic to previously established conclusions.*

Main conclusion: *the conclusion that it is the ultimate purpose of the argument to establish.*

Intermediate conclusion: *a conclusion that is arrived at by applying logic to accepted facts (premises, assumptions) and is then used to support the main conclusion.*

Background information: *facts that help establish the context of the argument but are not used in the logic itself. In other words, background information is not used to prove conclusions.*

Hypothesis: *a proposed conclusion that the argument attempts to prove.*

Example: *information that illustrates another element of the argument. An example is typically not used in the logic itself.*

Generalization: *a statement that takes facts about a specific situation and attempts to create a prediction about situations that fall into a general category.*

Complex logical roles. Fundamental logical elements can be used to create more complex logical roles. The following are examples of complex relationships that are tested in *role of a claim* questions. For each of the following relationships, try creating an argument that includes the relationship.

COMPLEX LOGICAL RELATIONSHIPS THAT ARE TESTED IN ROLE OF A CLAIM QUESTIONS

A premise in an argument that the main argument is attempting to attack

Evidence that supports another premise, such as a reason to believe a fact or an explanation of a fact

A premise that is used to create an intermediate conclusion

A premise that follows from another premise

A premise that proves the truth of a conclusion

A fact that is taken for granted by the argument as false

A statement that counteracts a possible objection to the argument

A claim that is inconsistent with the evidence presented in the argument

A statement that is refuted by the argument

A statement that illustrates a principle

A statement that qualifies a conclusion

A statement that is supported by a study

A statement that is the basis for an analogy that supports the conclusion

A statement that establishes the importance of a conclusion but is not evidence for the conclusion

A statement that sets out a problem to resolve

A statement that is compatible with both accepting and rejecting a conclusion

A hypothesis that the argument rejects

A conclusion that is a generalization

A conclusion that is supported by an intermediate conclusion

The answer choices for *role of a claim* questions may consist of descriptions of the fundamental logical elements or of the more complex logical roles. There are many other combinations of logical relationships that could be tested, although the examples above cover most of the relationships that actually have been tested on recent LSATs. You may find that the wording of an answer choice obscures the real relationship. As you work through practice LSAT questions that test *role of a claim*, refer to the lists above. This will help you be able to recognize the role relationships.

SAMPLE PASSAGE 10

Unfortunately, voters today have little real information to go on when choosing the best candidate for office, and as a result, voters often end up with officials whose values do not represent those of the voters. Studies have shown that traditional debates reveal a candidate's values better than staged debates or brief television ads. If candidates are required to participate in traditional debates, the values of elected officials will better match the values of the people who voted them into office.

The statement that voters often end up with officials whose values do not represent the voters' values plays which one of the following roles in the argument?

(A) It is a conclusion that is proven by another premise.

(B) It is a premise on which the argument relies.

(C) It is a premise that is used to create an intermediate conclusion.

(D) It sets out the problem that the argument hopes to solve.

(E) It is a hypothesis that the argument rejects.

Solution: Read the setup and identify the premises and conclusion. If you are able to understand how the statement in the question stem relates to the argument, scan the answer choices to find an answer that matches your understanding. If you are not clear on how the statement in the stem relates to the argument, begin by testing the answer choices.

Choice A refers to an intermediate conclusion. The cited statement is not an intermediate conclusion. For choice B, is the cited statement a premise? A premise is used later in the argument to support the conclusion. Choice B does not seem to be used later. Choice B can be left as a weak possibility. Choice C also takes the cited statement as a premise, one that is used to create an intermediate conclusion. The cited statement does not seem to be used to create another premise. Leave choice C in as a weak possibility. For choice D, is the cited statement a description of the problem that the argument hopes to solve? Yes, this seems to exactly describe the role of the cited statement. This is most likely the best answer. Quickly glance at choice E. The argument does not reject the cited statement. Choice D is the correct answer.

Some *role of a claim* questions may not test logical relationships directly but rather may test information that is specific to the argument. For example, an answer choice might read *helps explain why pigs are more intelligent than dogs*. Such a statement can be evaluated on its meaning rather than its logical elements.

Committed to Disagree

This question type involves two arguers and asks you to make determinations about the logic to which each arguer is committed and to what extent the two arguers are committed to the same or different logic.

SAMPLE PASSAGE 11

> Frank: Anyone who does not like fruit must not like people either.
> Shannon: You are wrong. I like fruit but I do not like people. Therefore, people who do not like fruit, do like people.
>
> Frank's and Shannon's statements provide the most support for the claim that they disagree over the truth of which one of the following?
> (A) People who do not like people also do not like fruit.
> (B) People who do not like people do like fruit.
> (C) People who like people also like fruit.
> (D) People who like fruit may like people.
> (E) People who do not like fruit like people.

Solution: Frank is committed to the if/then statement

If –like fruit → –like people

Frank must also be committed, then, to the contrapositive

Like people ∴ like fruit

These are the only two logical statements to which Frank is committed. For any other logical statement, Frank would have no opinion. In *committed to disagree* questions it is important to know both the arguments to which the arguer is committed and the arguments to which the arguer is *not* committed (about which the arguer has no opinion).

Shannon is committed to the if/then statement

If –like fruit → like people

along with its contrapositive

–like people ∴ like fruit

Table 2.12. Summary of the Situations for Which Each Arguer Has an Opinion and Does Not Have an Opinion

	Committed	**Not Committed***
Frank	If –like fruit → –like people Like people ∴ like fruit	If like fruit If –like people The White Sox are great
Shannon	If –like fruit → like people –like people ∴ like fruit	If like people If like fruit The White Sox are great

*This column can include anything other than the elements to which the arguer is committed, including elements that are irrelevant to the argument, such as the White Sox.

The information in Table 2.12 is a good start but a *committed to disagree* question does not simply ask you to identify what Frank believes or what Shannon believes. You must identify a statement about which Frank and Shannon disagree. This is a very important concept to understand thoroughly because (1) it is complex; (2) if you do grasp the concept well, the questions are easy to answer; and (3) this same type of logic appears in the Comparative Reading passage in the Reading Comprehension section.

What does it mean that Frank and Shannon *disagree* about a statement? It means that one of them is committed to believing that the statement is true and the other is committed to believing that the statement is false. If one of the two does not have an opinion about the statement, then the two do *not* disagree and the statement *cannot* be the correct answer.

Table 2.13. Chart of Frank's and Shannon's
Responses to the Five Answer Choices

	Committed to Believing the Statement Is True	Committed to Believing the Statement Is False	Not Committed
(A) People who do not like people also do not like fruit.		Shannon	Frank
(B) People who do not like people do like fruit.	Shannon		Frank
(C) People who like people also like fruit.	Frank		Shannon
(D) People who like fruit may like people.	Frank Shannon		
(E) People who do not like fruit like people.	Shannon	Frank	

Table 2.13 shows that the correct answer is the one for which one arguer is committed to believing the statement is true and the other arguer is committed to believing that the statement is false. In the table this is represented by one person being in the second column and the other person being in the third column (the final answer choice). If either arguer is in the "Not Committed" column, the answer choice cannot be correct. Test out each of the five statements above for yourself so that you are clear on why each arguer is committed to its truth, committed to its falsehood, or not committed.

There are several cases that potentially can trick you. No matter how vehemently one arguer may feel that a particular statement is false, there can be no disagreement if the other arguer does not have an opinion (is not committed to a position). Similarly, no matter how strongly one arguer feels that a statement is true, there can be no disagreement if the other arguer is not committed to a position. Finally, be careful in cases in which both arguers are committed to an opinion but it is the same opinion, as in the fourth statement in Table 2.13. In order for there to be a disagreement, the two arguers must be committed to the *opposite* opinions. One believes the statement is false and the other that it is true.

Some committed to disagree questions are based on deductive logic, such as in Sample Passage 11. Questions may be slightly more challenging when the arguments are not deductive, as in Sample Passage 12.

SAMPLE PASSAGE 12

Andrea: Independence is a valuable quality for all children to develop. Simple art such as finger painting is an ideal activity for children because they can create a finished artwork without needing help from an adult. Because they did the project by themselves, their sense of independence is enhanced.

Ted: But when children complete a finger painting, even if they did not get help from an adult, they have not done it by themselves. There can be no finger painting without the people who made the paints and the paper, the plants and minerals that the paints and paper are made from, the people who pay the taxes that make the school building and the teachers available, and so on. Adults should help children develop a sense of interdependence, rather than an exaggerated sense of self-importance.

The statements above provide the most support for concluding that Andrea and Ted disagree about whether

(A)   finger painting is an activity that children can do without help from an adult

(B)   when children do work without help from an adult, they have done the work by themselves

(C)   interdependence is a valuable quality for children to develop

(D)   when children do work by themselves, their sense of independence is enhanced

(E)   adults should help children develop valuable qualities

Solution: With the inductive arguments above, it is not as easy to summarize each arguer's belief as it was with the deductive argument in the previous Sample Passage. Start with the answer choices and work backward, determining for an answer choice what each arguer's position would be. In choice A, both Andrea and Ted would be committed to the truth of the statement. Andrea specifically makes the statement given in choice A and Ted admits that it is possible. For choice B, Andrea is committed to its truth. Ted explicitly states that even though a child may have done the work without the help of an adult, the child has not done the work by himself or herself. Thus, Ted explicitly finds the statement in choice B false. Andrea and Ted are committed to disagreeing on the truth of choice B, so B must be the answer.

Look quickly at the remaining choices. Ted is committed to the truth of choice C. Andrea does not state an opinion about interdependence. Presumably, she could think interdependence and independence are both valuable qualities. Because Andrea's position is unclear, choice C cannot be the answer.

Andrea clearly is committed to the truth of choice D. Ted's position is unclear. Choice D cannot be the answer. Both Andrea and Ted are committed to the truth of choice E, so the two arguers do not disagree.

Complete the Sentence/Argument

This type of question is based on a setup that establishes most of an argument but leaves the last sentence incomplete. You are to identify the answer choice that best fills in the blank at the end of the setup. You can easily identify this type of question by the blank line at the end of the setup paragraph.

For all questions in this category, the last line—the line that is incomplete—is the conclusion. The setup, then, gives you the premises and part of the conclusion and asks you to identify the answer choice that correctly completes the conclusion. The arguments are typically *not* deductive.

SAMPLE PASSAGE 13

Raising vegetables in the garden requires a delicate balance. If the gardener does not apply enough fertilizer, the plants will be stunted and unproductive. If the gardener applies too much fertilizer, the plants will become lanky and tasteless. The gardener must keep a constant eye on how plants are responding to the gardener's attention. This is not dissimilar to raising children. Parents must _____.

Which one of the following most logically completes the argument?

(A) be careful not to overfeed their children

(B) not withhold their attention from their children, even when parents are busy

(C) give both positive and negative attention to their children

(D) provide their children access to a wide variety of experiences

(E) carefully balance giving their children too much attention and giving their children too little attention

Solution: Because you have to complete the conclusion, your first task is to understand the premises and how the argument attempts to create a conclusion. In this example, the conclusion is based on an analogy. Raising plants is similar to raising children. Identify exactly in what way the two are similar.

The gardening part of the analogy is laid out first and more thoroughly in the setup. Gardening requires a "delicate balance" of applying too little fertilizer and too much fertilizer. Parenting, then, must be a "careful balance" of applying too little attention and too much attention. Choice E is the correct answer.

Choice A is a distracter, confusing feeding plants with feeding children. Choice B discusses only too little attention. In choice C, positive and negative attention is not the same as too much or too little attention. Choice D is somewhat off the mark, though if anything, it only addresses too much attention.

Type of Reasoning

This type of question asks you to identify the specific type of logic used in the argument. The arguments may be valid or flawed, although questions that specifically ask you to identify the flaw in an argument fall under the category of *flaw* questions. The answer choices refer to the types of reasoning that you reviewed in the "Types of Arguments" section of this chapter. The answer choices might include examples of flawed reasoning as well as valid types of reasoning. The answer choices also often include types of refutations, which are also covered under "Types of Arguments" earlier in this chapter.

To solve a *type of reasoning* question, review the setup, identify premises and conclusions, and try to get a sense of what type of logic the arguer has used. Then test the answer choices.

Sample Passage 14

When Europeans first began colonizing the New World, they thought of it as a paradise of wide open spaces, in contrast to the congested living conditions of many of the European cities of the time. However, the New World is now as congested as Europe. Similarly, the claims that we should colonize Mars because of its vast open spaces should be rejected. After a short while, Mars will be just as congested as Earth.

The argument proceeds by

(A) rejecting a proposal on the basis that the proposal has not been proven to be valid

(B) treating an assertion that is not correct as an assertion that is intentionally misleading

(C) challenging an assertion by providing additional evidence

(D) establishing a conclusion by eliminating alternative possibilities

(E) defending one argument by showing that the argument is similar to another, presumably valid argument

Solution: Compare each answer choice with the passage. For choice A, the argument rejects the proposal to colonize Mars, but not on the basis that the proposal has not been proven to be valid. For choice B, the argument does not imply that the people who say we should colonize Mars are being intentionally misleading. For choice C, the argument does challenge the assertion that we should colonize Mars. The argument does not provide additional direct evidence that Mars colonization would fail. Instead, it argues through an analogy. Go on to choice D. The argument does not eliminate other possibilities. For choice E, the argument does defend the argument against colonizing Mars by showing that it is similar to an argument for colonizing the New World. Choice E *describes* an analogy without using the word *analogy*. Choice E is the correct answer.

Relevant Information

This rare type of question presents an argument and then asks you to identify information that would be useful for evaluating the effectiveness or validity of the argument. Relevant information does not necessarily strengthen or weaken an argument. It is simply information that would be relevant.

SAMPLE PASSAGE 15

Only people who have worked for Company X for at least ten years and have not taken more than three consecutive days of sick leave in the last year will be allowed to take three weeks paid vacation next summer. John has worked at Company X for eleven years and has taken four days leave in a row in the last month. Therefore, John is not eligible for taking three weeks paid vacation next summer.

Evaluating the validity of the above argument requires a clarification of which one of the following?

(A) whether John took three weeks of vacation last year
(B) whether the leave John took last month was the only leave of more than three days that John took in the last year
(C) whether John's leave last month was for illness
(D) whether Company X can afford to pay for the vacations of all of the employees who are eligible
(E) whether John will be allowed to take unpaid vacation

Solution: Only answer choice C is relevant to the conclusion of the argument. If John's leave was for illness, then the conclusion is valid. If his leave was not for illness, then the conclusion is not valid. The answer to the issue posed in choice C completely determines whether the conclusion is valid or not. In addition to the wording of the stem in the example, typical wording of the stem for these questions include the phrase *useful in evaluating*.

Identify an Element of an Argument

This rare type of question asks you to identify an answer choice that represents a certain element of the argument. The examples in recent tests include asking you to identify a comparison that is made and asking you to identify which element of an analogy corresponds to another element of the analogy.

Consistent with Both Arguments

In this rare type of question, two arguers present arguments, just as in the *committed to disagree* questions, but in this case you are asked to find an answer choice that is consistent with both arguments.

SAMPLE PASSAGE 16

Kendra: All applicants who have less than three years of experience must submit at least three letters of recommendation.

Ursula: Any applicant who applies from out of state must submit a birth certificate.

Which one of the following scenarios is consistent with both the principle given by Kendra and the principle given by Ursula?

Solution: An answer choice that is consistent with both is:

Peter is applying from out of state, has four years of experience, and is submitting two letters of recommendation and a birth certificate.

An answer choice that is *not* consistent with both is:

Tammi has two years of experience, is applying from in state, and is submitting two letters of recommendation.

Whereas Tammi is not required to submit a birth certificate under Ursula's conditions, she is required to submit at least three letters of recommendation under Kendra's conditions. Thus, the answer choice is *not* consistent with both sets of conditions.

Question Formats

You have now reviewed all of the types of questions that appear in LR. There are also several special formats in which questions of any type can be presented.

"EXCEPT" Questions

Consider the following possible question stem:

> *All of the following strengthen the argument EXCEPT*

For such a question there are four answer choices that strengthen the argument. The one remaining answer choice—the one that does *not* strengthen the argument—is the correct answer.

EXCEPT questions require careful attention. First, the correct answer in the example above is *not* necessarily one that weakens the argument. It may be an answer choice that has no effect or is irrelevant. Prove which answer choices *do* strengthen the argument and cross them off.

Second, an EXCEPT question is logically confusing in that you have to keep a certain criterion in mind, such as *strengthening*, and yet you are looking for an answer that is *not strengthening*. This situation is a bit like someone telling you, "Don't think about elephants." All you can think about is elephants. It is very easy to get confused and end up choosing an answer choice that strengthens (or whatever the criterion for the question is). To avoid this, as you orient yourself to the question stem, make a notation in the scratch area of the test that there will be four *strengthens* and one *not strengthen*.

Only a few percent of LR questions use EXCEPT. On recent tests they have historically appeared only in questions based on *resolve a paradox, strengthen,* and *weaken* (all *effect of a new premise* questions), as well as *conclusion* and *consistent with both arguments* questions.

"LEAST" Questions

You may rarely find a question stem like the following:

> *Information on which of the following topics would be LEAST useful in evaluating the argument?*

As with EXCEPT questions, four answer choices would be useful and the one remaining answer choice would be correct. LEAST questions have the same logical pitfalls as EXCEPT questions. LEAST questions appear on some of the older practice LSAT material. In recent tests they have become rare.

One-Labeled Arguer

Many setups are labeled with a name or description of the arguer.

> *Ethel: John says we should all take nice vacations this year. However, John was once found cheating on checkers. Why should we take the advice of a cheater?*

> *Researcher: Our experiments show that Earth's rotation is slowing. At this rate, we will all need to find a new home in 14 billion years.*

The fact that the arguer is labeled does not affect the logic of the passage or the process that you use to answer the question. The label can be completely ignored, although some people may find the passage to feel "friendlier" when there is a label. Labeling a one-person argument has become more common in recent exams. Nearly a third of passages have a one-person label.

Do not confuse a one-label argument with an argument in which two elements are labeled. Two-label arguments have unique properties.

Two-Labeled Arguers

Just under 10 percent of LR questions have setups with two distinct arguments. Each argument is preceded by a label. The labels may be names or they may be descriptions of the arguer (such as researcher, scientist, journalist). In *application of a principle* questions, the labels are "Principle" and "Application."

> *Olivia: Average temperatures around the world have increased by at least several degrees during my lifetime. Clearly, we can expect temperatures to continue to rise.*

> *Patrick: I disagree. Last summer was the coolest that I remember. I barely had any opportunities to go swimming.*

More than two-thirds of the questions with two-labeled arguers occur in passages with either *application of a principle* questions or *committed to disagree* questions. Both types involve comparing two distinct arguments.

Of the remaining passages with two-labeled arguers, half are *flaw* questions. The flaw involves how one arguer responds to or misunderstands the other. Other passages with two-labeled arguers involve *type of logic* questions, asking you to identify the logic that one arguer uses in responding to the other.

Occasionally a *strengthen* or *relevant information* question uses a format with two-labeled arguers. You can use the same strategies for such questions in this format as you would for the same type of question in the normal format.

Obsolete: Two Question Stems for One Setup

Passages of this type have not appeared on the LSAT in several years but you will find them in older practice material. In this format, one passage was followed by two distinct questions, each with its own stem and answer choices. It is possible that a few such questions may reappear occasionally on current LSATs.

HOW TO SOLVE LOGICAL REASONING QUESTIONS

Chapter 1, "General Strategies," reviews the most common testing strategies for solving questions on the LSAT, including the LR section. Review Chapter 1 now to refresh your memory. Below you will learn how to apply these strategies to LR.

Starting an LR Question

When you start a new timed LR section, apply the timing strategies that you have studied in Chapter 1 and at the beginning of this chapter. Pick a question to work on first, set your watch to noon, and follow the steps below.

Problem-Solving Steps

There is a specific set of steps for working through a complex LR problem. On easy problems, it is not necessary to use all the steps. However, if you are getting questions wrong because of what seem like "careless errors," or if there are questions that you cannot get right even when you work them carefully, then learning the systematic set of steps will help you gain points.

Glance at the Question Stem

When you start a new LR question, glance quickly at the question stem. You do not need to analyze the stem at this point. The purpose of glancing at the stem is to get a quick sense of which type of question the stem represents. You may catch the word *weaken* or notice that the stem is asking for a conclusion, or you may notice the wording *Which one of the following, if true*, which gives you a general orientation to what the stem is asking for.

If the meaning of the stem is not too clear, go directly to the passage. You will come back to the stem later. However, if you do not at least glance at the stem, you will not have any sense of what you are looking for.

Read the Passage

Next, read through the passage to get a sense of the argument. If you have understood the stem, look for elements that you will need to identify in order to solve the question. You will come back to the passage again after orienting yourself to the question stem.

Orient to the Question Stem

After reading the passage the first time, come back to the question stem. At this point, it is vital that you understand the question stem thoroughly. This stage is one of the two most critical stages of problem solving. Being thorough here often makes the difference between a correct answer and an avoidable error.

Orienting to the question stem includes two specific steps. The first step is to ask yourself if you clearly understand what the question stem means. What type of question is it? Are there any aspects of the question that do not make sense?

Many question stems are worded in a complex way that disguises the type of question. Break the stem down carefully to make sure you understand it. If you have trouble breaking down a complex question stem, refer to the lists of wording variations for all of the question types listed in this chapter.

When a question asks you about an argument, you must distinguish to which argument it is referring. Many setups contain only one argument. Other setups, however, either include two or more arguments or refer to another argument that is not presented.

SAMPLE SETUP 1

Philosopher: Scientists recently hypothesized that the lifespan of the sun is a billion years shorter than they had previously thought. I have gone through their evidence and do not find it convincing. Therefore, I conclude that the sun will survive as long as scientists had previously thought.

Which one of the following, if true, would most seriously weaken the scientists' argument?

The stem asks you to weaken the scientists' argument, *not* the philosopher's.

Plan of attack: Once you have clearly understood the question stem and to which argument it refers, the second step is to consider what your plan of attack will be. It is often not a good idea to simply read the question stem and start evaluating the first answer choice. Generally, you need to review the setup to look for more specific information. The information that you need depends on the type of question.

Review the Passage

Having oriented yourself carefully to the question stem and considered what information you need from the passage, come back to the passage a second time. You may need to clarify what the conclusion is, what the premises are, what type of logic is being used, and if there are gaps in the argument. A gap indicates that there may be unstated assumptions or errors in the logic. Ask yourself if you "buy" the argument. On an intuitive level, does it make sense to you? Even if you know the argument is valid, it may strike you as flawed. This is important to notice. Similarly, even when you are told that an argument is flawed, it may sound perfectly valid. In both cases, this discrepancy is a clue as to what is going on.

Scan the Answer Choices

Once you have read the passage for a second time, you are ready to scan the answer choices. Scanning means to quickly glance at all five answer choices. There are several purposes for doing this. First, the answer choices might change how you understand the question. Second, you may spot an answer choice that seems to closely match your intuitions about the question. This does not mean that you should automatically choose that answer. Often intuition leads you in the wrong direction and equally often an answer choice is partially correct but has a fatal flaw that requires more careful analysis to detect. However, an answer choice that seems to match your understanding of the question is certainly a good place to start. Finally, scanning the answer choices helps refine your sense of what tools you will need for answering the question.

Test the Answer Choices

In most cases, scanning the answer choices does not lead directly to the correct answer. Your next step is to test the answer choices carefully. Starting with the first answer choice, apply a two-pass approach, described below.

The Two-Pass Approach

Make two passes through the answer choices. The first time you go through the answers, spend only enough time to determine for each answer choice whether that choice can be eliminated or must be left as a possibility. Do not be too quick to eliminate answers. If you find that you are missing many questions because you initially eliminated the correct answer, become more conservative. Only eliminate a choice if it is clearly wrong. If it seems wrong but you are not sure, leave it in and put a question mark next to it.

Ask yourself if an answer choice goes in the right direction or wrong direction. If an answer choice is consistent with the passage, it goes in the right direction. If an answer choice is inconsistent with or contradicts the passage, it goes in the wrong direction and can be eliminated. The fact that an answer choice goes in the right direction does not, of course, mean that it is the correct answer, but it must be left in, to be evaluated more carefully in the second pass.

SAMPLE PASSAGE 17

Dr. Manning claims that psychological challenges help keep us emotionally flexible and healthy. According to Dr. Manning, even though a difficult emotional experience may be uncomfortable or even have unfortunate results, the very fact of facing the situation with courage builds our repertoire of emotional tools and makes our lives better in the long run. Dr. Manning has clearly been an accurate observer of human behavior.

Which one of the following statements best represents the main conclusion of the argument?

(A) Dr. Manning is probably better adjusted emotionally than most people.

(B) Too much emotional discomfort can be harmful in the long run.

(C) Dr. Manning's claim fails to consider that painful emotional experiences may have results that negatively affect our lives.

(D) A highly traumatic experience would make a person emotionally stronger than a mildly uncomfortable experience.

(E) Dr. Manning's claim is valid.

Solution: Does choice A go in the right direction or the wrong direction? Choice A is consistent with the passage, even though it is probably not defendable. During the first pass, leave choice A in, though you can mark it with a question mark to show that it does not seem likely. This allows you to come back later to double-check it. It is not unusual for a correct answer to seem unlikely at first.

Choice B goes in the wrong direction. It contradicts the passage. Cross it out. Choice C is also inconsistent with the passage. Dr. Manning does consider the possibility mentioned in C. Cross off choice C.

Choice D seems an extreme statement but it is consistent with the passage in that it maintains a correlation between emotional pain and emotional growth. It is an unlikely answer but you cannot eliminate it without further testing. Mark it with a question mark. Choice E is consistent with the passage. The last sentence indicates that the author of the passage believes that Dr. Manning's observations are valid. Though this answer may seem too simple or obvious, it fits as the main point that the arguer is trying to convey. Choice E is the correct answer.

As you make your first pass through the answer choices, use marks to indicate answer choices that are out, that are in but unlikely, and that are in and seem to be good (one plus mark) or strong (two plus marks).

(E) 17. ... clearly been an accurate observer of human behavior.

Which one of the following statements best represents the main conclusion of the argument?

(A) Dr. Manning is probably better adjusted emotionally than most people.

? (B) Too much emotional discomfort can be harmful in the long run.

✗ (C) Dr. Manning's claim fails to consider that painful emotional experience may have results that negatively affect our lives.

(D) A highly traumatic experience would make a person emotionally stronger than a mildly uncomfortable experience.

++ (E) Dr. Manning's claim is valid.

Figure 2.8. Marks showing answer choices that have been eliminated (crossed out), are unlikely ("?"), are possible ("+"), or are strong ("++"). The correct answer is circled and then written by the question number.

The second pass. After completing the first pass through the answer choices, review what is left. How do the remaining answers compare and how do they differ? In some cases, simply reviewing the remaining answers leads to the correct answer. In other cases, you need to apply advanced strategies for examining each remaining answer choice and proving which one is correct. The most powerful strategy for finding the correct answer when you are down to two or three possibilities is the adversarial approach.

Adversarial Approach

The adversarial approach is described in detail in Chapter 1. Review it now. Below is a description of how to use it in LR.

When left with two, or sometimes three, answer choices, untrained test takers guess and move on. Such a strategy is not productive. If you are not able to get some of these more complex questions correct, you will have a hard time increasing your score. It *is* possible to figure out exactly why one answer choice is correct and exactly why the other answer choices are incorrect. It may take another thirty seconds to four minutes to get the correct answer but this strategy allows you to get many more correct answers.

The adversarial approach is based on the fact that, when there are two or three answer choices left, you have most likely developed a bias for one answer and against the others. This bias prevents you from seeing information you may have missed. To counteract your bias, start with an answer choice that you think is probably not correct and *defend* it. This forces you to look for evidence that the answer choice is correct. Similarly, when you come to the answer choice that you believe is probably correct, *attack* it. Prove that it must be wrong. The key to applying the adversarial approach effectively is that when you are defending, you must defend wholeheartedly and when you attack, you must attack wholeheartedly.

After applying the adversarial approach, you usually have a clearer picture of the strengths and weaknesses of each answer. Even if you run out of time (after three to four, or even five minutes) on a question without proving one answer correct, your guess is more likely to be correct.

What to Do if There Is No Clear Answer

If you have used the three to five minutes that are reasonable to spend on a single question and still do not have a clear answer, put your best guess. If you have only spent one or two minutes on the question and do not have a clear answer, continue working on the question.

In some cases, you may have worked carefully through all of the remaining answer choices and found that no answer choice seems to work. In other cases, it may seem that more than one answer choice can be defended. Assuming that you have not exhausted your allotted time for the question, it is *not* a good strategy in such cases to guess and move on. You have most likely made an error or missed important information. Start the question from scratch, using the remaining time. You may well be close to a correct answer if you can undo your error. Study the list of common errors discussed later in this section, so that you can more quickly identify what you may have missed.

Answer the Question

Once you have proven why one answer choice is correct and the others are wrong, you are ready to indicate your answer. Chapter 1 discusses strategies for marking the bubble sheet. Review those strategies. Once you have chosen the correct answer, circle the letter of your answer *and* write the letter next to the number of the question. As you bubble in your answers, your markings next to the answer choices might be difficult to read. Putting the letter of the correct answer next to the number gives you a clear reminder of which bubble to fill in.

Common Errors

Many test takers, when they review questions they have gotten wrong, feel that they have made a "careless error," which implies that they did not pay enough attention, and they resolve to be "more careful." In actuality, virtually all errors are the result of not applying a valid strategy or of applying a strategy incorrectly. Review *each and every* incorrect answer and determine the real reason why you got the question wrong. Below are the most common errors.

Too Little Time

For a question that you got wrong, did you spend enough time on it? Check your notes. Remember that you should write down the time that you spend on each question even when you are working untimed. If you only spent one or two minutes on the question, consider why you did not take more time. If you attempted the question under timed conditions, you could have taken three to five minutes on it. If you attempted the question under untimed conditions, then you could have worked on the question longer. In untimed practice it is sometimes helpful to spend even fifteen or twenty minutes or more wrestling with a question.

One typical reason for stopping too soon on a question is that you may have been convinced that you had the correct answer. If this happens regularly, start to monitor your confidence level on each question more carefully. If you are only 90 percent confident in your answer, then you still have some doubt and should take a little more time on the question. If you find that you really do feel completely confident in answers that turn out to be wrong, then you may be eliminating answer choices too quickly or not reading all of the answer choices.

Another common reason for stopping too soon is that you think you have done everything possible. In some cases, that may be true. In most cases, however, you could have pushed the adversarial approach further.

A third major reason for stopping too soon, especially on a timed section, is that you feel rushed for time. You feel that you should be getting on to other questions in the section. If you feel this way, you may not yet have worked out exactly what your timing strategy is. If you are convinced in theory that it is worth your while to spend two, three, or four minutes on certain difficult questions, but in practice you are feeling rushed after two minutes on a question, there is a gap between your theory and your practice. When you are in a timed section, you may be unconsciously reverting to old test-taking patterns.

Too Frazzled

Even if you are actually spending three to five minutes on some questions, if you are getting questions wrong, it may be because your brain is still worrying about time. See the comments in Chapter 1 on creating a "timeless four-minute bubble" around each question.

Not Oriented to the Question Stem

A very common cause of mistakes is that the test taker has not taken the time to orient well to the question stem. If this happens to you, you may find that you have misunderstood the question stem or interpreted it as a different type of question. If this happens regularly, take more time—even just a few seconds may be enough—to make sure you are clear on the question stem.

The Default Multiple-Choice Question

As discussed in Chapter 1, if you were given a set of five answer choices, without any setup or any question stem, and asked to choose the correct answer, you would naturally assume that you are looking for the answer choice that is a true statement. This is the default multiple-choice question, namely, *Which one of the following is a true statement?*

Some LR questions actually ask this. Many, however, ask something very different. Your brain, however, can easily forget what question it is trying to answer and, without your noticing, revert to the default multiple-choice question. If you get a question wrong and find that the answer you chose represents a true fact, whereas the question stem asked for a premise that would weaken the argument, you have most likely reverted to the default multiple-choice question.

A good strategy for preventing both reverting to the default question and getting confused as to what question you are answering is to periodically go back to the question stem and refresh your brain as to what you are looking for. When you move to the next answer choice, briefly glance back at the stem.

Inadequate Application of the Adversarial Approach

The adversarial approach is your most powerful tool but you need to train yourself to use it most effectively. The most common error in applying the adversarial approach is to mix attacking and defending. Consider that you are trying to attack the answer choice C, which you liked, and your inner dialogue goes as follows:

> *What could be wrong with C? Hmm. I really like it. It seems to work. It matches the setup. OK, what could be wrong with it? Maybe it's too extreme. I don't think so, though. It seems all right to me.*

Are you *really* trying to attack choice C? Your brain cannot get out of the "I like C" rut. When you do spot a possible weakness, your thinking immediately goes back to saying that you like C, instead of mercilessly pursuing your attack. The same, of course, is true of halfhearted defending. It may help to think of an attorney who is being paid a million dollars to prosecute someone, even though the attorney believes that the person is innocent. The more you can avoid mixing attacking and defending, the more effective your use of the adversarial approach.

In many cases, when you try to attack an answer choice, there is actually nothing wrong with it. Similarly, you may try to defend an answer choice for which there are no points of defense at all. However, you cannot know this in advance for an answer choice. You still must attack, attack, attack and defend, defend, defend. It may only take thirty seconds of attacking to determine that there is no point of attack and then you can be more confident in your findings.

Failure to Use Your Eyes Instead of Your Memory

The strategy of using your eyes, not your memory, is described in Chapter 1. If you find that you have gotten confused on information from the setup or the question stem, you might have tried to use your memory to fill in facts, instead of going back with your eyes to review the information.

Failure to Use Visual Aids

This error is similar to the previous one. If you are getting confused on information or remembering it incorrectly, you may need to use some visual aids. This means making notes in your scratch area or in the passage itself. Even doodling can help some people organize their thoughts. Visual information functions very differently from information in short-term memory. Learn to make more use of visual aids.

Distracters

As described in Chapter 1, a distracter is an incorrect answer that has been designed to appear correct because it contains elements that superficially seem to match what the question stem is asking for. Because many questions contain distracters, you cannot answer a question solely on the intuitive feeling that an answer choice seems correct.

Failure to Check All the Answer Choices

If you find that you are choosing an incorrect answer that is higher in the list of answer choices than the real answer, you might have decided your answer was correct when you saw it and then did not check the rest of the answers after it. The test writers hope that you will become vested in the distracter before you get to the correct answer.

Even if you feel very confident that you have found the correct answer before looking at all the answer choices, it is still a good idea to glance briefly at the remaining answers. A few extra seconds will either confirm that the remaining answers do not need to be examined or will indicate that there may be something in one of the remaining answers that you should consider.

Eliminating an Answer That Seems Too Easy

Some correct answer choices may seem too easy or too simplistic. Remember that there *are* easy questions on the LSAT. If you eliminate an answer choice only because it seems too simplistic and instead choose one that is more convoluted, you may well be wrong. If an answer choice meets the criteria that the question stem sets forth, it is the right answer, even if it seems too easy. If you are not convinced that an easy answer is the correct one, work through the other answer choices carefully to prove that they are not defendable.

Ratio Versus Actual Number

Consider the following problem. In town X, 30 percent of the people own BMWs. In town Y, 5 percent of the people own BMWs. In which town are there more BMWs? Do you see why the question cannot be answered? If town X has 10,000 people and town Y has 4 million people, then town Y will have more BMWs.

A ratio, such as 30 percent or two-fifths, is not the same as an actual number, such as twelve BMWs. Many LR questions give you ratios, including percentages, and try to trick you into making a conclusion about actual numbers.

HOW TO PRACTICE

Chapter 1 discusses several distinct ways of practicing, each of which helps you develop different skills. Review this information.

For LR, most of your studying should be untimed, so that you can learn as much as possible on each practice question. As you work on problems, refer back to the lists and descriptions in this chapter. When you do a timed section, use the guidelines in Chapter 1 to evaluate your timing strategy.

As you get closer to your official test, do several timed sections at a sitting, working up to doing full mock tests. Whenever you do a timed section, evaluate it for timing strategy. Then review each question that you got wrong.

To make maximum improvement, review this entire chapter periodically. Each time you go through it, you will learn more and improve your skills.

Reading Comprehension | 3

This chapter helps you understand the patterns that the Reading Comprehension section is testing. You will learn strategies for organizing your time, for orienting yourself to the passage, and for getting to the correct answer. A sample passage will be analyzed in depth to help you learn how to apply the strategies. Finally, you will have a chance to take an LSAT-style Reading Comprehension section test and review the answer explanations.

INTRODUCTION TO READING COMPREHENSION

The Reading Comprehension (RC) section of the LSAT comprises four sets of passages and questions, with a total of twenty-seven questions. Each set typically has from six to eight questions, and rarely five questions. The time limit is thirty-five minutes.

VOCABULARY FOR READING COMPREHENSION

Set: A passage and the questions that go with it. There are four sets per section.

Regular set: The traditional RC set, consisting of one long passage, followed by questions. An RC section contains three regular sets and one Comparative Reading (CR) set.

CR set: A Comparative Reading set, in which there are two shorter passages, Passage A and Passage B, followed by questions that typically refer to the relationship between the two passages.

Passage: The paragraph(s) that make up the reading selection for a set. A passage is followed by a series of questions.

Question stem: The sentence that poses the question you are to answer. The question stem does not include the five answer choices.

Question: A question stem and the five answer choices that go with it.

Section: The grouping of four RC sets that constitutes a thirty-five-minute testing section. An RC section typically has twenty-seven questions.

Three of the four sets consist of one long passage. The other set consists of two shorter passages, labeled Passage A and Passage B. This type of set is called Comparative Reading (CR) and differs slightly from the other sets.

The subject matter of the passages is drawn from the natural sciences (30 percent), social sciences (30 percent), humanities (20 percent), and law (20 percent). A fifth of all passages refer to law. A sixth refer to literature. The next most common topics are history, biology, geology, and sociology, followed by archaeology, art, ecology, political science, psychology, and technology.

EXAMPLES OF SUBJECTS FOR RC PASSAGES

Natural sciences: astronomy, botany, computers, ecology, geology, meteorology, technology, zoology
Social sciences: anthropology, archaeology, economics, education, history, languages, political science, psychology, sociology
Humanities: architecture, fine art, literature, music, philosophy, popular culture, spirituality, theater
Law: various

The RC combines some elements from the other sections of the test. Some question types in RC are identical to question types in LR. In addition, RC is set up in four sets, just as AR is.

Is It Possible to Improve on RC?

If RC were just a test of how well people read, it would be difficult to improve on it. The good news is that RC is very learnable. There are hidden agendas and secret patterns to RC. By mastering these RC strategies and combining them with timing strategy, you can increase your scores significantly.

⚟ Mastering Timing

A strong timing strategy is critical for getting your best score. To get the most out of this section, review the section on timing strategy in Chapter 1, "General Strategies," now.

The first step in timing strategy is to rank the difficulty of the passages. The difficulty of a passage is subjective. What is easy for one test taker might be impossible for another. Simply glance at the passage. If the topic seems unpleasant, it will be harder to understand. Also consider the complexity of the language. Some passages might be on an interesting topic but be written in a way that makes it hard to understand. The opposite is also true. A passage may be on a difficult topic but may be relatively easy to follow.

If two passages are equally difficult but one has more questions, choose the one with more questions, as it offers more possible points for the same setup time. However, never choose a harder passage just because it has more questions. The "more questions" rule only applies for passages of equal difficulty.

After taking a timed practice section, evaluate the effectiveness of your timing strategy. To do this, you need to know how much time you spent on each question. After marking an answer, make a note on scratch paper of the time it took. Score the section and then review your strategy.

🔑 *STEPS FOR TIMING*

1. Rank the passages.
2. Set up the easiest passage.
3. Do all the questions, but not necessarily in order. Give each question up to three or four minutes, or even five, if necessary.
4. When two minutes are left, fill in cold guesses.
5. Keep working until the end.
6. If starting a new passage with only a few minutes left, do not read the passage. Go right to a detail question. Do not rush to complete all the questions.

Count how many questions you got wrong, ignoring the questions that were blind guesses. If there are more than one or two wrong answers, then there is room for improvement. How? Suppose you have five wrong answers. In theory, you could have skipped two of those questions and used the time to get the other three correct. How much time did you spend on the questions you got wrong? If there are many on which you spent only one or two minutes, you may be rushing. Compare the person who works on twenty-seven questions and gets twelve right with the person who works on sixteen questions and gets all of them right. Who has the better score?

Work on timing strategy until you are missing no more than two or three of the questions on which you actually worked (that is, do not count the cold guesses you get wrong) on a timed section. If you find that you have spent two minutes or less on questions that you got wrong, you might find that you will get them correct by allowing more time. Do not worry right now if your score is not where it should be. Focus on accuracy. Look carefully at each wrong answer and try to determine why you were not able to get it correct. Was something confusing? Were there two answers that were close? The next step is to master the RC strategies that help you get more questions correct more quickly.

How to Practice

Most practice on the RC—maybe 80 percent—should be done untimed. Working untimed means practicing and perfecting strategies for getting the right answer, no matter how long it takes. It may take twenty or thirty minutes to thoroughly work on one question. This is beneficial. If a particular question becomes frustrating, rather than giving up, set it aside, take a break, and come back to it later.

Even when practicing untimed, write down the time spent on each question. On many questions, it may feel like you are taking too long; however, the watch might tell you that you solved the problem within three to five minutes. On the real test it is OK to spend that much time on the more difficult questions. Keeping track of time helps you adjust your internal sense of what is too much time and what is acceptable. It also shows, on questions that you get wrong despite your best efforts, whether you gave the question enough time.

Periodically do an RC section timed to evaluate your timing strategy under testing conditions. Do a timed section now as you begin your studying and then again every few weeks. Before starting a timed section, review your timing strategy. Use your watch to keep track of time on each question. During the last few minutes, put cold guesses for questions that there is not enough time to answer. Note which questions were cold guesses.

On your official LSAT your timing strategy will be exactly the same as on your timed practice except that you will not write down the time for each question on your official test.

Many LSAT takers get their best score by working on only two or three passages and guessing cold on the rest. The person who works on three passages and gets every question correct scores higher than the person who works on all of the questions but gets half of them wrong.

TACKLING THE PASSAGE

THE THREE STEPS FOR MASTERING RC

1. Set up the passage.
2. Analyze and understand the questions.
3. Prove the correct answer and find the flaws in the wrong ones.

How to Set Up the Passage

What is the most efficient way to set up a passage? What needs to be remembered, what needs to be understood, and what can be ignored? A typical RC passage contains twenty, thirty, or more specific facts. However, a passage tests only three or four of those facts. The rest of the questions test what can be called big-picture information, such as the main idea, the author's tone, or the function of a particular phrase. The test taker who tries to absorb all the facts is doing too much work. Consider a different approach: read for the big picture.

All questions are either big-picture questions or fact questions. For a fact question, even if you tried to remember the facts the first time through the passage, your memory will not be accurate enough to answer the question. A better, faster, and more accurate strategy is to go back and get facts as they are needed.

This means it is not necessary to memorize facts when reading the passage. Then why bother to read the passage at all? To answer a big-picture question, it is necessary to first have a clear sense of the big picture—the overall structure and movement of the passage. The real purpose of the initial skimming of the passage, then, is to find the big picture.

The big picture of a passage has certain predictable elements. Most RC passages—and perhaps all of them—are built around what can be called a dichotomy: a contrast or a tension between two opposing things, something "on the one hand" versus something else "on the other hand." Consider the discussion given in Chapter 1 about the two vehicles: the Toyota and the Subaru, one red and one silver, one a car and one a truck. This is a clear example of a dichotomy. Two things are compared and contrasted. There may or may not be similarities but there must be a fundamental contrast.

The dichotomy can take the form of a problem to be solved, a dilemma, a paradox, or a contradiction, as well as a simple contrast between two things.

SAMPLES OF DICHOTOMIES

1. Because the supply of petroleum is decreasing steadily, we will need increasingly more sources of energy in the future.
2. Until recently, scientists believed that asteroids traveled alone.
3. Whereas the inquisitorial system of law allows for more cooperation among all parties, the adversarial system often results in more information being brought to light.
4. The theory of evolution replaced earlier attempts to explain biological variations as remnants of primordial differences.
5. Beethoven believed that traditional standards of musical composition were not sacred, that they should be broken at the whim of the creative force, and yet today, many teachers of composition hold Beethoven's own standards up as guidelines to be rigorously learned and followed.

Identify the dichotomies in the above examples. Use expressions such as "On the one hand, there is a red Toyota pickup. On the other hand, there is a silver Subaru wagon." Organize dichotomies visually in your scratch area:

On the one hand	versus	On the other hand

LSAT passages use certain kinds of dichotomies regularly. One of the most common is the dichotomy between an old phenomenon and a new phenomenon. The theory of evolution is a new theory replacing an old theory. Beethoven's standards were new compared to the traditional (old) standards from before his time.

Another common type is a dichotomy between theories, such as in Sample 4 above. Very often, one theory is old and the other new. However, passages can also use contemporary theories that are being contrasted with each other. Because a new theory is usually not presented unless it corrects flaws in a previous theory, the author of a passage usually finds the new theory better.

The big picture involves not just a dichotomy but what the passage does with the dichotomy. All of this together creates what we can call the structure of the passage. Here are three examples of structures.

STRUCTURE 1

- A theory is presented.
- Facts supporting it are given.
- A fact that weakens it is given.
- The author concludes that the theory is good, despite the weakness.

Structure 2

- An attitude or belief from the past is presented.
- The current belief about the same subject is presented.
- Support for the superiority of the current belief is given.
- Additional support for the current belief is given.
- The author concludes that the current belief is superior.

Structure 3

- A dilemma is presented.
- A solution is given.
- Evidence to support the solution is given.
- The author points out a new problem that the solution would create.
- A way to overcome the new problem is given.
- The author concludes that the original solution has merits but also has drawbacks, and states that further research is needed.

The passage establishes the dichotomy and then builds a structure by incorporating elements such as definitions, explanations, clarifications, and examples. From there, it goes on to present elements such as solutions, partial solutions that create new problems, support for a view, objections to or criticisms of a view, rebuttals to objections, similarities and differences between A and B, and interim conclusions.

The flow of the passage is often predictable. If a theory, belief, or solution is defended, there are only two ways the passage can continue. Either the defense holds up or there is a problem with it. If there is a problem with it, there are only two ways the passage can continue. Either the problem can be overcome and the defense holds up, or the problem is fatal and the defense does not hold up.

The ending of a passage is often particularly important. A passage often introduces something new at the end or gives insights into the author's main point. The ending can confirm that a particular view or theory is correct or that it is correct but with some qualifications. Alternately, the passage may conclude that the view or theory is incorrect or that it is incorrect with some redeeming qualities. The passage may conclude that a further line of investigation is needed. It may propose a new synthesis that provides an alternative to either of the original two elements of the dichotomy. It may even suggest a whole new area that could be investigated as a result of the passage's line of inquiry.

Finding the Big Picture (Structure)

Skim the passage below in order to find the big picture. Start at the beginning of the passage and skim until you find something that could be a dichotomy.

EXAMPLE

  Relationships between elements of the natural world are often more complex than we realize, so that our actions affecting one element may have unexpected, and often negative, effects on another. For example, under natural conditions
(Line) grasslands are grazed by various animals, and yet in certain circumstances, this
(5) grazing may harm the health of the grassland. When grazing takes place under the unnatural conditions that result when grazing patterns are altered by people, the potential for harm is much greater.

  Many grasslands in the West have been grazed under conditions altered by people for well over a hundred years. Scientists recently have been studying the
(10) effects of grazing the American bison, commonly known as the buffalo, because it has a less harmful effect on grasslands than most other domestic grazing animals. Two factors have been measured—the health of the grasses and the health of the range area in general. Health of the grasses is measured by counting the number of grass clumps per acre still alive at the end of the season. Health of the range is
(15) measured by calculating the number of different species of plants per acre and the total mass of vegetation produced per acre for the season. By comparing bison-grazed range areas with ungrazed control areas, researchers found that the more palatable, fine-textured grasses, such as Indian Rice Grass, suffered significant damage, whereas less tasty, coarse grasses, such as Sacaton, showed virtually
(20) none. Overall range health declined in areas dominated by Indian Rice Grass but not in those dominated by Sacaton.

  It is still unclear whether a decrease in the health of grasses, even with the more vulnerable ones, necessarily results in a decrease in range health in the long run. Rangelands dominated by the slower growing, fine-textured species will obviously
(25) be more susceptible to permanent damage, but the ultimate effect on a rangeland depends on four identifiable factors. Areas with these characteristics would be most adversely affected: a high ratio of fine grasses to coarse grasses, a high ratio of grasses to non-grass plants, low annual rainfall, and high average seasonal temperatures. It would be a good idea to identify range areas with a combination
(30) of these characteristics and take special restorative measures with them, because they are most susceptible to being damaged by human-directed grazing.

The first paragraph does not contain any significant dichotomies. It gives a general statement and an example. It refers to a possible problem, but there is no binary choice—no choice between two distinct things.

The second paragraph starts with facts. Facts are not dichotomies. The passage does mention that bison are different from other domestic grazing animals. This fact could be the basis for a dichotomy but the passage does not pursue it. The passage goes on to mention two additional factors—the health of grasses and the health of rangeland. Whereas there are differences between these two factors, the passage does not pursue a conflict between them.

Only when the passage introduces the distinction between fine-textured grasses and coarse grasses is there a clear, black-and-white distinction. Fine grasses do not hold up to grazing. Coarse grasses do. The final paragraph does not pursue this dichotomy further but does return to the dichotomy between the health of grasses and the health of rangelands—a dichotomy that was mentioned earlier in the passage but not pursued at that time. Thus, health of grasses versus health of rangelands is also a significant dichotomy. The paragraph states that the solution is unclear. It identifies further factors that need to be considered.

The ending tells us that we can use information about the difference between fine- and coarse-textured grasses and the information about how the health of grasses influences the health of rangeland to help solve the problem of damage caused by human-directed grazing.

The big picture of the passage, condensed to its essentials, is:

> *Fine grasses are more susceptible to damage than coarse grasses in grazing conditions that have been altered by people. Damage to grasses alone doesn't determine whether the rangeland is damaged, but in conjunction with other factors, it can. We can use this information to protect vulnerable areas.*

Why is it important to identify dichotomies and the big picture? First, big-picture questions cannot be accurately answered without a clear grasp of the structure of the passage. Second, many of the detail questions are specifically designed to confuse the reader between the facts on opposite sides of the dichotomy. In the example in Chapter 1, what color was the vehicle that had four-wheel drive? Often the test uses terms that sound similar to create additional confusion. For example, a passage might contrast neurolinguistic therapy with linguistic neuropathology.

It is difficult to keep dichotomies clear in your memory. A diagram on paper, on the other hand, is an almost foolproof way of keeping two sets of data distinct. Once the dichotomy is clear, put it down on paper immediately.

Diagramming the Big Picture

Theoretically, it is possible to draw a complete diagram of the dichotomies and facts in a passage, along with their relationships. However, this is too time-consuming on the actual test. During the test, only the main dichotomies and basic facts need to be written down. Go back to the diagram of the differences between the two vehicles, the Toyota and the Subaru. It is a good example of a basic working diagram. Even though it is only a part of the whole setup, it is a complete diagram of that part. Such a diagram makes it impossible to become confused.

In order to develop a sense of how much to diagram and how much to leave out, start by fully diagramming one or two passages. After that, try cutting back to what feels like just the essentials. If you get questions wrong because the diagram was too incomplete, try diagramming a little more. If a diagram contains information that was never needed to answer the questions, try doing less.

Diagramming is similar to making an outline of a passage. However, instead of putting headings down the side of the page, make columns across the top. The columns are usually in pairs—one column versus the other column.

Below is an RC passage presented one sentence at a time in order to break down the process of identifying the structure.

> *Until 1959, most social scientists considered the family unit to be the only valid subject of sociological research.*

Is there a dichotomy? At first glance, this example may seem only to give facts. However, the statement "Until 1959" actually creates a dichotomy: what was true before 1959 versus what was true after 1959. This is a very common kind of dichotomy. It may be introduced with wording such as "until recently," "up to now," or "before the fourth century A.D."

Here is the second sentence of the same passage:

> *In the 1960s, sociologists at several major universities began interviewing single adults about their work habits, social relationships, and personal goals.*

This reveals the other half of the dichotomy—what was true after 1959. The dichotomy can be diagrammed:

Family unit   versus   Single adults

Additional information about each side of the dichotomy can be added:

<u>Family unit</u>   versus   <u>Single adults</u>

<1960   >1960

If the passage gives more facts about the earlier studies, those facts can go under "Family unit," and likewise for the later studies.

The third sentence of the passage is:

Modern researchers are divided as to whether young single adults consti-
tute a sociological reality distinct from single senior citizens.

This sentence introduces a new dichotomy between younger and older, but it falls under the "Single adults" column. It is a dichotomy within one-half of an existing dichotomy. One category splits into two:

<u>Family unit</u>   versus   <u>Single adults</u>

<1960   >1960

<u>younger</u>   <u>older</u>

The next sentence of the passage is:

Young singles typically can look forward to an increasing income and are
more flexible in developing new friends and interests.

This sentence gives specific information about the "younger" category. It also gives implied information about the "older" category, because they are contrasted:

<u>Family unit</u>   versus   <u>Single adults</u>

<1960   >1960

<u>younger</u>   <u>older</u>

increasing $ fixed $

more flexible,   less flexible
friends/interests

The passage continues:

> *However, most sociologists now believe that these differences are insignificant compared with the similarities among all ages of single people in free time and amount of social contact.*

What has happened here? The author has reconciled the dichotomy. The problem is solved, the two sides brought together and the tension resolved.

<u>Family unit</u>	versus	<u>Single adults</u>	
<1960		>1960	
		<u>younger</u>	<u>older</u>
		increasing $	fixed $
		more flexible, friends/interests	less flexible

To summarize, then, there is a basic dichotomy, a new dichotomy within a branch of the original dichotomy, and the coming together (merging or bridging) of the two sides of a dichotomy. All of these were diagrammed, along with the details that go into each category.

Dichotomies are often indicated by words or phrases like "however," "on the other hand," and "in contrast." These show a switch from one side to the other. *John is happy with his job. However, he is dissatisfied with his living situation.* Words or phrases such as "similarly," "likewise," "furthermore," and "in the same way" show that the author is continuing to talk about the same side. *John is happy with his job. Furthermore, he enjoys his living situation.*

Once a dichotomy has been introduced, there are usually only a few directions in which the passage could go next. It could give examples. It could explain theories. It could evaluate whether something is good or bad. It could bridge a dichotomy. It could create a dichotomy within a dichotomy. Keeping these possibilities in mind helps you recognize quickly where the passage is going.

Identifying dichotomies is such a powerful organizing tool that it can be used to understand the structure of a passage even when the content of the passage is too difficult or complex to follow. The next passage is based on the most complex recent theories in astrophysics. For most people, the details of the passage would be incomprehensible. To avoid being sidetracked by complex detail, skip the details and stick with the big picture. The passage has been modified below to simulate that. The actual details are replaced with simple variables, A and B.

EXAMPLE

> Until 1956, people thought that stars generated their energy by A. New research, however, indicated that Theory A could not explain Observation O. Theory B was put forward to explain Observation O. Theory B was widely attacked because calculations based on it came up with a different estimate for the life span of our sun than those based on previous observations. Prof. X reviewed the previous observations and found that the observations themselves were inaccurate, and once corrected, the new calculations matched those predicted by Theory B. Theory B not only gives us a more consistent explanation of how stars produce their energy, but also reassuringly gives life on Earth an extra 15 million years before our sun dies.

Even though the topic is highly complex, the structure of the passage is easy to spot by simply sidestepping the details.

How to Skim

Start skimming for the big picture at the beginning of the passage. If the first few sentences contain only facts but no dichotomies, continue until you find a dichotomy. Identify the two parts of the dichotomy clearly. It is helpful to take extra time on this step in order to be accurate.

Passages can be thought of as "an analysis of an interesting something." This phrase contains four implied questions that help build the big picture. What is the "something?" What makes it interesting? In what way is it analyzed? How does the analysis end up?

In the astrophysics passage, the "something" being analyzed was two theories. It was the contrast and tension between them that made the topic interesting. The analysis showed problems posed by Theory A and a partial solution (Theory B) with its own problems. The analysis concluded by showing how the problems with Theory B had been overcome.

Here are common answers to the four questions.

1. **What is the "something" that is interesting?**
    Theory
    Event
    Action
    Definition
    Phenomenon (social, political, natural, etc.)

2. **What is interesting about it?**
   Contrast (A versus B, old versus new)
   Dilemma/problem/inadequacy/unknown
   Paradox/discrepancy/paradoxical contradiction

3. **In what way is it analyzed?**
   Definitions/explorations/clarifications/examples
   Solutions
   Partial solutions with additional problems
   Support for a view
   Criticisms of or objections to a view
   Similarities between A and B
   Differences between A and B
   Interim conclusions

4. **How does it end up?**
   A view or solution holds up.
   A view or solution holds up with qualifications.
   A view or solution does not hold up.
   A view or solution does not hold up but has some redeeming
     qualifications.
   Further inquiry is needed.
   A new synthesis is proposed.

Highlighting

Highlighting is not strictly necessary on an RC passage, though it helps some people focus. If you highlight information that you never use, cut back. If you do not highlight, you can feel confident that identifying the dichotomies and the movement of the passage, along with some brief diagramming, is enough.

Setting Up Comparative Reading Sets

Set up the CR set in the same way that you set up the regular sets. Each of the two passages in CR is shorter than a regular passage. In addition to getting a sense of the big picture for each passage, orient yourself to how the two passages are related. In what way are they similar? In what way do they differ? There is usually an important contrast between the two. Consider the points of view of each author. What does each author believe? To what points is each committed?

UNDERSTANDING THE QUESTION TYPES

RC questions fall into two categories—detail questions and big-picture questions. Detail questions ask for facts that are specifically stated in the passage or that can be implied from information specifically stated. Big-picture questions test an understanding of the overall purpose and structure of the passage. When you begin to work on a question, start by orienting yourself to the question. Identify whether the question is a big-picture or a detail question. The following sections cover the types of questions that occur in each category, along with strategies for solving that type.

It would be nice to think that there is just one strategy for each type. Unfortunately, it is not that simple. One *main idea* question, for example, may throw completely different obstacles at the test taker than another *main idea* question. To master strategy, work carefully with hundreds of questions. The good news, though, is that there are certain things that all questions of a particular type have in common.

RC tests three thinking skills that are reflected in the questions:

1. **Comprehension:** Has the reader understood the facts presented in the passage?
2. **Evaluation:** Can the reader identify the relationships among the various elements of the passage?
3. **Application/Extension:** Can the reader apply information in the passage to other situations?

    The first of these is a detail skill and the others are big-picture skills.

Big-Picture Questions

Big-picture questions test your holistic understanding of the passage, as opposed to understanding of specific facts. There are six major types of big-picture questions, nine less common types, and six types exclusive to CR.

Question stems can have straightforward wording or obscure wording. Obscure wording makes it difficult to identify the question type. The examples below show you both the straightforward and more obscure common wording variations for question stems.

Major Big-Picture Question Types

The most common big-picture questions and percentage of occurrence are:

1. Main idea (12%)
2. Use of a word or phrase (9%)
3. Function (8%)
4. Agree with a view (8%)
5. Application/extension (7%)
6. Analogous situation (5%)

Together these account for nearly 50 percent of all RC questions.

Main Idea

Main idea questions constitute about 12 percent of all RC questions. Below are common wording variations for the question stem of *main idea* questions. Some question stems typically appear only in a CR set.

1. *The author's main point is . . .*
2. *The author's major contention is . . .*
3. *The main idea expressed in the passage is . . .*
4. *The primary purpose of the passage is to . . .*
5. *Which one of the following most accurately expresses the main point of the passage?*
6. *Which one of the following most accurately expresses the central idea of the passage?*
7. *Which one of the following most accurately states the main function of the passage?*
8. *Which one of the following statements most accurately summarizes the content of the passage?*

For Comparative Reading:

1. *Which one of the following most accurately states the main point of Passage A?*
2. *Which one of the following is the central topic of each passage?*

Strategy for main idea questions. To be correct, the answer must (1) be a statement that is true and consistent with the passage, and (2) match the structure (big picture). Beware of choosing an answer that is true or consistent but is not the main idea. A *main idea* question requires you to understand what the dichotomy in the passage is, as well as how the author treats the dichotomy, and what the conclusion of the passage is.

Use of a Word or Phrase

This type accounts for 9 percent of RC questions. Examples of main wording variations for *use of a word or phrase* questions are:

1. *In the context of the passage, the description of a work of art as "uplifting" mainly refers to its . . .*
2. *In using the phrase "the bane of his existence" the author of Passage A most probably means to refer to . . .*
3. *Which one of the following most accurately describes the author's use of the word "enfranchise" in line 17 and "disenfranchise" in line 36?*
4. *The author uses the word "interminable" (line 14) most likely in order to express . . .*
5. *By referring to the scientist's argument as "highly suspect" (line 36), the author most clearly intends to emphasize . . .*
6. *The author most likely refers to the Magna Carta (lines 20–23) and the Declaration of Independence, mentioned in lines 43–44, for which one of the following reasons?*
7. *Which one of the following expressions most accurately conveys the sense of the word "paramount" as it is used in line 43?*
8. *The passage most strongly suggests that the business owner believed that "net profit" should be defined in a way that . . .*
9. *The author describes the coincidence mentioned in the last paragraph as "extraordinary" in order to suggest that the coincidence . . .*

Strategy for use of a word or phrase questions. It is not enough to simply understand the literal meaning of the word. Examine its context. Consider the author's intent in using the word. Look at several lines immediately before the word. Sometimes it is necessary to refer to a previous paragraph.

Function

Questions that ask you to identify the function of an element of the passage account for 8 percent of questions. Common wording variations are:

1. *The author provides an example of a contemporary issue in lines 14–15 primarily in order to . . .*
2. *The author's discussion of rites of passage serves primarily to . . .*

3. Which one of the following describes the author's primary purpose in mentioning the fact that the Mexican gray wolf is endangered?
4. The first sentence of the passage functions primarily in which one of the following ways?
5. In discussing the opinions of the landlord, the author of Passage B seeks primarily to . . .
6. The main purpose of the first paragraph of the passage is to . . .

Strategy for function questions. A *function* question is similar to a *use of a word or phrase* question in that you must identify how certain information functions in the passage, or, in other words, what role the information serves. For a *function* question, the information that you are to evaluate is not limited to a word or phrase. It is less likely that line numbers will be cited. Orient yourself to the information that is cited. Referring to the previous question stems, you may need to consider what the author actually says about the contemporary issue, rites of passage, and so on.

As with *use of a word or phrase* questions, it is not enough to understand the literal facts about the contemporary issue, for example. You must understand what the author's intentions were for including the information and how the information fits into the passage as a whole. Does the information provide background information? Does it support a point? Does it attack a view? Does it resolve an issue? Look for clues in the lines immediately before the part of the passage that introduces the information. If necessary, look earlier in the passage.

Agree with a View

These account for 8 percent of questions. Variations are:

1. The author of the passage would be most likely to agree with which one of the following statements?
2. It can be inferred from the passage that Madame Curie would most likely have agreed with which one of the following statements about the fear that scientific discoveries can have negative consequences for humanity?
3. Given the information in the passage, the author would be most likely to agree with which one of the following statements about modern operas?
4. The passage most strongly suggests that pacifists would agree with which one of the following statements?
5. It can be inferred from the passage that Gandhi most likely held which one of the following views?
6. It can be inferred from the passage that the author would be most likely to view the "outlandish opinions" mentioned in line 15 as . . .

Strategy for agree with a view questions. These question stems may or may not specify a particular issue. Some, such as examples 1, 4, and 5 above, simply ask what a certain person would agree with. If no particular issue is specified, you have to base your answer on your big-picture understanding of the author's point. Eliminate choices that go in the wrong direction. For example, Gandhi would be unlikely to agree with a view that the best way to resolve issues is through armed combat. The view that negotiations with one's opponent can sometimes break down could be in the right direction—it involves peaceful negotiation—but is not necessarily the correct answer.

The correct answer must be defendable by information stated in the passage. Test each remaining answer. Look for information in the passage that would defend or attack a particular answer choice. For this type of question the correct answer can hang on subtle and unexpected elements, so be careful!

If the question stem does specify an issue, first review the information in the passage that describes the author's belief about the issue. Then eliminate answers that go in the wrong direction and test the remaining answer choices.

Application/Extension

This type of question tests your ability to absorb information from the passage and apply it to new situations. These questions often require you to extend the application of information beyond the way that the information is applied in the passage. *Application/extension* questions account for 7 percent of RC questions. The common wording variations of the stems are:

1. *As it is described in the passage, an interactive research methodology would be best exemplified by a research project that . . .*
2. *Given the information in the passage, to which one of the following would magnetic resonance imaging likely be most applicable?*
3. *The ethical principle supported in the passage would be most relevant as a standard for deciding that which one of the following is ethically ambiguous?*
4. *The author's description of consensus decision making suggests that which one of the following would be least appropriately described as a valid response to a person who refuses to understand the opinions of others?*
5. *Based on the passage, Einstein's attitude toward the quantum physicists' view would be most softened if the quantum physicists were to . . .*
6. *The author most probably means to include which one of the following groups among the "supporters of a transformational agenda" referred to in line 32?*
7. *Suppose that a team of physicists has detected a particle that does not follow the laws of either relativity theory or quantum mechanics. Which one of the*

following actions by the international physics community would most closely meet Einstein's criteria for "the ability to reevaluate established theory" as described in lines 23–26?

Strategy for application/extension questions. Because there are so many ways in which application and extension can be tested, the wording of the stems can vary greatly. Orient yourself carefully to the stem. What information is the question asking you to work with? What are you supposed to do with the information? In many such questions you need to understand the opinions and perspectives of either the author or of the people referred to in the passage.

Some application/extension questions ask you to identify an example of something that is described in general in the passage. Some ask you to match information in the passage with a situation in the answer choices, much in the way that *matching* questions function in LR. Some questions ask about the author's intentions. Some provide new information, such as example 7 above, and ask you to apply information from the passage to the new situation.

All of the *application/extension* questions require you to have a solid understanding of the relationships in the passage, as well as a clear understanding of what the question is asking. These questions require abstract thinking.

Analogous Situation

These ask you to identify a situation that is analogous to something in the passage. The answers represent situations and can be lengthy. This type accounts for 5 percent of questions. Variations are:

1. *Based on the passage, which one of the following scenarios is most similar to the way in which the early settlers attempted to establish security?*
2. *The passage indicates that the works of Plato and teachings of Socrates were similar in that . . .*
3. *As described in the passage, the university's policy for dealing with plagiarism is most closely analogous to which one of the following situations?*
4. *The relationship between the tribes that depend on fishing and the tribes that depend on hunting, as described in the passage, is most analogous to the relationship between which one of the following pairs?*

The second example does not ask you to identify an analogous situation but rather, asks you to identify why two situations are analogous.

Comparative Reading Question Types

The questions on CR sets can be drawn from any of the general question types. However, many of the question types are unique to CR. There are six specific CR-type questions.

In Common

About half of CR-type questions ask you to identify something that Passage A and Passage B have in common. The common elements can be premises, types of logic, main ideas, issues, or opinions, among other possibilities. Possible wording variations are:

1. *The argument described in Passage A and the argument made by the author of Passage B are both advanced by . . .*
2. *Which one of the following is mentioned in both passages as evidence to support the view that young children should play outdoors regularly?*
3. *Each passage suggests which one of the following about wild horses?*
4. *Both passages are concerned with answering which one of the following questions?*
5. *The passages have which one of the following goals in common?*
6. *Both passages identify which one of the following as a factor that is necessary for ethical action?*
7. *Which one of the following most accurately describes a perspective on ethics present in each passage?*
8. *Both passages mention television primarily in order to . . .*

Strategy for in-common questions. Orient yourself carefully to the question stem to understand what the question is asking. When you find an answer choice that you believe is correct, be sure to find the exact wording in each passage that proves that the answer is correct. Do not rely on your memory.

Agree

An *agree* question asks you to identify a statement that the authors of the two passages would both agree is true. This is similar to an *in-common* question in some ways but is a distinct type. Wording variations include:

1. *It can be inferred from the passage that the author of Passage A and the author of Passage B would accept which one of the following statements?*
2. *It is most likely that both authors would agree with which one of the following statements about health insurance?*

Strategy for agree questions. Correctly answering an *agree* question requires that you understand the concept of an arguer being *committed* to certain facts. The following abbreviated passages illustrate this concept.

EXAMPLE ━━━━━━━━━━━━━━━━━━━━━━━━━━━━━━━━━━━━━━

Passage A: Most people prefer fresh fruits to either canned or frozen fruits.

Passage B: Most people prefer frozen foods to canned varieties of the same food.

With which one of the following statements would both authors agree?

(A) Most people would prefer fresh oranges to canned oranges.

(B) Most people would prefer frozen oranges to canned oranges.

(C) When choosing non-fresh food, most people choose frozen food.

(D) Most people would prefer fresh carrots to canned or frozen carrots but if they could not have fresh carrots, most people would choose frozen carrots.

(E) When choosing fruit, most people have a preference as to how the fruit has been handled from the point where it was harvested to the point at which the person receives it.

━━

Try to answer the question. Defend your answer. The discussion is below.

Consider choice A. Choice A is completely consistent with Passage A. However, Passage B contains no information on preferences for fresh food. Arguer B is not committed to any conclusion about fresh food. Therefore, Arguer B cannot agree with the statement in choice A. It is not enough to say that Arguer B might agree with it. You have to prove that Arguer B is *committed to the truth* of choice A. That is not the case.

Choice B is completely consistent with Passage B. Oranges are a food and the frozen food in choice B is preferred over the canned variety of the same food. Arguer A, however, is not committed to any information about a preference between frozen and canned versions of a food. Passage A treats frozen and canned versions equally. Even though Arguer A might not disagree with the statement in choice B, Arguer A is not *committed* to the truth of choice B.

Choice C refers to non-fresh food. Arguer B is committed to the fact that when given a choice between frozen and canned food, people prefer frozen. However, Arguer B does not address the possibility that there are other types of processing that people might prefer over frozen. Arguer B is not committed to the truth of choice C. Arguer A is not committed to a viewpoint when it comes to choosing between different styles of processing, only between fresh and processed.

Choice D is closer to an answer that both arguers would agree on but it has a fatal flaw. It refers to a vegetable (carrots), whereas Arguer A only discusses fruit. Arguer B is committed to the truth of choice C because her argument is based on food, in general, not just fruit.

Choice E refers to fruit. It simply states that most people care about the state of the fruit. This is consistent with Passage A because people have a preference (they care) for fresh over frozen or canned. Choice E is also consistent with Passage B because people do not want canned fruit if they can have frozen. Both arguers are committed to agreeing with choice E.

Disagree

This question type is the opposite of *agree* questions. The two arguers are committed to *disagreeing* about the truth of a statement. *Disagree* questions can also ask about how the author of one passage would critique the other passage. *Disagree* questions are more common than *agree* questions. The wording variations are:

1. *The authors would be most likely to disagree over . . .*
2. *The author of Passage B and the kind of critical thinker described in Passage A would be most likely to disagree over whether . . .*
3. *Which one of the following is a statement that is true of scientific inquiry, according to Passage A, but that is not true of theological inquiry, according to Passage B?*
4. *It can be inferred that the author of Passage B would regard which one of the following as a logical error in the arguments made in Passage A?*

Strategy for disagree questions. The disagreement in these questions is typically between the authors of the two passages. However, the disagreement can also be between arguers who are referred to by the author of a passage, as in example 2 above. Also, the disagreement can be between two perspectives, without necessarily referring to the authors of the perspectives, as in example 3 above. In example 3, you are asked to find a statement that is consistent with one perspective and inconsistent with the other. Just as in disagreement between authors, in disagreement between perspectives, one perspective must be committed to the truth of the statement and the other perspective must be committed to the falsehood of the statement.

Difference Between Passages

These questions require you to identify a difference between the two passages. This is *not* the same as identifying a statement on which the two authors disagree. The wording variations are:

1. *Passage B differs from Passage A in that Passage B is more . . .*
2. *Which one of the following distinguishes the music students discussed in Passage B from the art students discussed in Passage A?*
3. *Which one of the following statements most accurately describes a difference between the two passages?*
4. *The perspectives on endangered species presented by the two authors differ in which one of the following ways?*

Strategy for difference between passage questions. As you orient yourself to the passages, look for the similarities and differences. There are often too many similarities and differences to list, so work backward from the answer choices, testing each one. Do *not* rely on your memory. Go back to the passages.

Relationship Between Passages

This type of question asks you about the relationship between the two passages. The question may simply ask you to identify the relationship, or it may ask you specific questions that require you to relate the two passages. Common wording variations are:

1. *Which one of the following most accurately describes a relationship between the two passages?*
2. *How does the content of Passage B relate to the purpose of Passage A?*
3. *The facts that are cited in Passage B relate to the generalization reported in Passage A in which one of the following ways?*

Strategy for relationship between passages questions. Orient carefully to the question and review the passages before looking at the answer choices. For example, in variation 3 above, you would review what the generalization is in Passage A. However, variations 1 and 2 are so general that there is nothing specific for you to review in advance. Go right to the answer choices and test them by finding the exact words in the passages that would defend the answer.

A Premise in One Passage Supports a Conclusion in the Other

Wording variations for this specific question type are:

1. *Which one of the following assertions from Passage B provides support for the view attributed to Einstein in Passage A, lines 23–25?*
2. *Which one of the following assertions from Passage A most closely exemplifies what the author of Passage B means in referring to eminent domain as "mass megalomania"?*

Strategy for a premise in one passage supports a conclusion in the other. Use the same strategies as for *relationship between the passages.* To support a conclusion, use the LR strategies for strengthening a conclusion. Identify the conclusion. Identify the premises that support the conclusion and identify the type of logic that the author uses to arrive at the conclusion.

Less Common Big-Picture Question Types

There are nine specific types of less common big-picture questions. Each of these individually accounts for 2 percent or fewer of all RC questions. As a group, they account for about 13 percent.

Agreement Between People

This rare question type asks you to identify a statement that two people would agree is true. The two people can include the author and people whose views are described in the passage. Typical wording is:

> *Based on the passage, it can be concluded that the author and Einstein would have the same attitude toward . . .*

Strategy for agreement between people. The strategy for this type is similar to the strategy for identifying with what statement an author would agree. In this case you must understand the viewpoint of both people. Review the viewpoints first and then go to the answer choices, eliminating ones that are clearly wrong. Test the other answer choices.

Assumption

RC assumption questions are similar to LR assumption questions. This is a rare type on RC. Typical wording is:

> *It can be inferred that the argument for legalized euthanasia in lines 54–56 relies on which one of the following assumptions?*

Strategy for assumption questions. Apply the same strategies that you use on an LR assumption question. Identify the premises and the conclusion. Look for a gap in the argument. Test the answer choices by negating them.

Helps to Answer

In this question type, the answer choices consist of questions. You are to choose the question that the passage provides enough information to answer. Common wording variations are:

1. *The passage provides information sufficient to answer which one of the following questions?*
2. *The passage provides information that most helps to answer which one of the following questions?*
3. *The discussion of quantum mechanics in the second paragraph can most justifiably be taken as providing an answer to which one of the following questions?*

Strategy for helps to answer questions. Test the answer choices by considering what the answer to the question in the answer choice would be. It is not necessary to come up with a precise answer, but you must determine that the question in the answer choice can be answered by information in the passage.

Identify a Difference

This type of question asks you to identify a difference between two elements in the passage. Common wording variations are:

1. *According to the passage, one of the ways that relativity theory differs from quantum mechanics theory is that . . .*
2. *The passage suggests that one of the differences between relativity theory and quantum mechanics is that the relativity theory . . .*

Strategy for identify a difference. Most people find this type relatively easy. Look for the exact wording that shows that the two elements differ.

Identify the Structure

This question type asks you to recognize elements of the structure and organization of the passage. Wording variations include:

1. *Which one of the following most accurately represents the structure of the third paragraph?*

2. *Which one of the following most accurately describes the organization of the passage?*

Strategy for identify the structure. To answer this question you must have a good sense of the big picture of the passage. Understand the dichotomies and understand how the author develops the passage.

Strengthen

This question type is similar to its counterpart in LR. It is not a very common question type, though its mirror image, *weaken*, accounts for 3 percent of RC questions. Common wording variations are:

1. *Which one of the following, if true, would most strengthen Feldenberg's assertion that raw foods contain more nutrients than cooked foods?*
2. *Which one of the following would, if true, most help to support the raw food theory?*

Strategy for strengthen questions. Apply the same strategies that are used for *strengthen* questions in LR. The premises in the passage must be assumed to be true. Determine whether there is an apparent gap in the argument. Analyze how the argument is put together, what the conclusion is, and how the argument tries to support the conclusion. Test the answer choices by showing how each one would strengthen the argument.

Support a Generalization

This rare question type asks you to identify a generalization that can be supported by statements in the passage. Typical wording is:

> *Einstein's perspective on quantum mechanics, as it is described in the third paragraph, gives the most support for which one of the following generalizations?*

Strategy for support a generalization. This question type is similar to a *what can be concluded* question in LR, with answer choices that are generalizations. Find the generalization that can be concluded based on the information in the passage. This type of passage may also ask you to match the concrete information in the passage with an abstract expression. For example:

> *Concrete information: Apples have vitamin C. Hawthorn berries have vitamin E.*
>
> *Abstract generalization: Many fruits are excellent sources of necessary nutrients.*

Tone

This question type asks you to evaluate the author's tone or attitude toward a topic or issue. Common wording variations include:

1. *Based on the passage, the author's attitude toward the proponents of raw food is most accurately described as . . .*
2. *The author's stance toward the financial services industry can best be described as . . .*
3. *The tone of the passage is best described as . . .*

Strategy for tone questions. Each passage has at least one "voice," representing the viewpoint of a particular person. Each voice has a specific tone, or attitude. Consider the following:

> *Most politicians try to be tactful when they are talking to the public, but not good old Congressman Harry Paxton. Harry recently told a group of constituents that they had the brains of a banana slug when it came to understanding the federal budget. He told them that one of their fellow citizens complained that the government was giving too much money to people on welfare who weren't doing anything to earn it. But the complainer was himself living on disability payments. The country would be a better place if we had more politicians like Harry.*

What are the voices in this passage? Does the author have a voice? In any passage, the author either has an opinion about the information or is neutral. A neutral passage is like a newspaper article. It presents only the facts without expressing an opinion. If the author's voice is not neutral, it will be either positive, in support of the information presented, or negative, critical of the information.

On the LSAT, if the author's voice is positive, it will be either totally positive or positive with some qualifications or reservations. In the previous article, the author is totally positive about Harry Paxton. No reservations are expressed. Suppose the last line had read:

> *The country would be a better place if we had more politicians like Harry, but he would be wise to tone down his approach or he may not get reelected.*

Then the author's voice would be positive with qualifications. Note that the phrase *"but not good old Congressman Harry Paxton"* in the first sentence already indicates that the author is positive. If the author's voice is negative, it will likewise be either totally negative or negative with some positive qualifications.

LSAT tone questions ask about the tone of a particular voice. In the previous passage, there are three distinct voices. One is the author's. Whose voice is reflected in the statement "they had the brains of a banana slug when it came to understanding the federal budget?" Whose voice is reflected in the statement "the government was giving too much money to people on welfare who weren't doing anything to earn it"? The first is Harry's voice. The second is the voice of the person on disability. Be careful to identify the various voices in a passage and to keep them separate. Most tone questions ask about the author's voice.

In tone questions, answers are often on a continuum.

EXAMPLE

(A) bitter
(B) mildly annoyed
(C) unconcerned
(D) cautiously supportive
(E) ecstatic

Note that these answers start with a totally negative tone, move through a mildly negative tone to neutral to a moderately positive tone, and then move to a fully positive tone. First identify where on the above continuum the author's voice falls. If the author is positive but mentions some drawbacks, this is the qualifiedly positive position, which is answer choice D. It is not necessary to agree with the exact wording, *cautiously supportive*. Go by the place on the continuum even if the wording does not seem to be perfectly accurate.

Weaken

Like *strengthen* questions, these questions are very similar to their counterparts on LR. Typical wording variations are:

1. *Which one of the following would, if true, most undermine the author's claim about the value of early music training?*
2. *Which one of the following, if true, would most weaken the position that the passage attributes to opponents of preventive medicine?*
3. *Which one of the following, if true, most seriously undermines the author's criticism of the United Nations' proposal for redistribution of health resources?*

Strategy for weaken questions. Use the same strategies that you learned for such questions on the LR section. Identify how the argument is put together. Find the premises and the conclusion. Identify the type of logic that the author uses to support the conclusion. Look for gaps in the logic. Do you "buy" the argument? If not, identify what exactly seems to be wrong with it. Test the answer choices. The correct answer, when added to the original argument, causes the argument to fall apart or at least weaken.

Detail Questions

All detail questions ask for facts. These may be facts that are specifically stated in the passage (*specific detail* questions) or facts that follow logically from the information that is explicitly stated (*implied detail* questions). Correct answers do not depend on outside knowledge. If you choose an answer based on your own outside information, it cannot be correct unless it can also be defended by information in the passage. Detail questions account for 25 percent of all RC questions. There are more *implied detail* questions than *specific detail* questions.

Specific Detail

Specific detail questions account for about 9 percent of RC questions. The wording *according to the passage* indicates that the question may be a specific detail question, as about 60 percent of specific detail questions use this wording. However, the same phrase is also found in some other question types. Common wording variations are:

1. *The passage states which one of the following?*
2. *According to the passage, Einstein recommended that . . .*
3. *The passage states that the purpose of peer review in scientific research is to . . .*
4. *Which one of the following is given by the passage as a reason for the decision to stop burning coal?*

Strategy for specific detail questions. The correct answer must be defendable by words stated in the passage. The test of a correct answer is to be able to physically point to the specific words in the passage that undeniably prove that the answer must be true.

Implied Detail

Implied detail questions account for 15 percent of questions. Variations include:

1. *The author suggests/implies that . . .*
2. *It can be inferred from the passage that . . .*

3. If the author's claim about wild boars is true, which one of the following is most likely to be true?

4. Which one of the following statements is most strongly supported by information given in the passage?

5. Which one of the following is most supported by the passage?

6. Which one of the following is most strongly implied by the passage?

7. The passage most strongly suggests that the author holds which one of the following views?

8. The passage provides the most support for inferring which one of the following statements?

9. Based on the passage, which one of the following is most likely to be true of negotiations based on the mediation methods mentioned in the second paragraph?

10. The second paragraph most strongly supports the inference that Einstein made which one of the following assumptions?

11. The passage indicates that relying on the reactions of animals to impending earthquakes may be unreliable due to . . .

Strategy for implied detail questions. As with *specific detail* questions, the answer must be defendable by pointing to specific words in the passage. However, the answer is derived from facts in the passage through the application of logic. It is not specifically stated in the passage.

> *Anyone who has worked at the XSQ Coal Mine during the past twenty years can participate in the upcoming class action suit. Jamie Peters began work at the mine five years ago.*

It can logically be concluded from the above two facts that Jamie Peters is eligible to participate in the suit. This fact is not stated in the passage, but it follows indisputably from the facts that are given.

There are two traps to watch out for with *implied detail* questions. First, a conclusion that goes too far beyond what is stated cannot be logically defended. In the above example, it cannot be defended that Jamie Peters suffered injuries or illness while working in the mine. That conclusion goes too far.

The other trap is to reject a conclusion because it seems to be explicitly stated rather than implied. It is highly unlikely that an LSAT question will ask you to distinguish between one answer choice that is explicitly stated and another that is derived through logic. If an *implied detail* answer choice is absolutely defendable, it must be correct, even if it appears to be a restatement of a fact in the passage. Generally, on closer inspection, it turns out that the answer is not an exact restatement. There is usually some small leap of logic.

Some answer choices may seem too obvious or too simple to be correct. However, if they can be defended by words in the passage, they must be the answer. There are many easy questions on the test. Do not try to make the question more difficult than it is.

Answers to detail questions are often highly literal. If an answer choice says *Most of the people in cities suffer from allergies,* it is necessary to prove by words in the passage that at least one more than half of the people in cities suffers from allergies. This is what "most" means literally—at least one more than half.

Because *implied detail* questions involve a certain amount of logical "leap," they can range from very literal, in which you are inferring something that almost seems to be stated, to very broad, in which the question almost becomes like an *application/extension* question. Orient yourself carefully to the question stem to determine how literal or how generalized you need to be.

EXCEPT and LEAST

Just as in the LR and AR sections, some RC questions are posed in terms such as *all of the following . . . EXCEPT* or *which of the following is the LEAST . . .* In both of these variations, four answer choices have a certain characteristic. The one answer choice that does not have that characteristic is the correct answer. These question variations can be tricky in two ways. First, you must keep a certain criterion in mind and then look for the opposite or lack of it. The second confusing aspect of these variations is that when, for example, a question sets up four answer choices that strengthen the argument and you are looking for the exception, the correct answer is not necessarily one that weakens the argument. Four answers may clearly strengthen and one may be neutral or irrelevant. In RC, EXCEPT and LEAST questions are rare, with LEAST questions being rarer.

GETTING THE ANSWER

Strategies for Answering Questions

(STEP 1) Orient to the question stem.

Orienting means taking time to make sure the meaning is clear or identifying what it is about it that may not be clear. Orienting includes getting a sense of which part of the passage the question relates to, how the question fits into the structure of the passage, and what might need to be done to answer it correctly. Orienting need not take more than fifteen to thirty seconds but it is a critical step. It is a big-picture strategy, in which you let the information in the question sink into your mind more thoroughly. Often, test takers get a question wrong because they were never clear from the start what the question meant or how it fit into the passage.

(STEP 2) **Decide on a plan of attack.**

Quite often in RC, the second step is to go back to the passage and look for information. For example, if the question asks, *Which of the following is a form of torture prohibited by the Geneva Convention*, the second step is to scan the passage for information about forms of torture and the Geneva Convention. What if there is nothing there? There must be, because the answer must be defendable by statements in the passage. If it does not seem to be there, look again. If there is only one reference to torture and the Geneva Convention, for example, *the rack is prohibited under the Geneva Convention*, the answer must be based on that reference.

(STEP 3) **Make one pass through the answer choices, using elimination.**

In RC, the answers must be correct for very literal and specific reasons. Look carefully for the exact reason that one of the answers must be correct. Look for the fatal flaws in the other answers. It is almost never the case that one answer is better than another. One is right. The others are dead wrong. Usually an answer is wrong because it either violates what is actually stated or is not defendable.

Typically, answers are wrong because they violate logic or they contain one word that is not defendable. For example, consider a passage that states *many people in the United States do not like to eat liver*. Suppose a question asks:

Which of the following is consistent with the passage?

Evaluate the answer that says:

A. Most Americans find eating liver unpleasant.

First consider the phrase "find eating liver unpleasant." The information that we have is that people "do not like to eat liver." Is this the same as saying that people find it unpleasant? Yes. It can be defended from the dictionary definitions of these terms that they are interchangeable. The same can be said about the terms *American* and *people in the United States*.

The term *most*, on the other hand, is dead wrong. *Most* means at least one more than half. The passage only states that "many" people do not like to eat liver. It cannot be defended that at least one more than half (the definition of *most*) do not like to eat liver. The flaw is a logical and semantic one.

STEP 4 Use the adversarial approach to evaluate the remaining answer choices.

When there are two remaining possible answers, the most powerful tool for finding the correct answer is the adversarial approach, described in the strategy section of Chapter 1. Be careful to keep the defending and attacking stages completely separate. When test takers find they cannot use the adversarial approach successfully, it is usually because of mixing the two stages.

Beware the Default Multiple-Choice Question!

Review the example given in Chapter 1. Sometimes an RC stem does ask the default question. However, if the question is something else, there is a danger that your brain will revert to the default question. Obviously, this would result in getting a wrong answer. Go back regularly to reread the question while working through the answer choices.

Important Tips for Better Reading

Be an active reader. Have a plan and have tools for implementing your plan. Here are some additional tools that will help you be a more effective active reader.

Do Not Read the Questions First

Does it help to read all the questions first before reading the passage? People who do this may feel that they will be able to spot the answers to detail questions as they read the passage. Many detail questions, however, are so specific that unless you are focusing on the question, the answer will not be easy to find. Thus, reading all of the questions in advance may only waste time.

If you start a new passage with only a few minutes left in the test, it would be a waste of time to set up the passage. In this case, go directly to a detail question and then search the passage for the information to answer that question.

Signal Words

As you skim the passage, look for words that show whether the author is continuing a line of thought or switching to a contrasting line of thought.

CONTINUATION WORDS

Adding more: Also, again, as well, further, moreover, in addition
Comparing: similarly, likewise, in the same way
Concluding: thus, therefore, then, hence, finally, in summation, in conclusion
Giving examples: for example, for instance, as an example, in other words

CONTRAST WORDS

However, nevertheless, but, on the contrary, on the other hand, although, despite, regardless

Reading More Quickly and Accurately

Many test takers find that the language in RC passages is so complex that it is difficult to understand. For people who are struggling with understanding the complex sentences, there are some helpful strategies.

1. Take a friendly approach to the passage.
2. Avoid detail. Look for the big picture.
3. Study and use sentence diagramming.
4. Do lots of untimed practice.

Clearly, interesting topics are easier to "get into" than boring ones. However, even with a boring topic, it is possible to take a friendly attitude. Pretend that you are interested! It may make your mind a little more receptive.

The purpose of skimming the passage is to see the big picture. Only read enough detail to be able to follow the flow of the passage. As with the passage on the theories of how the sun generates energy, stepping back from the complex details helps improve both reading speed and comprehension. Avoid getting bogged down in details.

Sentence diagramming is a powerful tool for breaking down a highly complex sentence. Diagramming a sentence means identifying the basic parts of the sentence—the subject, the verb, the object, modifiers, and connecting words—and drawing a picture of the relationships among these parts.

The following example shows how even an extremely complex sentence can be broken down into simple relationships. Let's start simply with "the child."

What does the child do? The child eats.

What does the child eat? The child eats bread.

When does this happen? During the war, the child eats bread.

What child does this? During the war, the child who lost her family eats bread.

Which war was it? During the war between the two ethnic groups, the child who lost her family eats bread.

This process could continue to the following result:

> During the last war between the two ethnic groups occupying the territory in the eastern region of what was formerly known as Herzegovina, the child who lost her family on the trek from the mountains to the sea coast during the evacuation of the most vulnerable populations eats bread that she found in an abandoned cow shed as a photographer from the western press, moved by the mixture of sorrow and wisdom in her expression, quietly and surreptitiously snaps her portrait for posterity.

Is it clear that the basic sentence is still "the child eats" and that every new bit of information tells more about an earlier bit? Try answering the questions:

What kind of war?
Which ethnic groups?
Which region?
What specific trek?
When did she lose her family?
Evacuation of whom?
What do we know about the bread?
What do we know about the photographer's motivation?
In what manner did the photographer snap her picture?

Formal diagramming teaches specific strategies for quickly identifying parts of sentences and relationships. If you find many sentences too complex to follow, find a good guide to diagramming. Diagramming should be practiced untimed. Diagramming is time-consuming but you may be able to use it on one or two questions to gain extra points.

Vocabulary

It is not necessary to study vocabulary. An unfamiliar word in a passage should not be an obstacle. There are almost always other clues in the passage to clarify what the word means. RC is not really a vocabulary-based task and studying hundreds of vocabulary words will not increase your score.

Reading Challenging Articles

Some people read challenging material, such as articles in technical or scientific journals, to help them perform better on RC. RC passages are designed specifically on dichotomies. Other challenging material is not likely to be organized in this way but may help improve analytical skills. The test taker's first priority should be to master the strategies given here.

Analytical Reasoning

4

This chapter teaches you the skills that you need to quickly and accurately answer Analytical Reasoning (AR) questions. In the chapter you will find a number of lists of detailed AR patterns. Use these lists as resources that you can refer back to as you practice. You do not need to memorize the lists. Glance at them now. As you work through actual problems and refer to the lists, the patterns will become increasingly familiar and useful for you.

INTRODUCTION TO ANALYTICAL REASONING

The AR section is one of the four scored sections (1 RC, 2 LR, 1 AR) on the LSAT. If there are two AR sections on your test, one of them will be unscored. Each AR section consists of four **games**, each of which contains a **setup**, including **conditions**, followed by five to seven questions, with twenty-three questions per AR section. There have been sections with twenty-two or twenty-four questions on older tests.

Many people initially find the AR to be intimidating. In actuality, the AR is very learnable. Once you have mastered the skills in this chapter, you will have clear, logical tools for systematically solving the questions.

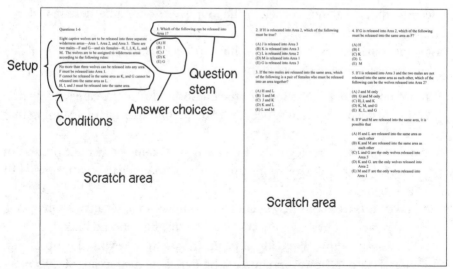

Figure 4.1. Anatomy of an AR game, showing the setup, conditions, questions, question stems, answer choices, and scratch area

The Three Necessary Skill Sets for Analytical Reasoning

The skill sets that you need to solve a game accurately and quickly are:

1. Organizing the Setup
2. Understanding the Question Types
3. Using a Systematic Problem-Solving Approach

Almost all errors that test takers make on the AR are the result of not having the right tools for one or more of the above skill sets. This chapter begins by reviewing general timing strategy and showing how to apply it to the AR.

⚿ TIMING STRATEGY

As on all sections of the LSAT, a strong timing strategy allows you to (1) gain points by working efficiently, (2) avoid errors caused by working too quickly or anxiously, and (3) reduce anxiety.

Adapting Timing Strategy to the Analytical Reasoning Section

General timing strategy is described in Chapter 1, "General Strategies." Review it now to refresh your memory. How should you adapt this strategy to the AR?

Rank the Games

As in RC, there are four sets (called games in AR). As soon as timing starts for a section, quickly glance at each of the four games and rank them in order of difficulty. There is a general tendency for the first game to be easiest and the last game to be hardest but because there are exceptions, you have to evaluate the games for yourself. Remember:

1. Do not try to read the setup or the questions. Judge the game at a glance.
2. The first game is often easy but do not fall into the trap of assuming that it is.
3. Look for the complexity of the variables. A game with multiple sets of players in complex relationships is harder than a game with one set of players.
4. Take hints from the answer choices. Complex-looking answers may look intimidating but may indicate what the diagram should look like.
5. If two games appear equally difficult, choose the one with the most questions. Do not, however, choose a harder game just because it has more questions.

Ranking the order of the games is an approximation. It would take too much time to determine exactly which games are the most complex. By quickly ranking the games, you avoid working on the hardest ones.

Working Each Game

Once you have ranked the games, start with the easiest. Do not move on to the next game until you have worked *every* question on the current game. Even on an easy game, there will be some questions that are difficult.

Test takers sometimes wonder if they should skip a harder question in their current game and then use their time to answer an easier question in another game. The problem with such a strategy is that it may well force you to set up a game that you would not otherwise have worked and that will be harder than the current game.

If a particular question is tough, work on other questions in the current game first. These questions may give you enough insight into the game for you to be able to then answer the more difficult question. You can work on the easiest questions first and then tackle harder ones. Generally, a question that asks you which of five answer choices does not break rules is easy. Questions that give you new information are easier to solve than questions that do not.

How Much Time Should You Spend on Each Question?

This is the most important element of your timing strategy. Review the instruction on timing strategy in Chapter 1. Most test takers will get the most points by allowing themselves three, four, or sometimes five minutes on a difficult question. You may only need to do this for a few questions on a section, but doing so often makes the difference between getting a few more questions right or not.

Test takers who spend only a minute or two on a question typically leave a string of wrong answers in their wake. Certain questions simply cannot be solved in less than two, three, or even four minutes. If you always quit after one or two minutes, you will not get the more difficult questions right. On the other hand, it is not a good idea to spend more than five minutes on any one question.

To implement a successful timing strategy, you have to know how much time you have spent on a question. At the start of each question, set your watch to noon. If you start to feel that a question is taking a lot of time, look at your watch to see how much time you have spent. Do not try to keep track of time mentally. Even if you can, it prevents you from giving your full attention to the problems.

How Many Games Should You Work On?

The fatal flaw for most test takers is that they attempt to answer too many questions. Who comes out ahead—the person who works on twenty-four questions and gets twelve right, or the person who works on fourteen questions and gets all of them right (plus 2 points for the questions they guess on)? Actually, once you have developed a strong timing strategy, the test itself will tell you how far you can get. Let's look now at what to do once you have finished the easiest game.

After the easiest game, work on the next easiest game. If you are still having difficulty with the AR section, you may run out of time during the second game. If you are already performing strongly on the games, you will be able to get to a third and possibly a fourth game. When you get to the last game on which you will have time to work, do the easiest questions first. As time runs out, be on guard against the urge to complete all the questions in the current game. Many people fall into this trap and attempt to cram in three or four questions in the last minutes. Usually they answer these questions incorrectly. Instead, pick the next easiest question in the game and give it the full time that it needs for you to be confident in your answer. There are no bonus points for completing a game!

If you (1) choose what to work on next and (2) give each question the time it needs, the test will show you how far you can get. If you are running low on time and try to go faster to answer additional questions, you risk answering many questions incorrectly. Why does this happen? You may have an expectation of how many questions you should answer. When you see that you are not going to get to that many in the remaining time, what happens? Untrained test takers get anxious and begin to rush. Trained test takers drop the expectation and stick with the reality. By working well on a few more questions, they maximize their score.

As you practice, you will get a more realistic sense of how many questions you can do. Of course, how many questions you answer in any particular section depends on many factors. Even if you work successfully on just two games, you can still achieve at least an average or above-average score.

When your timing is perfect, you get nearly every question that you work on right. Even so, you might find that you still are not at the score you would like. This means that you need to learn and master the strategies in this chapter. If you try to boost your score just by going faster, you will most likely lose points.

TIMING FOR SUPERIOR TEST TAKERS

If you are aiming for a near perfect score, note that we do not suggest that you *should* cut questions, only that, in some cases, you can get extra points by cutting some questions.

Consider a superior test taker who attempts all 23 questions, gets 20 correct, and spent an average of 90 seconds on each of the 3 incorrect questions. What would happen if the test taker cut 2 of those 3 questions and used the additional 3 minutes to get one more question correct? The total number correct would be 21, up one point from 20. In addition, there is approximately a 40 percent chance that one of the two answers that were guessed will be correct.

The suggestion to cut questions if necessary is not based on settling for an average score. On the contrary, it is an additional tool that the superior test taker can use to develop the absolutely most efficient timing strategy possible.

Guessing at the End

At the monitor's five-minute warning, put answers down for the questions you are not going to get to. Do not spend time looking at the questions. Simply fill in a bubble for each unanswered question randomly. Statistically there is no letter that is significantly more likely to be correct.

After filling in the remaining bubbles, go back to a question and continue to work on it until time is called. If you can eliminate even one answer choice, you will be a bit closer to another correct answer.

Summary of Timing Strategy for AR

1. Rank the difficulty of the games.
2. Work on the easiest game. Do all the questions in it before moving on. Take three to five minutes per question if necessary. Do not exceed five minutes per question. Use your watch to keep track of time on each question. There is no need to keep track of how much time you spend setting up the game or of how much time you spend on the entire game.
3. If time, go to the second easiest game. If time is running low, apply Step 6.
4. If time, go to the third easiest game. If time is running low, apply Step 6.
5. If there is time, go to the final game. If time is running low, apply Step 6.

6. If you start a game that there is not enough time to finish, choose the easiest questions. Do not rush to complete the game.

7. When the monitor gives a five-minute warning, fill in bubbles for questions that you have not already answered.

8. Continue working on a question until time is called.

ORGANIZING THE SETUP

The first and most important step in AR is to accurately organize the information in the **setup**. The setup consists of a paragraph, including a description of the game and some **conditions** that apply to the game, followed by a list of additional conditions. Conditions are **rules** that govern how the **elements** of the game can and cannot interact with each other. Elements consist of **players** and **fixtures**. The players, often people, are assigned to certain fixed positions (the fixtures).

Consider a game in which Freddie, Greta, Irene, Jason, and Kerry are each to perform during five specific time slots in a singing competition. The five people are the players. The five specific time slots are the fixtures. The sentence "Players are assigned to fixtures" can help you determine who are the players and what are the fixtures in a game. In the game above, "people are assigned to time slots." Players can be individual people, groupings of people, events, or objects, such as colors, flowers, fruit, or trees.

VOCABULARY FOR ANALYTICAL REASONING GAMES

Setup: the paragraph and following conditions that establish how the game works

Conditions (rules): the rules that determine how the elements relate to each other

Restrictions: a synonym for conditions that refers to the fact that conditions restrict the options that a player has

Elements: the players and fixtures of the game

Players: the elements that are assigned to fixed positions

Fixtures: the fixed positions to which players are assigned

Assignment: an attempted arrangement of players in the fixed positions. An assignment may be **valid**—it does not break rules—or it may be **invalid**—it breaks at least one rule

---

Why is organizing the setup so important? Many people rush through the setup so they can get on to answering questions. This is a common but disastrous pattern. If you have not accurately understood the setup and conditions, you will make mistakes, no matter how hard you work on the questions. If you have misunderstood even one of the conditions, you may well get several questions wrong or more! On the other hand, if you accurately understand the setup and conditions, create an effective diagram, and apply a systematic approach to solving questions, you can correctly answer every question on which you work.

STEP BY STEP APPROACH FOR ORGANIZING THE SETUP

1. Read the setup.
2. Identify the players and the fixtures. Use the template "(blank) is assigned to (blank)." The first blank represents players. The second blank represents fixtures.
3. Create the diagram. The diagram represents the fixtures. Create a supplemental diagram if needed.
4. List the players.
5. Going in order, identify each condition, make sure you understand it, and then rewrite it in an abbreviated form.
6. Briefly consider the relationships between conditions. For example, which conditions, if combined, would result in a new condition? Which elements have the most restrictions? Which elements have no restrictions?
7. Find any information that can be placed directly into the diagram.

The Setup and Conditions

Consider that the proctor has just announced, "You may now turn to the next section and begin." You have taken a deep breath to avoid rushing and to focus your mind. You have ranked the four games in order of difficulty. You have turned to the easiest game. Now apply the steps given in the previous chart.

Read through the setup so that you can identify the elements and can determine which elements are the players and which are the fixtures. Determining the players and fixtures helps you to create the diagram.

Using the blank margins of your test booklet—your **work space**—list the players. Use only the initial letter of each player in order to save space. There is never more than one player with the same initial letter. Use the separate list of players as a checklist when solving a question.

USING THE MARGINS OF YOUR TEST BOOKLET

The AR section requires more "scratch paper" space than the other sections of the LSAT. Because there is no scratch paper available, use the margins of your test booklet. This work space is limited. Practice condensing your scratch work. The diagramming strategies taught in this chapter are designed to use space efficiently. Write small but neatly. Do not take time to erase your scratch work unless you need that space. Current LSATs spread each game across two pages. Earlier LSATs put each game on one page.

Next consider each condition, in the order it is given in the setup. Look first for conditions that are given in the setup paragraph. When you are sure you understand a condition, summarize it. Write it in your work space, using symbols and abbreviations. Then do the same for the next condition. In theory, you could simply refer to the conditions on the test page, rather than repeating them in your work space. However, rewriting the conditions has two important advantages. First, it forces you to understand the condition clearly. Second, having the conditions listed in a concise form allows you to work with them more easily.

Once you have summarized all of the conditions, look for obvious relationships among conditions. For example, consider the two conditions:

> *If Kerry sings in the third time slot, Irene sings in the fifth time slot.*

And

> *If Freddie sings in the first time slot, Kerry sings in the third time slot.*

These conditions are related. Both conditions include Kerry. Combine these to derive a third condition:

> *If Freddie sings in the first time slot, Irene sings in the fifth time slot.*

If you do not spot any relationships among conditions at first glance, do not waste time looking more deeply. A game has many intricate relationships. These relationships will become apparent as you work the game. It is usually not productive to try to work out all of the relationships in advance.

Identify which players have the most restrictions. In the previous example, Kerry has more restrictions than Freddie or Irene. Also note which players have no restrictions. A player with many restrictions is more likely to create rule violations, whereas a player with no restrictions is less likely to do so. Although there are frequent exceptions to the above generalization, a good strategy is to first test players with the most restrictions when looking for rule violations.

The final step in organizing the setup is to identify any information that can go directly into the diagram. For example, if Greta must always sing in the second slot, you can put Greta into the diagram under 2 as permanent information.

Below is a diagram of a setup, showing the fixtures (1–7) across the top, some information about the game entered above the fixtures, the list of players on the left (F, I, M), and the list of rules, shown underneath the list of players. For the moment, do not be concerned about what the summaries of the rules mean.

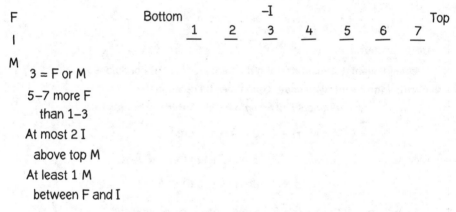

Figure 4.2. Example of the setup for a game

Symbols for Summarizing Conditions

The symbols that you use to summarize the conditions should be concise and yet unambiguous. You will find the symbols presented in this chapter to be helpful for most conditions. You can also modify these symbols or create your own. If you find that you have misinterpreted your notation, refine your system. There are hundreds of variations on how conditions are expressed. These variations often require you to be creative with your symbols. This chapter goes over practice questions that will help you learn some common summarizing tools. The explanations for the sample section test at the end of this chapter and for the practice tests in this book will help you refine your set of symbols. The symbols for summarizing if/then conditions are rather standard.

Types of Conditions

Conditions define the relationships among players. For most games the conditions fall into one of the following categories:

MAIN CATEGORIES OF CONDITIONS

1. **Defining quantity.** Specifies quantities.

    Freda has at least one apple but not more than three apples.

    $$F = 1\text{–}3$$

    Roster contains exactly one document.

    $$R = ex\ 1$$

    There are at most seven squirrels.

    $$\text{at most } 7\ S \quad \text{or} \quad S = O\text{–}7$$

    Defining quantity constitutes about 5 percent of all AR conditions.

2. **Comparing quantity.** Indicates quantities by comparison.

    Joggers has one more member than Hikers.

    $$J = H + 1 \quad \text{or} \quad J = 1 \text{ more than } H$$

    Group B has more members than group A.

    $$B > A \quad \text{or} \quad B \text{ more than } A$$

    Comparing quantity constitutes about 3 percent of conditions.

3. **Defining relative position in a sequence.** Indicates where a player fits into a sequence by comparing the player with another player.

    <u>**Sanders is immediately below Tanaka.**</u>

    $$S\ T$$

    Michael is below Nora but above Quincy.

    $$Q - M - N$$

    For the two diagrams above, "below" is defined as to the left.

    <u>**Randy is older than Teresa.**</u>

    $$R - T$$

"Older" is defined as to the left.

Defining relative position constitutes 40 percent of conditions. This type of condition predominates in **sequence** games (described later in this chapter).

4. **Assigning characteristics to a player.** Directly specifies characteristics that a certain player must have.

Jordan has a computer.

$$J = C \quad \text{or} \quad J = \text{comp}$$

Shawn plays solitaire.

$$S = \text{sol}$$

Wozniak orders the chocolate cheese cake.

$$W = \text{cake}$$

Assigning characteristics constitutes 30 percent of conditions.

5. **Defining two or more alternate options (either/or).** One of two conditions must be true.

Either Francine has worked at Tetwiler's longer than Ian has or Susan has worked at Tetwiler's longer than Thomas has.

$$\text{Either} \quad F - I$$
$$\text{or} \quad S - T$$

"Longer" is defined here as to the left.

Either/or conditions constitute 6 percent of conditions. Either/or questions can contain any of the above condition types. They do not exclude the possibility that both statements could be true.

6. **Defining two possible options but both cannot be true (either/or but not both).** One of two statements must be true but they cannot both be true.

Either Tanaka goes to the meeting on Thursday or Garcia goes to the meeting on Friday, but not both.

$$\text{Either} \quad T = \text{Tues}$$
$$\text{or} \quad G = \text{Fri}$$
$$\text{bnb}$$

(Note the use of the abbreviation "bnb" for "but not both.")

Either/or but not both conditions constitute 5 percent of conditions. This is a variation on regular either/or conditions that expressly prohibits both conditions from being true.

7. **If/then condition.** The occurrence or absence of one event determines the occurrence or absence of another event, for example, *If Roger goes to the store, Sandra does not go to the store.*

   If/then conditions constitute 25 percent of all conditions. If/then conditions are broken down into subtypes below. If/then statements may include components from the above condition types.

For each of the types of conditions described above, you will see many variations on how the condition is worded. Familiarize yourself with these variations. When you work with a condition in a practice test, analyze the wording to be sure you understand the condition. Use the following list of wordings as a reference. You do not need to memorize the variations. Glance through them now to become familiar with them and come back to the list as you are working on practice questions.

The seventh condition type—if/then statements—defines more complex relationships. The powerful strategies for understanding and manipulating if/then statements are described in depth in Chapter 2, "Logical Reasoning" (LR). If/then statements are critical in AR. A quarter of the questions in AR involve if/then logic. The above condition types are often combined with if/then logic. Review the if/then strategies in Chapter 2 now.

If/Then Conditions in Analytical Reasoning

Below are common variations of if/then conditions that you will find in AR. Note that the wording of an if/then can often be confusing. Apply the rules given in Chapter 2 for converting an if/then relationship into its standard form. Use the information listed below as a resource. It is not necessary to memorize it. Glance through it now. As you work with if/then statements on practice questions, come back to this list to help you sort out the various types of if/thens.

TEN PRINCIPAL TYPES OF IF/THEN CONDITIONS

Percentages are out of the total number of if/then conditions and are approximate. If/then conditions account for about 25 percent of all conditions.

1. **If A → B** If *A* occurs, then *B* must occur.

   Example: If Williams attends the conference, Young also attends the conference. (If W → Y)

   This is NOT the same as saying that Williams and Young must go together. If Williams does not attend the conference, Young can still go. Frequency: Accounts for 15 percent of AR if/then conditions

2. **AB** *A* and *B* must appear together.

   Example: Williams attends the same conference that Young attends. (WY or W = Y) Frequency: Accounts for ~13 percent of if/then conditions

3. **Not AB (or –AB)** *A* and *B* cannot appear together.

   Example: Williams does not attend any conference that Young attends. (–WY or not WY or W ≠ Y) Frequency: ~13 percent

4. **If A → not B (or –B)** If *A* occurs, then *B* does not occur.

   Example: If Williams attends the conference, Young does not attend the conference. (If W → –Y or not Y)

   This IS the same as saying that Williams and Young cannot be at the conference together. However, it is NOT the same as saying that one or the other must go. It is possible for both not to go. Frequency: ~13 percent

5. **If not A (or –A) → B** If *A* does not occur, then *B* must occur.

   Example: If Williams does not attend the conference, then Young attends. (If –W → Y)

   This is NOT the same as saying that they cannot both attend. If Williams does attend, Young can still attend. Frequency: ~7 percent

6. **If A → A = x** If *A* occurs, then *A* occurs with a certain characteristic (*x*).

   Example: If Williams attends the conference, then Williams attends on Saturday. (If W → W = Sat)

   Williams may or may not attend but if Williams attends at all, it must be on Saturday. In this type of rule, both sides of the if/then have to do with the same person. Frequency: ~5 percent

7. **If not A (or –A) → not B (or –B)** If *A* does not occur, then *B* does not occur.

   Example: If Williams does not attend the conference, then Young does not attend. (If –W → –Y)

   If Williams does attend, Young may or may not attend. Frequency: ~2 percent

8. **If A = x → either y or z** If A occurs with a certain characteristic (x), then one of two other characteristics (y and z) must occur.

   Example: If Williams attends the conference on Thursday, then Williams must be either the first or second presenter. (If W = Th, then W = 1 or 2)

   This rare type of rule could also specify only one additional characteristic on the right side. This differs slightly from the previous type in that the previous type only required that Williams be "in" the game, whereas this type requires that Williams meet a specific condition (in the game on Thursday). Frequency: ~2 percent

9. **If A = x → B = y** If A occurs with a certain characteristic (x), then B occurs with a different characteristic (y).

   Example: If Williams attends the conference on Thursday, then Young attends the conference on Saturday. (If W = Th → Y = Sat) Frequency: 26 percent

10. **If A → B and If not A (or –A) → not B (or –B)** A occurs if and only if B occurs.

    Example: Young attends the conference if, and only if, Williams attends the conference.

    The phrasing "if and only if" encompasses two different conditions. Young goes if Williams goes (if Williams goes, then Young must go) and Young goes only if Williams goes (if Williams does not go, then Young does not go.) Frequency: 2 percent

Standard form. As you learned in Chapter 2, the standard form of an if/then statement places the condition that happens first (the condition that is the determining factor) on the left side of the equation and the condition that happens second (the result) on the right side. Try the exercise below.

PRACTICE EXERCISE

Rewrite each sentence in the standard form.

Example: *John does not go to the party if Frances goes.*

  If Frances, then –John (or even more abbreviated: If F → –J)

1. If office R has a printer, it has neither a fax nor a copier.

2. If office R has a fax, then it also has a printer.

3. Either Ramon or Li must attend the party that Pearl attends.

4. Pearl must attend the same party that Li attends.

5. If Sandra attends the first meeting, then Liam attends the meeting immediately after the meeting that Sandra attends.

6. If Morgan does not perform, then Niles performs in the third time slot.

Answers:

1. If office R has a printer, it has neither a fax nor a copier.
   The logic: If A, then neither B nor C.
   The standard form: Write this as two separate statements. If R = printer, then –fax. If R = printer, then –copier.

2. If office R has a fax, then it also has a printer.
   The logic: If A, then B.
   This is already in standard form.

3. Either Ramon or Li must attend the party that Pearl attends.
   The logic: If A, then either B or C.
   The standard form: The determining factor is the presence of Pearl. If P, then R or L. Note that this cannot be broken into two statements. The existence of Pearl at the party predicts that one or the other of Ramon or Li must attend. Because the statement does not say *but not both,* there is the possibility that both may attend.

4. Pearl must attend the same party that Li attends.
   The logic: If A, then B.
   The standard form: Li is the determining factor. If Li, then Pearl.

5. If Sandra attends the first meeting, then Liam attends the meeting immediately after the meeting that Sandra attends.
   The logic: If $A = 1$, then $B = 2$.
   The statement is already in standard form. It is a variation on If A, then B.

6. If Morgan does not perform, then Niles performs in the third time slot.
   The logic: If $-A$, then $B = x$.
   It is in standard form but could be simplified as If –Morgan, then Niles = 3.

Three common if/thens. There are three common if/then relationships with which you should be familiar. The first is the relationship in which two things must go together. If you have pie, you have to have coffee. If you have coffee, you have to have pie. To express a "two must go together" relationship, both of these statements must be made.

> If pie → coffee
> If coffee → pie

Just asserting that if you have pie, you must have coffee does not establish that if you have coffee, you have to have pie.

Another common if/then relationship is one in which one or the other player must occur. If John does not go to the meeting, then Susan does.

> If –John → Susan

The contrapositive indicates that if Susan does not go, then John will. It is also possible that both go to the meeting.

The third common relationship is one in which two players cannot be together. In other words, they are mutually exclusive. If Shanna goes on the field trip, Jason does not.

> If Shanna → –Jason

It is not necessary to state that if Jason goes, Shanna does not because that is the contrapositive (Jason ∴ –Shanna) of the first statement. It is also possible that neither goes. Table 4.1 summarizes these three common relationships.

Table 4.1 Three Common Relationships

	Standard	Contrapositive	Note
Two must go together	If A, then B and if B, then A.	–B therefore –A, and –A therefore –B.	The contrapositives say that if B is not there, then A must not be there and that if A is not there, B is not there.
One or the other must occur. Both can occur.	If –A, then B.	If –B, then A.	The contrapositive captures the second part of this relationship.
The two cannot go together. Mutually exclusive. It is possible that neither goes.	If A, then –B.	If B, then –A.	The contrapositive captures the second part of this relationship.

The Diagram

Most games cannot be solved without a diagram. The diagram provides a working space for testing out possible assignments of players. The diagram allows you to fill in information and to spot rule violations.

There is one basic style of diagram that can be used effectively for all games. However, there are many variations on this basic diagram with which you need to become familiar. The advantage of this style of diagramming is that an entire assignment can always be shown on one line.

The diagram represents the fixtures, not the players. The players are assigned to places in the diagram. Therefore, to create the diagram, you must be clear on which elements are fixtures and which players. Do this by creating a sentence on the pattern "blank is assigned to blank," in which the first blank represents the players and the second represents the fixtures.

SAMPLE SETUP 1

The employees at Baxter Enterprises are John, Kevin, Lainie, Maria, and Nura. Baxter Enterprises has five separate offices situated in a row.

John cannot be in an office next to Maria.

The office that Lainie is in must have at least two offices between it and the office that Nura is in.

Kevin cannot be in the first or last office.

For Sample Setup 1, create a sentence on the pattern "blank is assigned to blank." The correct answer is in the next paragraph. There are only two elements: employees and offices. The trick is to determine which element is being assigned and which element represents the fixed positions (fixtures) to which players are assigned. If you get the relationship backward, you will probably still be able to solve the game but your diagram may not be as effective. People are often players but there are games in which an object is assigned to people, in which case the people are fixtures. As an example, consider a game in which each of four people can receive a hat, a coat, a scarf, and/or an umbrella. Do you see that the people are fixtures and the players are the items of apparel?

The best answer to the previous example is "Employees are assigned to offices." Typically, every fixture has at least one player assigned to it. One or more of the players, on the other hand, may not show up in a particular assignment. Use this fact to help determine which element represents the fixtures.

SAMPLE SETUP 2

Nel, Olga, Pablo, Roger, and Sung will each receive an expense-paid vacation to exactly one foreign country. The possible countries are France, Ghana, Iceland, Japan, Korea, Laos, and Morocco.

Given the above information, create a "blank is assigned to blank" sentence. The answer is in the next paragraph. If you decide that "X is assigned to Y" and then find that the diagram does not seem to be working well, try reversing your sentence and create a diagram in which X represents the fixtures.

The answer to the example above is "Countries are assigned to people." Every person will be assigned a country but two countries will not be assigned. Once you have created the sentence "blank is assigned to blank," you are ready to create a diagram. The diagram lists the fixtures horizontally. Below is a diagram for a game in which the fixtures consist of five offices, numbered 1 through 5.

$$\underline{1} \quad \underline{2} \quad \underline{3} \quad \underline{4} \quad \underline{5}$$

Figure 4.3. Basic diagram for a game with five fixtures

For all games the basic diagram is created by listing the fixtures across the top of the diagram. For more complex games you must modify the diagram.

Multiple Assignments to Each Fixture

Consider the following variation on a previous example:

SAMPLE SETUP 3

The employees at Baxter Enterprises are John, Kevin, Lainie, Maria, and Nura. Baxter Enterprises has five separate offices situated in a row. Each office receives exactly one chair. The chair can be orange, purple, red, salmon, or tangerine.

John cannot be in an office next to Maria.

The office that Lainie is in must have at least two offices between it and the office that Nura is in.

Kevin cannot be in the first or last office.

The chair in any office cannot be the same color as the chair in any adjacent office.

In the original example, people are assigned to offices. In this example, one chair of a particular color is also assigned to each office. Offices are still the fixtures, but there are now two types of players that are assigned: people and colors of chairs. Figure 4.4 shows how to modify the diagram for this case.

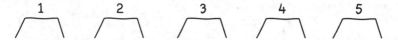

Figure 4.4. A diagram representing two players assigned to each fixture

Each fixture is given branches to show that it can receive multiple players. More complex games may require three, four, or, rarely, five branches.

For games in which there are multiple categories of players (such as *people* and *chairs*), many test takers try to use a grid, such as in Figure 4.5.

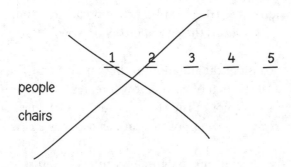

Figure 4.5. Grid. A grid is *not* the most effective diagram.

A grid is *not* the most effective diagram. It takes up too much space vertically. A grid is also more cumbersome for testing multiple possible arrangements, because each arrangement requires two lines. In Figure 4.6, compare the clearer and more compact linear branch approach with the grid approach.

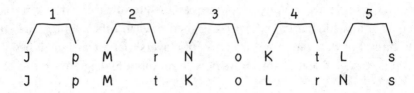

	1	2	3	4	5
people	J	M	N	K	L
chairs	p	r	o	t	s
people	J	M	K	L	N
chairs	p	t	o	r	s

Figure 4.6. The linear branch approach (on top)
versus the grid approach (below)

In Figure 4.6, consider the notation in the top diagram. The test taker has decided that the left branch of each pair will represent the person. The right branch represents the color of the chair. In addition, the test taker has capitalized the letters representing people and has used lowercase letters for the colors.

Some games with multiple assignments to each fixture may have only one category of players. For example, consider a game in which there are ten employees and five offices and two employees are assigned to each office. The list of players simply comprises ten employees. The two branches represent two employees. In many games with multiple assignments, however, there is more than one set of players. In the game in Figure 4.6, the players include a set of people and a set of chairs. Figure 4.7 shows the list of players.

People	Chairs
J	o
K	r
L	p
M	s
N	t

Figure 4.7. List of players in two sets

More Variations

Circular Games

You can use as many branches as needed to diagram games with multiple assignments to each fixture. Some games, however, will require additional variations. For example, in some games the fixtures are in a circle.

SAMPLE SETUP 4

> Five delegates to a conference—Sami, Tamara, Ursula, Vincent, and Wilbur—are to be seated around a circular table. No one else is seated at their table.
>> Ursula cannot sit next to Vincent.

Delegates are assigned to five positions. The basic linear diagram still works for this. Consider, though, what happens if Ursula is in seat 1. Can Vincent sit in seat 5? No. In the circle, seat 1 is next to seat 5. The diagram in Figure 4.8 does not show this. By drawing an arc between seat 1 and seat 5, you remind yourself that these are adjacent. A circular diagram would also show this but a circular diagram is much more cumbersome to work with. If you tend to still forget that seat 1 is next to seat 5 despite drawing an arc, you can draw a small supplemental diagram using a circle. However, your working space will still be the linear diagram.

$$1 \quad 2 \quad 3 \quad 4 \quad 5$$

Figure 4.8. Linear diagram showing seating around a circle

Multiple Rows

In some games the fixtures are not in a single row, such as five offices in a row, but rather are in multiple rows.

SAMPLE SETUP 5

> Nine passengers on a plane are seated in three adjacent rows, each row immediately behind the row in front of it. The passengers are Penn, Queen, Russell, Sheridan, Thomas, Upton, Vincent, Washburn, and Xerxes.
>> Penn cannot sit directly behind Vincent.
>> Russell cannot sit next to Sheridan.

Figure 4.9 shows all nine seats in one row but uses an arc to identify each row.

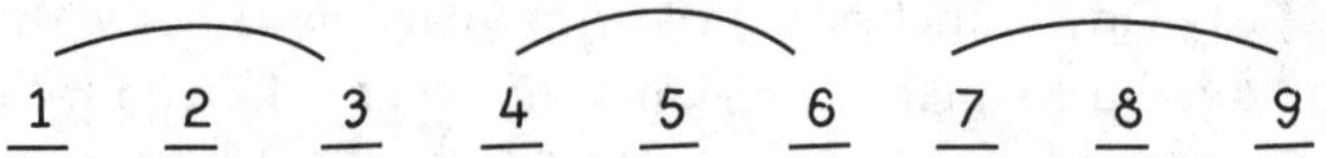

Figure 4.9. Three rows represented by one linear row

Consider the condition *Russell cannot sit next to Sheridan.* If Russell is in seat 3, can Sheridan sit in seat 4? Yes. Seats 3 and 4 are not next to each other. They are in separate rows. If Vincent is in seat 2, in which seat can Penn *not* sit? Do you see why it is seat 5? As with circles, a supplemental diagram can help you remember the orientation of the fixtures. However, the supplemental diagram (Figure 4.10) is not a good working space. Use the linear diagram to test assignments.

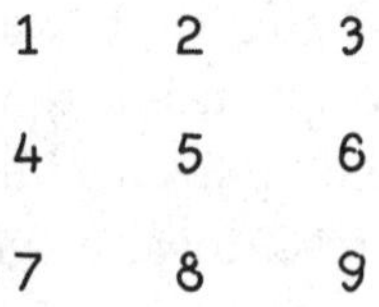

$$
\begin{array}{ccc}
1 & 2 & 3 \\
4 & 5 & 6 \\
7 & 8 & 9
\end{array}
$$

Figure 4.10. Supplemental diagram for multiple rows

Exclusions

In many games a particular assignment uses only some of the players and leaves the others out. If eight volunteers are assigned to five projects and each project has only one volunteer, then any valid assignment leaves out three of the players. It is helpful to keep track of who is out. You can do this easily by adding a special section to the diagram. Consider Figure 4.11:

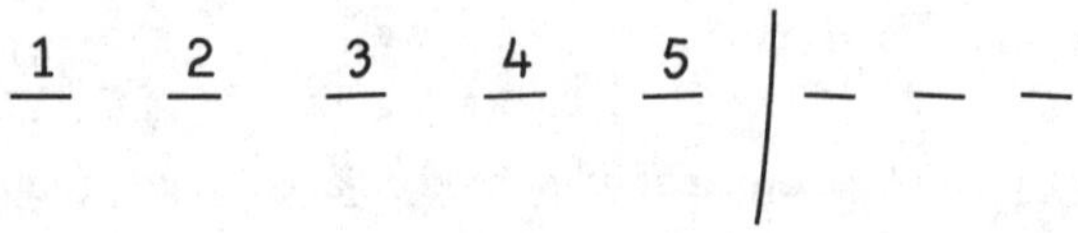

Figure 4.11. A diagram with a section for exclusions ("discard pile")

Notice the line after position 5. The dashes to the right of the line represent the three players who are left out of a particular assignment. The space to the right of the line is the **discard pile** or **out pile**. The space to the left is the

fixture diagram or the assignment. Avoid using the word *assigned* to refer to the discard pile. Players are either "assigned" (put in the fixture diagram) or "discarded." Consider the following example:

SAMPLE QUESTION 1

On a Saturday afternoon, five community projects will each be assigned exactly one of eight available volunteers: Karen, Lena, Marcel, Nava, Ofune, Peter, Randy, and Shan. No volunteer can be assigned to more than one project. The following conditions apply:

If Lena is not assigned, Marcel cannot be assigned.
Either Randy or Karen must be assigned but they cannot both be assigned.
Either Nava or Shan must be assigned but they cannot both be assigned.

Which of the following must be true?
(A) Ofune is not assigned.
(B) Peter is assigned.
(C) Lena is assigned.
(D) Karen is assigned.
(E) Nava is not assigned.

Solution: The condition *Either Randy or Karen must be assigned but they cannot both be assigned* tells you that one of these two players must be excluded. One place in the discard pile can be labeled R/K (Figure 4.12). Likewise, the condition *Either Nava or Shan must be assigned but they cannot both be assigned* tells you that one of these two must be out. A second place in the discard pile is labeled N/S.

$$\underline{1} \quad \underline{2} \quad \underline{3} \quad \underline{4} \quad \underline{5} \quad \bigg| \; \underline{} \; \underline{} \; \underline{}$$
$$\text{R/K} \quad \text{N/S}$$

Figure 4.12. Two places in the discard pile are defined.

Consider the remaining condition: *If Lena is not assigned, Marcel cannot be assigned.* What does this tell you? What happens if Lena is not assigned? She goes in the remaining position in the discard pile. Marcel must also go in the discard pile but there are no discard positions left. Therefore, Lena cannot be discarded. The correct answer is C. Lena must be assigned to a project.

$$
\begin{array}{ccccc}
\underline{1} & \underline{2} & \underline{3} & \underline{4} & \underline{5} \\
\text{K/R} & \text{S/N} & \text{L} & &
\end{array}
\quad\Bigg|\quad
\begin{array}{cc}
\underline{}\ \ \underline{} & \underline{}\ \ \underline{} \\
\text{R/K} & \text{N/S}
\end{array}
$$

Figure 4.13. Three slots are shown in the fixture diagram and two in the discard pile.

Because there are no further restrictions on any of the players, Ofune and Peter may or may not be assigned. One of the pair Karen/Randy must be assigned, as shown in position 1, but there is no restriction on which one. The same is true for Shan/Nava. Notice the notation. In the fixture diagram, Karen and Randy are represented as K/R. In the discard pile, they are represented as R/K. This reminds you that if K is in position 1, R is in the discard pile, and vice versa.

There is one important caution you must remember when using a discard pile. The conditions that apply in the fixture diagram do *not* apply in the discard pile. For example, if there is a condition that Lena and Shan cannot both be assigned, it *is* possible for both Lena and Shan to be in the discard pile. Note that once the discard pile is full, all other players must appear in the assignment.

More Supplemental Diagrams: Sequences

You learned about two supplemental diagrams in the paragraphs above: a supplemental circle diagram and a supplemental diagram showing multiple rows. A supplemental diagram organizes information in a way that is different from the working diagram. Keep supplemental diagrams small. Sometimes you can use the supplemental diagram to test assignments. The most common type of supplemental diagram organizes a **sequence** of players. For example:

> *Eight ingredients are added to a soup one at a time.*
> *Seven members of a club joined in different years.*
> *Seven trees have different heights.*
> *Nine cities have different populations.*

In these examples, you must determine the relative order in which the ingredients are added or in which the members joined the club. You must determine which tree is tallest, next tallest, and so on. You must determine which city has the largest population, next largest, and so on.

In games with sequences, the number of players is higher than usual in order to make the sequence more difficult to figure out. Consider the following:

SAMPLE SETUP 6

Eight ingredients—flour, garbanzos, jalapenos, kale, lemon, miso, noodles, and onion—are added to a soup, one ingredient at a time. Each ingredient is added exactly once.

Onion is added after garbanzos.

Miso is added after flour.

Jalapenos are added immediately after onion.

Noodles are added last.

Jalapenos are added after miso.

Build a supplemental diagram showing what you know about this sequence. The first condition (Step 1) yields

$$G - O$$

Use the convention of moving from left to right. Players on the left come first. The dash between the *G* and *O* is important. It represents the fact that other players could be assigned between *G* and *O*.

The next condition, *Miso is added after flour*, has no relationship to the diagram that you have started. It would have to be diagrammed separately, which is not helpful. Instead, look for another condition that shows a relationship to either *G* or *O*. Use *Jalapenos are added immediately after onion* and add the information to the diagram (Step 2).

$$G - OJ$$

There is no dash between *O* and *J* because the *J* comes immediately after *O*. Which condition should be added next? The condition with miso and flour still has no point of connection with the diagram. The condition *Noodles are added last* can be added (Step 3).

$$G - OJ - N \text{ //}$$

A longer dash between *J* and *N* shows that other players will probably be assigned there, because *N* is at the end of the sequence. The two slashes to the right of *N* indicate the end of the sequence, as well.

The second condition still has no point of intersection with the diagram, so add the condition *Jalapenos are added after miso* to the existing diagram. Jalapenos already appear in the diagram and miso must be to its left, but there is no information indicating where miso occurs in relation to garbanzos and onion. Start a new branch (Step 4), as shown below. Because onion is immediately before jalapenos, the new branch is linked to onion.

$$M$$
$$\diagdown$$
$$G - OJ - N \; //$$

You can now add the remaining condition to the diagram (Step 5).

$$F - M$$
$$\diagdown$$
$$G - OJ - N \; //$$

There are now two sequences that are known:

$$G - OJ - N$$

and

$$F - M - OJ - N$$

It is critical to note that the relationship between F – M and G – O is unknown. Flour could come before or after garbanzos. Miso could come before or after garbanzos. The key to a sequence is to distinguish what is known from what is unknown.

In a typical sequence game, there is one long string and one shorter string connected to the long string at one player. Most of the questions are relatively easy to answer if you are clear about what is known and what is unknown. For some sequence games, the supplemental diagram is all that you need. In other sequence games you must also use the main (linear) diagram.

The example above uses a supplemental diagram that moves from left to right. In other words, the leftmost player is the player that occurs first in time. For some games, it may be more logical to arrange the supplemental diagram up and down, such as when representing heights of people or objects. It is important that the orientation you use—vertical or horizontal—makes sense to you.

Variations on Sequences

The previous example is a basic sequence. There are a number of common variations of sequences. The section on "Types of Games," starting on page 232, teaches these variations and how to work with them.

Temporary Supplemental Diagrams

As you try to solve a question, you can create temporary supplemental diagrams to organize the information that pertains to that question. For example, if a question says *If kale is added before flour, . . .* you can create a temporary diagram that shows the sequence K – F – M – OJ – N. Be sure to cross out this information before going on to the next question.

Putting Information from the Setup into the Diagram

To review, the steps for organizing the setup are: Read the setup. Identify the players and the fixtures, using the template "(blank) is assigned to (blank)." Create the diagram. List the players. Going in order, identify each condition and rewrite it in an abbreviated form. Consider the relationships among conditions. Finally, find any information that can be placed directly into the diagram.

There are two kinds of information that go directly into the diagram before you start working on questions: permanent assignments, such as *Alfred is in office 3*, and rules and relationships, such as *Ben cannot go in office 5* or *Only Charlene or David can go in office 1*.

Permanent Assignments

Permanent assignments tell you exactly where a specific player must go. Many games contain permanent conditions.

SAMPLE SETUP 7 ▬▬▬▬▬▬▬▬▬▬▬▬▬▬▬▬▬▬▬▬▬▬▬▬▬▬▬▬▬▬

The employees at Baxter Enterprises are John, Kevin, Lainie, Maria, and Nura. Baxter Enterprises has five separate offices situated in a row.

John cannot be in the first or last office.

The office that Lainie is in must have at least two offices between it and the office that Nura is in.

Kevin is in the second office.

▬▬

The final condition is permanent information. Put it directly into the diagram, as shown in Figure 4.14.

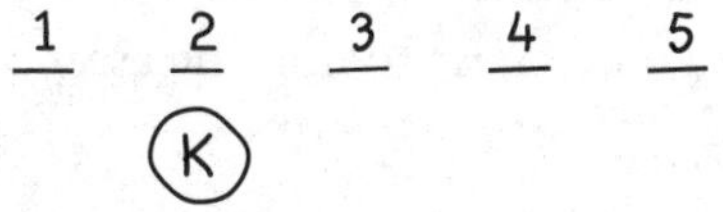

Figure 4.14. Placing a permanent assignment in the diagram

Kevin is placed under office 2. The letter *K* is circled to show that this is permanent information. Every assignment that you test must have Kevin in 2.

Rules and Relationships

Certain rules and relationships can be put directly into the diagram. Unlike permanent assignments, these rules and relationships do not tell you exactly where someone goes. They may, however, indicate where a player cannot go, as in the condition *John cannot be in the first or last office*. Because rules and relationships do not indicate a specific assignment, do not put them below the fixtures in the diagram. Instead, place them above the fixtures, as shown in Figure 4.15.

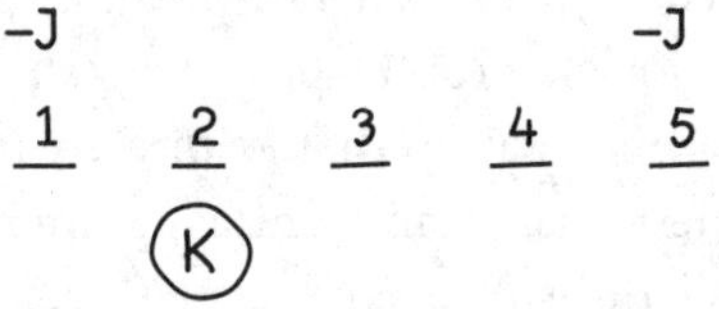

Figure 4.15. Placing rules and relationships in the diagram

Consider the condition *The office that Lainie is in must have at least two offices between it and the office that Nura is in*. There are several ways this can occur. Do not put them into the diagram. Only diagram the concrete information. Many test takers try to work out too many possibilities at the beginning of a game. If you stick only with known facts, your diagramming will be more efficient and more accurate. Do not try to put every condition into the diagram.

Types of Games

You have learned that you can use one type of diagram for all games. In one sense, then, there is only one "type" of game—one in which the relationships can be represented by a horizontal arrangement of fixtures to which players are assigned. You can, however, learn to recognize a number of distinct variations on how the players relate to one another, how the players relate to the fixtures, and how the fixtures relate to one another. It is more accurate to say that a given game consists of a combination of certain game characteristics, which can be thought of as building blocks. There are five main building blocks—or criteria—that you can use to find the essence of any game.

THE MAIN CRITERIA FOR EVALUATING GAMES

1. One-to-one correspondence. Is each player used exactly one time or not?
2. Ordering. Does the order of the fixtures matter or not?
3. Sequence. Do the conditions in an ordered game establish a sequence among at least three players?
4. Branching. Do the fixtures have more than one branch or not?
5. Variability. Are there a fixed number of fixtures and/or branches or is the number variable?

One-to-One Correspondence

One-to-one correspondence means that each player gets assigned to one fixture and each fixture (or branch of a fixture) receives only one player. Think of this criterion as a "perfect match" between players and fixtures. Every player gets used exactly once. No one is left over. No one is used more than once. A one-to-one correspondence is a simpler relationship than non-one-to-one correspondence, in which some players may be left over or used more than once. About 70 percent of recent LSAT games have one-to-one correspondence.

Consider the following variation on a previous example:

Sample Setup 8

Five volunteers—Karen, Lena, Marcel, Nava, and Ofune—are assigned to five community projects on one Saturday afternoon. Each project receives exactly one of these volunteers.

Do you see how this game has one-to-one correspondence? In many one-to-one games the number of players and number of fixtures is exactly the same, as above. In other one-to-one games the number of fixtures may be smaller than the number of players, but the fixtures may be divided into branches in a way that the total number of branches is the same as the number of players.

Sample Setup 9

Six attorneys—Franchetti, Jordan, Kellogg, Martin, Perea, and Riordan—are to serve as mentors for three debate teams. Each attorney serves on exactly one team and each team has exactly two of the six attorneys as mentors.

Figure 4.16 shows the diagram for this game.

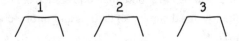

Figure 4.16. One-to-one correspondence with the same number of branches as players

There are exactly six attorneys, each appearing in exactly one of the six branches, even though there are only three fixtures—the three debate teams.

In other one-to-one correspondence games, each player is assigned exactly once, but the number of branches may be larger than the number of players. In some cases, the number of branches that will be assigned a player is unknown.

Sample Setup 10

Six attorneys—Franchetti, Jordan, Kellogg, Martin, Perea, and Riordan—are the only available attorneys to serve as mentors for two debate teams. Each available attorney serves on exactly one team and each team has at least one and at most four attorneys serving on it.

Figure 4.17. One-to-one correspondence with an inexact number of branches

In this game, the number of branches under each fixture is variable, ranging from a minimum of one to a maximum of four. The dotted lines in Figure 4.17 represent branches that *might* hold a player. The solid lines represent a branch that *must* hold a player. There are still exactly six players assigned to exactly six branches, but it is not known which of the total of eight possible branches will actually be used.

Non-One-to-One Games

If a game does not have a one-to-one correspondence between players and fixtures (or branches of fixtures), then the relationship between the players and fixtures is more complex. To understand these complex relationships, use the five criteria below. One-to-one correspondence means each player is used exactly once. Non-one-to-one correspondence means that either (1) some players are left out or (2) some are used more than once. If some players are left out, you need to know whether there is always the same number left out or whether the number left out varies. If players are left out, it may be helpful to use a discard pile.

If no players are left out, it is important to determine whether players are allowed to appear more than once. It is also important to determine whether each player must appear at least once. If so, then no player is left out and there is no discard pile. Finally, if players are allowed to appear more than once, is there a specific number of times that they must appear (e.g., *each player appears exactly twice*) or is the number of appearances variable?

FIVE CRITERIA FOR UNDERSTANDING NON-ONE-TO-ONE CORRESPONDENCE GAMES

1. Is there a specific number of players who are left out?
2. Is a discard pile helpful in the diagram for this game?
3. Are players prohibited from appearing more than once?
4. Must each player appear at least once?
5. Must each player appear a specific number of times? If so, how many?

Consider the following example.

SAMPLE SETUP 11

Eight volunteers—Karen, Lena, Marcel, Nava, Ofune, Peter, Randy, and Shan—are the only volunteers available to be assigned to five community projects on one Saturday afternoon. Each project receives exactly one of these volunteers, and no volunteer is assigned to more than one project.

This game does not have one-to-one correspondence. Test it using the criteria above. (The answer is in the next paragraph.)

In the example there are eight players and only five fixtures. Each fixture receives only one player. For any assignment there will be exactly three players who are not used. Here are the answers to the criteria questions:

1. Is there a specific number of players who are left out? Answer: exactly three
2. Is a discard pile helpful in the diagram for this game? Answer: probably
3. Are players prohibited from appearing more than once? Answer: yes
4. Must each player appear at least once? Answer: no
5. Must each player appear a specific number of times? If so, how many? Answer: no

When there is a specific number of players who are out in each assignment (question 1), the discard pile is often helpful (question 2).

Evaluate the following non-one-to-one correspondence examples using the five criteria on page 235.

Sample Setup 12

Five tables at a banquet are to be decorated with flower arrangements. Each table receives exactly one flower arrangement. The flowers that are available are freesias, geraniums, and lobelia. The arrangements must follow these rules:

Any arrangement with geraniums cannot contain lobelia.
Any arrangement with freesias must contain lobelia.
At least one freesia and one geranium must be used.
There must be at least twice as many arrangements with geraniums as there are arrangements with lobelia.

Answers to criteria questions:

1. Is there a specific number of players who are left out? Answer: no
2. Is a discard pile helpful in the diagram for this game? Answer: no
3. Are players prohibited from appearing more than once? Answer: no
4. Must each player appear at least once? Answer: yes. Although the setup does not specifically state this, the third rule states that geraniums and freesias must be used at least once and any arrangement with freesias requires a lobelia.
5. Must each player appear a specific number of times? If so, how many? Answer: no

If each player must appear at least once, no player is discarded, and no discard pile is needed.

SAMPLE SETUP 13

Six tables arranged in a single row at a banquet are to be decorated, each with a vase consisting of a single flower and some greens. The flowers that are available are freesias, geraniums, and lobelia. Each type of flower must be used the same number of times as each other type of flower.

Geraniums cannot be used on a table that is next to a table with lobelia.

Try to answer the five criteria questions for Sample Setup 13.

Answers:

1. Is there a specific number of players who are left out? Answer: no
2. Is a discard pile helpful in the diagram for this game? Answer: no
3. Are players prohibited from appearing more than once? Answer: no
4. Must each player appear at least once? Answer: yes
5. Must each player appear a specific number of times? If so, how many? Answer: two

In this game each player appears exactly two times. Of course, that also means that the answer to question 4 (*Must each player appear at least once?*) must also be "yes." If you find that the answer to the question 5 is "exactly once," then the game actually has one-to-one correspondence.

Memorize the five criteria for non-one-to-one correspondence games. Because one-to-one correspondence games have exactly the right number of players for the fixtures, non-one-to-one correspondence games typically have either (1) too many players or (2) too few players for the number of fixtures. The first and second questions involve cases with too many players (some players are left out). The remaining questions involve cases with too few players, namely, cases in which each player must appear more than once, must appear at least once, or must appear a predictable number of times.

It is quite possible that, even though there are too few or too many players, the number of times that any particular player appears is variable or unpredictable. In these cases the setup does not provide enough information to definitively answer "yes" to any of the five questions. In this situation, work out the relationship between the players and fixtures as you work the game.

Evaluating the game in advance for these criteria speeds up your understanding of the game.

Ordered Versus Unordered Fixtures

Once you have determined whether a game has one-to-one correspondence, consider whether the fixtures in the game are **ordered** or **unordered**. In an ordered game the order of the fixtures matters. In other words, it is important to know whether a player is assigned to fixture 1 or fixture 2, for example. In an unordered game it does not matter to which fixture a player is assigned. A player is simply "in" the assignment or "out" of the assignment. The order in which players are arranged does not matter in unordered games.

Unordered Games

Consider the following unordered game:

SAMPLE SETUP 14

Four members of a committee to plan next year's activities at the local senior center are to be chosen from among eight members of the center—Friedland, Gerhardt, Hong, Kovac, Manning, Neruda, Olsen, and Pappas.

If Pappas is chosen, Gerhardt is not chosen.

If Neruda is not chosen, Manning must be chosen.

Friedland and Hong cannot both serve on the committee.

Figure 4.18 shows the diagram.

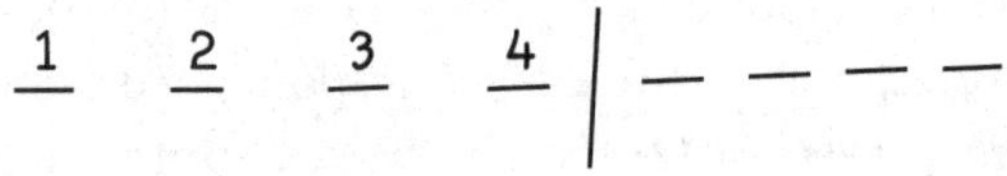

$$\underline{1} \quad \underline{2} \quad \underline{3} \quad \underline{4} \Big| \underline{} \; \underline{} \; \underline{} \; \underline{}$$

Figure 4.18. Unordered game with discard pile

Only four of the eight players can appear in any assignment. This is a non-one-to-one game and exactly four players are left out (put in the discard pile). The fixtures are unordered. Even though they are labeled 1 through 4, the order in which the players are assigned to the fixtures does not matter. Look at the conditions. There are none that indicate that one player must come before or after another or that one player must or must not be next to another. There is a condition that says that certain players cannot be on the committee together but that condition does not have to do with the order in which the players appear. An unordered game cannot have a one-to-one correspondence because there is always at least one player left out.

An unordered game is like throwing cards (players) into a hat. If you throw A, D, K, and M into the hat, the order that you throw them in does not matter, nor does the order in which they appear in the hat. The assignment A D K M is the same as K M D A.

In unordered games, nearly all of the conditions are if/then statements. The players are either in or out.

Ordered Games

Only about 10 percent of games are unordered. For the remaining 90 percent, the order in which players are assigned is critical. In other words, the great majority of games are ordered games. Ordered games are more complex than unordered games. Ordered games require you to understand the rules that govern how you assign players to fixtures. You cannot just "throw players into the hat." The rules determine how players relate to the fixtures (*Fontana cannot go in the last office*) and how the players relate to each other—who comes before whom (*Johnson comes before Gomez*); who can or cannot be next to whom (*Martin cannot be in an office next to Olivas. Weichman and Klemm must both be chosen*); and who can, cannot, or must appear if a particular player appears (*If Sheehan is chosen, Franco cannot be chosen*).

Sequences. In a little under 50 percent of the ordered games, the conditions show you a significant part of the **sequence** in which players must appear.

SAMPLE SETUP 15 ▬▬▬▬▬▬▬▬▬▬▬▬▬▬▬▬▬▬▬▬▬▬▬▬▬▬▬▬▬▬▬

Six singers are to perform in a concert in six time slots that are each exactly fifteen minutes long. Each singer performs exactly once and only one singer performs in each time slot. The possible singers are Jackson, Melendez, Norton, Oso, Petric, and Rogers. The singers are assigned according to the following conditions:

Jackson performs sometime after Oso.

Petric performs sometime before Melendez.

Oso performs immediately after Melendez.

Norton performs sometime after Oso.

Rogers performs sometime after Norton.

The conditions give clues as to the sequence. As you summarize the conditions, build a supplemental diagram that shows parts of the sequence. The first two conditions have no players in common. They result in two separate relationships:

O – J
P – M

If you look for two conditions that *do* have players in common, as in the first and third conditions, you can start to build a single supplemental diagram (Figure 4.19).

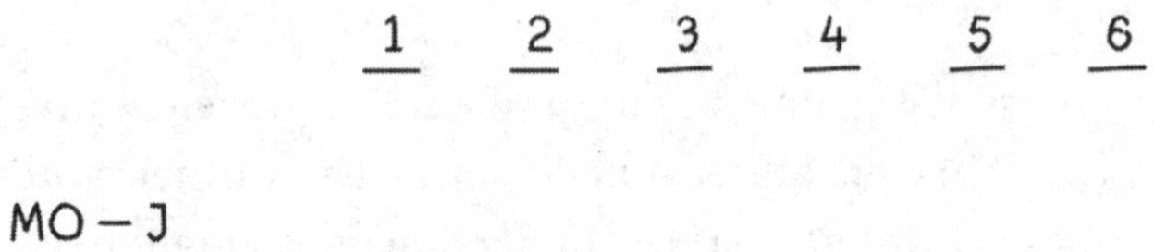

1   2   3   4   5   6

MO – J

Figure 4.19. Combine conditions 1 and 3.

The long dash between O and J indicates that there could be other players between them. The fact that there is no dash between M and O indicates that they are adjacent. We define a **sequence game** as one in which the relationship between at least three players is known, as in Figure 4.19.

Now the second condition can be added: Petric is before Melendez (Figure 4.20).

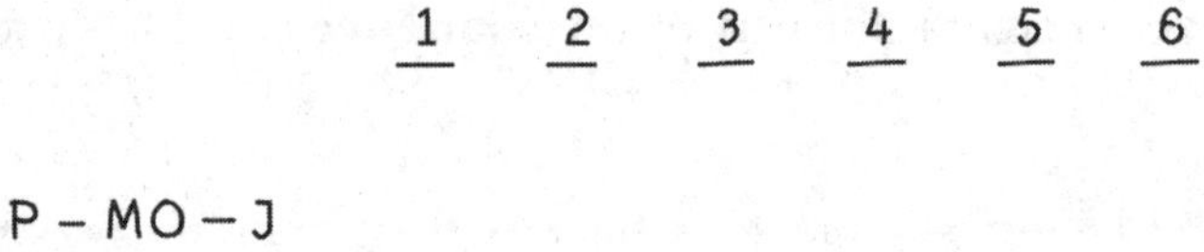

1   2   3   4   5   6

P – MO – J

Figure 4.20. Add condition 2.

At this point the relative order of four of the players is known. You do not yet know how many players appear where the dashes are and you do not know where in the main diagram the sequence P – MO — J will appear.

The fourth condition indicates that N comes after O (Figure 4.21).

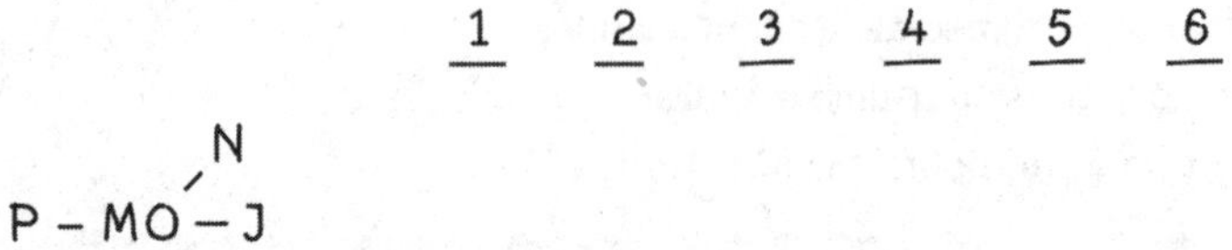

1   2   3   4   5   6

           N
P – MO – J

Figure 4.21. The fourth condition creates a new branch.

There are now two distinct branches in the supplemental diagram, and there are two sequences of four players.

P – MO – N and P – MO — J

The most important strategy for sequences is to recognize *what you do not know*. In this case, the relationship between N and J is not known.

Add in the final condition (Figure 4.22).

<u>1</u>   <u>2</u>   <u>3</u>   <u>4</u>   <u>5</u>   <u>6</u>

N – R
/
P – MO – J

Figure 4.22. Add the fifth condition.

There are now two distinct branches, one with five players and one with four. The relationships between J and N – R are unknown. If players are not adjacent and are not connected by a line, the relationship between them is unknown. Look for the positions that are not connected by lines.

The sequence game above gives you in advance most of the relationships in the sequence and includes all of the players. Many sequence games give only a few relationships and do not include all of the players.

Sequence games are a subset of ordered games. All sequence games are ordered. Unordered games cannot be sequence games. In ordered games, by definition, the players have to appear in a defined sequence. Why, then, are not all ordered games sequences? The conditions for some ordered games only show relationships between two players. Games in which the conditions define the relationships among three or more players function differently from games that do not. By studying games with three or more defined relationships as a distinct type of game—a sequence game—you will be better able to spot these games and solve them.

K – F   K – FA

B – O

AO

Non-sequence   Sequence

Figure 4.23. Ordered games: non-sequence versus sequence

To be a sequence game, the conditions must create a string that is at least three players long. In the leftmost example, there are several strings but they do not result in a string of at least three players.

Non-sequence ordered games. Approximately 60 percent of ordered games are not sequence games. In other words, either the conditions do not describe a string of relationships, or they show one or more strings of two players but no strings of three players. Non-sequence ordered games may have one-to-one correspondence (slightly more than 50 percent) or they may not have one-to-one correspondence (slightly less than 50 percent). By contrast, all sequence games have one-to-one correspondence.

Types of Ordering

The order in which players are assigned to fixtures in an ordered game can be based on many different criteria. Games can be ordered by time (*who goes first, who starts at 2:00 P.M.*), physical location (*who sits next to whom, who is on the first floor*), or any other general ranking (*which costs least, which received the highest rating*). In these examples, the fixtures are on a continuum, such as first to last, least expensive to most expensive, or leftmost to rightmost. It is not necessary, though, for fixtures to be on a continuum. For example, if the fixtures consist of five different movies, the movies are not necessarily in any order in time, space, or ranking. Fixtures that are not on a continuum might include movies, parks, swimming pools, and zoos.

Ordering in Relation to One-to-One Correspondence

There is a correlation between ordered/unordered games and one-to-one correspondence games. The flowchart in Figure 4.24 shows the possible combinations of one-to-one, ordered, and sequence games. From the top, follow the "Yes" branch of one-to-one correspondence. All such games are ordered. Some are sequences. Some are not.

From the top of the chart, follow the "No" branch. All games in the No branch either leave out some players or use players more than once. There are no sequence games in the No branch. From the label "Ordered," follow the No branch. These are unordered, "throw into the hat" games, in which players are either in or out. Going back to the label "Ordered," follow the Yes branch. These are ordered games without one-to-one correspondence. They cannot be sequence games, which all have one-to-one correspondence, and they function differently from the non-sequence ordered games that are under the one-to-one branch.

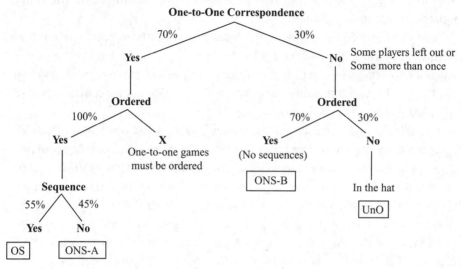

Figure 4.24. Flowchart for one-to-one correspondence,
ordering, and sequence games.
OS = ordered sequence; ONS-A = ordered non-sequence (left branch);
ONS-B = ordered non-sequence (right branch); UnO = unordered (in the hat)

All games with one-to-one correspondence are ordered. Because all of the players are assigned, the only factor that the test writers can use to distinguish one assignment from another is the order in which the players are arranged. Similarly, games that are unordered cannot have one-to-one correspondence because only some of the players will be "thrown into the hat." Games that do not have one-to-one correspondence are divided between ordered (70 percent) and unordered (30 percent).

Test yourself using the flowchart. The following categories appear in only one place on the chart. Find the end of the branch that represents:

1. Unordered games
2. Sequence games

The following category appears in more than one place on the chart. Find the three ends (not including the x-ed out branch) of the branches that represent:

3. Ordered games

Find the two places on the chart that represent ordered games that are not sequence games. Do you see that one is in the right branch and one in the left?

This means that one place represents non-one-to-one games and the other represents one-to-one games.

Find the four terminal ends of the branches in the flowchart. These represent the four most common categories of games. On the far left are the games labeled OS (ordered sequence) or sequence games (38 percent of all games). On the far right are the games labeled UnO (unordered; 9 percent). These are the *Throw Them in the Hat* games.

The middle two terminal ends are labeled ONS-A (32 percent) and ONS-B (21 percent). Both are ordered non-sequence (ONS) games. Like the sequence games, these two categories are ordered but they do not have the long chains of relationships that are found in sequence games. The two ordered non-sequence types have many similarities but they are different in that the ONS-A games have one-to-one correspondence and the ONS-B games do not. Because of the fact that all of the players in an ONS-A game are assigned exactly once, there is more likely to be some definition of the sequence, though not enough to classify the game as a sequence game. In an ONS-B game (without one-to-one correspondence) there are usually fewer players than fixtures and as a result, it is common that each player appears more than once, although there are some ONS-B games in which the players must be used more than once. ONS-B games do not usually give the relative order of players in the conditions.

When you begin a new game, first evaluate whether the game has one-to-one correspondence. Then evaluate whether the game is ordered or not. This will tell you which of the four major types of game it is: sequence, unordered (in the hat), or ordered non-sequence (one-to-one or non-one-to-one).

Fixtures

Variable Fixtures

After determining whether or not a game (1) has one-to-one correspondence; (2) is ordered; and (3) if ordered, establishes a sequence of at least three players (i.e., if it is a sequence game), determine whether the number of fixtures is exactly determined (fixed) or varies (variable). Fewer than 10 percent of games have variable fixtures, but be prepared to spot these.

Typically, games with variable fixtures are either:

1. Ordered games in which the players appear more than once but the total number of appearances of players is not known (see Sample Setup 16), or
2. Unordered games (in the hat) in which some of the players are chosen to participate but the total number can vary (see Sample Setup 17).

SAMPLE SETUP 16

Three coworkers—Marta, Nura, and Oliver—have volunteered to visit the parent of a colleague in the hospital on a particular day. Each visit lasts exactly one hour and each coworker visits at least once but not more than twice. Visits do not overlap and, except for the first visit, each visit begins immediately when the previous visit ends. No other coworkers will visit the parent in the hospital on this day. The following conditions apply:

Nura's first visit is some time after Marta's first visit.

Oliver does not visit in any hour immediately after an hour in which Marta visits.

No coworker visits in two consecutive visiting hours.

In this game there must be at least three visits and there cannot be more than six. The number of actual fixtures in a given assignment, then, could be 3, 4, 5, or 6 (Figure 4.25). The diagram uses three dots after fixture 3 to indicate that the additional fixtures may or may not be used in an assignment.

$$\underline{1} \quad \underline{2} \quad \underline{3} \quad \cdots \quad \underline{4} \quad \underline{5} \quad \underline{6}$$

Figure 4.25. Variable fixtures in an ordered game

SAMPLE SETUP 17

Six children—Lana, Marcus, Nick, Olivia, Patrick, and Rashelle—are eligible to go on a field trip to the natural history museum. No other children are eligible to go. At least one child goes on the trip. The children attend according to the following rules:

If Marcus goes, Nick does not go.

If Olivia goes, Lana does not go.

If Patrick goes, Rashelle also goes.

This game is unordered. Children are either "put in the hat" or not. There is at least one child who goes and the number of attendees cannot exceed the total number of eligible players (six). However, the actual number of children in a given assignment varies. In Figure 4.26, the three dots after fixture 1 indicate that there must be at least one fixture but that the subsequent fixtures may or may not be used. The discard pile is also variable, as there may be up to five players left out. Three dots at the right end of the discard pile help you remember that there may be more slots needed. The three slots that are shown are an arbitrary number.

$$\underline{1} \quad \cdots \quad \underline{2} \quad \underline{3} \quad \underline{4} \quad \underline{5} \quad \underline{6} \quad \Big| \underline{} \quad \underline{} \quad \underline{} \quad \cdots$$

Figure 4.26. Unordered game with variable fixtures and variable discard pile

There is only one significant difference between the above unordered game with variable fixtures and the previous ordered game (Figure 4.25) with variable fixtures. The unordered game has a slightly higher number of players and each player can appear only once (or not at all). The ordered game with variable fixtures has a smaller number of players, some of whom appear more than once.

A game with variable fixtures is unlikely to have one-to-one correspondence because in one-to-one correspondence the number of fixtures (or branches of fixtures) equals the number of players. Variable fixture games are typically found in the right branch of the flowchart—either unordered games or ordered non-sequence non-one-to-one (ONS-B) games.

Branched Fixtures

The setup of a game tells you whether or not the fixtures require branches. Approximately half of all games require branches and branches are found in every game type, though they are rarer in unordered games. Fixtures may require two, three, four, or more branches.

Fixed or variable branches. Just as fixtures can be fixed or variable, branches can also be fixed or variable. In only about 10 percent of games with branches are the branches variable. The rest have fixed branches. A branched game with a fixed number of branches per fixture might be diagrammed as in Figure 4.27.

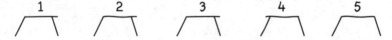

Figure 4.27. Fixed number of branches (two per fixture)

Compare Sample Setup 17 with Sample Setup 18, which has a variable number of branches.

Sample Setup 18

Eight runners are to be assigned to two teams, the Hares and the Tortoises. Each team must have at least two members.

The diagram for Sample Setup 18 is given in Figure 4.28.

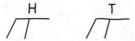

Figure 4.28. Variable number of branches (minimum of two)

Each team must have two members, represented by the solid branches. This accounts for four of the eight possible participants. How many optional branches are there? In theory, one of the teams could receive six runners. Leave space under each fixture to add in additional branches as needed. In some games there may be a maximum of one or two optional branches. Draw these as dotted lines.

SAMPLE SETUP 19

Five runners are to be assigned to two teams, the Hares and the Tortoises. Each team must have at least two members.

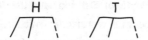

Figure 4.29. Variable branches with a small number of options

With five possible runners, there is only one runner left after the four required slots are filled. At most there can be one additional runner in H or T.

Ordered and unordered branches. If the fixtures are ordered, then determine whether the branches are ordered or unordered. It is very common for the branches of an ordered game to be unordered. If the fixtures of a game are unordered (in the hat game), then any branches will also be unordered.

SAMPLE SETUP 20

Six students—Frances, Gerald, Henry, Jocelyn, Lainie, and Martin—are to be assigned to three volunteer projects: raking, sweeping, and telephoning. Each student participates in exactly one project. Each project receives exactly two volunteers.

Gerald does not volunteer in any project in which Jocelyn volunteers.

If Lainie volunteers for raking, Martin does not volunteer for sweeping.

Henry volunteers for raking.

In this case, the order of the fixtures (raking, sweeping, telephoning) matters (Figure 4.30). Raking must be distinguished from sweeping, sweeping from telephoning, and telephoning from raking. However, it is not important whether a student is assigned in the first or second branch of a fixture. The branches are unordered.

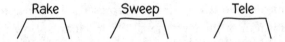

Figure 4.30. Unordered branches. The fixtures are ordered but the branches are not.

Consider Sample Setup 21.

SAMPLE SETUP 21

Six students—Frances, Gerald, Henry, Jocelyn, Lainie, and Martin—are to be assigned to three volunteer projects: raking, sweeping, and telephoning. Each student participates in exactly one project. Each project receives exactly two volunteers. One volunteer works on Saturday and the other works on Sunday.

Gerald does not volunteer in any project in which Jocelyn volunteers.

If Gerald volunteers for a project on Saturday, Martin must volunteer for the same project on Sunday.

If Lainie volunteers for raking, Martin does not volunteer for sweeping.

Henry volunteers for raking.

In this game, the two branches for each fixture represent Saturday and Sunday, respectively. One of the conditions distinguishes between Saturday and Sunday, so the order of the branches is now important. The branches are now ordered (Figure 4.31).

Figure 4.31. Ordered branches. The left branch must represent Saturday and the right branch Sunday.

Examples of Types of Games

You now know the characteristics that make up the four types of games:

Sequence: one-to-one correspondence, ordered, the relationship between at least three players is given

Unordered: "throw the cards in a hat," "in or out," non-one-to-one, unordered

Ordered Non-Sequence Games A: with one-to-one correspondence

Ordered Non-Sequence Games B: without one-to-one correspondence

Within each of these types there are common variations. In the paragraphs below, you will see all the variations and will be able to recognize these variations when you encounter them in practice sections. The examples consist of setups. The setups include representative conditions but not sample questions.

How to Use This Section

This section is a comprehensive listing of variations that you will find on actual LSAT AR sections. Trying to read through the whole section in one sitting would be overwhelming. Start by working a few variations for each of the four game types. Do not be concerned if you are not clear on the exact type of the game. It is more important that you feel comfortable with how to set up each game and with how a particular variation is different from other variations. With practice, you will recognize when a game is a sequence, is unordered, or is neither and has or does not have one-to-one correspondence.

You might also find it helpful to skim through the variations at first, getting a general sense of how they differ. This will help you absorb the many diagramming variations. You can come back to the variations later and work through a few at a time more carefully.

Use this section as a reference. Come back to it as you are working practice problems. See if you can identify the game type for the practice question you are working on. Then see if you can find the variation that is closest to it.

We have used the same general setup for most of the examples so that you can easily follow the changes between the various types of games. For each example, try to set up your own diagram before reading the explanation. Then, compare your diagram with the explanation that follows. If you would like to introduce some extra variety into the explanations, try creating your own setup using a different situation and different players. Then diagram your setup.

The in-depth instruction on the problem-solving process appears later in the chapter. For now, simply focus on becoming comfortable with the different types of games. If you already have experience with AR problem solving and are aiming for a superior score, challenge yourself as follows. For each type of game, create a series of six questions, drawing on the various question types, including five possible answer choices. Creating questions and answer choices is an excellent way to test your understanding and to challenge your skills. Then try to solve your own questions, or exchange questions with another superior test taker using this book, and test each other.

Sequence Games

All sequence games have one-to-one correspondence. Each player appears exactly once. The order in which the players appear is critical. Sequence games always have a primary diagram—the working diagram—that shows the fixtures. Sequence games usually require a supplemental diagram that summarizes what is known—and not known—about the players. The following samples focus mostly on the supplemental diagrams. Work out the diagrams in each sample for yourself.

Each sample represents a possible variation on sequence games. If you work through each of the samples, you will be prepared for any sequence game. For each variation, consider how it differs from others.

Remember to draw your own diagram first, before reading the explanation. Then compare your diagram with the one presented here.

SEQUENCE SAMPLE 1

Seven singers—Kovac, Larson, Ming, Nieto, Ofune, Parsons, and Rifkin—are to perform in seven distinct time slots at a single concert. Exactly one singer performs in each time slot. Each time slot is fifteen minutes long and time slots start at 7 P.M. and on each subsequent quarter hour. The singers appear according to the following conditions:

Ming performs before Larson.

Nieto performs before Parsons.

Parsons performs immediately after Rifkin.

Ofune performs either immediately before or immediately after Ming.

The strings of relationships that are given in the conditions include:

$$M - L$$
$$N - RP$$

In addition, the M – L sequence must take the form of either OM – L or MO – L. There is no point of connection between the sequences with M and L and the sequence with N, R, and P.

The sequences shown above are supplemental diagrams. The working diagram for the game (Figure 4.32) simply shows the seven time slots.

<u>1</u>   <u>2</u>   <u>3</u>   <u>4</u>   <u>5</u>   <u>6</u>   <u>7</u>

Figure 4.32. Main diagram showing seven slots in the sequence

SEQUENCE SAMPLE 2

Seven singers—Kovac, Larson, Ming, Nieto, Ofune, Parsons, and Rifkin—are to perform in seven distinct time slots at a single concert. Exactly one singer performs in each time slot. Each time slot is fifteen minutes long and time slots start at 7 P.M. and on each subsequent quarter hour. The singers appear according to the following conditions:

Ming performs before Larson.

Nieto performs before Parsons.

Ofune performs either immediately before or immediately after Ming.

There are exactly two time slots between Nieto and Rifkin.

The sequences defined are:

$$M - L$$
$$N - P$$

These relationships by themselves are not enough to make this a sequence game but the remaining conditions give us:

$$Either\ OM - L\ or\ MO - L$$

and

$$Either\ R\_\_N - P\ or\ N\_\_R\ and\ N - P$$

$$R\_\_N-P \quad or \quad N\_\_R^{\nearrow P}$$

Figure 4.33. R before N or R after N

SEQUENCE SAMPLE 3

Seven singers—Kovac, Larson, Ming, Nieto, Ofune, Parsons, and Rifkin—are to perform in seven distinct time slots at a single concert. Exactly one singer performs in each time slot. Each time slot is fifteen minutes long and time slots start at 7 P.M. and on each subsequent quarter hour. The singers appear according to the following conditions:

Ming performs before Larson.

Nieto performs before Parsons.

Larson performs before Nieto.

Parsons performs at some time after Ofune.

Kovac performs at some time after Ofune.

Figure 4.34 shows the sequences defined.

$$O - K$$
$$M - L - N - P$$

Figure 4.34. Sequence sample 3

Notice the string of four relationships, M through P. Notice that the relationship between O and M – L – N is unknown. O could occur either before or after any of these three. The same is true for K. You only know that K appears after O.

SEQUENCE SAMPLE 4

Seven singers—Kovac, Larson, Ming, Nieto, Ofune, Parsons, and Rifkin—are to perform in seven distinct time slots at a single concert. Exactly one singer performs in each time slot. Each time slot is fifteen minutes long and time slots start at 7 P.M. and on each subsequent quarter hour. The singers appear according to the following conditions:

Ming performs before Larson.

Ming performs before Parsons.

If Larson performs third, then Larson performs before Ofune.

If Larson does not perform third, then Larson must perform before Kovac.

The first two conditions do not give a string of three players, the requirement for a sequence game, but the third and fourth conditions do result in a string of three.

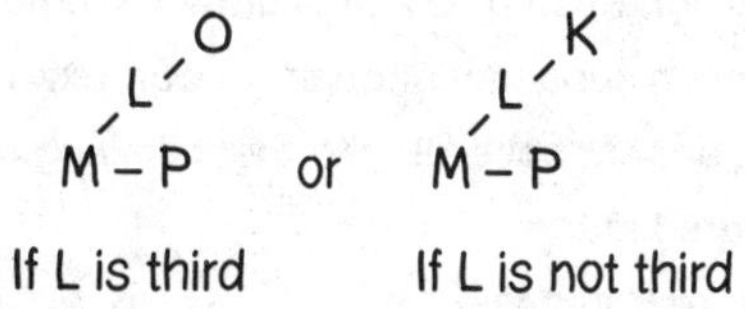

If L is third   If L is not third

Figure 4.35. Sequence sample 4

SEQUENCE SAMPLE 5

Seven singers—Kovac, Larson, Ming, Nieto, Ofune, Parsons, and Rifkin—are to perform in seven distinct time slots at a single concert. Exactly one singer performs in each time slot. Each time slot is fifteen minutes long and time slots start at 7 P.M. and on each subsequent quarter hour. The singers appear according to the following conditions:

Both Ming and Rifkin perform before Larson.

Both Ming and Parsons perform before Ofune.

If Ming performs before Rifkin, then Parsons performs before Nieto.

Parsons does not perform in the third slot.

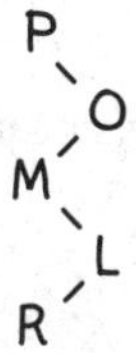

Figure 4.36. Sequence sample 5

Even though five players are represented in the diagram (Figure 4.36), there is not a chain that is at least three players long. Both R and M are before L, but the relationship between M and R is unknown. The last two conditions add additional information but still do not establish a chain of three players. Nevertheless, this game acts more like a sequence game than a non-sequence game, because information is given on nearly all of the players, and should be approached as a sequence.

SEQUENCE SAMPLE 6

Seven singers—Kovac, Larson, Ming, Nieto, Ofune, Parsons, and Rifkin—are to perform in seven distinct time slots at a single concert. Exactly one singer performs in each time slot. Each time slot is fifteen minutes long and time slots start at 7 P.M. and on each subsequent quarter hour. Exactly two singers receive an award. The singers appear according to the following conditions:

Ming performs before Larson.

Nieto performs before Parsons.

Ofune performs either immediately before or immediately after Ming.

There are exactly two time slots between Nieto and Rifkin.

If Ming receives an award, Nieto does not receive an award.

The singer appearing immediately after Rifkin does not receive an award.

This game is identical to Sequence Sample 2 except that it adds another factor—whether the singer receives an award—along with conditions that are related to the award. The award is represented by a second branch on each of the seven time slots (Figure 4.37). The award branch would be assigned either a + or –. In other words, + and – are the two possible players that can be assigned under the award branch.

Figure 4.37. Sequence sample 6 showing two branches

SEQUENCE SAMPLE 7

Seven singers—Kovac, Larson, Ming, Nieto, Ofune, Parsons, and Rifkin—are to perform in seven distinct time slots at a single concert. Exactly one singer performs in each time slot. Each time slot is fifteen minutes long and time slots start at 7 P.M. and on each subsequent quarter hour. The singers appear according to the following conditions:

Ming performs before Larson and Rifken.

Rifken and Nieto perform before Ofune.

Either Parsons performs before Rifken and Nieto, or both Rifken and Nieto perform before Parsons, but not both.

This sample is similar to previous ones except that the final condition adds two alternatives, each of which is represented by a small diagram of its own (Figure 4.38).

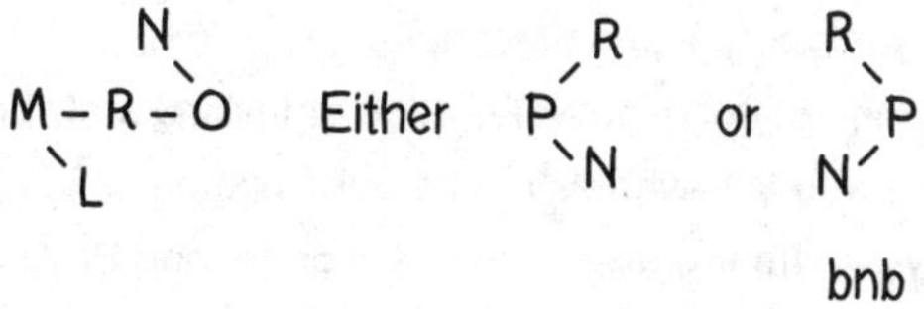

$$
M - R - \underset{\displaystyle L}{\overset{\displaystyle N}{O}}
\quad \text{Either} \quad
P \overset{\displaystyle R}{\underset{\displaystyle N}{}}
\quad \text{or} \quad
\underset{\displaystyle N}{\overset{\displaystyle R}{P}}
$$

bnb

Figure 4.38. Supplemental diagram with two parts

Seven singers—Kovac, Larson, Ming, Nieto, Ofune, Parsons, and Rifkin—are to perform in seven distinct time slots at a single concert. Each time slot is fifteen minutes and time slots start at 7 P.M. and on each subsequent quarter hour. The singers appear according to the following conditions:

Ming performs before Larson.

If Ofune performs before Ming, then both Larson and Rifken perform before Parsons.

If Ming performs before Ofune, then neither Parsons nor Larson perform before Rifken.

Here, either the second or third condition must apply. Thus, the first condition can be combined with each of the others to show two possibilities.

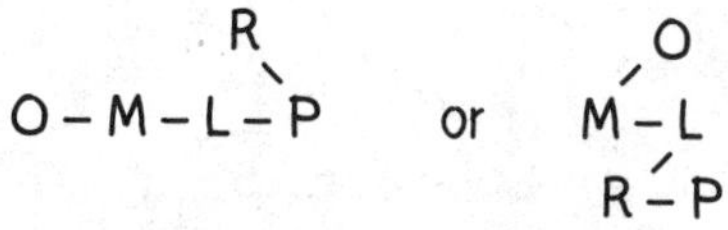

$$
O - M - L - \overset{\displaystyle R}{P}
\quad \text{or} \quad
M - L \overset{\displaystyle O}{\underset{\displaystyle R - P}{}}
$$

Figure 4.39. Two possibilities

SEQUENCE SAMPLE 9

A company is assigning departments to the six floors of a new building into which it is moving. Each department takes up exactly one floor and there are six departments: Legal, Management, New Accounts, Payables, Receivables, and Taxation. The following conditions must hold:

Either Legal is immediately above Taxation or immediately below Payables.

New Accounts is above Payables but below Taxation.

There is exactly one floor between New Accounts and Payables.

Management is on the top floor.

In this game, it is more natural to arrange the players vertically. There are a small but significant number of sequence games that are vertical. Usually vertical sequence games involve floors of a building, layers, or sometimes relative heights of players. In drawing the supplemental diagrams, look for the most concrete information first (Figure 4.40). Because the first condition allows for two distinct possibilities (L immediately above T or L immediately below P), the supplemental diagram will also show two possibilities. A vertical line between two players indicates that more than one additional player could be inserted. A short horizontal line between two players indicates that exactly one player goes in that position.

Figure 4.40. Vertical sequence supplemental diagram

Conditions for Sequences

In the sample setups above you saw many of the common kinds of conditions that are used in sequence games. Below is a more complete list. The most common sequence condition—and by far the easiest to understand—is simply that Player A is before (or after, above, or below) Player B. Almost all sequence games have at least one such condition. Many have two or more and in some sequence games all of the conditions are of this type.

All sequence games have at least three conditions and nearly two-thirds have four conditions. About a third of sequence games have a fifth condition and a few have a sixth condition. It is the combination of types of conditions that makes each sequence game unique.

In the list of conditions below, "before" can also be replaced with "after," or with "above" or "below." The example of receiving an award represents any additional characteristic that can be assigned along with a player, such as being "selected." In some cases players are divided into categories, such as experts and beginners. Here "award" represents the assignment of a category. When a condition also occurs in the negative, the word *not* is included in parentheses.

Use the following list as a reference. You do not need to memorize it. Glance through it now and come back to it as you work on practice sequence questions.

CONDITIONS THAT ARE USED IN SEQUENCE GAMES

- Frank is before Gretchen.
- Frank is before Gretchen but is not first.
- Frank is (not) assigned before the fourth place.
- Frank is before Gretchen but after Howard.
- Frank is immediately before Gretchen.
- Frank is (not) immediately before or immediately after Gretchen.
- Frank is immediately before either Gretchen or Howard.
- Frank is (not) in third place.
- Frank is in third or fifth place.
- Frank is not last.
- Frank receives an award.
- Frank, Gretchen, and Howard cannot be in second, fourth, or fifth place.
- There are at least three players before Frank.
- There are at least two players between Frank and Gretchen.
- Both Frank and Gretchen are before Howard.
- Either Frank and Gretchen are consecutive, or Frank and Howard are consecutive, but not both.
- Either Frank is before Gretchen and Howard, or Gretchen and Howard are before Frank, but not both.
- Either Frank is before Gretchen, or Frank is before Howard, but not both.
- Either Frank or Gretchen is immediately before Howard.

- Either Frank or Gretchen is in fifth place.
- There are (no/exactly two) awards given after Frank performs.
- There are exactly two students between Frank and Gretchen.
- If Frank is before Gretchen, then neither Howard nor Inez is before Jeremy.
- If Frank is before Gretchen, then Howard is before Inez.
- If Frank is (not) in third place, then Frank is (after) before both Gretchen and Howard.
- The award is given to the person in the sixth place.
- The award is given to either Frank or Gretchen and is given to the person in the third or fifth place.
- The expert performs immediately before the beginner.

You can see that the test writers can easily create many variations on the above types. Learn these types but be prepared for new twists.

Unordered Games ("Throw Cards in the Hat")

In unordered games, you are simply "throwing cards in the hat." In other words, some of the players will be "in," or selected, and the rest will be "out." Because there are always players left out, unordered games do not have one-to-one correspondence. Unordered games also often benefit from using a discard pile. The diagram for an unordered game typically has four to seven fixtures. Number the fixtures in order to distinguish the columns but it does not matter whether a player is assigned under fixture 2 or 5, for example. With occasional exceptions, in most unordered games the fixtures do not have branches. Unordered games may have two or even three categories of players. In some unordered games, the exact number of slots to be filled is variable. The conditions for unordered games are nearly all if/then statements.

For each variation, consider how it differs from other variations. Draw your own diagram first, before reading the explanation. Then compare your diagram with the one presented here.

UNORDERED GAME SAMPLE 1

A student must choose four elective courses to be taken during the next semester. The possible courses include Geography, Japanese, Legal Studies, Mandarin, Native Studies, Oceanography, Phonetics, and Russian. The following conditions apply:

If the student takes Geography, the student cannot take Russian.

If the student does not take Japanese, the student must take Russian.

If the student takes Phonetics, the student must take Mandarin.

If the student does not take Mandarin, the student does not take Native Studies.

Either the student takes Oceanography or Legal Studies, but not both.

This is a common, basic unordered game. The diagram consists of slots 1 through 4 and a discard pile of exactly four slots. The if/then statements represent a number of logical variations, including an "either/or but not both" statement. The students are fixtures and the courses are players.

UNORDERED GAME SAMPLE 2

A student must choose elective courses to be taken during the next semester. The possible courses include Geography, Japanese, Legal Studies, Mandarin, Native Studies, Oceanography, Phonetics, and Russian. The student must choose at least three courses. The following conditions apply:

If the student takes Geography, the student cannot take Russian.

If the student does not take Japanese, the student must take Russian.

If the student takes Phonetics, the student must take Mandarin.

If the student does not take Mandarin, the student does not take Native Studies.

Either the student takes Oceanography or Legal Studies, but not both.

In this game the number of fixtures varies. There must be at least three fixtures. At least one player must be out in an unordered game. As a result, the maximum number of fixtures is seven. It is safe to put seven possible fixtures in the diagram. They may not all be needed. The discard pile is also variable.

$$\underline{1} \quad \underline{2} \quad \underline{3} \quad \cdots \quad \underline{4} \quad \underline{5} \quad \underline{6} \quad \underline{7} \Big| \underline{} \; \underline{} \; \underline{}$$

Figure 4.41. Unordered game with variable
fixtures and a variable discard pile

UNORDERED GAME SAMPLE 3

A student must choose five elective courses to be taken during the next semester. The possible courses include four languages—Greek, Japanese, Lithuanian, and Mandarin—and four humanities—Native Studies, Organizational Management, Phonetics, and Sociology. The following conditions apply:

If the student takes Greek, the student cannot take Sociology.

If the student does not take Japanese, the student must take Sociology.

If the student takes Phonetics, the student must take Mandarin.

If the student does not take Mandarin, the student does not take Native Studies.

If the student takes any language, the student must take Organizational Management.

This game has two sets of players: languages and humanities. You must keep track of them separately because the last rule distinguishes between them. Otherwise, this game functions in the same way as a basic unordered game.

UNORDERED GAME SAMPLE 4

Eight employees—Ferguson, Griego, Handelin, Jong, Kowalski, Levy, Montoya, and Norton—have volunteered to attend a business conference. Each employee who has volunteered falls into exactly one of the following categories: manager, part-time employee, or union representative. Exactly five employees are to be chosen to attend. The following must obtain:

Kowalski is a manager.

Norton attends only if Norton is a part-time employee.

If exactly two managers attend, Kowalski does not attend.

Exactly two union representatives must attend.

This game has two sets of players: the employees and the designations of manager, part-time employee, and union representative. Each fixture must be assigned both a person and a designation. This game, then, requires two branches for each fixture. There are exactly five fixtures and exactly three discard slots.

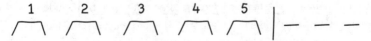

Figure 4.42. Unordered game with two branches

Conditions for Unordered Games

In the previous samples you have seen approximately half of the types of conditions that occur with unordered games. The majority of conditions involve an if/then statement. As with the sequence conditions, the test writers can create many variations. If you master the rules for working with if/thens, you will be able to correctly interpret most of the conditions in an unordered game.

Most unordered games have five conditions. Some have four or six. In the following conditions, players are either "in" or "out." In some games players are grouped by category. The conditions refer to a game in which some players are managers, some are part-time employees, and some are union representatives.

You do not need to memorize these conditions. Use the list below as a reference when you are working on unordered games. Glance through the list now to become familiar with the possible types of conditions.

CONDITIONS THAT ARE USED IN UNORDERED GAMES

- Howard is included only if Leonard is not included.
- Howard is included only if he is a manager.
- Howard is a manager.
- Howard is a manager and is included.
- There is at least one manager.
- There is at least one manager, one part-time employee, and one union representative.
- There are exactly two managers.
- Howard cannot be included if Leonard is included.
- Either Howard or Leonard is included, but not both.
- If Howard is included, then Leonard is included. (=Leonard must be included if Howard is included.)
- If Howard is included, then Leonard is not included.
- If Howard is not included, then Leonard is included. (=Leonard must be included if Howard is not included.)
- If Howard is not included, then Leonard is not included.
- If Howard is included, then neither Leonard nor Penny is included.
- If both Howard and Leonard are included, then at least one is not a manager.
- If either Howard or Leonard is included, then both must be included.
- If there are any managers included, then Howard must also be included.

Ordered Non-Sequence Games with One-to-One Correspondence

The games in this section are the ones labeled ONS-A (ordered, non-sequence, A = left branch, which is one-to-one correspondence) as shown in Figure 4.43.

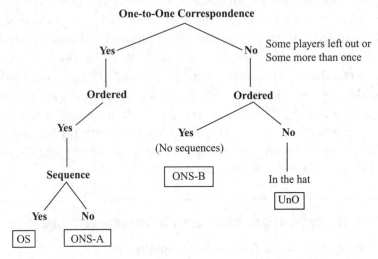

Figure 4.43. The games discussed in this section are ONS-A.

Games with one-to-one correspondence (OS and ONS-A) are all ordered. Because all of the players are used exactly once, it is the order of the players that is important. The first such type are sequence games (OS), which we have defined as establishing strings of relationships among at least three players. Some games have one-to-one correspondence but do not have a string with at least three players. These games (ONS-A) still have some elements of a sequence game but function differently enough that it is worth studying them separately. Study the examples below to find the differences and similarities between the two.

One difference between these two types is that nearly 75 percent of one-to-one non-sequence games (ONS-A) use branched fixtures, with variable branches in about a third of them. By contrast, only 5 percent of sequence games use branched fixtures and the branches are typically not variable. ONS-A games use the small number of fixtures with multiple and often variable branches to create complexity, whereas sequence games are complex because of their long linear relationships.

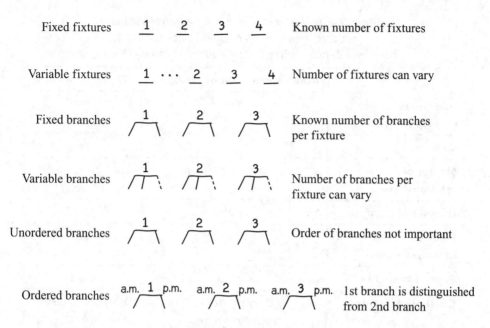

Figure 4.44. Summary of variations for fixtures and branches

In both of these game types each player is used exactly once (one-to-one correspondence), the order of the fixtures is important (ordered), and the number of fixtures is fixed. When the fixtures are branched, the branches—but not the fixtures—can be variable. In addition, the branches can be ordered or unordered.

Whereas in sequence games the fixtures simply represent the order in the sequence (e.g., 1 through 6), in the ONS-A games, fixtures are more likely to represent objects, such as people, presentations, companies, and teams. The players often fall into two or three categories, such as beginners and experts, singers and accompanists. In some games the branches might represent morning and afternoon, or a first presenter and second presenter. It is the relationships between categories of players, characteristics of branches, and fixtures that makes these games different from, and more complex than, sequence games. Table 4.2 summarizes the similarities and differences between sequence games and one-to-one non-sequence games (ONS-A).

Table 4.2. Comparison of one-to-one correspondence,
ordered sequence games and one-to-one
correspondence, ordered non-sequence games (ONS-A)

	Non-Sequence Games (ONS-A)	Sequence Games
One-to-one correspondence	Yes	Yes
Ordered	Yes	Yes
Strings of relationships	Short or none	Long (three players or more)
Number of fixtures	Fewer	More
Frequency of branched games	75%	5%
Type of branches	Variable	Fixed
Content of fixtures	Objects (people, presentations, etc.)	Places in sequence (first, second, etc.)
Categories of player	Two to three (e.g, singer and accompanist)	Only one
Categories per fixtures	Multiple (e.g., A.M. presentation and P.M. presentation on Day 1)	Only one
Conditions	Many if/then's	Few if/then's

Below are examples of the important patterns of ONS-A games. The patterns include games with fixed branches, variable branches that are unordered, variable branches that are ordered, and no branches. Draw your own diagram first, before reading the explanation. Then compare your diagram with ours.

Fixed Branches

ONE-TO-ONE NON-SEQUENCE SAMPLE 1

Six singers—Kovac, Larson, Ming, Nieto, Ofune, and Parsons—will each perform in one of three shows at a single concert. In each show exactly two of the singers will perform together. Each show lasts thirty minutes and the first show starts at 7 P.M. The shows run consecutively and do not overlap. Each singer performs exactly once. The singers appear according to the following conditions:

If Ming performs in the first show, then Larson performs in the second show.

If Ofune does not perform in the second show, then both Larson and Nieto perform in the third show.

Kovac performs in either the first or third show.

Parsons does not perform in any show that Nieto performs in.

The fixtures are the three shows and each show has two unordered branches, one for each of the two singers. This is a typical ONS-A game, using if/then statements and branches, rather than conditions showing who comes before whom.

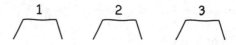

If M = 1 → L = 2

If O ≠ 2 → L + N = 3

K = 1 or 3

If N → –P

Figure 4.45. One-to-one non-sequence with two fixed branches

One-to-One Non-Sequence Sample 2

Six singers—Kovac, Larson, Ming, Nieto, Ofune, and Parsons—will each perform in one of three shows at a single concert. In each show exactly two of the singers will perform together. One singer will sing lead and the other will sing harmony. Each show lasts thirty minutes and the first show starts at 7 P.M. The shows run consecutively and do not overlap. Each singer performs exactly once. The singers appear according to the following conditions:

Either Ming performs in the same show as Larson, or Ming performs in the same show as Nieto.

Ofune sings harmony.

Either Parsons or Kovac sings lead, but they cannot both sing lead.

Kovac must perform before both Ming and Ofune.

This game still has two branches but they are now ordered. One branch represents the lead singer and the other, the person singing harmony. The conditions rely on either/or statements. The last condition is similar to a sequence condition.

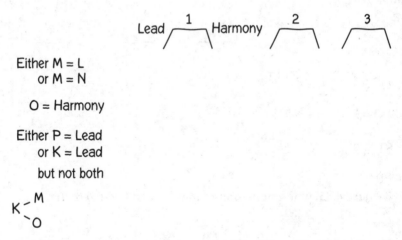

Figure 4.46. One-to-one non-sequence with two branches that are ordered

ONE-TO-ONE NON-SEQUENCE SAMPLE 3

Six singers—Kovac, Larson, Ming, Nieto, Ofune, and Parsons—will each perform in one of three shows at a single concert. In each show exactly two of the singers will perform together. One singer will sing lead and the other will sing harmony. In addition, each show is sponsored by exactly one of three local companies—Stanfield's, Topnotch, and Urban Style—and each company sponsors exactly one show. Each show lasts thirty minutes and the first show starts at 7 P.M. The shows run consecutively and do not overlap. Each singer performs exactly once. The singers appear according to the following conditions:

Ming performs in the show that is sponsored by Topnotch.

Parsons and Nieto do not perform in the same show.

The show sponsored by Stanfield's is after the show sponsored by Urban Style.

Kovac must perform before both Ming and Ofune.

This game introduces a third category of player—the sponsors—and has three branches—lead singer, harmony singer, and sponsor. The branches are ordered and represent different characteristics. The last two conditions show relative orders of players but not enough to make it a sequence game. The third condition gives a relative order of shows, not players, and does so in terms of the sponsors.

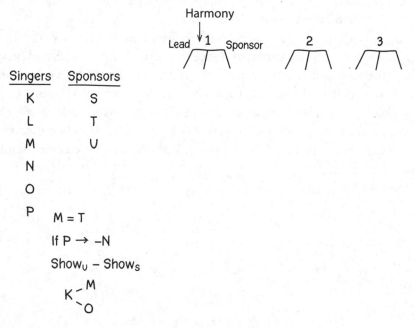

Figure 4.47. One-to-one non-sequence with three ordered branches

ONE-TO-ONE NON-SEQUENCE SAMPLE 4

Six singers—Kovac, Larson, Ming, Nieto, Ofune, and Parsons—will each perform in one of six shows at a single concert. In each show exactly one singer will perform. Each singer performs either with musical accompaniment or without. Each show lasts thirty minutes and the first show starts at 7 P.M. The shows run consecutively and do not overlap. Each singer performs exactly once. The singers appear according to the following conditions:

Kovac, Larson, and Ming are amateurs.

Nieto, Ofune, and Parsons are professionals.

Larson sings with accompaniment.

Parsons sings without accompaniment.

All of the singers who sing with accompaniment must perform before any of the singers who sing without accompaniment.

Any amateur who sings with accompaniment must perform before any professional who sings with accompaniment.

This game has three categories of player—amateur singers, professional singers, and the characteristic of being accompanied or unaccompanied. However, each fixture (representing one of the six shows) only needs to have a branch for the singer and a branch for being accompanied or not. It is not necessary to have separate branches for amateurs and professionals. The diagram, then, has two ordered branches for each fixture.

This game acts in some ways like a sequence game. The six players are assigned in a one-to-one correspondence to the six shows. The second branch is not the result of clumping players together, as in the previous sample games, but results from adding the characteristic of accompaniment. Unlike in sequence games, the conditions do not show the relationships among the players. Rather, the conditions present a complex set of rules that involve all three categories of players. The last two conditions are particularly complex. Study them carefully.

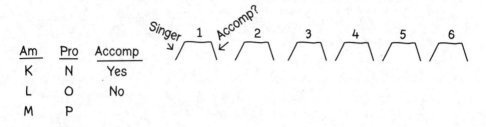

Am	Pro	Accomp
K	N	Yes
L	O	No
M	P	

L = Accomp

P = −Accomp

All Accomp before any −Accomp

Am + Accomp before any Pro + Accomp

Figure 4.48. One-to-one non-sequence with three categories of players and two fixed branches

ONE-TO-ONE NON-SEQUENCE SAMPLE 5

Six singers—Kovac, Larson, Ming, Nieto, Ofune, and Parsons—will each perform in one of three shows at a single concert. In each show exactly two singers will perform, one of whom is an amateur and one of whom is a professional. Each show lasts thirty minutes and the first show starts at 7 P.M. The shows run consecutively and do not overlap. Each singer performs exactly once. The singers appear according to the following conditions:

Kovac, Larson, and Ming are amateurs.

Nieto, Ofune, and Parsons are professionals.

Both Larson and Ming perform before Kovac.

Parsons performs before Nieto.

As in a sequence game, the conditions in this game primarily define relationships among players, but there is no string that connects three or more players. This game acts like a non-sequence game in that it clusters the players into three fixtures (the three shows), each with two ordered branches.

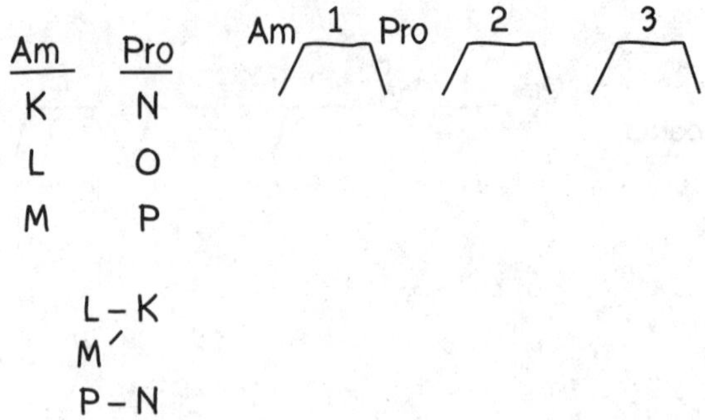

Am	Pro
K	N
L	O
M	P

L – K
M ╱
P – N

Figure 4.49. One-to-one non-sequence with sequence-like conditions

ONE-TO-ONE NON-SEQUENCE SAMPLE 6

Four singers—Kovac, Larson, Ming, and Nieto—are performing on stage at the beginning of a concert. No one else is on stage. At four randomly chosen times during the concert a judge will use one of four sounds—rasp, saxophone, trumpet, or viola—to indicate that exactly one singer must leave the stage and will not return to the stage for the duration of the concert. The following conditions obtain:

The first sound is saxophone.

Kovac is still on stage when the viola sounds.

Ming leaves the stage at some time after Nieto leaves.

If Kovac is still on stage when Ming leaves, the trumpet sounds before the viola.

If Kovac is not still on stage when Ming leaves, the viola sounds before the trumpet.

This unusual variation (it has only occurred once in recent years) starts with the full cast of players and has them leave one at a time, according to conditions. Think of this as an "unloading" game. The four fixtures, which represent the time at which a sound is played and a player leaves the stage, are divided into two ordered branches, one for the player and one for the sound. One of the last two conditions *must* be true. Notice how the diagram in Figure 4.50 uses the word *else* to show this relationship. S is placed under fixture 1 as permanent.

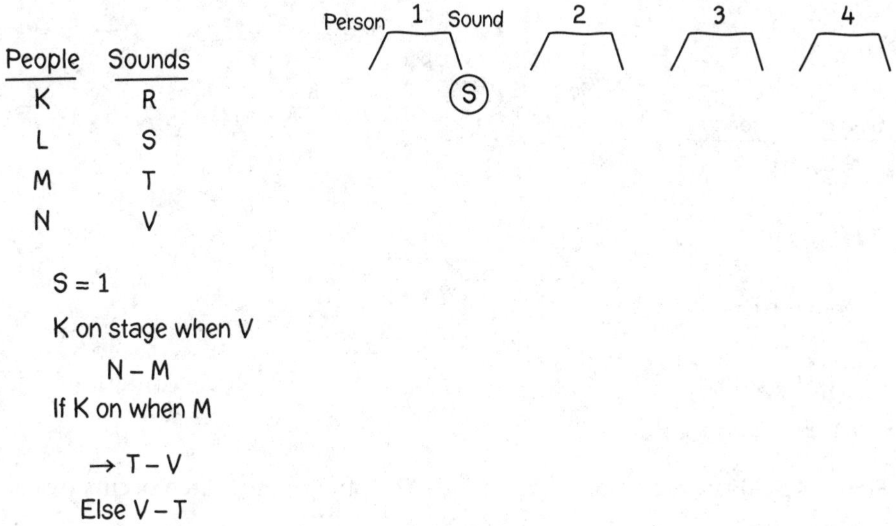

People	Sounds
K	R
L	S
M	T
N	V

Person 1 Sound 2 3 4

(S)

$S = 1$

K on stage when V

N – M

If K on when M

→ T – V

Else V – T

Figure 4.50. One-to-one non-sequence "unloading" game

ONE-TO-ONE NON-SEQUENCE SAMPLE 7

Three singers—Kovac, Larson, and Ming—will each perform in one of three shows at a concert on Friday and again at a concert on Saturday. On each day the shows run consecutively and do not overlap. In each show exactly one singer performs. In addition, each show is sponsored by exactly one of three local companies—Stanfield's, Topnotch, and Urban Style—and each company sponsors exactly one show on Friday and one show on Saturday. Each singer performs exactly once Friday and once Saturday. On Saturday no singer can appear in a show sponsored by the same company that sponsored the show in which that singer appeared on Friday. The singers and sponsors appear according to the following conditions:

Ming does not perform in any show that is sponsored by Topnotch.

Larson must appear in one of the shows sponsored by Urban.

The company that sponsored the show in which Kovac performed on Friday must sponsor the show in which Ming performs on Saturday.

Each of the players—singers and sponsors—appears twice in any arrangement. The game still has one-to-one correspondence. It is simply a one-to-one match that happens twice—once on Friday and once on Saturday.

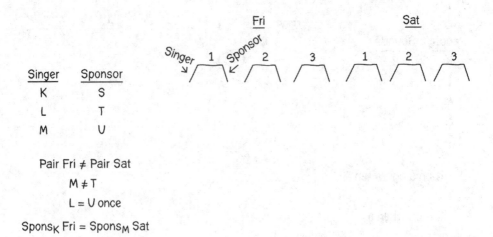

Singer	Sponsor
K	S
L	T
M	U

Pair Fri ≠ Pair Sat

  M ≠ T

  L = U once

$Spons_K$ Fri = $Spons_M$ Sat

Figure 4.51. Players appear twice because the one-to-one match occurs twice.

Variable Branches: Unordered

The one-to-one non-sequence samples above all have a fixed number of branches, usually two. Many one-to-one non-sequence games have variable branches. However, because these games have one-to-one correspondence, each player is assigned exactly once. If there are six players and exactly six fixtures, the assignment is straightforward. If there are six players and three fixtures, then the fixtures must have enough branches to make a total of six assignments. With variable branches, the number of branches per fixture varies.

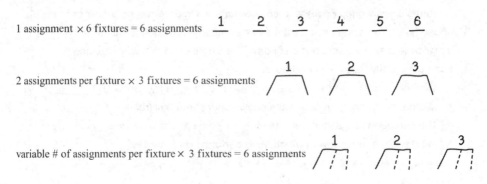

1 assignment × 6 fixtures = 6 assignments

2 assignments per fixture × 3 fixtures = 6 assignments

variable # of assignments per fixture × 3 fixtures = 6 assignments

Figure 4.52. Three ways to assign six players exactly once each: top—one player to each of six fixtures; middle—two players per fixture for three fixtures; and bottom—a variable number of players per fixture for three fixtures

In the following ONS-A game samples, the number of branches is variable and the branches are unordered. The number of fixtures is always fixed.

ONE-TO-ONE NON-SEQUENCE SAMPLE 8
WITH VARIABLE BRANCHES THAT ARE UNORDERED

Six singers—Kovac, Larson, Ming, Nieto, Ofune, and Parsons—will each perform in one of three shows at a single concert. Each show lasts thirty minutes and the first show starts at 7 P.M. The shows run consecutively and do not overlap. Each singer performs exactly once. Each show includes at least one singer. The assignment of singers conforms to the following:

If Ming performs in the first show, Larson also performs in the first show.

Ofune performs in the second show.

Parsons and Kovac do not perform in the same show as each other.

Kovac and Ofune perform in the same show.

There are exactly three shows but the number of branches under each show can vary. Each show must have at least one singer, so there must be at least one branch per fixture. Three players are used up in filling these slots. The three remaining players can be distributed in various ways. Theoretically, the three remaining players could all perform in the same show, resulting in one show with four players and two shows with one player each. The diagram does not necessarily need to show four branches under each fixture. It is enough to show one or two dotted (variable) branches and to know that there may be more branches. In the Figure 4.53 diagram, the line under the number for each show extends past the last dotted line. This helps remind you that there could be more branches. The branches in this game are unordered, meaning that the order in which players are assigned to a show does not matter.

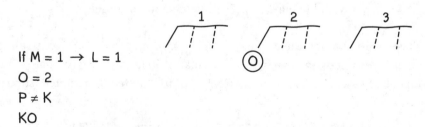

If M = 1 → L = 1

O = 2

P ≠ K

KO

Figure 4.53. One-to-one non-sequence with variable, unordered branches. Ofune is circled under show 2 to indicate that Ofune in 2 is a permanent condition.

ONE-TO-ONE NON-SEQUENCE SAMPLE 9
WITH VARIABLE BRANCHES THAT ARE UNORDERED

Six singers—Kovac, Larson, Ming, Nieto, Ofune, and Parsons—will each perform in one of two shows at a single concert. The shows run consecutively and do not overlap. In the first show up to three singers can perform. In the second show up to five singers can perform. Each singer performs exactly once. The assignment of singers conforms to the following:

Ofune performs in the second show.

Kovac performs in the first show.

Parsons and Kovac do not perform in the same show as each other.

There are only two fixtures—the first show and the second show—but the number of possible branches under each show is different. Unlike the previous sample, this game tells us exactly what the maximum number of branches is for each fixture—three and five, respectively. The setup does not initially state that either of the shows must have at least one performer, so all of the branches are optional at first (represented by dotted lines). If all of the slots in show 1 are filled, there will still be three players that must be assigned to show 2, so show 2 has at least three branches that must be filled. However, it is not necessary to figure this fact out before creating the diagram.

O = 2
K = 1
P ≠ K

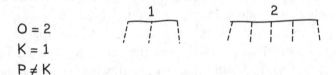

Figure 4.54. This represents the initial diagram. It is one-to-one non-sequence, and has two fixtures with different numbers of variable branches. The branches are unordered.

As you work through the diagram in Figure 4.54, players O and K are put into the diagram as permanent (circled) information (Figure 4.55). At that point, change the branches they are under from optional (dotted) to required (solid).

O = 2
K = 1
P ≠ K

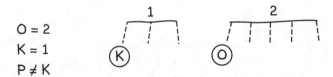

Figure 4.55. Permanent information added to the diagram and optional branches changed to permanent

ONE-TO-ONE NON-SEQUENCE SAMPLE 10
WITH VARIABLE BRANCHES THAT ARE UNORDERED

An archaeological team is excavating three layers—lower, middle, and upper—of an ancient site. Eight archaeology interns—Francesca, Gerard, Hung, Isabella, Jason, Karim, Laila, and Morton—are to be assigned to work on the layers. Up to four interns can be assigned to each layer. Each intern works on exactly one layer. The requirements for assigning the interns are:

The lower layer must be assigned more interns than the middle layer.

Gerard must be assigned to the same layer as Isabella.

Jason must be assigned to a higher layer than Morton.

Laila must be assigned to the middle layer.

Karim must be assigned to a layer on which no other interns work.

In this game the fixtures are arranged vertically. Earlier you learned about vertical sequence games. This non-sequence game differs slightly. The eight players are distributed among three fixtures, each divided into branches. Also, in this game there are no long strings of relationships. Long strings are found only in sequence games. About 10 percent of ONS-A games are vertical.

Each of the three layers has up to four branches. The setup does not state that each layer must have any certain number of interns, so the diagram initially shows all branches as optional (dotted lines).

For sequence games you learned to make a vertical supplemental diagram for vertical setups. A supplemental diagram is helpful in sequence games because sequence games are based on long sequences of relationships. For this non-sequence game a supplemental diagram is not applicable. You can represent the relationships among players horizontally. In the diagram below, lower is to the left and upper is to the right. See the rule M – J as an example. Jason is above (to the right of) Morton. The designations of lower, middle, and upper partially overlap with the alphabetical range of the players (G through M). Spell out *low*, *mid*, and *up*.

The first rule has been added into the Figure 4.56 diagram, above the fixtures. The space below the fixtures is used only for assignment of players.

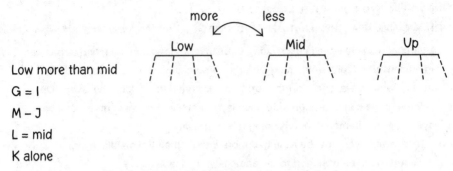

Low more than mid

G = l

M – J

L = mid

K alone

Figure 4.56. Initial diagram. A vertical setup.

The second rule cannot be put directly into the diagram. The third rule shows that Jason must be in a layer above M, so Jason cannot be in the first layer. You can enter –J above Low. The next rule puts Laila into the mid layer. The last rule—that K is alone—tells us that K cannot be in Mid (Laila is there) but also that K cannot be in Low because there must be more players in Low than in Mid. That leaves K in Up. The diagram is now:

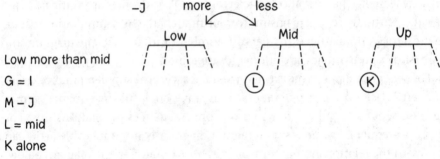

Low more than mid

G = l

M – J

L = mid

K alone

Figure 4.57. The second stage of entering information into the diagram

One branch of Mid and one of Up are now solid lines, with permanent information. Now that there is new information in the diagram (Figure 4.58), go back to the top of the conditions. The first condition indicates that there must be at least two players in Low. Make two branches solid. The second condition still does not go directly into the diagram. The third condition has already been applied. The fourth condition indicates that the last three branches of Up should be crossed out.

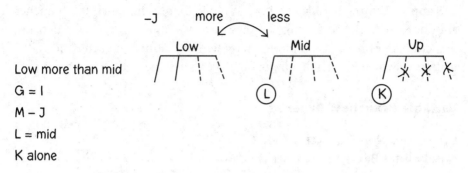

Low more than mid

G = I

M – J

L = mid

K alone

Figure 4.58. The third stage of entering information

Because there is new information in the diagram, go through the conditions again. What are the implications of the first rule? The maximum number of players in Low is four. Therefore, the maximum number of players in Mid is three. The final branch in Mid can be crossed off. It is still not clear how to apply the second rule. Gerard and Isabella could go either in Low or Mid. What about the third rule? Jason cannot go in Low. Mid is a possibility. Up is not a possibility. The final branches have been crossed off and Karim must be alone. Therefore, Jason must go in Mid. Make the second branch of Mid solid. The notation –J above Low is now not needed and can be crossed off.

Go back to the top of the rules again. The first rule now tells us that there must be at least three players under Low. Make one more branch of Low solid. What about the second rule? Gerard and Isabella must go together. What are the options? There is only one space left under Mid and none under Up. They must go under Low. The third rule dictates that M must go under Low. There are six players already accounted for. Two are left—F and H—for which there are no rules. One can go under Low and one under Mid. Make the final branch of Low solid and the third branch of Mid solid.

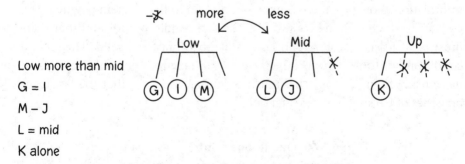

Low more than mid

G = I

M – J

L = mid

K alone

Figure 4.59. Final diagram for vertical game with all conditions entered

Samples 8 through 10 above have variable fixtures in which the branches are unordered. The following samples have variable fixtures in which the branches are ordered. Each branch represents a distinct characteristic and it matters to which branch of a fixture a player is assigned.

Variable Branches: Ordered

ONE-TO-ONE NON-SEQUENCE SAMPLE 11
WITH VARIABLE BRANCHES THAT ARE ORDERED

Six singers—Kovac, Larson, Ming, Nieto, Ofune, and Parsons—will each perform in one of three shows at a single concert. Each show lasts thirty minutes and the first show starts at 7 P.M. The shows run consecutively and do not overlap. Each singer performs exactly once. Each show includes at least one singer. Exactly one singer in each show must sing lead. The assignment of singers conforms to the following:

Either Ming or Nieto must sing lead in the show in which Larson performs.

Either Parsons or Kovac must sing lead in the show in which Ofune performs.

Ofune performs before Larson.

Kovac and Ofune perform in the same show.

One of the branches of each show represents the lead singer. The other branches are variable. Because three players are accounted for by the three solid branches (lead), there are three remaining players to assign to the variable branches. In Figure 4.60, Show$_L$ refers to the show in which Larson performs.

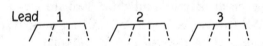

Show$_L$:

    Either M = Lead
      or N = Lead

Show$_O$:

    Either P = Lead
      or K = Lead

    O – L

    K = O

Figure 4.60. One-to-one non-sequence game
with variable branches that are ordered

ONE-TO-ONE NON-SEQUENCE SAMPLE 12
WITH VARIABLE BRANCHES THAT ARE ORDERED

Six singers—Kovac, Larson, Ming, Nieto, Ofune, and Parsons—will each
perform in one of three shows at a single concert. Exactly three accompanists—
Thompson, Ulibarri, and Vanh—are available to accompany the singers.
Each show lasts thirty minutes and the first show starts at 7 P.M. The shows
run consecutively and do not overlap. Each singer performs exactly once.
Each show includes at least one singer and exactly one accompanist.
Each accompanist is in exactly one show. The assignment of singers and
accompanists conforms to the following:

  The show with Vanh takes place before the show with Ulibarri.

  Vanh accompanies exactly one singer.

  The show in which Larson sings takes place before any show in which either
  Ofune performs or Thompson accompanies.

  Kovac cannot perform after any show in which Ming performs.

This game has two sets of players: singers and accompanists. The accompanists cannot be used as fixtures because the order in which they appear matters. The diagram uses the three shows as fixtures. Each show has a required
singer and exactly one required accompanist. However, there may be additional singers, shown by the variable branches.

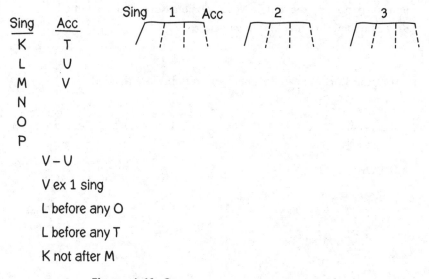

Figure 4.61. One-to-one non-sequence with
two sets of players and variable branches

The last two conditions warrant careful attention. To say that Larson appears before any position in which Thompson appears means that once Thompson appears, Larson cannot appear. The final condition has a similar meaning. Once Ming has appeared, Kovac cannot appear.

No Branches

Some ONS-A games have unbranched fixtures, which makes them look like sequence games. These games tend to use fewer if/then conditions than the ONS-A games with branches. Instead, they rely more on conditions that describe who must come before or after whom and who can, cannot, or must go into which fixture, supplemented by some if/then conditions. These features also make the non-branch games more similar to sequences. The primary difference is that there are not the long strings of relationships.

ONE-TO-ONE NON-SEQUENCE SAMPLE 13 WITH NO BRANCHES

Six singers—Kovac, Larson, Ming, Nieto, Ofune, and Parsons—will each perform in one of six shows at a single concert. Each show lasts thirty minutes and the first show starts at 7 P.M. The shows run consecutively and do not overlap. Each singer performs exactly once. The singers appear according to the following conditions:

Ming performs in a show before Larson.

Ofune performs either immediately before or immediately after Kovac.

Parsons performs either before Nieto or before Kovac, but not both.

Kovac performs in either the first or third show.

The six time slots are the fixtures. No branches are needed.

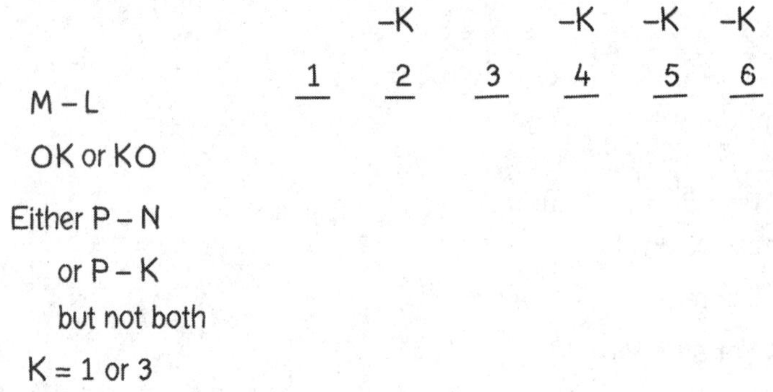

$$-K \qquad -K \quad -K \quad -K$$

1	2	3	4	5	6

M – L

OK or KO

Either P – N

or P – K

but not both

K = 1 or 3

Figure 4.62. One-to-one non-sequence game without branches

ONE-TO-ONE NON-SEQUENCE SAMPLE 14 WITH NO BRANCHES

Four employees of a company—Ferguson, Gray, Ibanez, and Jordan—are scheduled to each take a paid personal retreat during the first ten days of the upcoming month. Each retreat lasts either two or three complete, consecutive days. Each person takes exactly one retreat and, except for the first retreat, each retreat begins when the previous retreat ends. The first retreat begins on the first day of the upcoming month. The following conditions apply:

The retreats of Ferguson and Jordan last three days.

The retreats of Gray and Ibanez last two days.

Gray's retreat must start on an even-numbered day.

If Jordan's retreat is before Gray's, then Ibanez's retreat is before Ferguson's.

In this game there are four time slots—one for each player—but some slots are two days long and others are three days. In addition, it is important whether a player starts on an even- or odd-numbered day. The fixtures consist of all ten days, numbered from the first of the month through the tenth. Note the possible order drawn into the diagram in Figure 4.63. The dashes represent the number of days taken up for the time slot of the particular player.

1	2	3	4	5	6	7	8	9	10
I	–	F	–	–	G	–	J	–	–

F, J = 3 days

G, I = 2 days

G = even

If J – G →
  J – F

Figure 4.63. Unbranched game with unequal lengths for each time slot

On the LSAT you may also see time slots that start on the hour, half hour, or quarter hour. Some slots could last a half hour and others a full hour, or some a quarter hour and others a half hour.

ONE-TO-ONE NON-SEQUENCE SAMPLE 15 WITH NO BRANCHES

Three singers—Kovac, Larson, and Ming—are to perform during a concert. Kovac will perform one jazz piece and one rock piece. Larson will perform one folk piece and one modern piece. Ming will perform one swing piece and one tango piece. The performances run consecutively and do not overlap. The order of the performances follows these conditions:

The jazz piece is performed before the modern piece.

The rock piece is performed before the tango piece.

Ming cannot perform immediately after Larson.

At first you might think that this is not really a one-to-one correspondence game because each player appears twice. Notice how the Figure 4.64 diagram simplifies the game by listing the players as Kovac jazz, Kovac rock, Larson folk, and so on. In this way, there are six distinct players. The singers and types of music are not two separate sets of players. They cannot be "mixed and matched." The conditions pair them up for us and that pairing cannot be changed.

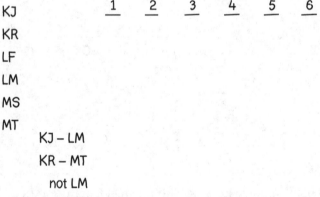

Figure 4.64. Unbranched game with predefined combinations of players and styles

ONE-TO-ONE NON-SEQUENCE SAMPLE 16 WITH NO BRANCHES

Three types of performers—singers, tap dancers, and musicians—are to perform during the eight time slots in an evening concert. There are exactly three singers, three tap dancers, and two musicians. Each performer performs exactly once. Because the setup for each type of performer is time-consuming, the following rules have been set:

There can be no more than three transitions from one type of performer to another during the evening.

The sixth performer cannot be of the same type as the fifth performer.

There are eight players, each used exactly once, but they do not have distinct designations. There are, for example, three singers but the game does not distinguish between the first, second, or third singer. It is important to keep track of how many singers are available for assigning. This game also introduces the concept of a transition between two different types and a limit on the number of transitions allowed.

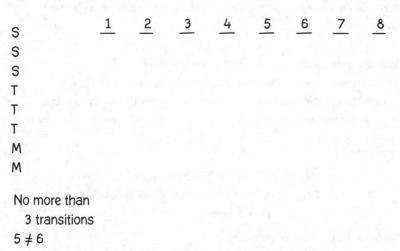

Figure 4.65. Unbranched game with generic types of players

Conditions for Ordered Non-Sequence Games with One-to-One Correspondence

The two tables below show the most common and less common types of conditions for ONS-A games. The test writers can create many variations on the patterns listed here. For the examples below, consider a game in which there are three trips—Grand Canyon, Yosemite, and Zion—and each trip has one guide and two travelers. The order in which the trips take place is important.

CONDITIONS FOR ORDERED NON-SEQUENCE ONE-TO-ONE CORRESPONDENCE GAMES
Most Frequent Conditions, in Relative Order of Frequency

- Howard does not go on the same trip as Leonard.
- Howard goes on the same trip as Leonard.
- Howard goes on the trip to Yosemite.
- Howard's trip takes place before Penny's trip.
- If Howard does not go on the trip to Zion, then Leonard goes on the trip to Yosemite.
- Howard is a guide.
- Howard goes on the trip that takes place second.
- Either Howard or Leonard is the guide on the trip that Penny takes.
- Howard is a guide and is on the same trip as either Leonard or Penny.

CONDITIONS FOR ORDERED NON-SEQUENCE ONE-TO-ONE CORRESPONDENCE GAMES
Less Frequent Conditions

- Howard does not go on the trip to Zion.
- The trip to Grand Canyon takes place before the trip to Yosemite.
- If Howard goes on a trip before Leonard, Howard goes on the trip immediately before Leonard.
- The trip that Howard is on cannot take place after the trip that Leonard is on.
- Howard must be one of the people who goes on a trip with Leonard.
- Howard's trip takes place before Leonard's trip and Penny's trip.
- There are exactly two people on the second trip.
- The trip that Howard is on is before any trip that either Leonard or Penny are on.

- Either Howard is a guide or Leonard is a guide, but not both.
- Howard's trip does not take place until after Leonard's trip.
- Howard is either on the first trip or third trip.
- Howard and Leonard cannot both be guides.
- The trip that Howard is on has exactly three people on it.
- Either Howard and Leonard are both guides or neither is a guide.
- There are exactly three guides and exactly five passengers.

The following conditions are found on games with certain complex relationships:

- The horse that Sanchez races on Day 1 is raced by Telgarsky on Day 2.
- Any beginner must come before the experts' opening speaker.
- All beginners must come before any experts.
- Tap dancing is on the floor immediately above the floor with an oil painting.
- There cannot be two beginners presenting in a row.

Ordered Games Without One-to-One Correspondence

The games in this section fall into the category of ONS-B, as shown in Figure 4.66.

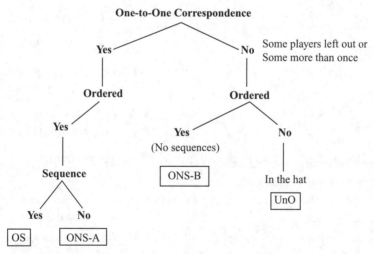

Figure 4.66. The games in this section are in the ONS-B category.

The previous section gave examples of ordered, non-sequence games with one-to-one correspondence (ONS-A). In this section we examine ordered, non-sequence games that are not one-to-one (ONS-B). ONS-B games are similar in many ways to ONS-A games. In the games in the previous section, each player was used exactly once. However, in ONS-B either some players are left out or some are used more than once, and it is important to determine which when setting up an ONS-B game.

ONS-B games may have fixed branches, variable branches, or no branches. Because the number of players in an assignment varies, these games tend to have a higher occurrence of variable branches and may also have variable fixtures.

Draw your own diagram first, before reading the explanation for the samples below.

Fixed fixtures	1 2 3 4	Known number of fixtures
Variable fixtures	1 ... 2 3 4	Number of fixtures can vary
Fixed branches	1 2 3	Known number of branches per fixture
Variable branches	1 2 3	Number of branches per fixture can vary
Unordered branches	1 2 3	Order of branches not important
Ordered branches	a.m. 1 p.m. a.m. 2 p.m. a.m. 3 p.m.	1st branch is distinguished from 2nd branch

Figure 4.67. Summary of variations of fixtures and branches

No Branches

About a third of ONS-B games have no branches. They may, however, have variable fixtures. If only some of the players are used, the unbranched diagram may include a discard pile, as in the unordered ("throw them in the hat") games.

NON-ONE-TO-ONE ORDERED GAMES SAMPLE 1
WITH NO BRANCHES AND FIXED FIXTURES

An office building has seven floors, with floor 1 being the lowest and floor 7 the highest. The seven floors are each occupied by one of seven companies. Each company engages in exactly one of either finance, investment, or management. There is at least one finance, one investment, and one management company in the building. The location of companies is determined by the following conditions:

The third floor can be occupied only by either a finance company or a management company.

There are more finance companies on the top three floors than there are finance companies on the lowest three floors.

At most two investment companies are above the uppermost management company.

There is at least one management company that is immediately between a finance company and an investment company.

This game assigns types of companies (players) to floors (fixtures). The floors are listed from left to right, which represents bottom to top, respectively. A vertical supplemental diagram is not necessary but might help prevent confusion. Each floor gets exactly one company, so there are no branches. It is not known how many times each of the players is used but there must be a total of seven players, so the fixtures are fixed.

An important aspect of this game is that the players—finance, investment, management—actually represent categories of players. You are allowed to use as many finance companies, for example, as the rules allow. In setting up categories of players, the LSAT uses categories such as types of fruits, colors, and trees.

The conditions in this game include if/then statements along with information about the relative order of players.

	Bottom			−I				Top
		1	2	3	4	5	6	7
F								
I								
M								

3 = F or M

5–7 more F
  than 1–3

At most 2 I
  above top M

At least 1 M
  between F and I

Figure 4.68. Non-one-to-one ordered Sample 1.
No branches.

NON-ONE-TO-ONE ORDERED GAMES SAMPLE 2
WITH NO BRANCHES AND DISCARD PILE

Five law students—Franticek, Griselli, Hao, Ionescu, and Jones—are available
to participate in three sessions of a conference on human rights—the morning,
afternoon, and evening sessions. None of the students can attend more than one
session and each session is attended by exactly one of the five students. The
conference manager must assign the students based on the following conditions:

Either Griselli or Jones, but not both, attends one of the sessions.

If Hao attends any session, Ionescu attends the session that immediately
follows.

If Franticek does not attend any session, Griselli attends the evening session.

Jones does not attend the morning session.

In this game only some of the players are used. Exactly three of the five
are used and exactly two are discarded. The conditions are primarily if/then
statements.

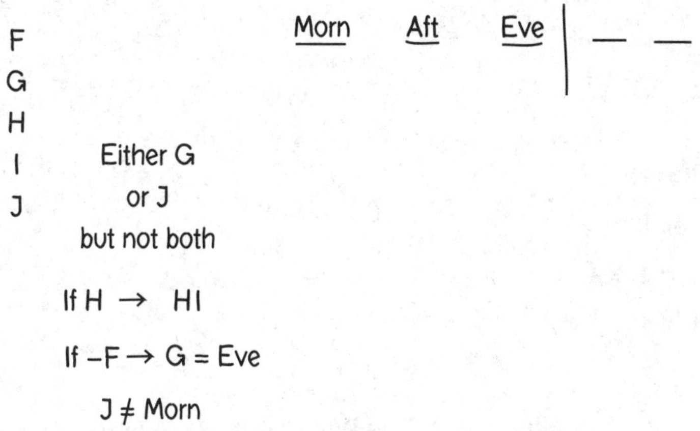

F
G
H
I   Either G
J   or J
       but not both

    If H → HI

    If –F → G = Eve

     J ≠ Morn

Morn   Aft   Eve | — —

Figure 4.69. Non-one-to-one game with
no branches and with a discard pile

NON-ONE-TO-ONE ORDERED GAMES SAMPLE 3
WITH NO BRANCHES AND VARIABLE FIXTURES

During his stay in the hospital, Frederick is able to receive at most one visitor per day from a list that consists of four of his friends: Gerald, Hermione, Inez, and Jackson. Each friend visits him at least once but no friend visits him more than twice. The visits are constrained by the following rules:

Hermione visits exactly once out of the first four visits.

The person who visits third is also the last person to visit.

At least once, Inez visits in the next available time after Gerald.

Each player appears at least once but may also appear a second time. The total number of visits is unknown. The visits—a minimum of four and maximum of eight—are the fixtures. Therefore, the number of fixtures is variable. Notice how the Figure 4.70 diagram shows the minimum and maximum number of visits and uses dots to indicate that the exact number is unknown and variable.

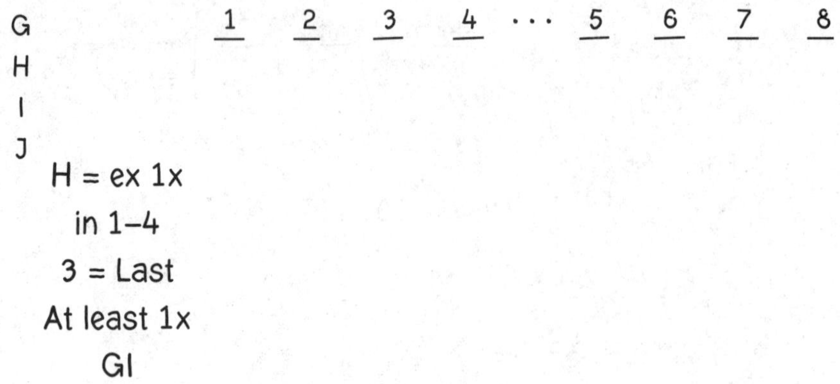

G
H
I
J

| | 1 | 2 | 3 | 4 | ... | 5 | 6 | 7 | 8 |

H = ex 1x

in 1–4

3 = Last

At least 1x

GI

Figure 4.70. Non-one-to-one game with
no branches and variable fixtures

Fixed Branches

About two-thirds of ONS-B games have branches. Most of these have variable branches, but a small number have fixed branches.

Non-One-to-One Ordered Games Sample 4 with Fixed Branches

Three playgrounds—Heights, Midtown, and Uptown—are scheduled to have their equipment repainted. Five colors of paint are available—green, orange, purple, red, and yellow. Each playground is repainted with exactly three colors and each color is used at least once among the three playgrounds. The following conditions apply:

Red is used at Uptown if, but only if, green is used at Heights.

At least one playground uses both orange and purple.

If a playground uses yellow, it also uses green.

Midtown uses orange.

The number of fixtures is known: three (Heights, Midtown, and Uptown). The number of branches is also known. There are exactly three for each fixture, totaling nine branches. Thus, the branches are fixed. However, it is not known how many instances of each color there will be. Each player is used at least once. The first condition is a complex if/then. It is broken into two statements in the diagram. Orange is entered as permanent information (circled) under Midtown.

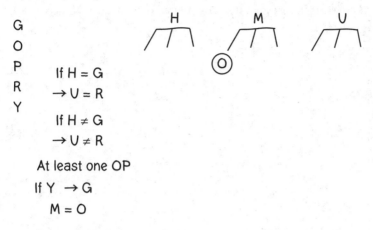

G
O
P
R
Y

If H = G
→ U = R

If H ≠ G
→ U ≠ R

At least one OP

If Y → G
    M = O

Figure 4.71. Non-one-to-one game with fixed branches

Variable Branches

About half of ONS-B games have branches that are variable. This makes sense because in a game without one-to-one correspondence, it may not be known how many times each player appears.

NON-ONE-TO-ONE ORDERED GAMES SAMPLE 5 WITH VARIABLE BRANCHES

Three playgrounds are scheduled to have their equipment repainted on three consecutive days in respective order: Heights, Midtown, and Uptown, one playground per day. Six colors of paint are available: green, magenta, orange, purple, red, and yellow. Each playground is repainted with at least two colors and each color is used at least once among the three playgrounds. The following conditions apply:

If a playground uses red, then it uses neither orange nor purple.

At least one playground uses both orange and purple.

If a playground uses yellow, it also uses green.

Orange is used in the first playground in which green is used.

The first day on which purple is used is some day before the first day on which yellow is used.

No color can be used on two consecutive days.

In this variation on Sample 4, the number of colors that can be used on a given playground is left variable. There must be at least two colors but there could be up to six colors per playground. Also, the playgrounds are painted in a specific time order. Because of this, the conditions can talk about a player (color) appearing before or after another player or about players appearing consecutively.

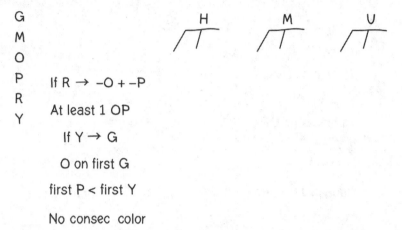

Figure 4.72. Non-one-to-one ordered game with variable fixtures

NON-ONE-TO-ONE ORDERED GAMES SAMPLE 6 WITH VARIABLE BRANCHES

A club's entry in a parade consists of exactly two parts: a pony and a cart. The parts will be decorated with ribbons, each of which has one color. The only possible colors for the ribbons are green, magenta, orange, purple, red, and yellow. One of the parts will have exactly one ribbon color and the other part will consist of a combination of ribbon colors. The decoration must obey the following rules:

If the pony is decorated with a combination of ribbon colors, there are exactly four ribbon colors in the combination.

No ribbon color used to decorate the pony can be used to decorate the cart.

The cart cannot be decorated with any ribbon that is green or yellow.

The pony cannot be decorated with any ribbon that is magenta or purple.

The players in this game are the colored ribbons, or simply colors. It is unknown whether or not each color must appear at least once. This game is unusual in that the two fixtures—pony and cart—take a different number of branches. One has no branches and the other has multiple branches. In addition, in one arrangement the pony may have no branches and in another, the cart may have no branches. This makes the game more complex. In any arrangement one fixture is unbranched but the other fixture has variable branches.

In the diagram, each fixture has one required branch (solid). The number of other branches is unknown. Rather than using dotted lines to represent possible branches, the diagram in Figure 4.73 leaves room for as many branches as may be needed.

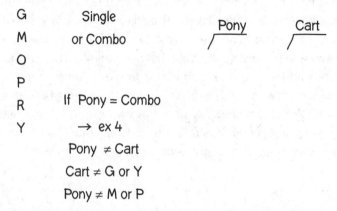

Figure 4.73. Non-one-to-one ordered game with unequal fixtures

Ambiguous Games

Occasionally a game can be set up in different ways depending on which element is considered to be the players and which the fixtures. It is possible that one way results in a one-to-one correspondence game and the other way results in a non-one-to-one correspondence game.

NON-ONE-TO-ONE ORDERED GAMES SAMPLE 7
AMBIGUOUS WITH VARIABLE BRANCHES

Six dancers—Margolies, Newton, Osaka, Perez, Rafik, and Strong—are each to be ranked on a solo performance. There are four possible ranks—one, two, three, or four pluses, with four pluses being the best. The assignment of ranks is constrained by the following conditions:

Each rank is used at least once but no more than twice.

Strong receives exactly two more pluses than Rafik.

At least one dancer receives more pluses than Perez.

Either Osaka receives the same rank as Perez, or else Newton receives the same rank as Strong, but not both.

This game could be diagrammed in two different ways. Because ranks are being assigned to people, the people could be fixtures—all six listed across the top of the diagram. Doing so results in a non-one-to-one game. However, in this game the ranks—one to four pluses—represent an order. Two pluses is better than one plus and two pluses is greater than one plus by a quantity of one. Ordered elements are usually fixtures. The players are assigned to the ordered fixtures.

In Figure 4.74, the ranks are used as fixtures. Each fixture is assigned at least one and up to two players, so the branches are variable. There is one required branch (solid) and one optional branch (dotted). However, each player is assigned exactly once. When organized this way, the game becomes a one-to-one game. Of course, the game itself has not changed. It is just organized differently. This fact highlights the similarities between one-to-one non-sequence ordered games and non-one-to-one ordered games.

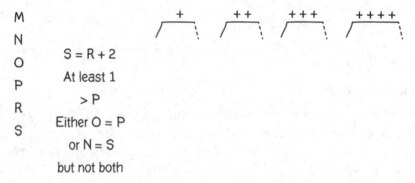

M
N
O   S = R + 2
P   At least 1
R   > P
S   Either O = P
      or N = S
      but not both

Figure 4.74. Ambiguous game that can be one-to-one or non-one-to-one

Conditions for Ordered Non-Sequence Non-One-to-One Correspondence Games

You have seen many of the common conditions in the samples above. The conditions for these games are different from conditions in the one-to-one games—both sequence and non-sequence—because in the non-one-to-one games, some players are left out or players may be used more than once. Conditions give rules about the first occurrence of a player or about which players are options for a certain fixture. Conditions also define who is used and who is not used. Study the conditions below to understand what relationships between players and fixtures the conditions are conveying. The test writers tend to be creative with conditions for the ordered non-one-to-one games. The ONS-B conditions that you see on actual LSATs will be variations on the patterns in previous tests.

Use the list below as a reference, coming back to it as you work on games. You do not need to memorize the list. Glance through the list now to become familiar with it.

CONDITIONS FOR ORDERED NON-SEQUENCE NON-ONE-TO-ONE CORRESPONDENCE GAMES
The conditions below use elements from Sample Game 5.
Variations on conditions are listed in parentheses.

- Red is (not) used at Midtown (or at Uptown).
- Uptown uses red if, but only if, Heights uses yellow.
- Yellow is used at the first playground that uses green.
- Green cannot be used at two playgrounds that are painted consecutively.
- Red is used exactly twice.
- Magenta and purple are the only colors that can be used at Heights.
- There are at least two colors but no more than four colors used at Midtown.
- There is at least one playground that uses both magenta and orange.
- There is at least one color that is used at both Heights and Uptown.
- Each color is used at least twice.
- Either red or green is used on any fixture that uses purple.
- Exactly two fixtures use green (and yellow).
- The first use of red is before the first use of green.
- Heights and Uptown have exactly one color in common.
- If red is (not) used at Midtown, purple is (not) used at Uptown (Midtown).
- If red is (not) used, so (neither) is yellow.
- Red is used more times than magenta is used.
- There is a playground with orange that is painted before any playground with green.
- There is a playground with orange that is painted immediately before a playground with green.

The conditions below use elements from Sample Game 3.
- Exactly once, Gerald visits immediately after Inez.
- Hermione does not visit first.
- At most two people visit after Jackson.
- The first and last visits are by the same person.
- Of the first four visits, exactly one is by Hermione.

The conditions below use elements from Sample Game 2.
- Either Franticek attends or Ionescu attends, but not both.
- If Griselli attends in the afternoon, Hao does not attend.

- If Hao attends, Hao attends in the evening.
- If Jones attends, Ionescu attends.
- If Ionescu attends, Franticek attends the session immediately after Ionescu's session.
- If Griselli does not attend, Hao attends in the evening.

  The conditions below refer to a game in which only some of eight colors are to be chosen and the colors are divided into primary and secondary colors.
- No more than four colors can be chosen.
- If the third place is a primary color, there are exactly four colors chosen.

UNDERSTANDING THE QUESTION TYPES

Each AR setup is followed by a series of questions. Each question consists of the statement of the question—called the **stem**—and the five answer choices. In this section you will learn all the possible types of questions, starting with the four basic types of questions, along with the variation "EXCEPT." Then you will learn certain special question types.

Refer to the following game to illustrate the question types.

SAMPLE SETUP 22

Six geology students—Jones, Kellogg, Lindquist, Ming, Nieto, and Pacheco—are to present papers at a six-day conference. Each student presents exactly one time and only one presentation is given on each day, according to the following conditions:

Jones presents before Ming.

Ming presents before Nieto.

Jones presents either immediately before or immediately after Pacheco.

Pacheco presents before Lindquist.

Either Kellogg presents last or Ming presents before Lindquist, but not both.

The Basic Question Types

The four basic question types are:

1. Could be true
2. Must be true
3. Cannot be true (= Must be false)
4. Could be false

In addition, some of the basic question types can be presented in the form of an EXCEPT statement. The basic questions may sound simple, but it is easy to get confused about what you are looking for, especially after hours of testing. Before you begin trying to solve a question, take time to orient yourself carefully to what the question stem means and how to approach it.

Could Be True

This question type asks you to select the one answer that could be true, given the conditions. What does this mean about the wrong answers? They violate rules. In this question type, four answers violate rules and one does not. Because there are four rule violations, it is helpful with this type of question to start by going through the rules and looking for answer choices that violate them. About 40 percent of all AR questions are **could be true** questions.

> *Example: Which one of the following could be the presenter on the third day?*

Must Be True

This question type asks you to select the one answer that *must* be true. In other words, the conditions force certain assignments, for example that G must go in position 3. Be careful to distinguish this from what *could be true*. In a **must be true** question, what do you know about the wrong answers? It is *not* the case that each wrong answer violates a rule. Some of the wrong answers may violate rules, and any answer that does violate a rule is wrong. However, other wrong answers may be valid possibilities. They are simply not *forced* to be true. About 20 percent of all AR questions are **must be true** questions.

> *Example: If Jones presents on Day 3, which one of the following must present after Kellogg?*

Cannot Be True (= Must Be False)

This question type asks you to select the one answer that CANNOT be true. (The word CANNOT is always written in all capitals to emphasize that the question is asking for a negation of what the test taker would normally look for.) In other words, the correct answer violates rules. The other answer choices could be true. They do not violate rules. Some of the wrong answers may even be forced to be true. Note the two ways that this question can be worded. Combined, these two wordings account for 18 percent of all AR questions, with 15 percent being **cannot be true** and 3 percent being **must be false**.

> *Example: Which one of the following CANNOT be the presenter on Day 4?*

Could Be False

This question asks you to find the one answer that could be false. This means that the other four answers cannot be false. They must be (are forced to be) true. The correct answer either has the option of being true or false or is forced to be false. Barely 1 percent of AR questions are **could be false** questions but they are included here because their logic is similar to the other basic questions.

> *Example: If Ming presents before Lindquist, which of the following could be false?*

Except

The use of the word EXCEPT (it is always written with all capitals) makes a question logically more complex. If someone asks you to identify all the red-heads in a class, you simply look for people with red hair. If someone asks you to identify all the people in the room EXCEPT redheads, you have to keep the criterion "redhead" in your mind and look for the opposite. It is similar to someone telling you, "Think of something that is not an elephant." All you can think of is elephants! With EXCEPT questions, you must (1) identify the criterion, and (2) be careful to remember that you are looking for the *opposite* of the criterion.

In recent LSATs, EXCEPT has been used only in the form of **could be true EXCEPT** and **must be true EXCEPT**. The former accounts for about 5 percent of all AR questions. The latter has only occurred a few times in recent years. In a **could be true EXCEPT** question, four of the answers could be true. The remaining answer is the correct one. It cannot be true. In other words, the correct answer violates one or more rules. In a **must be true EXCEPT** question, four of the answers are forced to be true. The remaining answer is one that is not forced to be true. It may be an answer that could be true or it may violate rules.

> Example: *Each of the following could be true EXCEPT:*
> Example: *If Nieto presents last, each of the following must be true*
> *EXCEPT:*

Table 4.3 shows the characteristics of the correct answer and the incorrect answers for each of these basic question types.

Table 4.3. Characteristics of Correct and Incorrect Answers

	Correct Answer	**Four Incorrect Answers**
Could be true	Does not violate rules	Violate rules
Must be true	Forced to be true	Could be true or violate rules
Cannot be true **(= Must be false)**	Violates rules	Do not violate rules
Could be false	Could be true or violates rules	Forced to be true
Could be true **EXCEPT**	Violates rules	Do not violate rules
Must be true **EXCEPT**	Could be true or violates rules	Forced to be true

Special Question Types

The basic question types, discussed above, account for about 85 percent of AR questions. There are over a dozen special types of questions that appear less frequently but with which it is important for you to be familiar. The special types include many of the more complex and challenging questions. These are the questions that will help you get your maximum score.

Complete and Accurate List

Some questions use the wording "complete and accurate list" or sometimes just "accurate list." This wording may simply refer to a complete assignment of players. For example, a complete assignment could be Kellogg, Pacheco, Jones, Ming, Lindquist, and Nieto. This is called a complete list because it does not exclude any player who could appear, and it is called an accurate list because it does not include any rule violations.

The wording "complete and accurate list" can also be used in a different way. Consider the question "Which one of the following is a complete and accurate list of people who could give the first presentation?" In this case the correct answer is not a complete assignment (six players in their specified order). Consider the following answer choices, which refer to **Sample Setup 22**.

(A) Jones
(B) Jones, Kellogg
(C) Jones, Kellogg, Pacheco
(D) Jones, Lindquist, Kellogg, Pacheco
(E) Lindquist, Kellogg, Pacheco

Only Jones, Kellogg, and Pacheco can present first. Only choice C can be the correct answer. Choices A and B are accurate (i.e., everyone in A and B can be first) but are not complete. Choice D is complete (it includes everyone who needs to be in the list) but is not accurate (Lindquist violates rules). Choice E is inaccurate (Lindquist violates rules) and incomplete (it is missing Jones).

In the above example, the complete and accurate list consisted of players. Some questions may ask for a complete and accurate list of fixtures to which a player may be assigned.

EXAMPLE

Which one of the following is a complete and accurate list of positions in which Jones can give her presentation?

(A)   1, 2
(B)   1, 3
(C)   1, 2, 3
(D)   2, 3, 4
(E)   1, 2, 3, 4, 5

Only choice C is both complete and accurate. The other answer choices either include fixtures that would result in rule violations or leave out fixtures in which Jones could present. A similar question might ask for a complete and accurate list of fixtures to which both Jones and Pacheco could be assigned or for a complete and accurate list of players who could be assigned to the third spot if Jones is assigned to the first spot.

Completely Determined If

Consider the following question:

EXAMPLE

If Lindquist does not present last, the order in which the students present their papers is completely determined if which one of the following is true?
(A) Lindquist presents fifth.
(B) Ming presents third.
(C) Pacheco presents first.
(D) Jones presents third.
(E) Kellogg presents fourth.

In this question type, when the information in the correct answer is put into the diagram, the rules determine exactly who must be in each remaining position, with no other options. To solve this type of question, test the answer choices by putting the information from that choice into the diagram. Then apply the rules to see if the assignment to every fixture is uniquely determined. The correct answer to the above question is choice D. About 3.5 percent of all AR questions are *completely determined if* questions and these questions appear on two thirds of recent tests.

There are several variations on the wording "completely determined." You may also see "completely resolved," "fully determined," "fully and uniquely determined," and "there is exactly one order if . . ."

Other *If* Questions

The completely determined questions are based on the consequences *if* each of the answer choices were true. Very rarely, there is a question that, rather than asking for a completely determined order, asks for a specific fact that would be true if one of the answer choices were true.

Ming presents third if which one of the following is true?

Equivalent Condition

This type asks you to replace a specific original condition with an answer choice that has the same result as the original condition. Consider the following question:

EXAMPLE

Which one of the following, if substituted for the condition that Pacheco presents before Lindquist, would have the same effect in determining the order in which the students present?

(A)   Pacheco presents before Kellogg.

(B)   Pacheco presents either immediately before or immediately after Lindquist.

(C)   Lindquist presents last.

(D)   Jones presents before Lindquist.

(E)   There is exactly one student who presents between Pacheco and Linquist.

To solve an **equivalent condition** question, you must be sure that your answer accomplishes all of the results of the original condition without adding any additional restrictions. In the above example, choice A does not necessarily result in Pacheco presenting before Lindquist. In choice B, Pacheco and Lindquist are adjacent, so Pacheco might be before Lindquist but might also be after. This answer is not restrictive enough. In choice C, Pacheco is before Lindquist but this answer imposes an additional restriction—that Lindquist presents in position 6—that is, not in the original conditions. The answer is too restrictive. In choice D, Jones presents before Lindquist. Because the only two possible configurations for Jones and Pacheco are JP or PJ, the result is JP – L or PJ – L. In both cases, P presents before Lindquist without any additional restrictions being introduced.

Equivalent condition questions have appeared on every recent test but there is usually only one per AR section, usually the last question in a passage.

How Many

Three minor question types ask you to find the number of possibilities that exist in a certain situation. The answer choices are numbers.

For How Many Can It Be Determined?

Consider the following example:

If Kellogg presents last, then for exactly how many of the total students can it be determined in which time slot he or she presents?

(A) two
(B) three
(C) four
(D) five
(E) six

In this question, new information is given—*Kellogg presents last*—and as a result, some players are forced into a specific position. You must calculate how many players are forced into one specific position and how many have options. Theoretically, you could get a question like this without new information.

A slight variation asks for how many players is the choice of fixtures limited to one or two. Both variations are rare. The latter variation has only appeared once in recent years.

How Many Orders Are There?

This question type asks you how many different valid assignments exist. The question may give additional information.

If Lindquist is the third presenter, then how many orders are there in which the remaining students could appear?

(A) one
(B) two
(C) three
(D) four
(E) five

This question type is rare but has been introduced recently and may appear again.

How Many Players for a Specific Fixture?

This question type refers to a specific fixture. The question might or might not provide new information. You must determine how many players could be assigned to the specified fixture. This question type does not ask you to identify the players—only to count them.

EXAMPLE

Exactly how many students are there any one of whom could present sixth?

(A) one

(B) two

(C) three

(D) four

(E) five

The question refers to the sixth fixture. No new information is given. A similar question could ask *If Kellogg presents last, exactly how many students are there any one of whom could present third?* In this case new information is given.

The **how many** questions account for about 2.5 percent of all AR questions. More than half of those are **how many players for a specific fixture**. This type appears in about half of all recent LSATs.

One or Both of a Pair

In a few special question types the answer choices consist of pairs of players.

At Least One Is In

In the answer choices for this type of question, at least one of the members of the pair must be included in the assignment.

SAMPLE QUESTION 2

A law professor will choose four law students from a group of eight—Frantishek, Goldstein, Hong, Ibarrez, Jackson, Kelly, Lovato, and Ma—to attend a conference on ethics. The following conditions apply:

If Goldstein is chosen, neither Jackson nor Kelly can be chosen.

If Kelly is not chosen, Hong must be chosen.

If Ma is chosen, Hong is not chosen.

If Jackson is not chosen, then both Goldstein and Frantishek are chosen.

Which one of the following is a pair of students of which the professor must choose at least one?

(A) Goldstein and Hong

(B) Jackson and Lovato

(C) Jackson and Hong

(D) Goldstein and Lovato

(E) Jackson and Kelly

Answer: The key to this question type is to understand that for the correct answer, it is not possible that both members be excluded. This question type is used with a game that has a discard pile. To test an answer, try to put both members of the pair in the discard pile. Test choice C. If Jackson and Hong are both out, then Goldstein is in. If Goldstein is in, Kelly is out. If Kelly is out, Hong must be in. However, Hong is in the discard pile. If a rule violation results, the two members cannot both be out and therefore, at least one of them must be in. Choice C is the correct answer. This question type accounts for slightly less than 1 percent of questions.

Both Can Be Out

In this question type the answer choices represent a pair of players both of whom *can* be together in the discard pile. This is the opposite of the previous type, in which the correct answer is a pair that *cannot* both be in the discard pile. In this type of question, four of the answer choices result in rule violations. One, the correct answer choice, does not result in a violation.

EXAMPLE

A pair of students who are not chosen to go to the conference could be

(A) Jackson and Hong

(B) Jackson and Goldstein

(C) Jackson and Frantishek

(D) Kelly and Lovato

(E) Kelly and Hong

Test each pair by putting it in the discard pile and determining what else must be true. Only Kelly and Lovato can be in the discard pile together. Each of the other pairs results in a rule violation.

Both Fixtures Can Be

In this rare type of question the answer choices also consist of pairs, but the pairs represent fixtures. Consider the following, which refers back to the game introduced in the beginning of the section:

EXAMPLE

Which one of the following is a pair of presentation slots both of which could be taken by Jones?

(A) 1 and 2

(B) 1 and 5

(C) 2 and 5

(D) 3 and 6

(E) 4 and 6

The correct answer consists of a pair of fixtures both of which could have a certain player (in this case, Jones) assigned to them. The pair need not be a complete list of the fixtures to which Jones can be assigned. In other words, choice A is correct even though Jones could also be assigned to slot 3. In the incorrect answers, one or both of the fixtures listed in the pair would result in a rule violation if Jones were assigned to that fixture.

Many other types of questions have pairs in the answer choices. The types explained above are distinctive in that they force you to decide if one or both members of the pair meet a certain criterion.

What Is the Minimum/Maximum Number?

This question type asks for the maximum or minimum number of players that are included in a valid assignment. A **minimum/maximum** question is usually only asked in a game in which the number of fixtures is variable.

SAMPLE QUESTION 3

Judges will choose from among six singers—Robert, Sandra, Tomas, Uma, Vincente, and Yuki—to determine who will be asked to audition for an upcoming performance. At least one singer but no more than five singers must be chosen. The following rules apply:

If Robert is chosen, then either Uma or Tomas is chosen, but not both.

If Uma is not chosen, Sandra is chosen.

If Yuki is chosen, Tomas is not chosen.

If Vincente is chosen, either Robert is chosen or Yuki is chosen, but not both.

1. What is the maximum possible number of singers who can be chosen?
   (A) five
   (B) four
   (C) three
   (D) two
   (E) one

2. What is the minimum number of singers who must be chosen if Robert is chosen?
   (A) one
   (B) two
   (C) three
   (D) four
   (E) five

Answer: In this game there must be at least one fixture and can be up to five. The first question is based solely on the original conditions. Based on these conditions, there is no combination of five singers that does not violate rules. (Test this by putting one player at a time in the discard pile by itself and testing the set of five remaining players.) The correct answer is choice B, four players. The second question gives new information. If Robert is chosen, Uma or Thomas is chosen. If Uma is chosen, the assignment is complete and accurate, so it is possible to have only two singers. Choice B is correct. **Minimum/maximum** questions account for barely 1 percent of all AR questions and the majority of those are **maximum** questions.

What Is the Earliest/Latest?

This question type asks you to identify the earliest or latest place in the sequence of fixtures that a player could appear. The example refers to Sample Setup 22.

EXAMPLE

The earliest Nieto could present is
(A) second
(B) third
(C) fourth
(D) fifth
(E) sixth

The order of players includes the sequences JP – M – N or PJ – M – N. Based on this sequence alone, Nieto cannot present until three other players have presented.

Similarly,

EXAMPLE

What is the latest time slot in which Jones can present?
(A) sixth
(B) fifth
(C) fourth
(D) third
(E) second

Jones has at least two other players who must follow and based on that alone, choices A and B are eliminated. Testing Jones in fourth place results in a rule violation. Pacheco must go in position 3 and this violates the rule P – L. The correct answer is D.

Earliest/latest questions are very rare. They have only occurred twice—once each—in recent years. However, the concept of earliest and latest position is an important one. In questions such as "Which one of the following cannot present fifth?" you need to calculate the earliest or latest that various players can appear.

New Information

As you read each question stem, determine if the question

1. does not provide new information, or
2. provides new information that can be entered directly into the main diagram, or
3. provides new information that cannot be entered directly into the main diagram, or
4. adds or modifies an original condition.

If there is no new information, answer the question based on the original conditions. New information that can be entered in the diagram includes facts such as *Kellogg presents sixth* that tell exactly to which fixture a player is assigned. Facts such as *Lindquist presents before Ming* give you new information but do not tell you where in the diagram either player goes. For such facts, use supplemental diagrams or temporary rules to keep track of the information.

A question may modify an original condition—for example, *If the original condition requiring Pacheco to present before Lindquist were changed to require Lindquist to present before Pacheco, which one of the following could be true?* A question may also add a new condition, such as *If Jones were required to perform before Lindquist, which one of the following must be true?* In both cases, use temporary supplemental diagrams and temporary rules. Cross out these temporary notes before you go to the next question. Remember that new information in a question applies only to that question.

Table 4.4 shows how common or rare each question type is. The first column shows what percentage of all recent AR questions the type constitutes. The second column shows in what percentage of recent tests the type has occurred. The third column shows whether the question type is becoming more common or less common on the most recent LSATs.

Table 4.4. Frequency of AR Question Types

	Percent of All AR Questions	Percent of All Recent Tests in Which the Type Occurs	Current Trends: Is This Type Becoming More Common or Less Common?
Could be true	41	100	No change
Must be true	21	100	No change
Cannot be true (= Must be false)	15	100	No change
Must be false (= Cannot be true)	3	53	Less common
Could be false	0.8	13	No change
Could be true EXCEPT	5	53	No change
Must be true EXCEPT	0.6	13	Less common
Complete and accurate list	1.5	27	More common
Completely determined if	3.5	60	Less common
Equivalent condition	2.3	47	More common
How many?	2.6	40	More common
One or both of a pair	1.5	20	More common
What is the minimum/maximum?	1.2	20	Less common
What is the earliest/latest?	0.6	13	Less common

How Question Types Are Distributed Among Each Type of Game

The question types do not show up equally in all four types of games. For example, a *cannot be true* question with new information that goes in the diagram can appear only in a *sequence* game or an *unordered* game. At the same time, a *cannot be true* game with new information that is *not* in the diagram can appear only in an ONS-A game. Some types of questions do not appear at all for certain types of games. Table 4.5 shows the question types that have such restrictions. You do not need to memorize this information, but these facts may help you orient yourself to a game more quickly. The "New Information" column refers to whether the question type uses no new information, new information that goes in diagram, new information that does not go in diagram, or all three.

Five of the rows below are associated with only one type of game. There are five other rows that are excluded from exactly one type of game. For most of the latter, it is the unordered games in which they cannot appear. Question type and new information combinations not listed below can appear with any type.

Table 4.5. Question Types with Restrictions on the Game Type with Which They Can Appear

Question Type	New Information?	Cannot Appear With	Only Appears With
One of a pair	All	Sequence, ONS-A, ONS-B	Unordered
Cannot be true	New in diagram	ONS-A, ONS-B	Sequence, unordered
Cannot be true	New NOT in diagram	Sequence, ONS-B, unordered	ONS-A
Could be true	New NOT in diagram	ONS-A	Sequence, ONS-B, unordered
Could be false	All	ONS-A, unordered	Sequence, ONS-B
Could be true EXCEPT	New in diagram	ONS-B, unordered	Sequence, ONS-A
Could be true EXCEPT	No new info	ONS-B, unordered	Sequence, ONS-A
Could be true EXCEPT	New NOT in diagram	Unordered	Sequence, ONS-A, ONS-B
How many	All	Unordered	Sequence, ONS-A, ONS-B
Must be false	New in diagram	Sequence, ONS-B, unordered	ONS-A
Must be false	New NOT in diagram	Unordered	Sequence, ONS-A, ONS-B
Must be false	No new info	ONS-A, unordered	Sequence, ONS-B
Must be true	No new info	Unordered	Sequence, ONS-A, ONS-B
Must be true EXCEPT	All	ONS-A, ONS-B	Sequence, unordered
What is the maximum	All	Sequence, ONS-A	ONS-B, Unordered
What is the minimum	All	Sequence, ONS-A, ONS-B	Unordered
What is the earliest/latest	All	ONS-A, ONS-B, unordered	Sequence

🔑 HOW TO SOLVE THE QUESTIONS: A SYSTEMATIC APPROACH

The secret to a perfect score on the games is to develop a systematic approach. Most test takers, when faced with a tough AR question, grasp at straws. They haphazardly put various elements into the diagram. They lose track of what works, what does not, and even of what they have already done. Often test takers go in circles, not getting closer to an answer. Eventually they give up.

With a systematic approach you know what tools you have available. You know when to use each tool, and you know in what order to use your tools. *Every* AR question can be efficiently solved with the right sequence of tools.

The Problem-Solving Tools

There are four major categories of tools for solving AR questions. There are also four supporting tools. Read through this section so that you become comfortable with the tools presented here. Refer back to this section as you work questions.

CATEGORIES OF PROBLEM-SOLVING TOOLS

The Major Categories of Tools
Applying the rules
Working with the answer choices
Using the main diagram
Using supplemental diagrams

The Supporting Tools
Enough to answer the question?
Most restricted players
What rules apply to a given player?
What are the options for a player or fixture?

Applying the Rules

One of the most powerful problem-solving tools is using the rules to evaluate answer choices and diagrams. There are three ways to do this.

Questions with Four Rule Violations: The Typical First Question

For some questions, four of the answer choices violate rules. In fact, in most—but not all—games, the first question in a set has five answer choices that contain possible complete assignments and asks you to find the one answer that could be true. This means the other four answer choices violate rules.

Test takers are often tempted to read through an answer choice and then check the rules to see whether the answer violates any rules. You will get to the answer more quickly if you use a different strategy. Start by looking at the first rule (not the first answer choice). It is important to work systematically. If you start with the rule that pops into your head first, you will have a harder time remembering what you have already tested. Start at the top of your list of rules and work each rule, one at a time, in order, from top to bottom.

When you look at the first rule, identify what a violation of that rule would look like. For example, for a rule *If John is chosen, Mary is not chosen*, a violation would consist of John being in the answer and Mary also being in. Now scan all five answers to see whether any choices violate the rule. Typically, for each rule there is one answer that violates it, although there are sometimes two or more answers that violate it. By carefully going through all the rules, you will quickly eliminate four answer choices, and the correct answer will be revealed.

The advantage of starting with the rules is that you can keep one rule in mind as you scan the answers. If you start with an answer choice and scan all of the rules for a violation, you have to orient yourself to each rule multiple times.

For any question in which there are four answers that violate the rules, start with the rules and look for violations. On the other hand, if only one of the answer choices violates a rule, there are other strategies that are more efficient. These are discussed below.

Use the Rules to Fill in Your Diagrams

When a question gives you new information—for example, *Gonzales is in place 3*—your first task is to put that information into the diagram and then fill in anything else that follows from the rules. Start *only* with information that *must* be true. There is a time and place for filling in options, but most test takers confuse themselves by mixing *necessary* information with *possible* information. Put Gonzales in 3. Scan the rules, starting at the top and working down one by one. A rule lower down may jump into your mind first, especially if it has to do with Gonzales. It is all right to work with that rule first, but then go back to the top, to the first rule. For each rule, ask yourself if there is any way in which that rule applies to what is in the diagram. If the rule does not clearly lead to something that must be true, move on to the next rule.

Suppose that there is a rule *If Gonzales is in 3, then Jasper is in 5*. Put Jasper in 5. Now you have new information in the diagram and so you should go back to the top of the rules again. Maybe when you looked at the first rule before, it did not apply, but now that Jasper is in 5, the first rule may give you new information. As you add players into your diagram, go through the rules again until the rules provide no new information.

Test an Assignment for Validity

Another way to use the rules to solve a problem is to test a certain assignment, such as an assignment that is given in one of the answer choices, and apply the rules to that assignment. In that way you can determine whether the assignment you are testing is valid or breaks rules. Consider the following question:

> *Which one of the following is a student who could present third?*
> *A. Jones*

To test choice A, put J in 3 and then apply the rules to see what else must be true. In order to prove that J can go in 3, you need to fill in the assignment in a way that you believe does not violate the rules. It is easy to make a mistake, so as a double check, once you have filled in an assignment that seems to work, apply the rules to test your assignment. Start with the first rule—at the top—and check it and each subsequent rule carefully against your assignment. If you have inadvertently created a rule violation, this process will find it.

Working with the Answer Choices

The second major problem-solving category is working with answer choices. There are five specific tools you can use to work with answer choices: scanning answers, testing answers, checking answers for violations, checking answers against the diagrams, and checking answers against previous viable assignments.

Scanning Answers

Often one of the first steps is to scan the answer choices. In scanning you are looking quickly at the answers. Scanning may show you an obvious rule violation. It may give you ideas of other strategies you can use. It may give you a sense of what answer choices are most likely to violate rules or to be forced to be true. Testing those answers first can save you time.

Testing Answers

When you test an answer choice, work systematically. It takes time and concentration to do this accurately, so it is important to first identify choices that can be eliminated and then to scan the answers to decide which remaining answers should be tested first. Answer choices can sometimes be eliminated by applying the rules and/or by checking answers against valid assignments that are either in your notes or in previous questions. If you have no clear idea of which answers to test first, start at the top of the remaining answers.

Could be true. If you are testing an answer choice to determine whether it *could* be true, either show that the answer would lead to a rule violation, and thus eliminate it, or use the answer to create a viable assignment.

SAMPLE QUESTION 4

Six students—Jefferson, King, Li, Montoya, Nussbaum, and Olivier—are to present papers, one student at a time, during six consecutive time slots.

Jefferson presents before King.

King presents before Nussbaum but after Li.

Olivier cannot present first.

Which one of the following is a pair of students who could present first and second, respectively?

(A)   King, Olivier

(B)   Montoya, King

(C)   Olivier, Jackson

(D)   Jackson, Li

(E)   Li, Nussbaum

Answer: Test choice A. Put K in first place and O in second place. Look for a rule violation. This order violates the rule *Jefferson presents before King.* Choice A is out because you have found a clear rule violation. Now test choice D. Put J and L in the first and second places, respectively. Check for a rule violation. Most likely you will not see a violation. At this point you cannot be sure if there is no violation or if you have simply not spotted a violation that exists. In general, if you prove that a certain fact leads to a rule violation, that proof is conclusive. However, if you create an assignment that does not *seem* to violate rules, there is still the possibility that you have missed a violation. For this reason, showing that a certain assignment is possible is never as conclusive as showing that an assignment violates rules. All you can say about a possible assignment is that you "think" it works. For this reason, it is helpful to find all the violations first.

Cannot be true. If you are looking for an answer choice that *cannot* be true, then four of the answer choices are viable assignments. Some may even be required to be true. It is still more conclusive to look for the one viola-tion, rather than to prove that the other answers could be true. As you test an answer, look at it quickly to see if it looks like it might work.

Referring to **Sample Question 4**, consider this question:

EXAMPLE

Which of the following is a pair of students who CANNOT present in the fifth and sixth positions, respectively?

(A)   King, Nussbaum

(B)   Nussbaum, Montoya

(C)   Montoya, Olivier

(D)   King, Olivier

(E)   Nussbaum, Olivier

Test choice A. Put K in fifth and N in sixth. There are no clear violations. Is it possible to fill in the remaining spaces in a way that creates a viable order? If you try to fill in an order, it will take a lot of time and once you have an order that you think may work, it takes more time to test it. Instead of filling in an order, evaluate whether there seem to be possibilities for creating a viable order. K and N are already assigned at the end of the sequence. J and L will not violate rules no matter where you put them. O and M do not have any restric-tions, other than that O cannot go first. There seem to be many options for creating a viable order. It only takes a moment to make this evaluation. You have shown that choice A is *probably* out. Move on to choice B. This strategy is helpful when four answer choices are viable.

When you get to the correct answer (the one that *does* violate a rule) the violation will, hopefully, be clear and you will have saved time. If all of the answer choices seem viable, then you have missed a violation in one of them and have to go back and test each answer choice in more detail. To do that, fill in a complete assignment and then go back to the rules—starting systemati-cally at the top—and check the assignment against all of the rules.

Must be true. If you are looking for an answer that *must* be true, then four of the answers either violate rules or could be true. The correct answer is forced to be true. Testing an answer choice to see if it must be true is tricky. Consider the game with the geology students that was introduced earlier in this chapter.

GAME WITH GEOLOGY STUDENTS

Six geology students—Jones, Kellogg, Lindquist, Ming, Nieto, and Pacheco—are to present papers at a six-day conference. Each student presents exactly one time and only one presentation is given on each day.

Jones presents before Ming.

Ming presents before Nieto.

Jones presents either immediately before or immediately after Pacheco.

Pacheco presents before Lindquist.

Either Kellogg presents last or Ming presents before Lindquist but not both.

QUESTION

If Kellogg presents sixth, which one of the following must be true?

(A)   Jones presents first.

(B)   Pacheco presents first.

(C)   Pacheco presents second.

(D)   Lindquist presents third.

(E)   Nieto presents fourth.

First, put K in 6. Now apply the rules. If K is in 6, the last rule tells you that L presents before M. M and N must go in 4 and 5, respectively. How would you test choice A? You want to prove or disprove that Jones must present first. What happens if you put J in 1? P must go next to J, which means in 2. There is only one place left for L, in 3. Test this assignment against the rules. There are no violations. Everything works. What have you proven? Only that J *could* go in 1. You have not proven that J *must* go in 1. This is a critical point in working with a *must* question.

To test an answer choice in a *must* question, you cannot simply put the answer into the diagram and show that it works. To prove that J *must* go in 1, you have to show that putting J any place *other* than 1 results in a violation. At this point you have MNK in 4–6. The only other options for J (besides 1) are 2 and 3. Put J in 3. What are the options for L? None. L has to come after J. You have proven that J cannot go in 3. However, you have *not* proven that J must go in 1. You must test J in 2. To show that Jones *must* go in 1 means showing that J cannot go in *any* other slot.

Put J in 2. P goes in 1. L goes in 3. Check this assignment against the rules. No rules are broken. You have proven that J does *not* have to go in 1, because J *can* go in 2.

Test choice D. Put L in any position other than 3. Every slot other than L in 3 violates rules. L *must* go in 3. Choice D is the answer.

Check Answers for Violations

In working with answer choices, you often have to test them for rule violations. Even though you may have started with the rules and eliminated answer choices that violate specific rules, there may be answer choices whose rule violations only show up when you consider more complex combinations of rules.

SAMPLE QUESTION 5

Four types of trees are to be planted in a new park. The seven available types of trees are Fraxinus, Ginkgo, Juniperus, Kalmia, Larix, Morus, and Poncirus. The trees must be chosen according to the following rules:

If Fraxinus is chosen, Kalmia is not chosen.

If Kalmia is chosen, Larix is chosen.

Either Fraxinus or Morus is chosen but not both.

If Ginkgo is chosen, either Morus is chosen or Larix is not chosen, but not both.

If Ginkgo is chosen, which one of the following statements could be true?

(A) Fraxinus and Kalmia are chosen.

(B) Kalmia is chosen and Larix is not chosen.

(C) Fraxinus and Morus are chosen.

(D) Fraxinus is chosen and Larix is chosen.

(E) Morus and Larix are both chosen.

Answer: Because four answers violate rules, start with the rules and look for violations. For the first rule, a violation would have F chosen and K also chosen. Choice A violates this. A violation of the second rule would have F chosen and L not chosen. Choice B violates the second rule. A violation of the third rule would have both F and M. Choice C violates the third rule.

A violation of the last rule would have both M chosen and L not chosen. There is no answer choice that specifically says *Morus is chosen and Larix is not chosen*. All the rules have been tested but there are still two choices remaining, D and E. One of the two must contain a violation but that violation is most likely based on a combination of rules. In order to detect a more complex rule, you must check the answer choices for violations.

Test choice D. Create a diagram, putting G in. Put both F and L in. Check the rules to see if a violation has already been created. If F is in, K must be out. Put K in the discard pile. The second rule does not apply because K is not in. Apply the third rule. F is in, so M must be out. Put M in the discard pile. Apply the final rule. M is not in, so the second half of the rule must apply, namely that L must be out. However, L is already in. Answer choice D violates the rules but the violation is not clear without testing the answer choice.

By starting with an answer choice and testing it against the rules, you can spot these more complex violations. The difference between (1) applying the rules to the answers and (2) checking the answers against the rules is a difference of the direction in which you are working.

Check the Answers Against the Diagrams

For many questions, you will create one or more diagrams of partial or complete assignments before you even begin looking at the answer choices. Diagrams represent things that must be true, along with some things that could be true. Once you have finished the diagrams, you can check the answer choices against the diagrams. Some answers may violate the information that must or could be true and these answers can be eliminated. The diagrams can also verify that a particular answer must be correct.

Check the Answers Against Previous Valid Assignments

Consider the following question, which refers to the game with the geology students:

EXAMPLE

> If Lindquist presents before Ming, which one of the following is a time slot in which Nieto can present?
> (A) first
> (B) second
> (C) third
> (D) fifth
> (E) sixth

The condition that L presents before M means that K presents sixth. In an earlier question we created a valid assignment that met that condition: JPLMNK. In that assignment, N presents fifth, so we have proof that N can present in the fifth position. The correct answer is choice D.

In other cases you can use previous valid assignments to eliminate certain answers. For example, consider a question that asks which must be true. If choice A reads *Pacheco presents third*, you can prove that choice A is out because in the valid assignment in the previous paragraph, P did *not* present third.

Because the answer to a typical first question for a game contains a full assignment, you can use that answer to test answers on other questions. (If you often have trouble getting the typical first question correct, do not use this strategy.) Also, use the valid assignments that you create in your diagram. Be careful to cross out any assignments that you try that result in rule violations.

This strategy works best when a question does not present new information. However, if a question does present new information and the answer to the typical first question matches that new information, this tool may help.

Using the Main Diagram

The third category of problem-solving tools is to use the main diagram. The main diagram is your most powerful tool for working through possibilities.

What Must Be True

When you start creating assignments, only put the information that must be true, if there is any. Referring to the geology game:

EXAMPLE

If Lindquist presents third, all of the following must be true EXCEPT:
  (A)   Nieto presents fifth.
  (B)   Ming presents fourth.
  (C)   Jones presents first.
  (D)   Pacheco presents before Nieto.
  (E)   Lindquist presents before Ming.

Put L in 3. P must appear before L and J must be adjacent to P. Therefore, M cannot be before L and so K must be in 6. Because L comes before M, there is the sequence L–M–N. M and N must be in 4 and 5, respectively. Check the rules. There is nothing else that must be true. The placement of J and P is optional. Leave the diagram as blank-blank-LMNK. Check the answer choices against the diagram. All answers must be true except C. J could present first but is not required to be first.

What Could Be True

For the above question it was not necessary to deal with the optional information—the placement of J and P. If entering only what must be true does not give you enough information to solve the question, use strategies for systematically showing options that could be true. At every point in the problem-solving process, you should be clear on whether you are looking for optional information or required information. Confusing the two is the cause of many errors. The question below requires entering options.

EXAMPLE

If Ming presents fourth and Kellogg presents before at least one other student, which of the following could be true?

(A) Pacheco presents first and Kellogg does not present third.

(B) Kellogg presents second and Nieto presents third.

(C) Kellogg presents first and Jones presents third.

(D) Jones presents first and Kellogg presents second.

(E) Pacheco presents first and Jones presents third.

Put M in 4. The rules do not provide the exact location of any of the other players. The last rule does tell us that if K is not in 6, L must come after M. The second rule tells us that N presents after M. There are only two places in the diagram after M so L and N must be assigned to 5 and 6, but we do not know in which order. Notice the notation used in Figure 4.75.

$$\underset{1}{\underline{\quad}} \quad \underset{2}{\underline{\quad}} \quad \underset{3}{\underline{\quad}} \quad \underset{\text{M}}{\underline{\quad}} \quad \underset{\text{L/N}}{\underline{\quad}} \quad \underset{\text{N/L}}{\underline{\quad}}$$

Figure 4.75. Diagram showing options in 5 and 6

The notation L/N indicates that either L or N could appear in 5. In 6, the notation is reversed—N/L. This indicates that if L is put in 5, N is put in 6. It is also fine to call 5 N/L and 6 L/N. It is not necessary to know exactly which players are in 5 or 6. By noting the possibilities, it is clear that J, P, and K cannot go in those slots. For some questions, showing the possibilities is enough to answer the question. For example, if this question had read *Which one of the following is a slot in which Lindquist could present?* then either 5 or 6 would be the correct answer.

Consider the possibilities for J, P, and K. There are a number of options. If you enter them using the slash notation above, the diagram would quickly become difficult to decipher. Instead, use parallel universes.

Parallel Universes

When the possibilities for a diagram become too complex, the diagram can be split into a number of "parallel universes." In the above example, what are the options for K? It seems that K could go in 1, 2, or 3.

You may already have an intuitive insight that one of those options cannot work. However, because it is not possible to *count* on having intuitive insights, use the parallel universe tool. Once you have mastered the tools taught here, you can get the right answer even if the intuitive insights do not come to you.

Using the fact that K's current options seem to be 1, 2, or 3, create three parallel lines in the diagram, one for each possible "universe." All the information other than the placement of K is the same in each universe.

1	2	3	4	5	6
K			M	L/N	N/L
	K		M	L/N	N/L
		K	M	L/N	N/L

Figure 4.76. Diagram with three parallel
universes based on K

The three parallel universes are based on the three options for K. Now fill in what else is known about each universe. In the top universe, slots 2 and 3 are J/P and P/J. In the bottom universe, J/P and P/J go in 1 and 2. What about the middle universe? If J is in 1, P must be adjacent to it. There are no two slots in which J and P can be adjacent. The middle universe violates rules and is out.

1	2	3	4	5	6
K	J/P	P/J	M	L/N	N/L
	~~K~~		~~M~~	~~L/N~~	~~N/L~~
O/P	P/J	K	M	L/N	N/L

Figure 4.77. Diagram with parallel universes.
One violates rules and is crossed out.

The two remaining universes represent all of the possibilities for this question. Each universe contains some optional information but the diagram is now complete enough that the answer choices can simply be compared to the diagrams and the correct answer easily identified. Choice C—K first and J third—appears in the first universe. It can be true and is the correct answer. The other answer choices do not appear as options in either universe. They cannot be true.

When you create parallel universes, do so around the player that has the fewest options. Be cautious about creating more than three universes. Doing so can be time-consuming and can create diagrams that are difficult to use. There are questions, though, in which creating four, five, or even six universes may be the quickest way to solve the question.

Use these diagramming tools in the order that they have been presented here. First enter only what must be true. If that is not sufficient to answer the question, then enter possibilities, using the slash notation (L/N). If that is still not enough, make parallel universes. Even though parallel universes are the most complex to create, they are the most powerful tool for answering a question quickly and accurately.

The great advantage of creating fairly complete diagrams is that the answer choices can simply be checked against the diagrams and the correct answer identified. If the resulting diagram is not complete enough to answer the question, you must test answer choices, which takes more time but is often the only viable strategy.

Using Supplemental Diagrams

In the earlier section on diagrams you learned how to use supplemental diagrams to represent circular arrangements, multiple rows (such as rows on an airplane), and sequences. Supplemental diagrams are powerful tools for solving questions.

Counting Places in a Sequence

Supplemental diagrams of short or long sequences show how many players must come before or after a particular player.

GAME WITH GEOLOGY STUDENTS

Six geology students—Jones, Kellogg, Lindquist, Ming, Nieto, and Pacheco—are to present papers at a six-day conference. Each student presents exactly one time and only one presentation is given on each day.

Jones presents before Ming.

Ming presents before Nieto.

Jones presents either immediately before or immediately after Pacheco.

Pacheco presents before Lindquist.

Either Kellogg presents last or Ming presents before Lindquist but not both.

What is the latest slot in which Jones can present?

(A) sixth

(B) fifth

(C) fourth

(D) third

(E) second

Look at the conditions for this game. They include supplemental diagrams for several sequences.

$$J - M - N$$
$$JP \text{ or } PJ$$
$$P - L$$
$$\text{Either } K = G$$
$$\text{or } M - L$$
$$bnb$$

Figure 4.78. Conditions for game with geology students (bnb = "but not both")

The first line combines the first two conditions: J presents before M, and M presents before N. To find the latest that J can present, look for the number of players that must come after J. There are two: M and N. P does not have to come after J. Based on the diagram J – M – N, J cannot present in 5 or 6 because M and N must both follow J. Test J in 4 for rule violations. In fact, there is one. As an exercise, try to find the violation.

When you find temporary information in a question, you can create a new, temporary supplemental diagram with the new information and its consequences. This is helpful because new information often cannot be put directly into the main diagram. Cross out temporary diagrams when you are finished with them so that you do not get confused by them in later questions.

Example ▬▬▬▬▬▬▬▬▬▬▬▬▬▬▬▬▬▬▬▬▬▬▬▬▬▬

If Kellogg presents last, what is the latest that Lindquist can present?

(A)   fifth

(B)   fourth

(C)   third

(D)   second

(E)   first

▬▬▬▬▬▬▬▬▬▬▬▬▬▬▬▬▬▬▬▬▬▬▬▬▬▬▬▬▬▬▬▬▬▬▬▬▬▬

If K is last, then L presents before M.

$$PJ/JP - L - M - N - K$$

Figure 4.79. Temporary supplemental diagram

You can read from the diagram that there are three players who must come after L. L can present no later than third. Now test L in 3 to see if any other rules would create a violation. Counting places in the Figure 4.79 diagram also allows you to determine how many players must appear before M, for example.

In addition to counting places, supplemental diagrams allow you to determine which players are options for specific places. In the diagram above, the options for places 1, 2, and 3 are L, P, and J. The diagram also shows required orders, such as P presenting before L, and optional orders, as with J, who may or may not present before P.

Early Versus Late

In Figure 4.79, notice that L tends to come early in the sequence and N, for example, tends to come late. If an answer choice has N presenting before L, there is an increased chance that the answer choice violates a rule. When you scan for answer choices that are likely to violate rules, consider whether players tend to come early or late in the sequence.

The early versus late concept can be applied to a question such as *What is the maximum number of students who can present after Pacheco but before Nieto?* Because you want to find the most possible places between P and N, put P as early as possible and put N as late as possible. To find the smallest number of places between the two, you would choose the latest possible position for P and the earliest possible position for N, as shown in Figure 4.80.

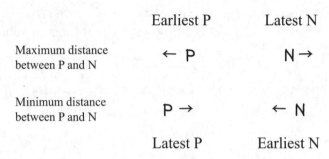

Figure 4.80. Creating maximum or minimum distances between players

Other Temporary Diagrams and Rules

Some temporary information cannot go into a supplemental sequence diagram but can be written as a new rule or a new sequence. Based on the new rule or sequence, other temporary rules or sequences might follow. All of this information can be helpful in solving the question. Write temporary sequences and rules below the original rules and cross them out when you are finished with them.

Consider a question that adds the condition that P must come after J. Figure 4.81 shows how this condition can be entered as temporary supplemental information. The consequences of the new condition can also be entered.

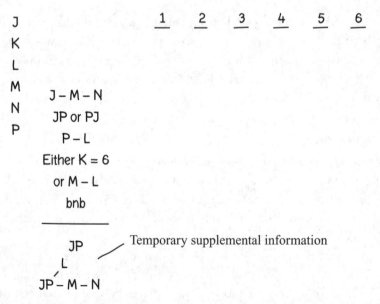

Figure 4.81. Temporary supplemental information. Temporary information should be crossed off after finishing the question to which it applies.

Enough to Answer the Question?

As you work through a question, it is often not necessary to fill in all possible information in your diagram. Sometimes after one or two steps, you have enough information to solve the question. Stop after every couple of steps to see if you already have enough to answer the question. Check the answers against the diagram. Even if you do not yet have enough to answer the question, you may be able to eliminate some answer choices, which helps you know what to focus on.

Most Restricted Players

Players that have the most restrictions on them—meaning that there are a number of rules that govern the player—are more likely to either break a rule or be forced into a certain fixture. As you scan the answer choices, look for players that have the most restrictions. Be aware, though, that a player that has no restrictions is sometimes the one that violates a rule or is forced into a position.

What Rules Apply to a Given Player?

This is a rather obvious and simple strategy but it is a powerful strategy that many people forget to use. When you are working through a diagram, look for the rules that apply to specific players. Suppose that you are working on a game in which L and J, among other players, have not yet been assigned, and places 2, 3, and 5 have not yet had players assigned to them. Start with one player. Use L as an example. Check the rules that apply to L. L must come after P. This information helps you determine what the options are for L. You can use the same strategy for the fixtures. Check for rules that apply to fixture 5. J cannot appear in 5.

What Are the Options for a Player or Fixture?

Asking yourself what the options are for a particular player or fixture helps you figure out how a question works. In some cases there are only a few specific options for a particular player or fixture, so all of the options can be readily diagrammed and then the answers can be determined directly from the diagrams. If there are only a few options for a player, use them to create parallel universes.

There are two different contexts in which you look for options. You can look for the options for where a particular player can go or you can look for the options for which players can be assigned to a particular fixture.

EXAMPLE

If Kellogg and Lindquist present as far apart from each other as possible, all of the following could be true EXCEPT:

(A) Kellogg presents before Jones.

(B) Kellogg presents immediately before Pacheco.

(C) Ming presents immediately after Jones.

(D) Nieto presents after Kellogg.

(E) Nieto presents after Lindquist.

Try to put K and L into the diagram. What are the options for K and L, given that they must be as far apart as possible? The two furthest positions are 1 and 6. What are the options for fixture 1? Check the rules that apply to fixture 1. Any player who must come after another player cannot be in 1. L must come after P, so L cannot go in 1. There are no restrictions against K going into 1. L cannot present first and so K must present first. There are no restrictions against L being sixth.

$$\frac{1}{K} \quad \frac{2}{} \quad \frac{3}{} \quad \frac{4}{} \quad \frac{5}{} \quad \frac{6}{L}$$

Figure 4.82. Place Kellogg and Lindquist
as far apart as possible.

Which remaining player has the most restrictions? J must come before M and N and must also be adjacent to P. What are the options for J? Count the places in the sequence. J must be followed by two players. What is the latest that J can appear? The latest is 3, because M and N must occupy 4 and 5, respectively. What are all of the options for J? They are 2 and 3. Create a new universe parallel to the existing one.

$$\begin{array}{cccccc} \frac{1}{K} & \frac{2}{} & \frac{3}{} & \frac{4}{} & \frac{5}{} & \frac{6}{L} \\[2mm] \frac{1}{K} & \frac{2}{} & \frac{3}{} & \frac{4}{} & \frac{5}{} & \frac{6}{L} \end{array}$$

Figure 4.83. The original universe split into two universes

Now create the two options for J.

1	2	3	4	5	6
K		J			L
K	J				L

Figure 4.84. The two possible universes based on Jones

In the first universe, what are the options for M and N? They must go in 4 and 5, respectively. There is only one option for P: 2. In the second universe, there seem to be several options for M and N (ignoring the other conditions)— M in 3 and N in 4, M in 3 and N in 5, M in 4 and N in 5. These are too many to work with. Instead, look for a player with more limited options. What are the options for P? P must be adjacent to J and so it has only one option: 3. Then M and N must be in 4 and 5, respectively.

1	2	3	4	5	6
K	P	J	M	N	L
K	J	P	M	N	L

Figure 4.85. Two universes with all options filled in

The answers can now be compared directly to the diagrams. You can find the correct answer quickly and easily because all possible options are shown.

The Problem-Solving Process

Use the tools that you just learned to systematically work through a question. Below is a general series of steps that you can apply to a question. For each step, the basic tools that you can use in that step are listed and described.

Two Paths to an Answer

There are two distinct paths for getting to a correct answer. The first path is to create a diagram that is accurate and complete enough that the answer can simply be read from the diagram. This is the best problem-solving method but cannot be used on every question. When the diagram path cannot be used, the alternative path is to test answer choices. The two paths are described below.

The Diagram Path

The first path is to create diagrams that are complete enough that the answer choices can simply be compared to the diagrams, eliminating the wrong answers and discovering the correct one. Complete diagrams can consist of (1) a single assignment in which it is determined which player is assigned to every fixture, (2) a single assignment in which it is determined which players are assigned to some fixtures and for other fixtures there is a list of the players who could be assigned, or (3) several assignments (lines) that represent all the possibilities (parallel universes). These can include fixtures to which a specific player must be assigned and fixtures for which there is a list of possible players that can be assigned.

	1	2	3	4	5	6
A single assignment, all players determined	U	W	X	V	Z	Y

	1	2	3	4	5	6
A single assignment, some options	U	W/V	X	V/W	Y	Z

	1	2	3	4	5	6
Parallel universes. Top universe has options. Bottom universe, all are determined.	U	W	V/X	X/V	Y	Z
	U	X	W	V	Y	Z

Figure 4.86. Three types of diagrams that can be used when following the diagram path

The Testing Answers Path

The second path to getting an answer is to test each answer choice. This can be time-consuming, especially if the correct answer turns out to be in the D or E position. Creating diagrams, when it is possible, is a faster and more accurate way to get an answer. However, on many questions there is not enough—or any—information to create a sufficient diagram. On other questions, it would be theoretically possible to show all of the options but it would be too time-consuming or complex. For example, on some questions it would require ten or more parallel universes to capture all of the options.

When diagramming is not practical, you may be able to eliminate some answers by using diagrams, but you then need to test answer choices to get to the correct answer. When testing answers, first eliminate answer choices if possible, and then decide which answer choices to test.

Remember that proving that an answer choice does not violate rules is always tentative. You may have missed a violation. On the other hand, proving that a violation exists is usually accurate.

When you work on a question in which four of the answer choices are viable orders, most of the answer choices may have wide-open options and few restrictions. Often you will have the clear impression that there are a number of ways for creating a viable option. However, it would be time-consuming to actually create an order and then test it. When there are four answer choices that could be true and a particular answer choice seems to have lots of options, it is better to assume that the order is viable (and thus not the correct answer) and move on to test the next answer choice. Hopefully, when you get to the answer choice that breaks rules, it will be clear. If you have made a mistake, all of the answer choices will appear to be viable and you must go back and look at each one more closely.

The Four Steps for Problem Solving

There are four steps for problem solving. These steps help you determine which of the two paths you should use and then help you implement the best path.

THE FOUR STEPS FOR PROBLEM SOLVING

STEP 1 **Diagramming.** Fill in as much of the diagram as possible. If this does not provide enough information to answer the question, continue with the next steps.

STEP 2 **Elimination.** Apply strategies to eliminate answer choices.

STEP 3 **Scanning.** Glance at the remaining answer choices to orient yourself.

STEP 4 **Testing answer choices.** Apply strategies to test the remaining answer choices.

Start working on a question by going through the steps in order. Then, you can go back to any of the steps as needed.

Diagramming, eliminating, scanning, and testing answer choices make up your basic problem-solving strategy. This section creates a catalog of the specific tools that you can use for each of the four steps, along with the tools for general problem solving.

Step 1. Create Diagrams

If there is new information in the question stem, the first step is to put that information into a diagram. If the new information can go directly into the main diagram, put it there. Apply the rules in order to enter any other information that *must* be true. If not too complex, put in some information that *can* be true (e.g., L/N and N/L). Look for rules that apply to players in the diagram. Determine which players have the most restrictions. Determine what the options are for the most restricted players and fixtures. If not too complex, create parallel universes.

How much time and effort should you put into making diagrams? Start with what is simple, obvious, and quick. Check frequently to see if you already have enough information to get the answer or at least to eliminate additional answer choices. If you are not sure whether you are doing more work than you need to, move on to the next step. You can always come back and fill in more.

If there is new information that cannot be put into the main diagram, create temporary supplemental diagrams and rules. If there is no new information, go to Step 2.

Below are the specific tools for diagrams. Glance through these now and come back to them as a resource when you are working on problems. It is not necessary to memorize these now.

SPECIFIC TOOLS FOR DIAGRAMS

Diagram—put in new information. Enter new information directly into the main diagram.

Diagram—apply rules, musts. Use the rules to determine what else must be true given what is already in the diagram. When you use this tool, stick with only that which must be true. Do not enter options.

Diagram—apply rules, with options. When you use this tool, you add to the main diagram information that could be true but does not have to be. Keep this tool distinct from the previous tool. Use options to indicate that there are two players, L and R, for example, who could be options for a particular fixture (L/R). Also, when you are trying to create a viable assignment, such as proving that M could go in slot 5, you are entering options. In this case, be sure to check your finished assignment against the rules to make sure the assignment does not create a violation.

Diagram—parallel universes. If you try to enter too many options in an assignment, the assignment can become difficult to work with. Creating parallel universes (multiple lines that show various options) keeps your information clear. Each universe includes information that must be true but can also include information that could be true. If it takes more than three or four universes to cover all possibilities, this tool may be too time-consuming. The alternative is to test answer choices.

Diagram—supplemental diagrams or rules. If a question gives new information but that information cannot be put directly into the diagram, for example, *If Jones presents immediately before Ming, . . .* make temporary supplemental diagrams or write temporary rules to keep track of the information. Check the permanent supplemental diagrams and rules to see if anything else follows from the new information and write down anything that does follow. Be sure to cross out temporary diagrams and rules when you are done with the question to which they apply.

Step 2. Eliminate Answers

If a question does not provide new information, start with this step. Many of your tools allow you to eliminate answers. You can start with the rules and look for violations. This is particularly effective when there are four answers that violate rules, as in *which one of the following could be true.* Alternately, you can start with an answer choice and look for rules that apply to it. Checking previous valid assignments, such as in the correct answer to the typical first question, as well as the valid assignments you create in your diagrams, can sometimes eliminate one or two answers. Checking answers against a diagram, even if the diagram is only partially filled in, can help eliminate answers. You may be able to eliminate answers by using the supplemental diagrams and the temporary diagrams and rules.

Below are the specific tools for elimination. Use these as a resource when you are working on problems. You do not need to memorize these now. Glance through them so that you can start to become familiar with them.

SPECIFIC TOOLS FOR ELIMINATION

Elimination—apply the rules to four violations. This is the main, and often only, tool needed for the typical first question. Start with the first rule. Work the rules in order.

Elimination—apply rules, general. When there are not four violations, apply the rules in a more general way. Start with the rules that are most relevant to the question. **Elimination—check previous valid assignments.** Use the answer to the typical first question, as well as any other valid assignments that you have created in your notes, to confirm or eliminate answer choices. This tool is only helpful in about a tenth of the questions. However, when it does work, it saves valuable time by reducing the number of answer choices you need to test. Sometimes this tool leads directly to the correct answer.

Elimination—check answers against the diagram. In nearly half of all AR questions this is the final step that gives you the answer. If you have been able to fill in the main diagram or temporary supplemental diagrams, you can check each remaining answer choice against the diagrams. The answer will be clear unless you have made an error in the diagram. This tool will not give you a definitive answer if there is not enough information to fill in the diagram. However, it may help eliminate some answer choices. In that case you may need to test each of the remaining answers.

Step 3. Scan the Answer Choices

Quickly look through the answer choices to determine what to test. Scanning also allows you to compare answers and to get a sense of what you need to do to solve the question. If it is necessary to test answer choices, scanning helps you determine which choices have the most restrictions on them and are most likely to either break rules or be required to be true. It is not always possible to determine which choices should be tested first. However, this step is an important one because it often saves time.

TOOL: SCANNING

Scan. This tool saves time by telling you which answer choices to focus on first.

Step 4. Test Answer Choices

For many questions, creating a diagram and/or eliminating choices leads to a definitive answer and you will be done before Step 4. Before doing Step 4, consider whether it is possible to create a more complete diagram instead. Testing answer choices is not necessarily difficult but can be time-consuming if you have to test many answer choices. On the other hand, testing answer choices is almost always effective. You can get the answer.

When you create a viable assignment, be sure to check it against all of the rules. After testing all answer choices, you will have the correct answer.

Following are the specific tools for testing answer choices. Use these as a reference as you work on problems. Glance through the tools to become familiar with them. It is not necessary to memorize them now.

SPECIFIC TOOLS FOR TESTING ANSWER CHOICES

Test answers—negate a MUST. To prove that an answer choice must be true, prove that if it is NOT true, a violation will result.

Test answers—create a possible assignment and double-check against rules. Prove that an answer choice could be true by making up an order that you think is viable and testing it against all of the rules to be sure there is no violation.

Test answers—prove a violation. Show that an answer choice must result in a violation. To do this, show that, given the answer choice, certain other facts MUST follow. Do not confuse this tool with showing that an answer choice might lead to a violation.

Test answers—other. A small number of answer choices have to be tested in other ways.

General Problem-Solving Steps

There are some general tools that can be used at various stages of the problem-solving process. They are summarized below. Scan them now to become familiar with them. Use the list below as a reference when you are working on problems. It is not necessary to memorize them now.

GENERAL TOOLS FOR PROBLEM SOLVING

General—count places in a sequence. Counting places in a sequence can eliminate answer choices. It can show how many parallel universes exist. Use this tool in the Diagram and Elimination steps.

General—look for most restricted information. Players or fixtures with the most restrictions are the most likely to either cause rule violations or force something to be true. Use this tool in the Diagram, Elimination, Scan, and Test Answers steps.

General—look for rules that apply to a player/fixture. When you are trying to test an answer or to put information into the diagram, look for rules that apply to a particular player or fixture. For example, if a question puts Ferguson in Wednesday, review the rules that apply to Ferguson and to Wednesday. Use this tool in the Diagram, Elimination, Scan, and Test Answers steps.

General—options for a player. In filling in the options for a diagram, find the player with the most limited options and identify which fixtures are options for that player. A player with only two options can be used to create parallel universes. Use this tool in the Diagram and Scan steps.

General—options for a fixture. For a specific fixture, identify the players that could possibly go in that fixture. A fixture for which there are only two possible players can be used to create parallel universes. Use this tool mainly in the Diagram step.

General—enough to answer the question? Check regularly to see if you already have enough information to answer the question or at least to eliminate some answer choices. Use this tool in the Diagram, Elimination, and Test Answer steps.

General—count the possibilities. This tool is used for questions in which you have to determine a number, for example, how many players can be assigned to a particular fixture, or for how many players is the exact assignment determined. (This is not the same as counting places in a sequence.)

General—early versus late. This tool helps you spot answer choices that are likely to violate rules because the choice tries to place a player who tends to be late in the sequence before a player who tends to be early in the sequence. Also use the concept of early versus late to find the earliest or latest that a player can appear.

Below is a decision tree that outlines the common problem-solving paths and tools, as described above. The tree refers to the steps **Diagram**, **Eliminate**, **Scan**, **Test Answers**, and to the **General** tools.

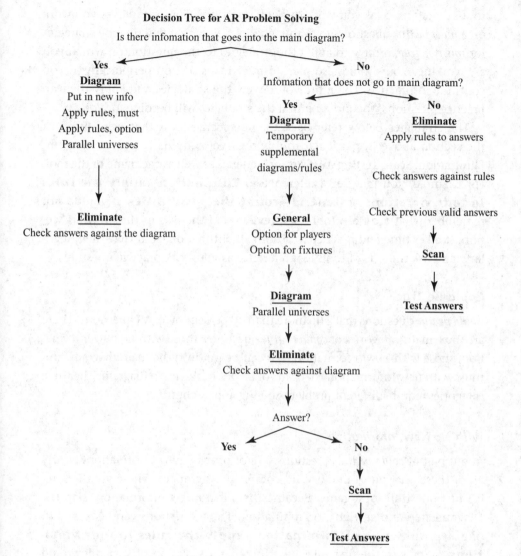

Decision Tree for AR Problem Solving

Is there infomation that goes into the main diagram?

Yes

Diagram
Put in new info
Apply rules, must
Apply rules, option
Parallel universes

Eliminate
Check answers against the diagram

No

Infomation that does not go in main diagram?

Yes

Diagram
Temporary
supplemental
diagrams/rules

General
Option for players
Option for fixtures

Diagram
Parallel universes

Eliminate
Check answers against diagram

Answer?

Yes

No

No

Eliminate
Apply rules to answers

Check answers against rules

Check previous valid answers

Scan

Test Answers

Scan

Test Answers

Strategies for Solving Specific Question Types

By following the previous steps and creatively using the problem-solving tools, you can crack any AR question. In the section below, you will learn strategies for solving specific types of questions quickly and accurately.

The strategies in this section are very in-depth. They represent the tools needed for virtually every AR question that has appeared on recent LSATs. Do not try to memorize these strategies. Read through them to get a sense of how each strategy works. You will get the most out of this section by coming back to it as a reference as you work through questions. For example, as you work on a *must be true* question, go to the sections below that describe the strategies for *must be true* and try to apply the strategies to the question on which you are working. You should also plan to reread this section periodically as you continue to practice. The more you review the strategies and apply them to practice questions, the more natural the strategies will become for you.

The strategies below refer back to the specific tools that were listed in the section above. A particular tool is referred to by its category (Diagram, Elimination, Scan, Testing Answers, or General) as well as the name of the tool. For example, you may see a reference to **Elimination—apply the rules to four violations** or **General—count the possibilities**. If you do not remember what a certain tool does, review it in the lists in the previous section. It takes time and practice to absorb all of the tools, so review them regularly and use the lists of tools as a reference as you work practice questions.

Could Be True

Could be true questions make up more than 40 percent of all AR questions. There are three main categories of *could be true* questions: those with no new information, those with new information that can be put into the main diagram, and those with new information that cannot be put in the main diagram. The three categories require different problem-solving approaches.

With No New Information

About half of *could be true* questions do not provide new information. Nearly all of these ask you to find a valid complete assignment. These are the typical first question for a game. Because there is no new information, skip the Diagram step and go right to Elimination. These questions can be solved in one step with one tool: **Elimination—apply the rules to four violations**. Start with the first rule. Identify what a violation of that rule would look like and then look for the violation in the answer choices. Review the detailed instructions for this tool earlier in the chapter.

There are some *could be true* questions with no new information that do not ask for a complete assignment. These questions might ask for a partial assignment, which fixtures a player could be assigned to, or any other fact about players. Because there is no new information, diagramming is not likely to help. You may be able to eliminate some answers by applying rules: **Elimination— apply rules, general**. (There are still four violations even though the choices are not complete assignments.) You might also eliminate answers by using **General—count places in a sequence**. The final tool for these questions is testing answers—either **Test answers—create a possible assignment and double check against rules** or **Test answers—prove a violation**. In other words, because four answer choices violate rules and one does not, when you test an answer, you either prove it causes a violation or you prove that it could work.

With New Information That Goes in the Main Diagram

About 30 percent of *could be true* questions provide new information that can be put directly into the main diagram (e.g., *Jones presents third*). In these questions the first step is Diagram and the first tool is **Diagram—put in new information**. The problem-solving process involves applying the rules to find what else must be true (**Diagram—apply rules, musts**). Some questions also require applying the rules to put in some options (**Diagram—apply rules, with options**) and/or creating parallel universes (**Diagram—parallel universes**). By using these tools you create a diagram that is complete enough to answer the question. The final tool is **Elimination—check answers against the diagram**. These questions typically do not require you to test answer choices.

Below are some typical sequences of tools that can be used to solve *could be true* questions with new information that goes into the main diagram. These are sequences that have been used to solve actual, specific LSAT questions. The exact order of steps and the specific steps that are included reflect the unique properties of specific questions. For the questions on which you work, start with the sequences below and then adapt them using the problem-solving tools.

The sequences are similar to summaries of a chess game. They outline the "moves" that you can make to efficiently solve questions. They are not meant to represent the only way to solve a problem. Rather, the sequences show you the thinking process of a skilled test taker. As you work on questions, identify and write down the steps you are using. Then compare them with these sequences.

It is not necessary to memorize the sequences you see here. It is best to use these lists of sequences as a reference, coming back to them later as you work on specific problems. You do not need to understand them thoroughly right now but it may be helpful to glance through them briefly, identifying the similarities and differences among the sequences.

To better understand how these sequences apply, consider an example that uses the first sequence, **Without parallel universes, variation 1**.

GAME WITH GEOLOGY STUDENTS

Six geology students—Jones, Kellogg, Lindquist, Ming, Nieto, and Pacheco—are to present papers at a six-day conference. Each student presents exactly one time and only one presentation is given on each day.

Jones presents before Ming.

Ming presents before Nieto.

Jones presents either immediately before or immediately after Pacheco.

Pacheco presents before Lindquist.

Either Kellogg presents last or Ming presents before Lindquist but not both.

If Ming presents third, which one of the following could be the students who present fifth and sixth, respectively?

(A) Kellogg, Lindquist

(B) Nieto, Kellogg

(C) Jones, Kellogg

(D) Jones, Nieto

(E) Lindquist, Kellogg

Follow the steps in variation 1.

Step 1: Diagram—put in new information. The new information is that Ming presents third. Put Ming in 3 in the main diagram.

Step 2: Diagram—apply rules, musts. Apply the rules that involve Ming. Ming must be after Jones and before Nieto. However, these rules do not give you any information that *must* go in the diagram. Apply the last rule. With Ming in 3, could Ming be after Lindquist? No. Both Jones and Pacheco must come before Ming. Ming appears before Lindquist and, according to the last rule, Kellogg cannot appear last. There is no other information that must be true. Go on to the next step, which looks for information that *could* be true.

Step 3: [Diagram—apply rules, with options]. This step is optional for this sequence. (It is listed in brackets.) This means that the sequence can be used either with or without the third step. In this step, look for information that lists options, because Step 2 exhausted the information that *must* be true. According to the first rule, Jones presents before Ming, so Jones must go in either 1 or 2. According to the third rule, Pacheco and Jones present in adjacent time slots. Enter J/P in 1 and P/J in 2. (It would be equally valid to put P/J in 1 and J/P in 2.) There are three time slots remaining (4, 5, and 6) and three players remaining (Nieto, Lindquist, and Kellogg). Kellogg cannot go in 6, so put N/L in 6. In 4 and 5 put K/L/N. Now each fixture shows either the one player who must go there or the options that can go there.

Step 4: Elimination—check answers against the diagram. This tool involves checking the answer choices against your now complete diagram (which includes options). You can quickly determine from the diagram that choices B through E are not valid options. Only choice A matches the diagram.

The exact sequence of tools that is required by any particular question depends on the specifics of that question. The sequences presented below are common ones and reflect sequences that have been used to solve actual AR questions. As you work through questions, you will find your own variations.

With New Information That Does Not Go in the Main Diagram

Information such as *If Jones presents before Ming* . . . does not tell you exactly to which fixture Jones is assigned. For that reason, you cannot put the information directly into the main diagram. You can, however, put this information into a temporary supplemental diagram or you can create a temporary rule. Sometimes the temporary diagram reveals information that can be put into the main diagram. In addition, even though the new information does not go directly into the main diagram, it may be sufficient to allow you to create parallel universes.

Information that does not go in the diagram is typically not as specific as information that does go in the diagram. In about a third of these questions you can create a diagram that is complete enough that you can check the answers against the diagram, just as you can do for questions with new information that goes in the main diagram. However, for the other two-thirds, you need to test answer choices as your final step.

The general problem-solving process, then, is to create temporary diagrams and rules that may eliminate some choices and will help you test answers more quickly.

Must Be True

About 20 percent of AR questions ask you to choose an answer that must be true. About half of these provide new information that goes directly into the diagram. A quarter of the questions provide new information that does not go into the main diagram, and the final quarter provide no new information.

No New Information

Four answer choices could be true or may violate rules. Only one answer choice is forced to be true. In these questions there is no new information, which means that something is forced to be true solely based on the original conditions. You may be able to eliminate some answers based on previous valid assignments. For example, if a previous valid order included Jones in 3, then an answer choice that reads *Jones presents fifth* is not an answer that must be true. If previous valid orders do not apply, scan the answers to see what choices are most likely to invoke rules and then test the answer choices by negating them. In other words, prove that the answer does *not* have to be true.

New Information That Goes in the Main Diagram

Because these questions provide new information that can be entered directly into the main diagram, you have more information to go on and it is easier to eliminate wrong answers and spot correct ones. In these questions, start by entering the new information into the main diagram and then applying the rules to find what must be true. In some cases you will need to also enter some options and/or create parallel universes. You then can compare the answer choices to the diagrams and find the correct answer. For some of these questions you can also use temporary supplemental diagrams or temporary rules.

New Information That Does Not Go in the Main Diagram

These questions are more challenging than those that provide information that goes directly in the main diagram. Use temporary supplemental diagrams and rules to organize the new information and to determine what else must be true. You may be able to enter some information in the main diagram, showing what must be true, what could be true, or creating parallel universes. Use the tools for considering what options particular players have or what options can be assigned to particular fixtures. In almost all of these questions your last step is to compare the answer choices to the temporary or main diagram.

Cannot Be True

About 15 percent of AR questions ask you to choose an answer choice that cannot be true. Usually, no new information is given. This means that diagramming is not used very much with these questions. Rely on eliminating and testing answers.

In these questions, four answers could be true. One violates rules. It is difficult to prove that an answer choice could be true because you might overlook a violation. Therefore, it is more efficient to find answer choices that are more likely to break rules and to test them first. You can apply the rules in order to find violations but because there are many rules and only one answer choice that violates them, this is not as efficient as when there are four violations.

After eliminating answer choices, you will need to test the answer choices that are most likely to break rules. Test them for violations.

Some *cannot be true* questions can be solved by testing answers to prove a violation. Others are solved by counting places in a sequence.

Could Be True "EXCEPT"

About 5 percent of AR questions are worded *Each of the following could be true EXCEPT*. Four of the answer choices could be true. One choice—the correct response—cannot be true. These questions are logically identical to *cannot be true*. However, the *could be true EXCEPT* questions are equally divided among questions that have no new information, new information that goes in the main diagram, and new information that does not go in the main diagram. As a result, in these questions you can take more advantage of diagramming. Because you create diagrams, your last step is **Eliminate—check answers against diagram**.

Completely Determined If

About 3 percent of AR questions ask you to find the one answer choice that, if true, would result in the assignment of players being completely determined. In over 90 percent of these questions there is no new information. For most *completely determined if* questions, then, there is nothing to diagram. Because the answer choices do not necessarily violate rules, elimination is usually not helpful either. Your primary tool for these is to test the answer choices. Before testing, scan the answer choices to look for information that forces assignments to happen. To test an answer, put it in the diagram and try to show that it leads to only one, complete assignment. If the answer seems to leave options, move on to another answer.

If there is new information, put it into the main or temporary diagrams. Then continue with scanning and testing answers.

Must Be False

About 3 percent of AR questions ask you to find the one answer choice that *must be false*. The other answer choices are not forced to be false. They either must be true or could be true. (Note that if an answer choice could be false, it also could be true.) A *must be false* question is logically the same as *cannot be true* and *could be true EXCEPT*.

The *must be false* questions tend to have either no new information or new information that does not go in the main diagram. The questions that do not have new information can be solved in the same way as *cannot be true* questions. Eliminate answers based on previous valid assignments, if possible, and then scan the answer choices and test them, trying to prove a violation.

The *must be false* questions that have new information can be solved in the same way as the *could be true EXCEPT* questions. For those that have new information that goes in the diagram, (1) put the new information in the diagram, (2) apply the rules, (3) create parallel universes if feasible, and then (4) check the answers against the diagram. For those that have new information that does not go in the diagram, (1) create temporary supplemental diagrams or rules, (2) apply the original rules if possible, (3) create parallel universes if possible, and then (4) either check the answer choices against the diagrams, or (5) if there is not enough information in the diagrams, scan and test the answers, trying to prove a violation.

Equivalent Condition

About 4 percent of AR questions ask you to find a condition that is equivalent to one of the original conditions. The question stem does not provide new information. Typically, diagramming and eliminating are of little value. Your primary tool is testing each answer choice to see if it creates an equivalent condition without adding any additional restrictions and without leaving out any of the original restrictions. It may help to scan the answer choices to see what to test first.

How Many Players for a Fixture

About 2 to 3 percent of AR questions ask how many players could be assigned to a given fixture. Usually this type of question does not provide new information. The sequences used to solve this type of question are a little different from previous sequences. Note the use of the General tools. When there is new information, the strategies shift to creating diagrams and checking answers against them.

For How Many Can It Be Determined

Fewer than 1 percent of questions ask you to calculate the number of players for whom it can be determined to exactly which fixture they are assigned. One variation asks "For how many players are there exactly two options?" This type of question may give new information or not. If the new information does not go directly into the main diagram, use temporary diagrams or you may be able to create parallel universes that show all the possibilities.

Because you have to count all possibilities, this type of question is difficult to answer if you cannot represent all the possibilities either through parallel universes or through temporary diagrams. Once you have complete diagrams, count how many options there are.

Could Be False

About 1 percent of AR questions ask you to identify the answer choice that could be false. This means that the other choices cannot be false. They must be true. The remaining (correct) choice does not have to be true.

Because four answer choices are forced to be true, the question has to set up a lot of restrictions. For this reason, *could be false* questions usually give new information that goes in the main diagram. The best strategy is to fill in the main diagram as much as possible and if necessary, create parallel universes. Check the answer choices against the diagrams. This is quicker than testing answer choices.

Complete and Accurate List

About 1 percent of AR questions fall into this category. Do not confuse this type of question with the typical first question, which presents five complete assignments. The typical first question may use the wording *complete* or *accurate* or *complete and accurate*. The *complete and accurate* question type differs from the typical first question in that the former does not present complete assignments. The *complete and accurate* question presents a complete list of players who can be assigned to a specific fixture (*a complete and accurate list of students who can present third*) or a complete list of fixtures to which a player can be assigned (*a complete and accurate list of slots in which Jones can present*). The word *complete* means that no options are left out of the list. The word *accurate* means that every option in the list belongs there. Four of the answer choices either violate rules or leave out a required element.

This question type can also present a subset of a full assignment (*which of the following could be an accurate list of the students who present third, fourth, and fifth*). When the question asks for a subset of a full assignment, only the word *accurate* is used, not the word *complete*.

The *complete and accurate* questions usually do not provide new information. When there is no new information, eliminate as many answer choices as possible by applying the rules or by using previous valid assignments. Because there is so little diagrammable information in these questions, you must test the answer choices, so it is important to scan the answer choices first to save time and then test the answer choices. When there is new information, put it into the diagram and apply the rules. The diagram helps you eliminate some answers but does not provide enough information to solve the problem. You still need to test the remaining answers.

What Is the Maximum/Minimum

This rare type of question historically has asked for the minimum or maximum number of fixtures that there could be. This applies only in a game with variable fixtures. It has also asked for the maximum number of spaces between two players or between two instances of a player. Usually there is no new information.

One or Both of a Pair

This rare type asks you to identify a pair of players of which at least one must be in the assignment. Both could be in but it is not possible for both to be out. In the incorrect answer choices, one or both members *could* be in but do not have to be. This type implies that something *must* be true and some of the questions use the word *must*. Some use the wording *at least one*, as in *Which one of the following is a pair of students at least one of which must present fourth?*

A *one or both of a pair* question is found only in games with a discard pile. There is usually no new information and so little to diagram. Test answers to prove a violation. Put both members of the pair you are testing into the discard pile. Then apply the rules to prove a violation. If an answer choice seems to have many options, move on to the next answer. It is not necessary to work it out thoroughly. When you test the correct answer choice, it does not take much time to spot the violation. If none of the answers seem to have violations, you have missed something. Go back and work them more carefully.

Must Be True "EXCEPT"

In this rare type, four answer choices are forced to be true. The correct answer is one that could be true or that is false. In order to create four facts that are forced to be true, the question typically presents new information that goes directly in the main diagram. To solve this type of question put the information in the diagram, apply the rules, and then check the answer choices against the diagram.

What Is the Earliest/Latest

This rare question type asks you to find the earliest or latest fixture in which a player can appear. There is usually no new information. Count places in the sequence and consider how early or late the player can appear. If a player must have two other players coming after it, for example, and if there are six fixtures, then the player cannot appear any later than position 4. However, it is possible that there are other restrictions that would prevent the player from appearing in 4, so you have to check the possibilities.

Avoiding Errors

You now have all the tools you need to understand how to set up different types of games, to interpret different types of questions, and to get answers systematically and efficiently. Your final challenge is to learn how to avoid errors.

Even the most skilled master of Analytical Reasoning will make occasional mistakes. To get your absolute best score on AR, you need to:

1. Learn the warning signs of an error.
2. Learn the most common errors.
3. Identify the types of errors you make and develop strategies for avoiding them.

The Warning Signs of Errors

There are two clear warning signs that you have made an error (short, of course, of looking up the answer). If you have eliminated all five answer choices, you have made an error on one of the choices. If there seems to be more than one answer choice that works, you have made an error. As tempting as it may be to think that the test writers have erred, the odds are against you.

Errors on the AR section are more serious than on either of the other LSAT sections because if you have misunderstood the game, you may have gotten several questions wrong without realizing it. When you do find a question for which no answer seems to work or more than one seems to work, take it very seriously. Do not simply guess in frustration and move on. You need to find what your error was in order to be sure that you have not gotten other questions wrong. This may seem too time-consuming but the alternative is to risk missing nearly every question on a specific game. This has happened to many test takers!

If no answer or more than one answer seems to work, review the question stem to make sure you understood it correctly. Then go back to the conditions and look for any misinterpretations you may have made. Finally, redo your work.

The Most Common Errors

Keep an eye out for the most common errors.

Misinterpreting One of the Conditions in the Setup

Be careful in your analysis of if/then conditions. Be sure you understand the contrapositive of each if/then. Be particularly careful in setting up sequences, as the wording can be misleading. In the condition *George must appear after Henry but before Fred*, the word order of George and Henry is the opposite of their logical relationship. Henry has to come before George. George comes before Fred but alphabetically Fred comes before George. Watch out for the more logically complex conditions, such as *either . . . or . . . but not both*.

If you find yourself misinterpreting your own notations and shorthand, come up with different notation that is less ambiguous. If you cannot come up with a clear abbreviation for a condition, write the condition out in words.

Misinterpreting the Question Stem

Some question stems are logically complex. Be sure to orient yourself to the stem before you begin solving the question. However, orienting yourself at the beginning of the question may not be enough. Many people lose track of what the question is asking part way through solving it. The more complex the logic of the question, the more likely that you will forget what it is asking and find yourself looking for the wrong thing. As you are working a problem, reread the question stem periodically.

Failing to Check All of the Rules

When you test an assignment to see if it is viable, it is important to check all of the rules. If you cut corners on this, you are likely to miss a violation. On the other hand, if you are trying to prove that an assignment violates rules, you only need to find one violation. Once you have found a violation, you do not need to check more rules. Do not confuse these two different processes.

Failing to Consider All the Options

In many questions you need to see all options. For example, in order to answer a *must be true* question, it is helpful if you have written out all the parallel universes. A common error is the failure to include some options. For example, a test taker may assume that George can only appear in position 1 or 2, missing the possibility that George can appear in 3.

Failing to Distinguish What Must Be True from What Could Be True

If you put George into a diagram as a possibility, there is the danger of later assuming that George must be in that position. Develop notation that ensures that you can distinguish necessary information from possible information. Always be clear whether you are working on *must* information or *could* information.

Applying Main Diagram Rules to the Discard Pile

In games with a discard pile, the rules that apply to the main diagram do not apply to the discard pile. For example, the rule *If George is in, then Fred must be in* means that the appearance of George in the main diagram requires the appearance of Fred in the main diagram. However, if you are testing an assignment by putting George in the discard pile, it is *not* true that Fred must go in the discard pile as well.

Learning Your Own Error Tendencies

The best way to perfect your strategy and avoid errors is to carefully analyze every error that you make. When you get a practice question wrong, try to reconstruct how you approached the question and identify exactly where you went wrong. You may not have used effective timing strategy (e.g., feeling too rushed for time to read carefully and work carefully). You may have failed to use the correct strategies or failed to use the correct strategy accurately. However, for some questions your strategy may have been perfect but you may have made an error. Be careful to note when you misinterpret a condition. If you do not understand the conditions, no amount of strategy will get you to the right answer!

It is not accurate enough simply to say that you made a "careless" error. What caused you to make that error? Spend at least as much time analyzing your errors as you do working on questions. Once you have mastered strategies, learning your own tendencies for making errors and developing ways to avoid those errors is the best and fastest way to your absolute top score.

The AR Problem-Solving Troubleshooter

This section describes a process that you can use when you are unsure of the correct answer on an AR question or when you simply cannot find a correct answer at all. As you practice questions untimed, use the troubleshooter to:

- Make sure you get the correct answer.
- Push yourself to master the AR strategies and patterns.
- Internalize the systematic problem-solving process so that you can use it under timed conditions.

For most people, simply working on a question and then checking the answer is not enough for mastering strategy. To get the most out of your practicing, especially when working untimed, look very carefully at each step of the process. When you are confused, uncertain, or unconfident, identifying what is confusing you and learning how to work through the confusion helps you develop powerful problem-solving skills. The troubleshooter walks you step by step through the stages of backtracking through a problem.

When you are working on an AR problem untimed, you should check the troubleshooter every time that:

1. Your level of confidence in your answer choice is less than 100 percent, or
2. You cannot find an answer at all, or
3. More than one answer choice seems to work.

Before you look up the correct answer, ask yourself if any one of the above points is true for the question you are on. If so, use the troubleshooter. It will help you learn more, increase your understanding of AR, and deepen your problem-solving skills. You can even print a copy of the troubleshooter to keep with you, though it is also helpful to have this book handy so that you can review strategies.

The Troubleshooter

Step 1

If you have chosen an answer but your level of confidence in your answer is low (less than 100 percent confident), go to Step 1a. If more than one answer seems to be correct, go to Step 1b. If you simply are not sure of the answer, go to Step 2.

Step 1a
- Review the question stem to make sure you have understood it.
- Review your proof of each answer that you are considering.
- Redo the proof from scratch, to make sure you do not repeat an error.
- If you have a proof for more than one answer, there is an error! Go to Step 1b.

- If you have eliminated all answer choices but the remaining answer does not seem defendable, you may have accidentally eliminated the correct answer. Start from scratch, reconsidering all of the answer choices.
- If you still do not have an answer, go to Step 2.

Step 1b
- If more than one answer seems to be correct, or if none of the answers seems correct, you may have misinterpreted a condition. This is a serious error because you may have gotten other questions wrong without realizing it.
- If more than one answer seems correct, double-check your proof for each one.
- If you do not find an error in one proof, reread the question stem, to make sure you did not misinterpret it.
- If no answer seems correct, reread the question stem.
- Go back to the setup and review each condition carefully from scratch. Look for any conditions you may have missed or misinterpreted.
- If any condition is confusing, analyze it carefully. For if/then conditions, review the information in the AR chapter about if/thens. If necessary, review the instruction on if/thens in the LR chapter.
- Check to see if your supplemental diagrams are accurate.
- If you do not find an error in your setup and still do not have the correct answer, go on to Step 2.
- If you have already done Step 2, go on to Step 3.

Step 2
- Review the question stem. Did you understand it correctly? If necessary, identify the type of question stem and review its description in the chapter.
- Review the strategy for solving the particular type of question stem.
- Work the problem again from scratch, applying the strategy for the particular question stem as described in the chapter.
- Create any possible diagrams. If there is no information that can be put in the main diagram, is there information that can go in a supplemental diagram?
- If there is information that can go in the main diagram, first enter *only* the information that *must* be true.

- Now enter options, such as L/P in slot 3. Only enter options for which you have complete confidence. A set of options must not include any elements that cannot go in the slot and they must include *all* elements that can go in the slot. If you are not clear on the options, do not list any.
- Evaluate whether it is feasible to create all the parallel universes that reflect all of the possibilities. If there are fewer than six possibilities, create them. If there are too many possibilities to create in a reasonable time, skip to Step 3.
- Once you have all of the parallel universes listed, you should be able to check each answer against the diagrams and find the correct answer. If you do not find a correct answer, recheck all of your work, or if necessary, redo the work from scratch to avoid making the same error. Review the chapter instruction on creating parallel universes.
- If you still do not find an answer, go to Step 1b to see if you made an error in setting up the passage. Then return to Step 3.

Step 3

- Because there is no or little diagram, you must test the answer choices. Review the chapter instruction on testing answer choices.
- Identify by name the type of question in the question stem. Review the instructions for testing answer choices for the particular question type.
- Carefully test each answer choice. If you are not clear whether the answer is or is not correct, take more time with it.
- If you still do not have an answer, go to Step 4.

Step 4

- Take a short break from the problem and then come back to it and start it from the beginning. Do not use the same setup diagrams or notes. Use clean scratch paper.
- Identify the type of passage. Does it have one-to-one correspondence? Is it ordered? Is it a sequence?
- Create the main diagram. Is the number of fixtures fixed or variable? Are branches required? Is there a discard pile? What are the players and the fixtures?
- Can you make a supplemental diagram?
- Redo your list of the players. Do the players fall into separate categories?

- Redo your list of the rules. If there are rules that you are unclear about, examine them carefully and double-check your interpretation. If you are unclear on an if/then rule, review the if/then instruction in the AR chapter and in the LR chapter.
- Put any permanent information into the diagram. Put any rules, such as T cannot go in 3, above the diagram.
- Rework the question. Be careful of your logic at every step.

Step 5

- Identify exactly what aspects of the problem gave you trouble. Even if you are not able to solve the problem, if you can identify your difficulty, you will increase your problem-solving ability.

ANSWER SHEET—PRACTICE TEST

Section I

1 Ⓐ Ⓑ Ⓒ Ⓓ Ⓔ	8 Ⓐ Ⓑ Ⓒ Ⓓ Ⓔ	15 Ⓐ Ⓑ Ⓒ Ⓓ Ⓔ	22 Ⓐ Ⓑ Ⓒ Ⓓ Ⓔ
2 Ⓐ Ⓑ Ⓒ Ⓓ Ⓔ	9 Ⓐ Ⓑ Ⓒ Ⓓ Ⓔ	16 Ⓐ Ⓑ Ⓒ Ⓓ Ⓔ	23 Ⓐ Ⓑ Ⓒ Ⓓ Ⓔ
3 Ⓐ Ⓑ Ⓒ Ⓓ Ⓔ	10 Ⓐ Ⓑ Ⓒ Ⓓ Ⓔ	17 Ⓐ Ⓑ Ⓒ Ⓓ Ⓔ	24 Ⓐ Ⓑ Ⓒ Ⓓ Ⓔ
4 Ⓐ Ⓑ Ⓒ Ⓓ Ⓔ	11 Ⓐ Ⓑ Ⓒ Ⓓ Ⓔ	18 Ⓐ Ⓑ Ⓒ Ⓓ Ⓔ	25 Ⓐ Ⓑ Ⓒ Ⓓ Ⓔ
5 Ⓐ Ⓑ Ⓒ Ⓓ Ⓔ	12 Ⓐ Ⓑ Ⓒ Ⓓ Ⓔ	19 Ⓐ Ⓑ Ⓒ Ⓓ Ⓔ	26 Ⓐ Ⓑ Ⓒ Ⓓ Ⓔ
6 Ⓐ Ⓑ Ⓒ Ⓓ Ⓔ	13 Ⓐ Ⓑ Ⓒ Ⓓ Ⓔ	20 Ⓐ Ⓑ Ⓒ Ⓓ Ⓔ	27 Ⓐ Ⓑ Ⓒ Ⓓ Ⓔ
7 Ⓐ Ⓑ Ⓒ Ⓓ Ⓔ	14 Ⓐ Ⓑ Ⓒ Ⓓ Ⓔ	21 Ⓐ Ⓑ Ⓒ Ⓓ Ⓔ	28 Ⓐ Ⓑ Ⓒ Ⓓ Ⓔ

Section II

1 Ⓐ Ⓑ Ⓒ Ⓓ Ⓔ	8 Ⓐ Ⓑ Ⓒ Ⓓ Ⓔ	15 Ⓐ Ⓑ Ⓒ Ⓓ Ⓔ	22 Ⓐ Ⓑ Ⓒ Ⓓ Ⓔ
2 Ⓐ Ⓑ Ⓒ Ⓓ Ⓔ	9 Ⓐ Ⓑ Ⓒ Ⓓ Ⓔ	16 Ⓐ Ⓑ Ⓒ Ⓓ Ⓔ	23 Ⓐ Ⓑ Ⓒ Ⓓ Ⓔ
3 Ⓐ Ⓑ Ⓒ Ⓓ Ⓔ	10 Ⓐ Ⓑ Ⓒ Ⓓ Ⓔ	17 Ⓐ Ⓑ Ⓒ Ⓓ Ⓔ	24 Ⓐ Ⓑ Ⓒ Ⓓ Ⓔ
4 Ⓐ Ⓑ Ⓒ Ⓓ Ⓔ	11 Ⓐ Ⓑ Ⓒ Ⓓ Ⓔ	18 Ⓐ Ⓑ Ⓒ Ⓓ Ⓔ	25 Ⓐ Ⓑ Ⓒ Ⓓ Ⓔ
5 Ⓐ Ⓑ Ⓒ Ⓓ Ⓔ	12 Ⓐ Ⓑ Ⓒ Ⓓ Ⓔ	19 Ⓐ Ⓑ Ⓒ Ⓓ Ⓔ	26 Ⓐ Ⓑ Ⓒ Ⓓ Ⓔ
6 Ⓐ Ⓑ Ⓒ Ⓓ Ⓔ	13 Ⓐ Ⓑ Ⓒ Ⓓ Ⓔ	20 Ⓐ Ⓑ Ⓒ Ⓓ Ⓔ	27 Ⓐ Ⓑ Ⓒ Ⓓ Ⓔ
7 Ⓐ Ⓑ Ⓒ Ⓓ Ⓔ	14 Ⓐ Ⓑ Ⓒ Ⓓ Ⓔ	21 Ⓐ Ⓑ Ⓒ Ⓓ Ⓔ	28 Ⓐ Ⓑ Ⓒ Ⓓ Ⓔ

Section III

1 Ⓐ Ⓑ Ⓒ Ⓓ Ⓔ	8 Ⓐ Ⓑ Ⓒ Ⓓ Ⓔ	15 Ⓐ Ⓑ Ⓒ Ⓓ Ⓔ	22 Ⓐ Ⓑ Ⓒ Ⓓ Ⓔ
2 Ⓐ Ⓑ Ⓒ Ⓓ Ⓔ	9 Ⓐ Ⓑ Ⓒ Ⓓ Ⓔ	16 Ⓐ Ⓑ Ⓒ Ⓓ Ⓔ	23 Ⓐ Ⓑ Ⓒ Ⓓ Ⓔ
3 Ⓐ Ⓑ Ⓒ Ⓓ Ⓔ	10 Ⓐ Ⓑ Ⓒ Ⓓ Ⓔ	17 Ⓐ Ⓑ Ⓒ Ⓓ Ⓔ	24 Ⓐ Ⓑ Ⓒ Ⓓ Ⓔ
4 Ⓐ Ⓑ Ⓒ Ⓓ Ⓔ	11 Ⓐ Ⓑ Ⓒ Ⓓ Ⓔ	18 Ⓐ Ⓑ Ⓒ Ⓓ Ⓔ	25 Ⓐ Ⓑ Ⓒ Ⓓ Ⓔ
5 Ⓐ Ⓑ Ⓒ Ⓓ Ⓔ	12 Ⓐ Ⓑ Ⓒ Ⓓ Ⓔ	19 Ⓐ Ⓑ Ⓒ Ⓓ Ⓔ	26 Ⓐ Ⓑ Ⓒ Ⓓ Ⓔ
6 Ⓐ Ⓑ Ⓒ Ⓓ Ⓔ	13 Ⓐ Ⓑ Ⓒ Ⓓ Ⓔ	20 Ⓐ Ⓑ Ⓒ Ⓓ Ⓔ	27 Ⓐ Ⓑ Ⓒ Ⓓ Ⓔ
7 Ⓐ Ⓑ Ⓒ Ⓓ Ⓔ	14 Ⓐ Ⓑ Ⓒ Ⓓ Ⓔ	21 Ⓐ Ⓑ Ⓒ Ⓓ Ⓔ	28 Ⓐ Ⓑ Ⓒ Ⓓ Ⓔ

Section IV

1 Ⓐ Ⓑ Ⓒ Ⓓ Ⓔ	8 Ⓐ Ⓑ Ⓒ Ⓓ Ⓔ	15 Ⓐ Ⓑ Ⓒ Ⓓ Ⓔ	22 Ⓐ Ⓑ Ⓒ Ⓓ Ⓔ
2 Ⓐ Ⓑ Ⓒ Ⓓ Ⓔ	9 Ⓐ Ⓑ Ⓒ Ⓓ Ⓔ	16 Ⓐ Ⓑ Ⓒ Ⓓ Ⓔ	23 Ⓐ Ⓑ Ⓒ Ⓓ Ⓔ
3 Ⓐ Ⓑ Ⓒ Ⓓ Ⓔ	10 Ⓐ Ⓑ Ⓒ Ⓓ Ⓔ	17 Ⓐ Ⓑ Ⓒ Ⓓ Ⓔ	24 Ⓐ Ⓑ Ⓒ Ⓓ Ⓔ
4 Ⓐ Ⓑ Ⓒ Ⓓ Ⓔ	11 Ⓐ Ⓑ Ⓒ Ⓓ Ⓔ	18 Ⓐ Ⓑ Ⓒ Ⓓ Ⓔ	25 Ⓐ Ⓑ Ⓒ Ⓓ Ⓔ
5 Ⓐ Ⓑ Ⓒ Ⓓ Ⓔ	12 Ⓐ Ⓑ Ⓒ Ⓓ Ⓔ	19 Ⓐ Ⓑ Ⓒ Ⓓ Ⓔ	26 Ⓐ Ⓑ Ⓒ Ⓓ Ⓔ
6 Ⓐ Ⓑ Ⓒ Ⓓ Ⓔ	13 Ⓐ Ⓑ Ⓒ Ⓓ Ⓔ	20 Ⓐ Ⓑ Ⓒ Ⓓ Ⓔ	27 Ⓐ Ⓑ Ⓒ Ⓓ Ⓔ
7 Ⓐ Ⓑ Ⓒ Ⓓ Ⓔ	14 Ⓐ Ⓑ Ⓒ Ⓓ Ⓔ	21 Ⓐ Ⓑ Ⓒ Ⓓ Ⓔ	28 Ⓐ Ⓑ Ⓒ Ⓓ Ⓔ

Practice Test

▬◣◣◣◤◤◤◤◤◤◤◤◤◤◤◤◤◤◤◤◤◤◤◤◤◤◤◤◤◤◤

SECTION I

Time —35 minutes
27 Questions

> **Directions:** Each set of questions in this section is based on one passage or on a pair of passages. Answer the questions based on what is <u>stated</u> or <u>implied</u> in the passage or in the pair of passages. More than one answer choice could conceivably answer the question in some cases. However, you should choose the <u>best</u> answer. The best answer is the response that answers the question most accurately and completely. When you have chosen the best answer, fill in the space on your answer sheet that corresponds to your answer.

A patent confers the right for the patent holder to prevent others from making, selling, or otherwise making use of the patented technol-
Line ogy without the permission of the patent holder. In principle, patents
(5) benefit society. They encourage innovators to create and perfect new products with the knowledge that the innovator will be able to profit from the results. At the same time, the patent process requires that the patent holder reveal the details of the innovation so that, after the patent expires, the public will continue to benefit from the product and the technology behind the product.

(10)   In practice, the process of issuing patents has been criticized from numerous perspectives. Whereas informed people might consider the ability for people to own, control, and profit from their work to be the epitome of capitalism, there are those—including the government of the Netherlands in the 1800s—who have believed that patents are inconsis-
(15) tent with capitalistic free trade policy. Presumably, they would prefer a system in which innovators can try to profit from their work but cannot stop others from copying or even stealing it.

GO ON TO THE NEXT PAGE

A more substantial criticism of patents is that many patents are based on improvements to technologies that are already patented, which com-
(20) plicates the issue of ownership. For example, suppose that Eduardo has been granted a patent on a new type of fishing pole. Sandra then invents a technology that improves the new fishing pole and is granted a patent on it. Sandra's technology is quite likely useless without Eduardo's technology. This raises the question of whether it is legitimate to issue a
(25) patent for a product that cannot be used without the permission of the holder of a different patent. It is also legitimate to propose that Sandra did not own the right to create an improvement on Eduardo's product.

In the case above, it is not clear who owns Sandra's invention because she cannot use it without coordinating with Eduardo. Because the goal
(30) of a patent is to grant exclusive ownership rights to an individual, when a new patent is based on a previous patent owned by a different person, the patent system is not functioning as intended. In this era of rapidly expanding technologies, it is quite possible that most patents fall into this category.

(35) There is a practical aspect to this theoretical objection to patents. With increasing confusion over the ownership of patents based on patents based on still other patents, there is an increase in litigation over patent rights. In many cases, the cost of litigation is greater than the value of the patented technology. While the issuing of patents achieves its goals in
(40) some cases, it would be better to eliminate patents altogether. If society were to buy valuable, new innovations outright, the innovators would receive an immediate lump sum payment for their efforts, and society could put the innovation to immediate use.

GO ON TO THE NEXT PAGE

1. Based on the passage, it can be concluded that the author and the government of the Netherlands in the 1800s would both agree that
   (A) it is the responsibility of a national government to reduce costly litigation when possible
   (B) granting patents can, in some case, confuse the issue of ownership of a technology
   (C) the most substantial criticism of patents is that they are inconsistent with a policy of capitalistic free trade
   (D) a person who has created a new technology should have the right to profit from that technology
   (E) for a person who has created a new technology to own a patent on that technology is not consistent with a policy of capitalistic free trade

2. Which one of the following most directly expresses the central idea of the passage?
   (A) Patents encourage innovators to create and perfect new products, while ensuring that society has access to the technology behind new products.
   (B) Although patents encourage innovators to create new products, patents are not consistent with policies of free trade and should be eliminated.
   (C) While some objections to patents are simply theoretical, there are objections to patents that are based on practical concerns.
   (D) Although patents offer certain benefits, at present patents often do not serve their intended purpose and could be replaced by other approaches for encouraging innovation.
   (E) If society paid innovators a lump sum for their innovations, both the innovators and society would benefit.

GO ON TO THE NEXT PAGE

3. Which one of the following, if true, most seriously undermines the author's criticism of patents for technologies that are based on previously patented technologies?

(A) When a person obtains a patent for a new technology that is based on a previously patented technology, it is almost never clear who has the right to make decisions about the new technology.

(B) In many cases of litigation over patented technology, the cost of litigation is not greater than the value of the technology.

(C) In many cases, patents are owned by corporations, not individuals.

(D) When a person obtains a patent for a new technology that is based on a previously patented technology, the owner of the previously patented technology is almost always willing to compromise with the owner of the new technology in making any decisions about how the new technology is to be used.

(E) When a person obtains a patent for a new technology that is based on a previously patented technology, the owner of the previously patented technology almost always allows the owner of the new technology to make any decisions about how the new technology is to be used.

4. Which one of the following is most strongly implied by the passage?

(A) If an entrepreneur wants to use, for commercial purposes, a patented technology owned by another person, the entrepreneur must agree to disclose the details of the technology once the patent has expired.

(B) If a merchant wants to sell a product that uses a patented technology owned by another person, the merchant must pay the patent holder.

(C) If a manufacturer wants to make a product that uses a patented technology owned by another person, the manufacturer must obtain permission from the patent holder.

(D) A patent is not inconsistent with free trade policy unless a patent holder refuses to allow others to use the patented technology.

(E) If an innovator creates a new technology and charges others to use it, the innovator's actions are inconsistent with free trade policy.

GO ON TO THE NEXT PAGE

5. The author's attitude toward the issuing of patents in this modern era can best be described as
   (A) absolute support
   (B) qualified agreement
   (C) complete neutrality
   (D) reserved antagonism
   (E) total disapproval

6. Based on the information in the passage, the author would be most likely to agree with which one of the following statements about a later patent—held by one person—based on an earlier patent—held by a different person?
   (A) Since the 1800s, most patents have been based on earlier patents.
   (B) It is probable that either the holder of the later patent or the holder of the earlier patent will initiate a lawsuit against the other.
   (C) The issuing of the later patent confuses the issue of the ownership of the earlier patent.
   (D) It is the owner of the earlier patent who actually owns the technology for which the later patent was issued.
   (E) It is not clear that the holder of the later patent actually owns the technology for which the later patent was issued.

7. According to the descriptions of the purposes of a patent given in the passage, all of the following would achieve the goals of a patent EXCEPT:
   (A) The holder of a patent made a profit from selling the patented technology but only by forcing all competitors out of business.
   (B) After receiving a patent on a technology, the holder of the patent borrowed money to manufacture samples of the new technology.
   (C) The holder of a patent who never earned a profit from the patented technology published a complete description of the details of the technology.
   (D) The holder of a new patent that is based on an earlier patent wins a suit filed by the holder of the earlier patent challenging the new patent holder's exclusive ownership of the newly patented technology.
   (E) The holder of a new patent that is based on an earlier patent enters into an agreement with the holder of the earlier patent that allows both patent holders to profit from sales of the newly patented technology.

GO ON TO THE NEXT PAGE

8. In using the word *legitimate* in line 24, the author of the passage most clearly means that
   (A) the assertion that Sandra does not own the right to create an improvement on Eduardo's product is a reasonable one
   (B) issuing Sandra a patent for a product that she cannot use without Eduardo's permission does not meet the goals of a patent
   (C) there is a legal basis for arguing that Sandra does not own the right to create an improvement on Eduardo's product
   (D) there is a legal distinction between receiving a patent and receiving permission to use the patent
   (E) it may not be ethical for Sandra to create an improvement on Eduardo's product

GO ON TO THE NEXT PAGE

Unlike the cities of the Old World, most American cities have evolved around the use of the automobile. With only a few notable exceptions, public transportation in American cities has not appreciably reduced pri-

Line vate car traffic nor the noise and pollution that go along with car traffic.
(5) Because of the spread of American urban areas, even aggressive public transportation initiatives are unlikely to reduce private car traffic in the future. Cars are simply faster, more flexible, and, in many cases, cheaper than taking the bus.

The most significant drawbacks of car traffic are congested streets,
(10) noise, chemical pollution from car exhaust and from pumped gasoline, and a dependence on petroleum. Dependence on petroleum is a problem because petroleum is a limited resource that, when it runs out, will require a Herculean restructuring of the technologies that currently depend on it. In addition, dependence on petroleum has political impli-
(15) cations because it ties our economy to a small number of petroleum-producing countries.

One solution for the problems of heavy car traffic seems appealing, at least at first glance. Electric car technology is quiet and it is clean. A freeway full of electric cars would be, at least in our imaginations, like a
(20) breath of fresh air. While the freeway would not be any less congested, the noise of gasoline engines would be replaced by the sound of wind, and a clean wind at that. The hidden problem with electric car technology is the issue of how and where the electricity is generated. Even if every car today were replaced with an electric one, if the electric energy
(25) to run the cars were generated by gasoline-powered generating stations, the consumption of gasoline would not drop at all. The pollution from burning fossil fuel would simply be transferred from one location to another.

Electric cars can only reduce the problems associated with gasoline-
(30) powered cars if the electricity needed to run them is generated in clean and renewable ways. One potential source of such energy can be found in the car itself. When the driver of a car applies the brakes, the work performed to slow and stop the car generates a large amount of kinetic energy. In standard cars, this energy is lost as heat. However, regenerative
(35) braking systems capture some of this energy and convert it directly into electricity, which can be stored in a battery or used directly to power the

GO ON TO THE NEXT PAGE

car. Regenerative braking systems have the potential to generate large amounts of electricity at virtually no cost. In Sweden, massively heavy trains—carrying coal from the coal fields in the north—that have regen-

(40) erative braking can generate enough electricity when loaded to return the train, once empty, to its origin. In fact, the trains often have excess electricity that can be pumped back into the power grid.

9. The author's main purpose in the passage above is to
   (A) provide the background of a problem and point out the drawbacks to a solution to the problem
   (B) defend a solution to a problem against criticisms of that solution
   (C) describe a problem, criticize a possible solution, and present an alternate solution
   (D) explain how certain solutions to a problem also solve additional problems
   (E) describe several problems caused by automobiles and consider two alternatives to the use of automobiles

10. Based on the passage, which one of the following is the author most likely to believe about automobiles in cities?
    (A) They are better than public transportation in several ways.
    (B) Despite public transportation initiatives, automobiles will continue to contribute to noise and pollution.
    (C) Converting to electric automobiles would reduce the consumption of gasoline by urban car owners.
    (D) An automobile in a city causes more pollution than an automobile in the country.
    (E) Electric cars using regenerative braking have the potential to reduce congestion in city traffic.

GO ON TO THE NEXT PAGE

11. It can be inferred from the passage that which one of the following is most likely true of cities of the Old World?
    (A) Most cities in the Old World do not have congestion, noise, and pollution.
    (B) Some cities in the Old World have been more aggressive about introducing electric cars than have American cities.
    (C) More people in cities of the Old World use public transportation than use private cars.
    (D) Many cities of the Old World evolved around the use of horses for transportation.
    (E) Most cities in the Old World did not evolve around the automobile.

12. Based on the passage, which one of the following scenarios is most similar to the situation of electric cars that use electricity derived from gasoline-powered generators, as described by the author?
    (A) In a city that relies on horses for transportation and whose streets are polluted with horse manure, gasoline-powered automobiles are introduced.
    (B) In a country with diminishing forests, plastic construction materials are introduced to replace wooden construction materials, but the fabrication of the plastic construction materials requires the burning of wood.
    (C) A city buys a new fleet of buses so that taking public transportation becomes faster, more flexible, and cheaper than driving a personal automobile.
    (D) A community replaces their coal-burning electricity-generating plant, which had caused serious air pollution, with arrays of solar panels that generate enough electricity that there is an excess that can be sold to neighboring communities.
    (E) A city provides a tax credit for residents to buy solar-powered electric lawn mowers to replace gasoline-powered lawn mowers that create noise and pollution, but even with the tax credit, the electric lawn mowers are too expensive for most residents.

GO ON TO THE NEXT PAGE

13. In the first paragraph, the author states that public transportation initiatives are unlikely to reduce private car traffic in the future primarily in order to
    (A) highlight the distinction between Old World cities and American cities
    (B) provide background on the conflict between those who want to increase the role of public transportation and those who want to introduce less-polluting automobiles
    (C) predict that pollution from automobiles cannot be reduced unless public transportation is made a viable option
    (D) suggest that public transportation can reduce congestion but cannot reduce pollution
    (E) emphasize that solutions to the problems caused by automobiles must involve changing the nature of automobiles

14. The author uses the phrase "massively heavy" in the second from the last sentence of the passage in order to suggest that
    (A) regenerative brakes can stop even an extremely heavy vehicle
    (B) the more energy that is required for regenerative brakes to perform their braking function, the more energy they generate
    (C) an empty train requires less energy to operate than a heavily loaded train does
    (D) even a very heavy vehicle can be operated by electricity
    (E) coal is massively more polluting as an energy source than electricity is

Passage A

Most people, if asked to give the defining characteristic of fiction, would probably say that a work of fiction is primarily a story that is not true. Some even go on to say that what predicts that fiction will be
Line entertaining is the *fact* that it is not true, and that the further a story
(5) strays from what is true, the more entertaining it can be expected to be.

Undoubtedly there is some correlation between how imaginative a work of fiction is and how entertaining it is. However, some reflection on this issue leads to the conclusion that the mere fact that a story departs from reality does not, for most people, guarantee that the people will
(10) be entertained by the story. Consider a story in which roads are made of a crushed-brick compound instead of asphalt or concrete or in which peach trees bear fruit in May instead of July. So what? There is nothing inherently entertaining about a fact simply because it does not conform to real life.

(15) What, then, is the quality that turns a compilation of facts that are not true into an interesting work of fiction? The answer, it may be argued, is in how real the untrue facts are. Consider a story in which a dog talks. Such a story is fascinating, but not because dogs do not really talk. It is fascinating because talking is an intimate aspect of our reality and
(20) dogs are an intimate aspect of our reality. By bringing these two aspects together, a work of fiction creates an entertaining world that is *more* real, not less real, than our ordinary world.

Passage B

How does science fiction differ from other types of fiction? It is not necessarily in the degree to which the fictional world differs from our ordinary
(25) one. After all, the world of the Roman empire, or even the world of Victorian England, is dramatically different from ours but does not necessarily constitute science fiction. Even the worlds of fantasy literature, which are different from *any* world that has existed on Earth, are not necessarily science fiction.

(30) The key to science fiction does lie in the imagination but there is another element that defines science fiction. It is the application of imagination to human knowledge. That is to say that science fiction looks into the human mind, into the storehouse of knowledge, of tools and technologies, and uses imagination to push the human mind into the
(35) future. The science fiction writer sees the mind as a movement, from the primitive discoveries of the past toward a distant and unknown future.

GO ON TO THE NEXT PAGE

The task of science fiction, then, is to show us a glimpse of where we are going, how we are evolving, and what our fate is to be. While science fiction entertains, its primary goal is to allow us to fulfill our destiny, *(40)* or as science fiction writers might portray it, the multiverse of possible destinies that unfold just beyond the outer limits of our knowledge. The further that a science fiction story takes us from our current reality, the more entertaining it is.

15. Both passages are primarily concerned with exploring which one of the following topics?
    (A) the distinction in literature between details that are not factually true and details that are factually true
    (B) how writers of certain types of fiction view the human mind
    (C) how accurate most people's definition of certain types of fiction is
    (D) what it is that defines certain types of literature
    (E) the difference between fiction in general and science fiction

16. Passage A offers which one of the following as an explanation for what makes a work of fiction entertaining?
    (A) juxtaposing two elements of our reality that are not normally juxtaposed
    (B) pushing the boundaries of human knowledge into the future
    (C) the further a story strays from the truth, the more entertaining it is
    (D) creating a world that is more imaginative than our ordinary world
    (E) drawing on elements that are intimate aspects of our reality

GO ON TO THE NEXT PAGE

17. Which one of the following is a statement from Passage A that supports the conclusion of the author of Passage B?
    (A) Most people, if asked to give the defining characteristic of fiction, would probably say that a work of fiction is primarily a story that is not true.
    (B) The fact that a story departs from reality does not, for most people, guarantee that the people will be entertained by the story.
    (C) There is some correlation between how imaginative a work of fiction is and how entertaining it is.
    (D) A work of fiction creates an entertaining world that is *more* real, not less real, than our ordinary world.
    (E) Fiction uses imagination to push the human mind into the future.

18. The argument outlined in Passage A and the argument made by the author of Passage B are both put forth by
    (A) showing that details that are untrue are in some ways more real than details that are literally true
    (B) refining definitions that are partially true to make the definitions more accurate
    (C) citing evidence that discredits an erroneous definition
    (D) comparing and contrasting one specific form of fiction with fiction in general
    (E) establishing a definition by eliminating all possible alternate definitions

19. Which one of the following statements is most strongly supported by information given in the passages?
    (A) There are people who consider fantasy fiction to be close to science fiction but not the same as science fiction.
    (B) There are people who would not consider a story based on the Roman Empire to be science fiction.
    (C) There are people who may expect a work of science fiction to be entertaining but are not entertained by it.
    (D) Some people believe that the fact that a story is not true defines it as science fiction.
    (E) There are some people who believe that the primary purpose of science fiction is to entertain.

GO ON TO THE NEXT PAGE

20. Which one of the following most accurately states a relationship between Passage A and Passage B?
    (A) The statement in Passage A—that by bringing two aspects of ordinary life together, a work of fiction creates an entertaining world that is *more* real, not less real, than the ordinary world—is relevant to the definition of science fiction in Passage B.
    (B) The statement in Passage A—that the mere fact that a story departs from reality does not, for most people, guarantee that the people will be entertained by the story—is inconsistent with the definition of science fiction in Passage B.
    (C) The example of a road made of crushed brick in Passage A supports the assertion in Passage B that science fiction looks into the human mind, into the storehouse of knowledge, of tools and technologies, and uses imagination to push the human mind into the future.
    (D) The conclusion in Passage B expands on the conclusion of Passage A by applying the conclusion of Passage A to a more specific situation.
    (E) The statement—that the further a story strays from what is true, the more entertaining it can be expected to be—is questioned by both passages, rejected by Passage A, and forms part of the conclusion of Passage B.

21. The approaches taken by the two authors toward defining their respective areas of literature differ in which one of the following ways?
    (A) The author of Passage A does not believe that science fiction meets the definition of fiction, whereas the author of Passage B believes that it does.
    (B) The author of Passage A believes that imagination is one element of fiction, but not the most defining element, whereas the author of Passage B identifies imagination as the most key element in defining science fiction.
    (C) The author of Passage B supports the conclusion of the passage with logic, whereas the author of Passage A uses only personal opinions to support the conclusion of the passage.
    (D) The author of Passage A specifies the goal of fiction, whereas the author of Passage B only hints at the goal of science fiction.
    (E) The author of Passage A disagrees with the author of Passage B on whether a work of fiction is more real or less real than the ordinary world.

GO ON TO THE NEXT PAGE

The United States has a two-party electoral system, in which nearly all elected officials are members of one of the two major parties. The framers of the Constitution may not have deliberately created a two-party sys-
Line tem. However, the congressional electoral system has inevitably pushed
(5) us toward such a system. The candidate with the plurality of votes in a district wins the right to represent the district, and all other parties, no matter how much of the popular vote they have received, have no representation at all.

By contrast, in a party-proportional representation system, a party
(10) that wins 10 percent of the vote wins 10 percent of the seats in the legislature. Such a system encourages the formation of multiple political parties, since each party has a much greater chance of winning at least some representation. The question remains, however, as to which system of representation is actually best—a two-party system or a multiparty
(15) system.

Some scholars have suggested that a two-party system such as that in the United States leads to greater political stability, which benefits economic growth, and to a more centrist approach to issues. However, most democracies have multiparty systems. In many cases, there are still
(20) two major political parties that dominate the legislature. However, even the presence in the legislature of a few alternative parties can cause the system to function differently than a strictly two-party system.

What are the benefits of a multiparty system that might outweigh the political stability and economic growth of a two-party system? A multi-
(25) party system represents a broader range of views than does a two-party system. In a two-party system, voters have only two choices. In a society in which consumers expect at least thirty choices of breakfast cereal, it is strange that consumers are satisfied with only two choices for governing their country.

(30) Beyond simply limiting choices and narrowing the political debate, a two-party system has a more insidious danger. It is prone to polarization, to one party or both backing up to an extreme position in order to mobilize supporters. If Party A begins labeling Party B as extreme and evil, voters who believe what they hear have no choice but to commit
(35) themselves to Party A. This is not likely to happen in a multiparty system, because many voters may become suspicious of both Party A and Party B. After all, a common first sign of a party that has become extreme is that it calls its opponents extreme.

GO ON TO THE NEXT PAGE

A simple innovation that has the potential to open a two-party system
(40) to more diverse representation and less polarization is instant-runoff voting (IRV). In IRV, voters mark a first, second, and third choice (or more).
If any candidate wins a majority of the votes, that candidate wins the
election. If not, the candidate with the fewest votes is dropped. For any
ballot that had marked the dropped candidate as first choice, that ballot is
(45) now counted as a vote for the ballot's second-choice candidate. With IRV,
voters can vote for third-party candidates without the fear of wasting their
vote or inadvertently aiding the election of a candidate to whom they are
opposed. IRV opens the doors to a more representative, multiparty system.

22. Which one of the following most accurately expresses the main idea of
the passage?
(A) A two-party electoral system is not appropriate for a democracy,
and most democracies do not use it.
(B) While a two-party electoral system may have some advantages, it
also has disadvantages and can be modified to a better system by
means of certain voting innovations.
(C) Both two-party and multiparty electoral systems have
disadvantages that can be addressed by instant-runoff voting.
(D) A two-party electoral system leads to a more stable government
and a stronger economy, even though such a system has some
drawbacks.
(E) A two-party electoral system is more prone to polarization than is a
multiparty system.

23. The author mentions the framers of the Constitution in the first
paragraph primarily in order to
(A) provide background on the development of the two-party system
in the United States
(B) support the assertion that the two-party system is fundamental to
the democratic institutions of the United States
(C) counter a possible objection that a multiparty electoral system is
unconstitutional
(D) establish that as far back as the time that the Constitution was
written, Americans tended to fall into two major political divisions
(E) contrast the American Constitution with the constitutions of other
democracies that have multiparty electoral systems.

GO ON TO THE NEXT PAGE

24. According to the passage, which one of the following is true of a party-proportional representation system?
    (A) Voters can mark their first, second, and third choices for an office.
    (B) It prevents the domination of politics by two major parties.
    (C) Every political party will earn at least some representation in the legislature.
    (D) Even a minor political party has a greater chance of winning a seat in the legislature than in the American congressional electoral system.
    (E) It offers voters better-qualified candidates than does the American congressional electoral system.

25. The author's descriptions of the drawbacks of the two-party system give the most support for which one of the following generalizations?
    (A) A system that is used by fewer people may still be a better system than one that is used by many more people.
    (B) When it is not clear which of two systems is better, it is a good idea to blend the two systems.
    (C) Most people will not put up with limitations in their political life that are more restrictive than the limitations in their economic life.
    (D) People are unlikely to change a political system that has been in place for many years.
    (E) When faced with only two choices, consumers are more likely to adopt an extreme viewpoint than when the same consumers are faced with multiple choices.

GO ON TO THE NEXT PAGE

26. Which one of the following is most strongly implied by the above passage?
    (A) Many voters would be willing to have their second-choice candidate win the election.
    (B) Voters in most democracies have chosen to have a multiparty electoral system.
    (C) In the American electoral system, politicians of one party try to consider the views of their constituents who are members of the other party.
    (D) A country with a multiparty electoral system does not have as much economic growth as a country with a two-party electoral system.
    (E) In multiparty electoral systems, votes cast for members of the smaller parties are usually wasted.

27. The passage most helps to answer which one of the following questions?
    (A) In a party-proportional representation system, what is the minimum percentage of the vote that a party must receive in order to earn at least one seat in the legislature?
    (B) What is the reason that people who expect variety when they purchase products do not expect variety when they vote?
    (C) What happens in a multiparty system if one party accuses another party of being extreme?
    (D) Has instant-runoff voting been successful in converting two-party systems into multiparty systems?
    (E) What is a sign that a vote for a third-party candidate may be wasted?

 **STOP**

If you finish before the 35-minute time period is over, you may go back and check your answers in this section only. You may not work on any other test section.

SECTION II

Time —35 minutes
26 Questions

Directions: The questions in this section are based on the reasoning contained in brief statements or passages. More than one answer choice could conceivably answer the question in some cases. However, you should choose the <u>best</u> answer. The best answer is the response that answers the question most accurately and completely. You should avoid making any assumptions that, by commonsense standards, are implausible, superfluous, or incompatible with the passage. When you have chosen the best answer, fill in the space on your answer sheet that corresponds to your answer.

1. Lee: Dr. Jansen does not meet the needs of his
    patients. He was not able to correctly diagnose several patients who
    turned out to have rare endocrinological disorders.

    Morrison: Dr. Jansen is a general practitioner,
    not an endocrinologist. If he is not able to diagnose a patient's
    condition, he refers the patient to a specialist.

    Which one of the following principles, if valid, most helps to justify
    the reasoning in Morrison's response to Lee?
    (A) A general practitioner should not be expected to meet the needs of
        all patients.
    (B) Only a specialist can correctly diagnose a rare condition.
    (C) It is up to a patient to decide whether or not to consult a specialist.
    (D) Referring a patient to a specialist meets the needs of that patient.
    (E) Even a specialist cannot meet the needs of all patients.

GO ON TO THE NEXT PAGE

2. A study conducted by the state government found that 35 percent of the new businesses started in Smithtown over the last three years failed within the business's first year. However, a study conducted by a private group found that only 10 percent of businesses started in Smithtown during the same three years failed within the business's first year.

Which one of the following, if true, most helps to resolve the apparent discrepancy described above?

(A) The government study was initiated in order to predict the future tax revenue from new businesses, whereas the private study was initiated specifically to determine the rate of failure of new businesses.

(B) The government study included Smithtown and three neighboring towns, whereas the private study included only Smithtown.

(C) There was more funding available for the government study than there was for the private study.

(D) The people who conducted the government study had never conducted such a study previously.

(E) The government study and the private study did not use the same definition of "failure."

3. When dogs are frightened, they invariably exhibit one of two reactions. They either bark or hide. Recently, when a particularly loud clap of thunder sounded near Marsha's house, her dog raised its ears but did not bark. Instead, the dog walked quickly into another room. It can be concluded, then, that the dog went to the other room in order to hide.

The conclusion is most strongly supported by the reasoning in the argument if which one of the following is assumed?

(A) The dog has been trained not to bark.

(B) Hiding is more comforting to a frightened dog than is barking.

(C) The dog was frightened by the thunder.

(D) If a frightened dog is going to bark, it will do so the moment it is frightened.

(E) It is unlikely that a dog will both bark and hide when frightened.

GO ON TO THE NEXT PAGE

4. There are many reasons why students often choose online courses over traditional classroom courses. Online courses offer students flexible schedules for reviewing lecture material and for taking exams. Because of the large number of students that can be accommodated by an online course, the course fees are relatively low. Finally, online courses allow students to interact with students from many parts of the country.

The statements above, if true, provide support for each of the following EXCEPT:

(A) Some students enjoy interacting with students from other parts of the country.

(B) Traditional classroom courses do not offer flexible schedules for reviewing lecture material.

(C) Traditional classroom courses accommodate fewer students than do online courses.

(D) Some traditional classroom courses offer flexible schedules for taking exams.

(E) Some students prefer to pay lower fees for courses.

5. Psychologist: Some psychologists claim that when children spend too much time on the computer, the children's behavior becomes more aggressive. However, to date there is no research evidence that supports this claim. Parents can be assured, then, that allowing their children to spend time on the computer will not increase aggressive behavior in their children.

Which one of the following is a questionable technique used in the psychologist's argument?

(A) accepting a claim solely because the opponents of the claim have failed to defend their argument

(B) defending a view by ignoring information that attacks the view

(C) asserting that lack of evidence defending a view is sufficient to prove that the view is incorrect

(D) failing to provide evidence to support the claim that no relevant research exists

(E) citing as an authority a source that is not in fact an authority in the relevant field

GO ON TO THE NEXT PAGE

6. A labor-saving technology is, by definition, a technology that allows a task to be completed with less time input from humans than would have been required without the technology. A piece of equipment that allows a certain person to perform a task in thirty-five minutes, when the same person would have required forty-five minutes to complete the task without the technology, is not a labor-saving technology if
   _____ .

   The argument's conclusion is most strongly supported if which one of the following completes the passage?
   (A) some people operating the equipment would require forty-five minutes to perform the task
   (B) the person could have saved time by not performing the task at all
   (C) other technologies would have allowed the person to perform the same task in twenty-five minutes
   (D) the person operating the equipment must spend fifteen minutes cleaning the equipment between tasks
   (E) fifteen of the thirty-five minutes is spent in setting up the equipment

GO ON TO THE NEXT PAGE

7. Regular aerobic exercise reduces blood pressure. Because it is necessary to reduce blood pressure in order to avoid strokes, a person who gets regular aerobic exercise will avoid strokes.

The flawed pattern of reasoning in which one of the following is most closely parallel to the flawed pattern of reasoning in the argument above?

(A) If Sherry completes her term paper, she will pass Dr. Powdrell's course. Any student who completes a term paper gets one hundred bonus points, and Dr. Powdrell only passes students who have gotten one hundred bonus points.

(B) Avoiding carbohydrates lowers total cholesterol. Because lower total cholesterol reduces the risk for a heart attack, a person who avoids carbohydrates reduces the risk for a heart attack.

(C) All great artists experienced personal suffering. Because some people who want to become great artists have not experienced personal suffering, there are some people who will not become great artists.

(D) Any plant that receives adequate nitrogen will grow. Because any plant that grows has received sunshine, any plant that receives adequate nitrogen also has received sunshine.

(E) A society cannot prosper unless all individuals in the society prosper. Because it is true that when society prospers, the greater good is attained, if all individuals prosper, the greater good will be attained.

GO ON TO THE NEXT PAGE

8. Gardener: If the temperature falls below 28 degrees Fahrenheit for at least two hours, the result is a hard frost. I forgot to set out my outdoor thermometer last night, but I know that a hard frost kills tomato plants, and my tomato plants are dead this morning, so the temperature must have been below 28 for at least two hours.

The gardener's reasoning is questionable in that it fails to consider the possibility that

(A) a hard frost kills many types of plants other than tomato plants

(B) if a tomato plant is in a sheltered location, it can survive a hard frost

(C) tomato plants can be killed overnight by a number of conditions other than hard frost

(D) other plants near the tomato plants were not killed

(E) without a thermometer, it is not possible to determine the exact overnight low temperature

GO ON TO THE NEXT PAGE

9. There are two conditions that are necessary for a manager of a company to approve a new business project. The project must not compete with another of the company's current projects, and the manager must have evidence that the venture can be profitable.

The principle stated above, if valid, most helps to justify the reasoning in which one of the following arguments?

(A) Our manager should approve the new project. The project does not compete with any of our other projects, and there is evidence that the project will generate significant income.

(B) The proposed new project does not compete with any of our other projects. Nevertheless, our manager should not approve the project because the evidence defending the project's profitability is not extensive.

(C) It was a mistake for our manager to have approved the new project. It is true that the project does not compete with any of our other projects, but we have just found out that the facts used to support the project's profitability were inaccurate.

(D) Our manager should not approve the proposed new project. While it does not compete with any of our current projects, all of the evidence indicates that the project would not be profitable.

(E) Even though the evidence supporting the profitability of the new project is impressive, the manager should not approve the project. It is highly likely that the project would compete with other projects that have been proposed.

GO ON TO THE NEXT PAGE

10. The island of Marbay has what most people consider to be an ideal climate. While the island lacks the seasonal variation that many parts of the world enjoy, its temperature is always mild, there is nearly always a light, fresh breeze, and the rain comes only at night. Few other locations offer this combination of climatic conditions.

Which one of the following, if true, most strengthens the argument above?
(A) Many people prefer a climate that does not have seasonal variation.
(B) Most people consider a dry climate to be more ideal than a wet climate.
(C) Mild temperatures, light breezes, and nighttime rain are the primary characteristics of what most people would consider to be an ideal climate.
(D) The island of Marbay is the only location in the world that has this specific combination of characteristics.
(E) What some people consider to be a mild temperature may be considered too hot by other people.

11. While inequities in the law are often obvious, it can take years of legislative research and planning before a remedy for an inequity can be incorporated into existing law. Even though such remedies can correct previous inequities, they frequently introduce new and unanticipated inequities.

Which one of the following is most strongly supported by the information above?
(A) Long-term planning may not reduce the number of legal inequities.
(B) Inequities in the law are not intentional.
(C) The number of inequities in the law increases with time.
(D) The more obvious an inequity in the law is, the longer it takes to remedy the inequity.
(E) Inequities in the law that are not obvious are often ignored.

GO ON TO THE NEXT PAGE

12. Marissa: Scientific inquiry is both an intuitive and an intellectual activity. Science is unique among human endeavors in that it tests intuition through a rigorous, intellectual process.

Frederick: The problem with science is the intellectuals. Intellectuals are out of touch with the practical needs of people. True science is a practical activity, not an intellectual one.

Frederick's reply to Marissa's argument is most vulnerable to criticism on the grounds that his reply
(A) uses language that is biased
(B) mistakes a cause in Marissa's argument for an effect
(C) uses the word *intellectual* in a way that is different from Marissa's use of the word
(D) assumes that because Marissa has not adequately defended her view that her view is incorrect
(E) uses an unrepresentative group to defend his conclusion

13. The great majority of influenza cases could be prevented by a simple flu shot. The beginning of the flu season coincides with the beginning of the holiday shopping season. It would be an economic boon to our local merchants if everyone were to get a flu shot this season.

The conclusion of the argument is most strongly supported if which one of the following is assumed?
(A) Most people do their holiday shopping even if they are sick.
(B) Anyone who gets a flu shot will not get the flu.
(C) The majority of flu cases occur after the holiday season.
(D) Local merchants lose money when people have the flu during the holiday shopping season.
(E) Nearly all people who get flu shots do so at a local facility.

GO ON TO THE NEXT PAGE

14. A new traffic radar technology for identifying cars that are speeding was tested against traditional traffic radar. Based on cars driven on a track by professional drivers, the study found that every car identified by the new technology as speeding actually was. On the other hand, 20 percent of the cars identified as speeding by the old technology were not in fact speeding. The new technology is clearly superior and should be implemented immediately.

Which one of the following, if true, most weakens the argument?
(A) Neither technology is effective for drivers who have radar detectors.
(B) The new technology is 20 percent more expensive than the old technology.
(C) Thirty percent of the cars identified by the new technology as not speeding actually were speeding, whereas all of the cars identified by the old technology as not speeding were in fact not speeding.
(D) The radar equipment used in testing the old technology was ten years old, whereas the radar equipment used in testing the new technology was new.
(E) The effectiveness of traffic radar technology depends in part on the skill of the person using the technology.

GO ON TO THE NEXT PAGE

15. The reason that our town does not attract new residents is most likely that potential new residents get the impression that our town is on the decline economically. There are two facts that prove that this is the reason. First, many of our homes have yards that are overgrown and untended. Second, the prospective residents who are shown a copy of the town's economic report, which clearly shows a strong pattern of growth, are much more likely to buy a home here than are prospective residents who are not shown the report.

Which one of the following, if true, most strengthens the reasoning in the argument above?
(A) Many homeowners are so busy with new projects at their jobs that they do not have time to keep their yards up.
(B) Many of the homes with overgrown and untended yards are abandoned because the owners of the homes lost their jobs.
(C) Many people associate overgrown and untended yards with economic decline.
(D) The town's economic report is too technical for most people to understand.
(E) Many prospective residents who saw homes with overgrown and untended yards refused to look at the town's economic report.

16. Rancher: Coyotes are the main predator of gophers, helping keep the gopher population down. Over the past several years, wildlife managers have removed most of the coyotes from our ranch. During the same time, though, the gopher population has continued to go down.

Which one of the following, if true, most helps to resolve the apparent discrepancy in the passage above?
(A) There are more coyotes on the ranch now than there were ten years ago.
(B) The coyotes were relocated in order to reduce the gopher population in another area.
(C) The rate of decline in the gopher population has not changed in the past five years.
(D) The populations of other animals on which coyotes prey have increased in the last three years.
(E) Coyotes drive away owls and snakes, both of which are predators of gophers.

GO ON TO THE NEXT PAGE

17. The five salespeople in our organization have roughly the same sales skills and so have roughly the same odds of winning this year's annual sales competition. However, because Sylvia is the only salesperson who got a head start, she has the best odds of winning. Therefore, Sylvia will win the competition.

The reasoning in the argument is flawed in that it
(A) fails to provide evidence that Sylvia is the only salesperson who got a head start
(B) presumes, without warrant, that no salesperson has better sales skills than Sylvia
(C) ignores the possibility that an event with a higher probability of occurring than other events may still have too low a probability to guarantee its occurrence
(D) attempts to predict the occurrence of an event solely by a comparison of the likelihood of all possible events
(E) assumes, without evidence, that all members of a group are equal

18. For a number of years physicians have encouraged their patients to get more physical exercise. However, after several highly publicized events in which people seriously injured themselves doing exercises in which they were not properly trained, some doctors have stopped recommending exercise. This is not right. After all, a small number of people injure themselves every day simply eating fruit or drinking water. This does not mean physicians should stop recommending eating fruit and drinking water.

Which one of the following principles most helps to justify the reasoning in the argument above?
(A) A physician should recommend activities that have the potential to improve the health of a patient.
(B) An activity should be recommended only if the advantages of the activity outweigh the risks of the activity.
(C) It ought to be the responsibility of a patient to decide which recommended activities to do.
(D) Anyone who begins a new exercise program should receive training in performing the exercise.
(E) A physician ought not to refrain from recommending an activity that has health benefits solely on the basis that the activity has the potential to cause harm.

GO ON TO THE NEXT PAGE

19. Baxter: When new immigrants come to this country, they face two challenges. They must first learn the cultural norms of their new country. Having learned those norms, they must then incorporate those norms into the context of the norms of their native country and arrive at a synthesis of the old and new norms. This same process, then, applies to other minority cultures in our country.

    Beardsley: Even though most immigrants are members of minority groups, their experience does not apply to members of minority cultures who were born in this country.

    Beardsley's response to Baxter's argument
    (A) challenges its assumptions about the experience of immigrants to this country
    (B) challenges it by providing an alternative explanation for one of its premises
    (C) challenges it by pointing out an inherent contradiction in its premises
    (D) challenges the basis on which Baxter argues from a specific situation to a more generalized conclusion
    (E) challenges it on the basis that the conclusion would lead to an undesirable result

20. Most newspapers today have suffered a significant drop in readership with the advent of the Internet. With this drop in readership, there has been a corresponding drop in revenue from advertisers. Many newspapers have set up their own websites. They must be doing so for the extra revenue they can earn by selling advertising space on their Web pages.

    Which one of the following, if true, most weakens the argument?
    (A) Advertisements on a Web page bring in less income than similar advertisements in a newspaper.
    (B) Most newspapers have found that when people who are otherwise not readers of the newspaper visit the website, they are more likely to become regular readers of the newspaper.
    (C) Newspapers that set up websites also typically use social media sites to promote their newspaper.
    (D) Some journalists on newspapers began their careers as journalists on websites.
    (E) There are no newspapers that have transitioned completely from print to Internet.

GO ON TO THE NEXT PAGE

21. When top executives at Company X travel for business, they are required to use a corporate jet. No employee who has worked at Company X for fewer than five years is allowed to use a corporate jet when traveling for business. Sarah is a top executive at Company X and has worked at the company for exactly three years.

    If the statements above are true, which one of the following statements must also be true?
    (A) Sarah sometimes travels for Company X business using a corporate jet.
    (B) Sarah never uses a Company X corporate jet.
    (C) Sarah sometimes travels for Company X business.
    (D) If any employee of Company X uses a corporate jet, it is for Company X business.
    (E) If Sarah uses a Company X corporate jet, it is not for Company X business.

22. Physicist: The gravitational effect of many astronomical objects cannot be accounted for by the amount of visible matter that the objects contain. Because of this, astrophysicists have postulated the existence of *dark matter*, a type of matter that does not emit light. However, there has never been any direct evidence of dark matter. It is just as likely that gravity simply acts differently on immense astrophysical scales than it does on Earth.

    The claim that the gravitational effect of many astronomical objects cannot be accounted for by the amount of visible matter that the objects contain plays which one of the following roles in the physicist's argument?
    (A) It is a premise that establishes the truth of the argument's conclusion.
    (B) It is an intermediate conclusion that is used as a premise to support the main conclusion.
    (C) It is a hypothesis that the argument as a whole rejects.
    (D) It is a premise in an argument that the argument as a whole attempts to weaken.
    (E) It is a statement that illustrates a principle.

GO ON TO THE NEXT PAGE

23. Some say that in all things we should strive for simplicity. However, by definition, striving is not simple. The act of striving moves us away from simplicity. Therefore, it is not possible to attain simplicity.

Which one of the following is an assumption that is required by the argument above?
(A) It is not possible to attain simplicity without striving.
(B) There are some forms of striving that are simple.
(C) There is not more than one way to define simplicity.
(D) It is not possible to strive without attaining simplicity.
(E) It is not possible to strive for simplicity in some things.

24. Principle: It is not unethical for a judge to rule on a case when the judge has received a large payment of money from one of the parties in the case if the judge is unaware of the payment.

Application: It was not unethical for Judge Clark-Thompson's wife to accept $250,000 from Company Z for a fifteen-minute speech, even though Company Z is the plaintiff in an important case that is being tried by Judge Clark-Thompson.

Which one of the following, if true, most justifies the application of the principle in the above argument?
(A) Judge Clark-Thompson did not rule in favor of Company Z.
(B) Company Z pays all speakers a minimum of $250,000 regardless of the length of the speech.
(C) Judge Clark-Thompson was not aware that his wife had had any contact with representatives of Company Z.
(D) Judge Clark-Thompson's wife put the money into a bank account in the judge's name but did not tell him about either the speech or the payment.
(E) The speech given by the judge's wife took place after the judge had ruled on the case involving Company Z.

GO ON TO THE NEXT PAGE

25. Astronomers who discover a new comet can become famous but only if they discover a type of comet that is rare. Short-period comets and longer-period comets are relatively common. If an astronomer wants a chance to become famous by discovering a new comet, the astronomer should look for a hyperbolic comet.

Which one of the following most accurately states the overall conclusion of the argument above?

(A) Hyperbolic comets are relatively rare.
(B) If an astronomer wants to become famous for discovering a comet, the astronomer should discover a hyperbolic comet.
(C) Short-period and longer-period comets are not as rare as other types of comets.
(D) An astronomer who discovers a rare comet will become famous.
(E) An astronomer cannot become famous unless the astronomer discovers a rare comet.

GO ON TO THE NEXT PAGE

26. Water-tolerant plant species that cannot grow in more than three inches of water can generally tolerate drought. Water-tolerant plant species that must grow in more than eight inches of water generally cannot tolerate drought. This plant grows in five inches of water, so it may be able to tolerate drought for a short period.

The reasoning in which one of the following is most similar to the reasoning in the argument above?

(A) A bookstore with less than $20,000 in inventory typically cannot make more than $25,000 per year. A bookstore with more than $20,000 in inventory can make more than $25,000 per year. This bookstore has more than $20,000 in inventory, so it can probably make more than $25,000 per year.

(B) A bookstore with less than $20,000 in inventory typically cannot make more than $25,000 per year. A bookstore with over $100,000 in inventory can typically make at least $150,000 profit per year. This store has over $100,000 in inventory and it makes over $150,000 per year, so it must be a bookstore.

(C) A bookstore with less than $20,000 in inventory typically cannot make more than $25,000 per year. A bookstore with over $100,000 in inventory can typically make at least $150,000 profit per year. This bookstore makes over $150,000 per year, so it must have over $100,000 in inventory.

(D) A bookstore with less than $20,000 in inventory typically cannot make more than $25,000 profit per year. A bookstore with over $100,000 in inventory can typically make at least $150,000 profit per year. This bookstore has $60,000 in inventory, so it can probably make a profit of almost $90,000 per year.

(E) A bookstore with less than $20,000 in inventory typically cannot make more than $25,000 profit per year. A bookstore with over $100,000 in inventory can typically make at least $150,000 profit per year. This bookstore has less than $20,000 in inventory, so it can probably make a profit of $15,000 per year.

STOP

If you finish before the 35-minute time period is over, you may go back and check your answers in this section only. You may not work on any other test section.

SECTION III

Time —35 minutes
23 Questions

Directions: The groups of questions in this test section are each based on specific sets of conditions. Making a rough diagram may be useful for answering some of the questions. For each question choose the answer choice that is most accurate and complete. Fill in the space on your answer sheet that corresponds to your answer.

QUESTIONS 1–6

Seven trees of different species—Larix, Morus, Nyssa, Olea, Poncirus, Robinia, and Salix—are to be planted along a parkway. There are seven specific spots allocated for the trees, and the spots are numbered 1 through 7, from west to east. The assignment of trees to spots must proceed according to the following conditions:

Poncirus is planted to the east of Salix.

Nyssa is planted in either the fifth or seventh spot.

Larix is planted east of Poncirus but west of Nyssa.

If Poncirus is planted in the third spot, Poncirus is planted to the east of Robinia.

If Poncirus is not planted in the third spot, Robinia is planted to the east of Poncirus.

1. Which one of the following is a possible assignment of the trees to the planting spots?
   (A) Olea, Salix, Morus, Poncirus, Robinia, Larix, Nyssa
   (B) Salix, Robinia, Morus, Poncirus, Larix, Olea, Nyssa
   (C) Salix, Robinia, Poncirus, Morus, Nyssa, Larix, Olea
   (D) Salix, Morus, Poncirus, Larix, Olea, Robinia, Nyssa
   (E) Morus, Robinia, Poncirus, Larix, Nyssa, Salix, Olea

2. Which one of the following CANNOT be true?
   (A) Poncirus is in the second spot and Robinia is in the last spot.
   (B) Poncirus is in the third spot and Robinia is in the first spot.
   (C) Poncirus is planted between Robinia and Salix.
   (D) Salix is in the first spot and Robinia is in the second spot.
   (E) Morus is in the first spot and Robinia is in the second spot.

3. If Robinia and Poncirus are planted in adjacent spots, then which one of the following could be true?
   (A) Salix is planted in the third spot.
   (B) Larix is planted in the third spot.
   (C) Salix is planted in the fourth spot.
   (D) Nyssa is planted adjacent to Robinia.
   (E) Nyssa is planted in the fifth spot and Salix is planted in the second spot.

4. If Morus is planted in the first spot, then which one of the following could be true?
   (A) Olea is planted in the fourth spot.
   (B) Olea is planted in the fifth spot.
   (C) Salix is planted in the third spot.
   (D) Robinia is planted in the last spot.
   (E) Poncirus is planted in the third spot.

5. Which one of the following must be true?
   (A) There are at least five trees planted east of Salix.
   (B) There are exactly two spots in which Salix can be planted.
   (C) If Robinia is planted next to Nyssa, Salix is planted in the first spot.
   (D) If Salix is planted next to Morus, Larix is planted next to Robinia.
   (E) If Morus is planted in the seventh spot, Salix is planted in the first spot.

6. Which one of the following must be false?
   (A) Poncirus is planted east of Morus and west of Olea.
   (B) Larix is planted east of Poncirus and west of Robinia.
   (C) Nyssa is planted east of Morus and west of Robinia.
   (D) Morus is planted east of Salix and west of Olea.
   (E) Robinia is planted east of Salix and west of Poncirus.

GO ON TO THE NEXT PAGE

Questions 7–13

Six members of the university swim team—Paul, Rachel, Shen, Thomas, Uli, and Victoria—will compete in a swim meet next Saturday. Each team member will swim one lap during one of six consecutive time slots. During each time slot, only one member swims. The order in which the members swim must meet the following constraints:

Rachel swims either immediately before or immediately after Victoria.

If Paul does not swim in the third time slot, then Shen swims in the fifth time slot.

Either Rachel swims before Paul, or Rachel swims before Thomas, but not both.

7. Which one of the following could be the order in which the team members swim, from first to last?
   (A) Uli, Shen, Paul, Thomas, Rachel, Victoria
   (B) Uli, Shen, Thomas, Victoria, Rachel, Paul
   (C) Thomas, Rachel, Paul, Shen, Victoria, Uli
   (D) Thomas, Uli, Rachel, Victoria, Shen, Paul
   (E) Victoria, Rachel, Thomas, Paul, Shen, Uli

8. If Paul swims in the first time slot, then which one of the following must be true?
   (A) Thomas swims either fourth or sixth.
   (B) Rachel swims either second or third.
   (C) Uli swims second.
   (D) Thomas swims after Uli.
   (E) Uli swims before Shen.

9. Which one of the following CANNOT be true?
   (A) Rachel swims immediately after Uli.
   (B) Paul swims immediately before Shen.
   (C) Paul swims immediately before Thomas.
   (D) Rachel swims immediately after Thomas and immediately before Victoria.
   (E) Shen swims immediately after Uli and immediately before Paul.

10. For which one of the following are there five possible time slots to which the member could be assigned?
    (A) Victoria
    (B) Uli
    (C) Thomas
    (D) Shen
    (E) Paul

11. If Uli swims before Shen, the order in which the team members swim is fully determined if which one of the following is also true?
    (A) Thomas swims sixth.
    (B) Victoria swims fifth.
    (C) Paul swims third.
    (D) Rachel swims third.
    (E) Shen swims second.

12. If Thomas swims before Paul, which one of the following must be true?
    (A) Paul swims sixth.
    (B) Thomas swims first.
    (C) Shen swims either immediately before or immediately after Paul.
    (D) Uli swims immediately before or immediately after Thomas.
    (E) Either Rachel or Victoria swims fourth.

13. If Paul swims immediately before Shen, then for exactly how many of the team members can it be determined in which time slot he or she swims?
    (A) one
    (B) two
    (C) three
    (D) four
    (E) five

GO ON TO THE NEXT PAGE

Questions 14–18

A radio station plays foreign language news for one hour starting at 8 P.M. every evening. The station's program scheduler must decide which language is assigned for each of the seven days of the upcoming week, beginning with Monday. The possible languages are Norwegian, Polish, Romani, Slovak, Thai, Urdu, and Welsh. Each day exactly one language is used. Each language is used exactly once during the week. The conditions are:

Romani and Norwegian are both assigned earlier in the week than Polish.
Norwegian and Thai are both assigned earlier in the week than Urdu.
Welsh is assigned to Thursday.
Either Romani is assigned earlier in the week than Welsh, or Thai is assigned earlier in the week than Slovak, but not both.

14. Which one of the following could be the assignment of languages to the days of the week, in order, from Monday to Sunday?
    (A) Slovak, Norwegian, Thai, Welsh, Romani, Polish, Urdu
    (B) Slovak, Thai, Romani, Welsh, Urdu, Norwegian, Polish
    (C) Thai, Norwegian, Slovak, Welsh, Urdu, Polish, Romani
    (D) Romani, Slovak, Norwegian, Welsh, Polish, Thai, Urdu
    (E) Thai, Norwegian, Romani, Welsh, Urdu, Polish, Slovak

15. If there are exactly two days between the day that Urdu is assigned and the day that Romani is assigned, then which one of the following could be true?
    (A) Slovak is assigned on Wednesday.
    (B) Norwegian is assigned on Tuesday.
    (C) Urdu is assigned on Friday.
    (D) Slovak is assigned on Saturday.
    (E) Polish is assigned on Saturday.

16. Which one of the following pairs of languages CANNOT be assigned to Monday and Tuesday, respectively?
    (A) Romani, Slovak
    (B) Slovak, Thai
    (C) Norwegian, Thai
    (D) Thai, Romani
    (E) Romani, Norwegian

GO ON TO THE NEXT PAGE

17. If Polish is assigned to Wednesday, then which one of the following could be false?
    (A) Slovak is assigned to Friday.
    (B) Thai is assigned to Saturday.
    (C) Urdu is assigned to Sunday.
    (D) Romani is assigned to Monday.
    (E) Welsh is assigned to Thursday.

18. If Thai is assigned earlier in the week than Slovak, then which one of the following could be true?
    (A) Norwegian is assigned to Friday.
    (B) Thai is assigned to Friday.
    (C) Thai is assigned to Wednesday.
    (D) Romani is assigned to Wednesday.
    (E) Urdu is assigned to Wednesday.

GO ON TO THE NEXT PAGE

Questions 19–23

A conference planner must invite at least three employees of Company X to an upcoming business conference. The employees who are available to attend are Fernandez, Gilliam, Hong, Idriss, Jankowic, King, Logan, and Monroe. The selection of attendees must conform to the following conditions:

If Hong is selected, neither Fernandez nor Logan is not selected.

King cannot be selected if Idriss is selected.

Idriss must be selected if Hong is selected.

Fernandez is selected only if Monroe is not selected.

If either King or Gilliam is selected, both must be selected.

19. Which one of the following could be the list of the employees who are invited to the conference?
    (A) Hong, Idriss, Jankowic
    (B) Gilliam, Hong, Jankowic, King, Monroe
    (C) Hong, Idriss, Logan, Monroe
    (D) Fernandez, Idriss, Monroe
    (E) Idriss, King, Gilliam

20. If Hong is invited, then which one of the following must be true?
    (A) At most four employees are invited.
    (B) At most five employees are invited.
    (C) Monroe is invited.
    (D) Jankowic is invited.
    (E) Jankowic is not invited.

21. If there must be at least four employees who attend the conference, which one of the following is a pair of employees of which the conference planner must select at least one employee?
    (A) Fernandez and Idriss
    (B) Fernandez and Gilliam
    (C) Hong and King
    (D) Idriss and King
    (E) Idriss and Monroe

GO ON TO THE NEXT PAGE

22. If Fernandez is selected but Jankowic is not, which one of the following could be true?
    (A) Exactly two employees are not selected.
    (B) Exactly five employees are selected.
    (C) Idriss is selected and Gilliam is selected.
    (D) Idriss is selected and Logan is not selected.
    (E) Gilliam is selected and Logan is not selected.

23. What is the maximum number of employees who could be selected to attend the conference?
    (A) four
    (B) five
    (C) six
    (D) seven
    (E) eight

If you finish before the 35-minute time period is over, you may go back and check your answers in this section only. You may not work on any other test section.

SECTION IV

Time —35 minutes
25 Questions

Directions: The questions in this section are based on the reasoning contained in brief statements or passages. More than one answer choice could conceivably answer the question in some cases. However, you should choose the best answer. The best answer is the response that answers the question most accurately and completely. You should avoid making any assumptions that, by commonsense standards, are implausible, superfluous, or incompatible with the passage. When you have chosen the best answer, fill in the space on your answer sheet that corresponds to your answer.

1. Store manager: Our strongest sales are in the
   evening. Since we changed our store hours last month in order to remain open one hour later in the evening, there have always been customers shopping during the last hour. However, our net profit per day has actually decreased.

   Which one of the following, if true, most helps to explain the decrease in net profit described above?
   (A) People who shop late in the evening tend to buy fewer items than people who shop earlier in the day.
   (B) Most of the people who shop during the last hour of the day would have come to the store earlier in the evening if the store had closed at its original closing time.
   (C) The net profit of any store is lower on some days than on other days.
   (D) Net profit is not the best way to measure the popularity of a store.
   (E) The cost of operating the store for an additional hour is greater than the income from sales during that hour.

2. After Ed suffered a minor heart attack, his physician reviewed Ed's diet, and advised Ed to cut back on certain foods. Like many people in the same position, Ed is not likely to change his eating habits, given that the foods he was advised to avoid were among his favorites. In such circumstances, it is important for family members not to nag the patient about the patient's diet. If, but only if, left alone, most such people begin to make small, healthful changes gradually.

Which one of the following most accurately expresses the overall conclusion of the above argument?

(A) Most people who have had a serious health problem eventually begin to make healthful changes.

(B) Nagging a family member about diet can prevent the family member from making healthful changes.

(C) Ed's original diet was not as healthy as it could have been.

(D) If Ed's family nags him about his diet, Ed will probably not make any effort to change his diet.

(E) Ed's family should accept his decisions about his health because he is reacting in the way that most people in his situation would react.

3. There are two widely separated islands in the Pacific Ocean that are both home to a species of flower with a sweet nectar that is located at the end of a long tube. On both islands, there is a butterfly species that has developed an unusually long tongue that allows it to suck the nectar from these flowers. This is an amazing example of two distinct populations independently developing the same adaptive mechanism in response to the same environmental challenge.

The argument's conclusion is properly drawn if which one of the following is assumed?

(A) There has never been any interbreeding between members of the two butterfly species on the two islands.

(B) The two flower species with the long tubes are not genetically related.

(C) If the butterfly species on either island had not developed the long tongue, they would not have had any food source.

(D) There is no other animal that is better adapted than the long-tongued butterflies to suck nectar from the long-tubed flowers.

(E) All of the butterflies on both islands are capable of long-distance flight.

GO ON TO THE NEXT PAGE

4. Mayor: I have advice for anyone planning to run for mayor after my term is up. When you talk with voters, it is natural for you to want to please them. However, this invariably leads to making promises that you cannot keep. Voters recognize unrealistic promises and are unlikely to vote for you.

Which one of the following is most strongly supported by the statements in the passage?

(A) If a mayoral candidate makes promises that are realistic, the voters are likely to vote for that candidate.

(B) Most mayoral candidates make promises that they cannot keep.

(C) If voters recognize that a mayoral candidate's promises are unrealistic, those voters will be unlikely to vote in the mayoral election.

(D) If a mayoral candidate wants to please the voters, the voters will be unlikely to vote for that candidate.

(E) If a mayoral candidate does not want to please the voters, the voters will be likely to vote for that candidate.

5. A new computer programming language, OYSTER, is very powerful because of its highly abstract syntax. Advanced programmers will get better and faster results with OYSTER. However, programmers who are not advanced will find OYSTER harder to work with. Because most computer programs are written by less-advanced programmers, and because programs written by advanced programmers must often be modified by less-advanced programmers, it would be better for advanced programmers to avoid OYSTER.

Which one of the following principles, if valid, most helps to justify the conclusion in the argument above?

(A) A programming language that is very powerful should be used only by those people who will find it to be superior to other programming languages.

(B) A programming language that is very powerful should not be used at all if some of the people who need to use it find it to be more powerful than necessary for their projects.

(C) A programming language that is very powerful should not be used at all if it is harder to work with than other programming languages for some of the people who are likely to need to use it.

(D) A programming language that is better than other programming languages should not be used at all if the people who write programs with the language are more advanced than the people who must modify the programs written in the language.

(E) Programmers who are advanced should not write programs that are so abstract that less-advanced programmers cannot understand or modify the programs.

GO ON TO THE NEXT PAGE

6. Politician: A recent survey of likely voters showed my opponent to be ten points ahead of me. However, the survey is not likely to be accurate. The survey was conducted by phone. Younger people are much less likely to answer a phone call from an unrecognized number than are older people, and my strongest support is from younger people.

Which one of the following arguments is most similar in reasoning to the reasoning in the argument above?

(A) A recent survey of people visiting an art museum indicated that more of them like classical art than like modern art. The results of the survey cannot be considered meaningful, since the art museum is best known for its collection of classical art and has almost no modern art on display.

(B) A recent survey asked college students to name their "favorite politician." Over 70 percent considered the state's governor to be their favorite politician. The results of the survey, however, can hardly be considered accurate. None of the students responding to the survey asked for a clarification of the term *favorite*. In addition, none of the people conducting the survey explained how the term should be interpreted.

(C) The recent survey of dog owners is flawed. The survey showed that the majority of dog owners like to walk their dogs in the evening. However, the survey was done outdoors during the evening, when people who do not like to walk their dog in the evening would be less likely to be outdoors.

(D) A recent survey asked a number of journalists what profession, other than journalism, they most admired. The survey concluded that 80 percent of journalists admire physicians. The results of the survey are, however, not likely to be accurate, because the people surveyed were not themselves physicians.

(E) A recent survey indicated that 75 percent of Americans believe that UFOs exist and that they are flown by extraterrestrials. The survey, however, is unlikely to have any meaning. The mere fact that a high percentage of people believe in a certain phenomenon is not an indication of the existence of the phenomenon.

GO ON TO THE NEXT PAGE

7. To ensure strong bones, it is important to have an adequate level of available calcium in the body. Because most people get significant amounts of calcium from their diets, they only need to ensure that they get enough vitamin D.

The argument depends on assuming which one of the following?
(A) There are fewer dietary sources of vitamin D than there are of calcium.
(B) Calcium from foods is preferable to calcium from supplements.
(C) It is not possible to have strong bones without a healthy diet.
(D) To ensure strong bones, it is necessary to get as much vitamin D as calcium.
(E) Without enough vitamin D, calcium cannot be made available for the body.

8. Phuong: The primary purpose of a garden is to nourish the spirit. A successful garden may or may not produce vegetables, fruits, or flowers. If, by lovingly tending the garden, the gardener feels relaxed and at home, then the garden has fulfilled its primary purpose.

Jacob: There is no reason to grow a garden other than to nourish the spirit. The spirit is nourished when one's hard labor results in a product that one can enjoy eating or looking at.

Phuong and Jacob disagree with each other over whether
(A) a gardener's feeling relaxed and at home is sufficient to conclude that the garden has served its purpose
(B) the primary reason for gardening is to nourish the spirit
(C) a garden that produces vegetables, fruits, and flowers may have fulfilled its purpose
(D) the primary reason for growing a garden is to produce healthy food
(E) gardening involves hard labor

GO ON TO THE NEXT PAGE

9. In order to discourage speeding, the police periodically increase the number of patrol cars checking traffic with radar guns. Usually, the patrol cars are placed where drivers can see them, as a deterrent. Unfortunately, the conspicuous presence of patrol cars seems to result in an increase in certain kinds of accidents. Apparently, knowing that they are being watched causes some drivers to get into an accident.

Which one of the following, if true, most strengthens the argument above?

(A) Most drivers become nervous when they know they are being watched by the police.

(B) Drivers who are speeding are more likely to cause accidents than are drivers who are not speeding.

(C) Drivers who regularly use radar detectors in their cars are less likely to become nervous in the presence of patrol cars than are drivers who do not regularly use radar detectors.

(D) When a driver becomes nervous, the driver is more likely to switch lanes frequently.

(E) When a driver's eyes focus on the speedometer, the driver's peripheral vision diminishes significantly.

GO ON TO THE NEXT PAGE

10. A work of art cannot be considered significant unless at least one professional art critic has given the work a positive review. Among those works that have received a positive review from such a critic, it can be said that any work that has been praised by more than one museum curator is certainly a significant work of art.

Which one of the following situations conforms most closely to the principles outlined in the passage above?

(A) Susan's sculpture, *Gull on a Hot Rock*, has been highly praised by all of the visitors to the museum where it is displayed. However, no museum curator has as yet commented on her sculpture. Therefore, *Gull on a Hot Rock* is not a significant work of art.

(B) Jefferson's print, *Todacheene*, has been praised by each of the five museum curators who recently reviewed it. Even though none of the museum curators is a professional art critic, their praise establishes that *Todacheene* is a significant work of art.

(C) Ruth Anne's print, *Praying Mantis*, recently received significant praise from two museum curators, one of whom is a well-known professional art critic. Therefore, *Praying Mantis* is a significant work of art.

(D) Li's painting, *Delta*, has been highly praised by several professional art critics, one of whom is also a museum curator. Therefore, it is likely, though not definite, that *Delta* is a significant work of art.

(E) Julianna's print, *Blue Chickens*, is not a significant work of art. Therefore, it cannot have received the praise of any professional art critic.

GO ON TO THE NEXT PAGE

11. Attorney: In many jury trials there is circumstantial evidence both for and against the defendant. Often, the only objective evidence is from eyewitnesses, but because members of juries are rarely convinced by testimony from people who they do not consider reliable, eyewitness testimony usually does not convince a jury.

Which one of the following, if assumed, allows the attorney's conclusion to be properly drawn?

(A) People who do not believe that they can reliably report what they have observed at a crime scene usually do not offer to be witnesses.

(B) Eyewitnesses who testify in jury trials often have personal characteristics that cause the members of the jury to doubt the eyewitness's reliability.

(C) People who serve on juries generally do not consider people who have committed crimes to be reliable witnesses.

(D) Most people who serve on juries find circumstantial evidence to be unreliable.

(E) In jury trials in which the circumstantial evidence does not clearly establish the guilt or innocence of the defendant, the jury must rely on eyewitness reports.

GO ON TO THE NEXT PAGE

12. Even though American public primary education is nearly universally co-educational, with boys and girls in the same class, some educators believe that students would learn more in classes that were either all male or all female.

    Which one of the following, if true, would provide evidence against the belief that students would learn better in classes that were all male or all female?
    (A) At the primary level, there are usually few male teachers available to teach classes consisting only of boys.
    (B) When there are both boys and girls in a classroom, the boys tend to learn more and the girls tend to learn less than if the boys and girls were taught in separate classrooms.
    (C) When there are boys and girls in a classroom, the teacher calls on the boys more often than on the girls.
    (D) The presence of girls in a classroom reduces the aggressive behavior among boys in the same classroom.
    (E) When students know they are being observed by students of the opposite sex, they often want to perform better on tests and quizzes.

GO ON TO THE NEXT PAGE

13. Before the recent citywide election, prominent advertisements warned nearly all residents that the proposed sales tax increase to fund a performing arts center would benefit only middle-class residents. Despite this warning, nearly all of the residents of the city's Old Town area, most of whom have incomes significantly below the middle-class level, voted for the increase.

Which one of the following, if true, best explains the voting pattern of the Old Town residents?
(A) Many city residents who have middle-class incomes voted against the increase.
(B) Nearly all people consider themselves to be middle class, even if their incomes are significantly above or below the middle-class level.
(C) Many people who have middle-class incomes are not in fact middle class.
(D) Many people who would enjoy having a performing arts center nevertheless do not want to pay for one.
(E) The Old Town area has always had a lower sales tax rate than other parts of the city.

14. Surgeon: I will not be able to operate on Edgar tomorrow. Even though Edgar has followed the presurgical protocol perfectly, the protocol does not guarantee favorable conditions for surgery unless the patient is completely free of infection the day before the surgery.

The argument relies on which one of the following assumptions?
(A) Edgar has an infection that cannot be cured by the day of surgery.
(B) Edgar has at least a small amount of infection.
(C) If the conditions for Edgar's surgery were favorable, the surgeon would operate.
(D) The presurgical protocol does not include measures for avoiding infection.
(E) Tomorrow is the only day that the surgeon would be able to operate on Edgar.

GO ON TO THE NEXT PAGE

15. Even though many talented musicians do not know how to read musical notation, there are many advantages to be gained by learning to read music. Just as learning to read English allows a person to "hear" the words of a story when no one is present to tell the story, learning to read music _____ .

Which one of the following most logically completes the final sentence of the above passage?
(A) allows a person to determine the sounds of a composition when no one is present to play the composition
(B) allows a person to write down a piece of music that the person has composed when there is no one present to hear the piece
(C) allows a person to "hear" the emotion that a composer intends to convey when the composer is not present
(D) allows a person to see the notes of which a composition is composed
(E) allows a person to "see" with the imagination when it is not possible to hear with the ears

GO ON TO THE NEXT PAGE

16. Historian: In comparing the appalling slaughter of combatants during World Wars I and II with the comparatively low mortality rate for combatants in recent wars, some historians have postulated that the difference is because modern politicians have learned lessons from the past. However, a careful analysis of the top political leaders responsible for several modern wars shows that these leaders had almost no understanding of the historical events of the two world wars. Most likely the lower mortality rate for combatants today is due to other factors, including, perhaps, combat technology.

Which one of the following most accurately states the main conclusion of the historian's argument?

(A) Today's lower mortality rate for combatants is due to improved combat technology.

(B) It is possible that modern political leaders have learned important lessons from the history of the two world wars.

(C) The lower mortality rate for combatants today, compared to during the two world wars, is not due to an understanding of history on the part of politicians.

(D) It is possible for wars to become less destructive, whether through improved technologies or through lessons learned from previous wars.

(E) Modern political leaders do not have an adequate understanding of even fairly recent history.

GO ON TO THE NEXT PAGE

17. Rancher: The reintroduction of wolves is a bad thing. Sure, it creates jobs for federal agencies, but the program costs us livestock without giving us anything beneficial in return.

Biologist: That is not true. Reintroducing wolves not only enriches the biological diversity of our ecosystem but also helps cull out weak and unfit livestock in a natural way.

Evaluating the effectiveness of the biologist's response requires clarification of which one of the following issues?
(A) whether the cost to ranchers in terms of lost livestock is less than or greater than the benefit to federal agencies in terms of new jobs
(B) whether either enriching biological diversity or culling out unfit livestock in a natural way benefits ranchers
(C) whether the value of enriched biological diversity is less than or greater than the value of culling out unfit livestock in a natural way
(D) whether the cost to ranchers in terms of lost livestock is less than or greater than the benefit to ranchers from culling out unfit livestock in a natural way
(E) whether enriching biological diversity and culling out unfit livestock have any economic value to ranchers

18. An exit poll of voters at our recent city election showed that those voters who had read a summary of the bond issue for funding a new bridge downtown voted for the bond issue, whereas those voters who had not read the summary voted against the bond issue. The summary must have convinced voters that the bond issue was worth voting for.

Which one of the following, if true, most seriously weakens the argument above?
(A) Once voters decided to support the bond issue, they subsequently wanted to read more about it.
(B) Many voters who opposed the bond issue had decided how they would vote on the bond issue before going to the polls.
(C) There were some people who read the summary of the bond issue and then decided to vote against it.
(D) A high percentage of people who voted in the recent city election did so by absentee ballot and did not go to the polls on election day.
(E) Many voters refused to talk with the people conducting the exit polls.

GO ON TO THE NEXT PAGE

19. Outside of the two-hour rush hour period, the average speed on the highway is 50 miles per hour. During rush hour, the average speed is 30 miles per hour. Cars traveling at an average of 30 miles per hour get better gas mileage than cars traveling at an average of 50 miles per hour. However, stop-and-go driving decreases gas mileage. During the second hour of rush hour, but not the first hour, cars are subject to frequent stop-and-go driving.

Which one of the following can be most properly inferred from the argument above?

(A) Cars on the highway outside of rush hour are not subject to frequent stop-and-go driving.

(B) During the second hour of rush hour, cars on the highway get worse gas mileage than cars on the highway outside of rush hour.

(C) During the first hour of rush hour, cars on the highway get better gas mileage than cars on the highway during the second hour of rush hour.

(D) The maximum speed of cars on the highway during rush hour is less than the maximum speed of cars on the highway outside of rush hour.

(E) The average speed of cars on the highway during the first hour of rush hour is higher than the average speed of cars on the highway during the second hour of rush hour.

20. Attorney: The public should be able to judge the extent to which corporations act ethically. However, because violations of ethics often do not involve violations of laws, the courts have been reluctant to force corporations to report their ethical practices. Unless that changes, it is unlikely that the public will be able to judge the extent to which corporations act ethically.

    The reasoning in the argument is most vulnerable to criticism on the grounds that it

    (A) presumes, without providing justification, that corporations violate the ethical standards of the public
    (B) fails to consider whether public judgment of the ethics of corporations would change the behavior of corporations that are judged to act unethically
    (C) presumes, without providing justification, that corporations are unable to judge the extent to which their own actions are ethical
    (D) fails to provide a rationale for the claim that violations of ethics are often not violations of laws
    (E) fails to consider that there may be other ways to obtain information about a corporation's ethical practices other than a court-ordered report

GO ON TO THE NEXT PAGE

21. With the advent of modern medicine, health care providers have been able to cure diseases and conditions that would have previously been fatal. As a result, the average life expectancy has increased dramatically. As medicine continues to evolve, it will some day be able not just to cure diseases but to protect people from getting the diseases at all. Because a person who has not had a disease is healthier than a person who has recovered from a disease, this new form of medicine will cause the average life expectancy to increase even further.

    Which one of the following, if true, most strengthens the argument stated above?
    (A) The countries with the best health care have the longest average life expectancy.
    (B) Having avoided getting diseases contributes significantly to living a long life.
    (C) Modern medicine has completely eradicated certain diseases.
    (D) People who have recovered from a serious disease often have antibodies that protect them from similar diseases.
    (E) People who have avoided contracting influenza because of a vaccination are typically healthier during influenza season than are people who contracted influenza and recovered from it.

22. The number of sightings of unidentified flying objects has increased dramatically in recent years. At the same time, the attempts to explain these objects as human phenomena have repeatedly failed. Regardless of who or what is piloting these objects, they have clearly begun visiting us more and more frequently in recent years.

    The reasoning in the above argument is questionable in that it takes for granted that
    (A) the frequency of sightings of unidentified flying objects will continue to increase
    (B) the increase in the frequency of sightings corresponds to an increase in the frequency of visitation by unidentified flying objects
    (C) something or someone is piloting the unidentified flying objects
    (D) there is no explanation for unidentified flying objects that could establish them as human phenomena
    (E) unidentified flying objects pose no danger to humanity

GO ON TO THE NEXT PAGE

23. The chances of a new small business surviving for a year are 30 percent. It is a shame that none of the fifteen new small businesses that started up in the last three months are likely to still be in business a year from now.

Which one of the following contains a logical flaw that is most similar to the logical flaw in the argument above?

(A) None of my greyhounds have won more than one race out of four. It is unlikely, then, that any of my six greyhounds will win the race that I have entered them in on Saturday.

(B) Of my ten favorite artists, only one has ever received public recognition. Therefore, it is unlikely that I will see the works of the other nine of my favorite artists when I go to the museum on Friday.

(C) All five of the high schools in our city are governed by our board of education, and all five have excellent academic success. Therefore, the academic success must be the result of the policies of the board of education.

(D) Three separate juries have acquitted the man accused of bribing jurors, so it must be that the man is actually innocent.

(E) Of the employees at Corporation Z, 40 percent have worked there for under a year. Andrea is an employee of Corporation Z, so there is a 40 percent chance that she has worked there for under a year.

GO ON TO THE NEXT PAGE

24. Ecologist: There is no question that the situation of the Rio Grande silvery minnow is precarious. Its numbers are lower now than when it was first declared endangered in 1994, and it is currently found in only 5 percent of its original habitat. The demise of this fish, which once dominated a 3,000-mile stretch of river, is a sure sign that our entire ecosystem—on which we depend for food, water, and survival—may well be in danger of collapse.

Which one of the following best describes the role played in the argument by the statement that the situation of the Rio Grande silvery minnow is precarious?

(A) It is the main conclusion of the argument and is defended by specific facts.

(B) It is a fact that the argument acknowledges and then attempts to rebut.

(C) It is a premise that supports a conclusion that is then used to support the main conclusion of the argument.

(D) It is a conclusion that is defended by facts and is used as a premise in support of the main conclusion of the argument.

(E) It is a hypothesis that the argument uses to support a conclusion.

25. The pursuit of truth is the most noble endeavor of humanity. However, no person can pursue truth if that person is obsessed with finding food and shelter. If society were but to guarantee adequate food and a warm, safe shelter to each and every person, then all of humanity would pursue the most noble endeavor.

Which one of the following most accurately expresses a flaw in the argument's reasoning?

(A) It applies a condition that is true in an individual case to a general case in which the condition is not true.

(B) It presumes, without warrant, that all members of a group have the same characteristic because some members of the group have that characteristic.

(C) It fails to consider that an event that is probable is not inevitable.

(D) It relies on information about a group that is not representative of the population as a whole.

(E) It treats a condition that is necessary for the occurrence of a certain endeavor as a condition that is sufficient to guarantee the occurrence of that endeavor.

STOP

If you finish before the 35-minute time period is over, you may go back and check your answers in this section only. You may not work on any other test section.

WRITING SAMPLE

Time —35 minutes

General Directions: You will have thirty-five minutes to organize and write an essay on the topic described on the next page. Read the topic and all of the directions carefully. It is generally best to take a few minutes to organize your thoughts before beginning to write. Be sure to develop your ideas fully and leave time at the end to review what you have written. **Do not write on any topic other than the topic given. It is not acceptable to write on a topic of your own choice.**

No special knowledge is needed or expected for this essay. Admission committees are interested in your reasoning, clarity, organization, use of language, and writing mechanics. The quality of what you write is more important than the quantity.

Keep your essay in the blocked and lined area on the front and back of the separate Writing Sample Response Sheet. That is the only area that will be reproduced and sent to law schools. Be sure to write legibly.

Scratch Paper
Do not write your essay here. Scratch work only.

WRITING SAMPLE TOPIC

General Directions: The situation described below gives two choices. Either one of the choices can be supported based on the information given. In your essay, consider both choices and then argue in favor of one over the other. Base your argument on the two specified criteria and on the given facts. There is no "right" or "wrong" choice. Either choice can be reasonably defended.

Slotown's city council wants to revitalize Slotown's public transit system because HugeGro Company recently announced that it will locate three or more of its new assembly facilities in different Slotown boroughs. Slotown has narrowed its transportation choices between light rail and buses. Using the facts given below, compose an essay in which you argue in favor of choosing one alternative over the other on the basis of the two criteria below:

- Slotown wants to maximize its transportation flexibility in the event that a HugeGro plant closes or changes location in the future.
- Slotown wants to minimize its fuel costs and hydrocarbon footprint.

RoadRail Corporation offers turnkey packages consisting of light rail trains, tracks, stations, and repair facilities for intracity applications. RoadRail's claim to fame is its recent installation at a major city in the southwestern United States. Officials from that city brag about RoadRail's low fuel costs, high rider capacities, and rapid turnaround times. RoadRail's sales team brags that RoadRail trains are at least thirty times more fuel efficient than buses. RoadRail has a modular track system that could provide flexible passenger routes that can be moved around regular streets once the initial hub and maintenance facilities are built, but the southwestern city officials have been silent concerning this feature.

Green Bus Co. builds natural gas-powered buses for urban use. Green buses are articulated and known for their maneuverability, as well as their large carrying capacities. Green has sold natural gas-powered buses for over twenty years and has refined the buses' efficiencies. Green's salesperson says that both the cost of natural gas and the hydrocarbon footprint of each bus will rapidly decrease in the next few years. Buses are indeed becoming more fuel efficient, but the old axiom that trains use less fuel than buses requires Green to present up-to-date facts and figures to city governments.

Scratch Paper
Do not write your essay here. Scratch work only.

Use the lined area below to write your essay.
Continue on the back if you need more space.

ANSWER KEY—PRACTICE TEST

Section I: Reading Comprehension

1.	D	8.	A	15.	D	22.	B
2.	D	9.	C	16.	A	23.	A
3.	E	10.	A	17.	B	24.	D
4.	C	11.	E	18.	B	25.	E
5.	D	12.	B	19.	C	26.	A
6.	E	13.	E	20.	E	27.	C
7.	E	14.	B	21.	E		

Section II: Logical Reasoning

1.	D	8.	C	15.	C	22.	D
2.	E	9.	D	16.	E	23.	A
3.	C	10.	C	17.	C	24.	D
4.	D	11.	A	18.	E	25.	B
5.	C	12.	C	19.	D	26.	D
6.	D	13.	D	20.	B		
7.	A	14.	C	21.	E		

Section III: Analytical Reasoning

1.	A	7.	D	13.	D	19.	A
2.	E	8.	A	14.	D	20.	A
3.	A	9.	C	15.	B	21.	D
4.	C	10.	E	16.	D	22.	E
5.	D	11.	B	17.	D	23.	B
6.	A	12.	C	18.	E		

Section IV: Logical Reasoning

1.	E	8.	A	15.	A	22.	B
2.	B	9.	E	16.	C	23.	A
3.	A	10.	C	17.	B	24.	D
4.	D	11.	B	18.	A	25.	E
5.	C	12.	E	19.	C		
6.	C	13.	B	20.	E		
7.	E	14.	B	21.	B		

CALCULATING YOUR SCORE

1. Check your answers against the Answer Key on the previous page.
2. Use the Score Worksheet below to calculate your raw score. Your raw score is the total number of questions that you answered correctly.
3. Use the Conversion Table below to convert your raw score into a score on the 120–180 scale. Remember that these scores are approximate.

Score Worksheet

Section	Number of Questions	Number Correct	Number Incorrect	Number Not Answered*
Section I: Reading Comprehension	27			
Section II: Logical Reasoning	26			
Section III: Analytical Reasoning	23			
Section IV: Logical Reasoning	25			
Total:	101			

*You should not leave any questions unanswered. There is no penalty for guessing.

Conversion Table

Raw Score Range	Scaled Score	Raw Score Range	Scaled Score	Raw Score Range	Scaled Score	Raw Score Range	Scaled Score	Raw Score Range	Scaled Score
0–15	120	30	133	50	146	72–73	159	90	172
16	121	31–32	134	51–52	147	74	160	91–92	173
17	122	33	135	53	148	75–76	161	93	174
18	123	34–35	136	54–55	149	77	162	94	175
19	124	36	137	56–57	150	78–79	163	95	176
20	125	37–38	138	58	151	80	164	96	177
21	126	39	139	59–60	152	81–82	165	97	178
22–23	127	40–41	140	61–62	153	83	166	98	179
24	128	42	141	63–64	154	84–85	167	99–101	180
25	129	43–44	142	65	155	86	168		
26	130	45	143	66–67	156	87	169		
27–28	131	46–47	144	68–69	157	88	170		
29	132	48–49	145	70–71	158	89	171		

EXAM ANALYSIS

Every practice section that you take is an opportunity for you to evaluate your testing strategy. If you take a section under timed conditions, that also gives you an opportunity to evaluate your timing strategy. The last section of Chapter 1 (General Strategies) provides a detailed worksheet and plan for reviewing your performance and identifying exactly what strategy error led to each wrong answer. The sections of Chapter 1 on timing explain how to evaluate your timing strategy. Be sure to evaluate your timing strategy for every section that you take under timed conditions.

Use the plan in Chapter 1 to review every question that you answered incorrectly. The plan lists twenty-two specific errors. For each question that you answered incorrectly, you should review the parts of Chapter 1 and the other relevant chapters that cover the strategies with which you had trouble. The key to success is identifying your errors and reviewing again and again.

Use the following chart to summarize your performance based on four main categories of error. Enter the number of incorrect answers in each column. Some questions may fall under more than one category.

Summary of Incorrect Answers

Section	Total Incorrect	Didn't Take Enough Time	Misread Information	Got Down to Two Answers	Didn't Have a Strategy
I: RC					
II: LR					
III: AR					
IV: LR					
Total:					

After you have reviewed your timing strategy, enter the results in the chart on the next page. The questions for which you simply filled in a bubble without working on the question should be counted under Cold Guesses. If you spent more than fifteen seconds working on a question, do *not* count it under Cold Guesses. Under Number Correct and Number Incorrect, do not include Cold Guesses. The number in the Cold Guesses column, then, includes both incorrect and correct answers. In the final column, enter the number of incorrect answers on which you spent under two minutes.

Analysis of Timing Strategy

Section	Number Correct (not cold guesses)	Number Incorrect (not cold guesses)	Cold Guesses	Number of Incorrect Under 2 Minutes
I: RC				
II: LR				
III: AR				
IV: LR				
Total:				

If most of your incorrect answers took under two minutes, you should plan to spend more time on questions. If you have more than two or three questions incorrect—excluding Cold Guesses—you can increase your score by working on fewer questions but spending a little more time on the questions that you do work on. See the example below.

Example of Revised Timing Strategy

Section	Number Correct (not cold guesses)	Number Incorrect (not cold guesses)	Cold Guesses	Number of Incorrect Under 2 Minutes	Total Correct (including cold guesses)
First attempt	11	6	7	5	12
Revised attempt	11 + 2	0	7 + 4	0	15

By guessing cold on four more questions, the test taker in the example above had time to work the remaining two questions correctly. Approximately one out of five Cold Guesses results in a correct answer.

ANSWERS EXPLAINED

Section I: Reading Comprehension

1. **(D)** This is a rare *agreement between two people* question. Choice D is correct because the policy of the government of the Netherlands allows the innovator to make a profit, and the author's proposal allows the innovator to make a profit (a lump-sum payment).

   Choice A is incorrect because it is consistent with the author's statements but there is no information about the attitude of the government of the Netherlands toward choice A. Choice B is incorrect for the same reason. Choice C is incorrect because the author believes that confusion of ownership is a more substantial issue. Choice E is incorrect because the author does not believe it.

2. **(D)** This is a *main idea* question. Choice D captures the entire context of the passage, including the positive aspects of patents, the negative aspects, and an alternative.

   Choice A is incorrect because it discusses only the positive aspects. Choice B is incorrect because it discusses the positives, one negative, but not the main negative, and does not include the alternative. Choice C is incorrect because it only compares two negatives without mentioning the positives or alternatives. Choice E is incorrect because it only includes the alternative.

3. **(E)** This is a *weaken* question, based on weakening an argument in the passage, similar to *weaken* questions in LR. The author's argument is based on the statement that the goal of a patent is to grant exclusive ownership. Choice E establishes that owners of previous patents on which a new patent depends usually do not interfere with the decisions of the owner of the new patent. Therefore, exclusive ownership is preserved in practice.

   Choice A is incorrect because it supports the author's argument. Choice B is incorrect because even if the cost of litigation is not more than the value, it is still a significant cost, and therefore choice B strengthens the author's argument. Choice C is incorrect because it does not attack the author's premise that patents based on other patents dilute exclusive ownership. Choice D is incorrect because the owner of the older patent, while willing to cooperate, requires compromise, which strengthens the argument that the new patent holder does not have exclusive ownership.

4. **(C)** This is an *implied fact* question. Choice C is correct, and choice B is incorrect, because the passage states that a patent holder can prevent others from making, selling, or using a patented technology without

permission. Payment is optional. Choice A is incorrect because it is the patent owner who must disclose the technology. Choice D is incorrect because the passage states that some people believe a patent is inherently inconsistent with free trade policy. Choice E is incorrect because it refers only to an innovator, not to a patent owner.

5. **(D)** This is a *tone* question. The answer choices are typically on a continuum, as in this question, ranging from positive without qualifications to positive with qualifications to neutral to negative with qualifications and finally to negative without qualifications. For this question, the author is negative about patents in the modern era but also cites some positive aspects. The correct answer choice is the one that is negative with qualifications, choice D.

6. **(E)** This is an *agree with a view* question. Choice E is correct, based on the statement "In the case above, it is not is clear who owns Sandra's invention . . ." In the passage, Sandra is the holder of the later patent.

    Choice A is incorrect because the author states that most patents are based on previous patents "in this era of rapidly expanding technologies." It is not defendable to conclude that that era began in the 1800s. Choice B is incorrect because it is not defendable to say that litigation is probable, only that it is possible. Choice C is incorrect because the author states that it is the ownership of the later patent that is questionable. Choice D is incorrect because the earlier patent confuses the ownership of the later patent, but the passage does not support that the holder of the earlier patent takes over ownership of the later patent.

7. **(E)** This is an *extension/application* question in an EXCEPT format. There are three goals of patents stated in the passage:

    1. Patents grant exclusive ownership. This is a necessary condition. Without exclusive ownership, the patent has not met its goal.
    2. Patents encourage creating and perfecting a product and allow the patent holder to make a profit.
    3. Patents require that the patent holder disclose the details of the innovation.

    Choice E does not meet any of these criteria. Because choice E does not confer exclusive ownership, it cannot meet the goals of a patent.

    Choice A meets the goal of making a profit. The fact that competitors were forced out of business is irrelevant to the goal of a patent. Choice B meets the goal of creating and perfecting the technology. Choice C meets the goal of disclosing the details. The fact that the patent holder did not make a profit does not detract from meeting the goal of disclosure. Choice D meets the goal of exclusive ownership.

8. **(A)** This is a *use of a word/phrase* question. The word *legitimate* in this instance simply means that the assertion is reasonable, as in choice A.

    Choice B is incorrect because it refers to the use of the word *legitimate* in the previous sentence. Choice C is incorrect because the word *legitimate* does not refer to a legal basis for the assertion. Choice D is incorrect because it refers to the previous sentence. Choice E is incorrect because the word *legitimate* does not refer to an ethical basis for making an assertion.

9. **(C)** This is a *main point* or *main idea* question. For this question, the correct answer is not just a summary of the conclusion but rather captures the structure of the argument. Choice C is correct because it includes the beginning of the passage, in which the author describes the problem, the portion of the passage in which the author describes electric cars as a solution but indicates a drawback of electric cars, and the final portion, in which the author presents an alternative to the generation of electricity for cars with fossil fuels, namely regenerative braking.

    Choice A is incorrect because it does not include the alternate solution. Choice B is incorrect because no one criticizes the author's solution of regenerative braking. Choice D is incorrect because the fact that regenerative braking solves another problem (generation of electricity for non-transportation uses) is not the author's main point. Choice E is incorrect because the author does not recommend an alternative to automobiles but rather an alternative to gasoline engines.

10. **(A)** This is an *agree with a view* question. The author would most likely agree with choice A. The author lists three advantages of cars over public transportation—fast, flexible, cheap—that are true of all types of cars.

    Choice B is incorrect because, even if people continue to use cars instead of public transportation, electric cars have the potential to reduce noise and pollution. Choice C is incorrect because the author believes that some electric cars would consume the same amount of gasoline—in terms of generating the electricity for the car—as current cars. Choice D is incorrect because there is no information in the passage that indicates that a car in the city performs differently than a car in the country. Choice E is incorrect because, although electric cars based on regenerative braking would reduce noise and pollution, the author states that electric cars do not reduce congestion.

11. **(E)** This is an *implied fact/inference* question. Choice E is correct because the passage makes a clear contrast between cities of the Old World and cities in America that "have evolved around the use of the automobile."

Choice A is incorrect because there are many sources of congestion, noise, and pollution other than cars. Choice B is incorrect because there is no information in the passage to support it. Choice C is incorrect because there is no information about the relative percentages of people in Old World cities using cars versus public transportation. Choice D is incorrect because, while it is inferred that these cities did not evolve around the automobile, there is not enough information to defend that they evolved around the use of horses. It is possible that Old World cities did not evolve around transportation at all.

12. **(B)** This is an *analogous situation* question. The role of electric cars that use gasoline-powered electricity is that they appear to be a solution to the use of gasoline but in fact still use gasoline, but in a less obvious way. Similarly in choice B, the plastic materials seem to avoid using wood but in fact use wood in their manufacturing process.

Choice A is incorrect because the automobiles introduce a different kind of pollution, not the same kind in a less obvious way. Choice C is incorrect because it does not involve replacing one technology with a different technology. Choice D is incorrect because the new technology avoids the problems of the old technology. Choice E is incorrect because the problem with the new technology is expense, rather than that it causes the same problem as the old technology in a less obvious way.

13. **(E)** This is a *function* question that asks you to identify the role in the argument of a specific statement. In the statement cited in this question, the author establishes that public transportation is unlikely to be a solution to the problems caused by gasoline-powered automobiles. The only remaining solution is to change the automobiles themselves, as described in choice E.

Choice A is incorrect because the author only mentions the distinction between Old and New World cities as background to discussing the problem of pollution. Choice B is incorrect because the author does not discuss any such conflict. Choice C is incorrect because the author states that public transportation is unlikely to ever be a solution. Choice D is incorrect because the author does not suggest these aspects of public transportation.

14. **(B)** This is a *use of a word/phrase* question. The author states that the train is massively heavy to show that under such conditions, regenerative brak-

ing produces large amounts of electricity. The implication is stated in choice B—the heavier the load, the more energy can be generated.

Choice A is incorrect because, although the statement is defendably true, it is not the author's point. Choice C is incorrect because there is no information about the energy required to operate the loaded train. Choice D is incorrect because it is not apparent, or likely, that the loaded train is operated by electricity. Choice E is incorrect because the author does not refer to the polluting quality of coal. Coal is only mentioned because it constitutes the load on the train.

15. **(D)** This is a Comparative Reading *in common* question. It asks for an element that is central to both passages. Choice D is correct because Passage A is mainly concerned with identifying what it is that defines fiction, and Passage B is mainly concerned with identifying what it is that defines science fiction.

Choice A is incorrect because neither passage is concerned with distinguishing true from untrue details. Choice B is incorrect because only Passage B discusses this. Choice C is incorrect because only Passage A discusses most people's definitions. Choice E is incorrect because Passage A does not compare fiction to science fiction.

16. **(A)** This is a *specific detail (stated fact)* question. Choice A is correct because Passage A specifically states that bringing together two separate elements of our reality (*talking* and *dogs*) is what makes fiction entertaining.

Choice B is incorrect because it refers to Passage B. Choice C is incorrect because it refers to most people's definition of fiction, with which the author of Passage A disagrees. Choice D is incorrect because Passage A states that imagination is not the sole defining element of fiction. Choice E is incorrect because it is not enough to simply draw on elements of our reality, such as "talking." Elements must be combined in unique ways, as described by choice A.

17. **(B)** This is a rare *element from Passage A supports argument in Passage B* question. Choice B supports the assertion in Passage B that imagination by itself is not enough to make a story science fiction.

Choice A is incorrect because it is not consistent with Passage B to say that being untrue is enough to make a story effective. Choice C is incorrect because being imaginative is not the defining characteristic of science fiction. Choice D is incorrect because it describes the view of the author of Passage A. Choice E is incorrect because it is not a statement from Passage A, but rather from Passage B.

18. **(B)** This is a Comparative Reading *in common* question that asks you to identify a type of reasoning that is used in both passages. Choice B correctly states that both passages start with definitions that are partially correct and then both passages refine those definitions.

Choice A is incorrect because it refers only to Passage A. Choice C is incorrect because neither passage includes an erroneous definition, only a definition that is partially correct. Choice D is incorrect because Passage A does not discuss a specific form of fiction. Choice E is incorrect because neither passage eliminates all possible alternatives.

19. **(C)** This is an *implied fact/inference* question that is applied to a Comparative Reading section. Choice C is correct because Passage A states that some people believe that the fact that a work of fiction contains details that are not true predicts that the story can be expected to be entertaining. In the second paragraph, Passage A establishes that, for most people, untrue details do not guarantee that people will be entertained. Therefore, there are some people who may expect a work to be entertaining (based on the fact that it contains untrue facts) and yet not be entertained by it.

Choice A is incorrect because there is no evidence to support that anyone considers fantasy to be close to science fiction, and because the author of Passage B allows for the possibility that certain examples of fantasy could also be science fiction. Choice B is incorrect because there are no people mentioned in either passage who would be committed to believing that a story is not science fiction simply because it is based on the Roman Empire. Choice D is incorrect because the passages only defend that some people believe that the fact that a story is not true defines a work as fiction. Choice E is incorrect because there are no people mentioned in either passage who believe this. The author of Passage B believes that entertainment is not the primary purpose of science fiction.

20. **(E)** This is a Comparative Reading *relationship between passages* question. Choice E is correct in that both passages question the statement in the beginning. Passage A rejects the statement and concludes the opposite, that fiction is truer to life than ordinary life. Passage B incorporates the statement into its conclusion in the final sentence.

Choice A is incorrect because the statement is not relevant. Passage B does not define science fiction in the same terms. Choice B is incorrect because the statement is consistent with Passage B. Choice C is incorrect because the crushed-brick technology is not necessarily one that "pushes the human mind into the future" and its mention in Passage A does not necessarily support the definition of science fiction. Choice D is incorrect because the conclusion of Passage B is based on different criteria from the criteria used to define fiction in Passage A.

21. **(E)** This is a Comparative Reading *identify the difference between the passages* question. Choice E is correct because Passage A states that a work of fiction is more real than ordinary life, and Passage B states that the further a story takes us from ordinary life, the more entertaining it is.

Choice A is incorrect because the author of Passage A does not express an opinion about science fiction. Choice B is incorrect because both authors believe that imagination is one element but not the defining element. Choice C is incorrect because the author of Passage B does not use logic to any greater extent than does the author of Passage A. Choice D is incorrect because it is the author of Passage B who specifies a goal, whereas the author of Passage A does not.

22. **(B)** This is a *main idea* question. Choice B correctly incorporates all of the main points of the passage.

Choice A is incorrect because the passage does not state that a two-party system is inappropriate, only that it has some disadvantages. Choice C is incorrect because IRV does not address the drawbacks of multiparty electoral systems. Choice D is incorrect because it presents a positive view of two-party systems, whereas the passage presents a negative view. Choice E is incorrect because, although a true statement, it is not the main idea.

23. **(A)** This is a *function* question that requires you to identify the function of a certain reference. The author indicates that the framers of the Constitution did not specifically create a two-party system. This provides background for the discussion that follows, explaining how the two-party system in the United States came about. Choice A correctly describes this.

Choice B is incorrect because the passage does not make such an assertion. Choice C is incorrect because the statement about the framers of the Constitution does not attempt to prove that the Constitution supports a two-party system. Choice D is incorrect because the statement about the framers of the Constitution does not mention that they fell into two major political divisions. Choice E is incorrect because the passage does not do what choice E says.

24. **(D)** This is a *specific detail (stated fact)* question. Choice D is a direct restatement of the facts in the second paragraph.

Choice A is incorrect because it refers to IRV. Choice B is incorrect because, although party-proportional representation can lead to a multiparty system, a multiparty system is not free from domination by two major parties. Choice C is incorrect because a political party could run a candidate and yet not gain enough votes to earn a seat. Choice E is incorrect because the passage does not support that the candidates in a party-proportional system are any better qualified than in the American congressional system.

25. **(E)** This is a rare *identify a generalization* question. The question asks you to find a generalization that is supported by something in the passage. Choice E is a generalization that is supported by the claim that when there are only two parties, it is easy for the parties to become polarized. In other words, that claim is a specific example of the generalization stated in choice E.

Choice A is incorrect because the passage supports the opposite view. Most democracies use a multiparty system and the author finds that system superior. Choice B is incorrect because the author does not recommend blending two-party and multiparty systems. Choice C is incorrect because the passage supports the opposite. People expect many choices in breakfast cereal but accept only two choices in candidates. Choice D is incorrect because there is nothing in the passage that supports it.

26. **(A)** This is an *implied fact/inference* question. Choice A is implied because the IRV system assumes that many people have more than one candidate who they would accept.

Choice B is incorrect because nothing in the passage defends that democracies with multiparty systems have those systems because the voters chose the system. Choice C is incorrect because it contradicts the statement that the party that loses an election has no representation. Choice D is incorrect because, even though the passage mentions a view that two-party systems have stronger economies, there is not enough information to defend that any country with a multiparty system does not have as much economic growth as a country with a two-party system. Choice E is incorrect because it is not supported by the passage. The passage states only that in a two-party system, a vote for a third-party candidate may be wasted.

27. **(C)** This is a *helps to answer* question. Choice C is correct because the passage explains that in a multiparty system, if one party accuses another of being extreme, voters distrust both parties. The other answer choices are incorrect because the passage does not contain information that would answer the questions posed.

Section II: Logical Reasoning

1. **(D)** This is a *strengthen by principle* question. Morrison's argument must address Lee's conclusion that Dr. Jansen does not meet the needs of his patients. Morrison states that Dr. Jansen refers patients to specialists when he cannot diagnose the patient's condition. The principle stated in choice D—that referring patients to a specialist constitutes meeting the needs of the patient—completes the argument.

Choice A is incorrect because Morrison's goal is to show that Dr. Jansen does meet his patients' needs. Choice B is incorrect because it leaves open the possibility that Dr. Jansen is not meeting the needs of his patients. Choice C is incorrect because it does not address whether or not Dr. Jansen is meeting the patients' needs. Choice E is incorrect because it leaves open the possibility that Dr. Jansen does not meet his patients' needs.

2. **(E)** This is a *resolve a paradox* question. The paradox is that the two separate studies seem to have evaluated the same set of businesses and yet found widely different results. Choice E explains the discrepancy because if two different definitions of failure were used, the same set of data would lead to different conclusions.

Choice A is incorrect. Even though it points out a difference between the two studies, the difference does not by itself explain why the results were different. Choices B and C are incorrect for the same reason as choice A. Choice D is incorrect because it does not address a difference between the two studies.

3. **(C)** This is a *sufficient assumption* question. For this particular question, the correct answer is also a necessary assumption. Negating choice C gives *The dog was not frightened by the thunder*. This makes the argument fall apart, which proves that choice C is necessary for the argument to work. From the standpoint of a *sufficient assumption* question, the statement that the dog was frightened by the thunder is sufficient to make the argument work. Often there is no significant difference between a sufficient and a necessary assumption.

Choice A is incorrect. The negation of choice A—*the dog has not been trained not to bark*—does not affect the argument. Choice B does not affect the argument unless it is known that the dog is frightened. Choice D simply confirms that the dog does not bark, which was already established by the passage. Choice E is irrelevant to the situation because the dog did not bark.

4. **(D)** This is a *conclusion* question in an EXCEPT format. Four answer choices can be concluded from the premises in the passage. Choice D is correct because it cannot be concluded from the passage. The passage states that online courses offer flexible exam schedules, but there is no evidence that traditional courses do.

   Choices A and E can be concluded because all of the characteristics of online courses that are described in the passage are reasons why students prefer online courses. Choice B can be concluded because, when the passage states that online courses have flexible schedules, the implication is that traditional courses do not. Similarly, for choice C, the statement that online courses accommodate more students implies that traditional courses accommodate fewer.

5. **(C)** This is a *flaw* question. Choice C correctly identifies that the psychologist has assumed the claim about computers is incorrect because there is no proof that it is correct.

   Choice A refers to accepting that a claim is correct because there is no proof that it is incorrect. Choice B is incorrect because the psychologist does not ignore information but rather believes that there is no relevant information. Choice D is incorrect because failing to back up a premise with facts is not a logical error. Choice E is incorrect because the psychologist does not cite any authorities in support of his or her case.

6. **(D)** This is a *complete the sentence/argument* question. Because labor saving is defined as saving time to complete a task for the person involved, if fifteen minutes for cleaning is added to the thirty-five minutes for performing the task, as in choice D, the total time for one task is fifty minutes, which is not a savings of time over the forty-five minutes that the task took to complete without the equipment. There is a difference, then, between the time to perform the task (thirty-five minutes) and the time to complete the task (fifty minutes.)

   Choice A does not violate the definition of labor saving because presumably the people who took forty-five minutes to complete the task with the equipment would have taken longer than forty-five minutes to do so without the equipment. Choice B is incorrect because the definition of labor saving does not depend on whether the task is a necessary one. Choice C is incorrect because the definition of labor saving does not depend on whether or not there is a more labor-saving technology available. Choice E does not change the fact that the time to perform the task is thirty-five minutes.

7. **(A)** This is a *parallel flaw* question. The logic in the original passage is:

$$aerobic \rightarrow reduce$$
$$-reduce \rightarrow -avoid\ stroke$$
$$\therefore\ aerobic \rightarrow avoid\ stroke$$

The fallacy in the argument is that it interprets *–reduce → –avoid stroke* as *reduce → avoid stroke*. In terms of A and B, the original argument is:

$$A \rightarrow B$$
$$-B \rightarrow -C$$
$$\therefore\ If\ A \rightarrow C$$

Choice A correctly parallels this flaw:

$$complete \rightarrow points$$
$$-points \rightarrow -pass$$
$$\therefore\ If\ complete \rightarrow pass$$

Choice B is valid logic:

$$avoid \rightarrow lower$$
$$lower \rightarrow reduce\ heart\ attack$$
$$\therefore\ If\ avoid \rightarrow reduce\ heart\ attack$$

Choice C is incorrect because it is based on a correlation—great artists correlate to personal suffering—not on an if/then statement.

Choice D is logically valid:

$$Nitrogen \rightarrow grow$$
$$-sunshine \rightarrow -grow$$
$$= grow \rightarrow sunshine\ (\text{contrapositive})$$
$$\therefore\ If\ nitrogen \rightarrow sunshine$$

The logic in choice E is similar to the logic in the original passage but is distinct in an important way:

$$-individuals \rightarrow -society$$
$$society \rightarrow greater\ good$$
$$\therefore\ If\ individuals \rightarrow greater\ good$$

Compare the structures of the original and of choice E, in terms of A and B logic.

Original	Choice E
If A → B	If –A → –B
If –B → –C	If B → C
∴ If A → C	∴ If A → C

In the original, it is the second statement that is misinterpreted. In choice E it is the first statement that is misinterpreted.

8. **(C)** This is a *flaw: fails to consider* question. The correct answer is one that, if true, would weaken or destroy the logic in the argument. Choice C is correct because if a condition other than a frost had occurred that was capable of killing the tomato plants, then the conclusion would be invalid.

    The other answer choices, if true, would not affect the conclusion.

9. **(D)** This is a *match a concrete example to a principle* question. The principle is in the setup and the answer choices are concrete examples. Choice D matches the principle. The criterion of evidence of profitability is lacking, so the project should not be approved.

    Choice A does not match the principle. The principle states that if criteria A and B are not met, the project cannot be approved. Choice A states that because criteria A and B have been met, the project should be approved. Choice B claims that because the evidence of profitability is not extensive, the project should be disqualified. However, this goes further than the actual criteria, which state simply that there must be evidence, without specifying how extensive the evidence must be. Choice C does not match because at the time that the manager approved the project, the manager had evidence that supported profitability. Choice E does not match the principle because it talks about competing with future projects, whereas the principle only requires not competing with current projects.

10. **(C)** This is a *strengthen* question based on the matching of terms, which is rare. Choice C is correct because the passage's conclusion is that the climate is ideal, and the only premise is the list of climatic conditions. By adding the statement in choice C—that the stated combination of characteristics constitutes what people consider to be an ideal climate—the conclusion is strengthened.

    Choice A is incorrect because seasonal variation is described as something desirable. The island has an ideal climate despite not having variation. Choice B is incorrect because the passage does not state whether Marbay has a wet or dry climate, so choice B is irrelevant. Choice D is incorrect because Marbay's uniqueness does not add to or detract from the idealness of its climate. Choice E goes in the wrong direction, weakening the argument.

11. **(A)** This is a *conclusion* question that asks for something that can be inferred from the information in the passage. Choice A is correct because the remedy that results from long-term planning to address one inequity may introduce one or more new inequities.

    Choice B is incorrect because, even though inequities introduced through legal remedies may be unintentional, there may be other inequities that were originally intentional. Choice C is incorrect because it does not follow from the passage that the number of inequities will necessarily increase. Even though new inequities may be introduced, there may be a net decrease in the number of inequities. Choices D and E are incorrect because there is nothing in the passage to support them.

12. **(C)** This is a *flaw: vulnerable to criticism* question. Choice C is correct because Marissa uses the word *intellectual* to refer to the use of the reasoning process, whereas Frederick uses the word to refer to a person who is out of touch with practical issues.

    Choice A is incorrect because Frederick does not use biased language. Choice B is incorrect because Marissa does not present a cause-and-effect argument. Choice D is incorrect because Frederick's attack on Marissa's argument is not based on her lack of defense for her view. Choice E is incorrect because Frederick does not base his argument on an unrepresentative group.

13. **(D)** This is a *sufficient assumption* question. Choice D is correct because, if local merchants lose money when people have the flu, then reducing the number of people who have the flu leads to the conclusion that the merchants will make more money.

    Choice A is incorrect because it goes in the wrong direction. If people shop when they are sick, then preventing people from getting sick will not affect the merchants' income. Choice B is incorrect because it does not lead to the conclusion. Choice C is incorrect because it is irrelevant. There are still enough flu cases during the holiday season to affect sales. Choice E is incorrect because there is no relationship between the local facilities at which people get shots and the local merchants.

14. **(C)** This is a rare type of *weaken* question that is based on a statistical argument. The key to this type of question is the concept of false positive results versus false negative results. The new technology had no false positives. All of the cars identified as speeding actually were. However, the new technology had many false negatives. Many cars that it indicated were not speeding actually were. Weakening the argument depends on pointing this out, as choice C does.

    Choices A and E are irrelevant, as they affect both technologies in the same way. Choice B is a factor that might cause a police department to question whether or not to buy the new technology, but choice B does not weaken the logical argument. The argument is based only on the fact that the new technology appears to be better. Weakening an argument requires weakening the logic on which the argument is based. Choice D would strengthen the argument, as it implies that if new equipment had been used for testing the old technology, the results might have been different.

15. **(C)** This is a *strengthen* question based on a cause-and-effect argument. The argument's conclusion is that the impression that the town is declining economically causes people not to move to the town. The first premise to support this cause-and-effect argument is that many yards are overgrown. To support the conclusion, it is necessary to add that overgrown yards create the impression that the town is declining economically. Choice C adds this premise.

    Choice A is incorrect because the argument has to do with *impressions* of prospective residents. Prospective residents would not know that the homeowners had good jobs. They would only see that the yards were overgrown. Choice B is incorrect for the same reason. Choice D does not change the fact that there is a correlation between people getting a copy of the report and buying a home in the town. Choice E is incorrect for a similar reason.

16. **(E)** This is a *resolve a paradox* question. The paradox is that, as the coyote population decreased, it would be expected that the gopher population would increase. Instead, the gopher population continued to decrease. Choice E is correct because it states that the decrease in the coyote population resulted in an increase in the population of other predators of gophers.

    Choice A is irrelevant to the fact that there are fewer coyotes on the ranch now than there were three years ago. Choice B is irrelevant. Choice C does not explain why the rate of decline has stayed the same. Choice D does not explain the decrease in gopher population.

17. **(C)** This is a *flaw* question. Choice C is correct because Sylvia may have the highest odds—for example, 24 percent—compared to the other four—for example, 19 percent each—but 24 percent odds is not high enough to conclude that she will win. There is a 76 percent chance that Sylvia will not win.

    Choice A is incorrect because it is not necessary for a logical argument to provide supporting evidence for a premise. Choice B is irrelevant. The argument has already established that all five salespeople have the same skills. Choice D is incorrect because predicting events based on their odds is not a logical flaw. Choice E is incorrect because the argument does not assume that the salespeople are equal simply because they are members of the same group.

18. **(E)** This is a *strengthen by principle* question. Choice E matches the situation described in the passage and is the correct answer.

    Choice A is incorrect because it fails to address the possibility of injury. Choice B is incorrect because the passage's conclusion does not depend on weighing the risks. Choice C is incorrect because it does not strengthen the conclusion. Choice D is incorrect for the same reason.

19. **(D)** This is a *type of logic* question. Baxter generalizes from the specific experience of immigrants to the broader case of all minority groups. Beardsley challenges this generalization by stating that immigrants are different from native-born minorities. Choice D correctly states Beardsley's method of logic.

    Choice A is incorrect because Beardsley does not question Baxter's description of the immigrant experience. Beardsley also does not do what is stated in choices B, C, and E.

20. **(B)** This is a *weaken* question. The argument states that the reason for establishing a website is to earn money from advertising on the Web page. Choice B weakens the argument by providing an alternative explanation for how the website generates additional income.

    The other answer choices do not weaken the argument.

21. **(E)** This is a *must be true* question. The setup is deductive. The rules are:

    If top exec + travel for business → *corporate jet*
    If < five years + travel for business → *–corporate jet*

    Choice E must be true. If Sarah uses a corporate jet, it could not be for business because then both if/then statements would apply, and the result would be a contradiction (both *jet* and *not jet*). Sarah could use a corporate jet for nonbusiness purposes, such as a company-sponsored vacation.

Choice A could not be true. Choice B could be true but does not have to be, as Sarah might use the jet for nonbusiness purposes. Choice C cannot be true, as it would trigger both rules. Choice D does not have to be true. As in choice A, an employee could use a corporate jet for a nonbusiness purpose.

22. **(D)** This is a *role of a claim* question. The claim that is quoted in the question stem is a fact (premise). Based on this fact, astrophysicists have concluded that dark matter exists. The physicist attempts to weaken this conclusion by providing a flaw in it (*no direct evidence*) and an alternate hypothesis. Choice D correctly describes this role.

Choice A is incorrect because, although the quoted statement is a premise, it does not establish the physicist's conclusion. Choice B is incorrect because the quoted statement is neither an intermediate conclusion nor a support for the physicist's conclusion. Choice C is incorrect because the quoted statement is a fact, not a hypothesis. Choice E is incorrect because the quoted statement does not illustrate a principle.

23. **(A)** This is a *necessary assumption* question. Test the answer choices by negating them. If the negation destroys the argument, that answer choice is the assumption. The negation of choice A is that it is possible to attain simplicity without striving for it, which destroys the conclusion that it is impossible to attain simplicity.

The negation of choice B is that there are no forms of striving that are simple, which strengthens the argument. The negation of choice C is that there are many ways to define simplicity, but this does not affect the argument. The negation of choice D is that it is possible to strive without attaining simplicity, which strengthens the argument. The negation of choice E is that it is possible to strive for simplicity in some things. This does not affect the conclusion that doing so does not lead to simplicity.

24. **(D)** This is an *application of a principle* question. Choice D adds the elements that are missing in the application in order to make it match the principle. Namely, for the principle to apply, the money must go to the judge—which is included in choice D—and the judge must not know about the money—which is also included in choice D.

Choice A is incorrect because it is not necessary—in order for the principle to apply—that the judge rule in favor of the party that provided the money. Choice B is incorrect because the principle does not require that the payment be reasonable or usual. Choice C is incorrect because the principle is not based on contact with a party but with a payment from a party. Choice E is incorrect because it does not matter when the speech takes place but rather when the payment takes place.

25. **(B)** This is a *main conclusion* question. You must identify the conclusion that is the main point of the argument. The last sentence of the argument is the conclusion, and is paraphrased in choice B.

Choice A is an unstated premise of the argument, as is choice C. Choice D is not a valid statement. The passage states:

$$\text{If discover comet and } -rare \rightarrow -famous$$

In other words, if you discover a comet and it is not rare, you cannot become famous. This is *not* the same as saying that if you discover a comet that *is* rare, you *will* become famous. Choice E is not valid because an astronomer may become famous in a way other than discovering a comet.

26. **(D)** This is a *parallel reasoning* question. The original passage sets up two categories, each with a certain characteristic:

$$\text{under three inches} = \text{drought tolerant}$$
$$\text{over eight inches} = \text{not drought tolerant}$$

The conclusion is that a case that falls between the two categories—*five inches*—has a characteristic that is midway between the characteristics of the original two categories—*somewhat drought tolerant*.

Choice D is parallel:

$$\text{Under } \$20,000 \text{ inventory} = \text{under } \$25,000 \text{ profit per year}$$
$$\text{Over } \$100,000 \text{ inventory} = \text{over } \$150,000 \text{ profit per year}$$

The conclusion is an intermediate case—*$60,000*—and an intermediate characteristic—*$90,000 profit per year*.

Choice A is incorrect because the conclusion is not an intermediate case. Choice B is incorrect for the same reason and, in addition, comes to a different kind of conclusion. Choice C also does not have an intermediate case and argues from the characteristic backward to the case, rather than from the case to the characteristic. Choice E does not have an intermediate case and assigns an arbitrary characteristic—*$15,000 profit per year*—without defending that that amount is proportional to the inventory.

Section III: Analytical Reasoning

QUESTIONS 1–6

This is a sequence game, which means that it must have one-to-one correspondence and be ordered. There are seven fixtures, numbered 1 through 7 from left to right, with left corresponding to west and right corresponding to east. The diagram is as follows:

L   West   N   East

M   1   2   3   4   5   6   7

N

O

P

R   S – P

S   N = 5, 7

       P – L – N

       If P = 3 → R – P

       If P ≠ 3 → P – R

     R

    S – P – L – N

     If P = 3

       R

    S – P – L – N

     If P ≠ 3

Note that there are two possible strings, depending on whether P is or is not in 3.

NOTE: Refer to Chapter 4 for an explanation of the problem-solving tools (shown in bold).

1. **(A)** This is the typical first question. Use **Eliminate—apply rules, four violations**. The rule S–P is violated by choice E. The rule $N = 5, 7$ is not violated in any answer. The rule P–L–N is violated by choice C. The rule *If P = 3* is violated by choice D. The rule *If P not = 3* is violated by choice B.

2. **(E)** This is a CANNOT be true question with no new information. Because there is nothing to diagram, use **Test answers—prove a violation**. First, though, check the answers briefly against the supplemental diagrams to see which are most likely to violate rules. The two supplemental diagrams are:

R   R
\   /
S – P – L – N   S – P – L – N

If P = 3   **If P not = 3**

Choice A is consistent with the right diagram. Choice B is consistent with the left. Choice C is consistent with the right. Choice D is consistent with the left. Choice E leaves some ambiguity. Test choice E first.

Put M in 1. Put R in 2. Scan the rules, starting with the first rule. No rule gives clear information until *If P not = 3* → *P – R*. Because P is *not* before R in the diagram, P must go in 3. Go back to the top of the rules. The first rule is violated. There is no place to put S before P. Choice E cannot be true.

3. **(A)** This is a *could be true* question with new information that is not in the diagram. Use **Diagram—supplemental diagram or rules** to adjust the supplemental diagrams to represent P and R as adjacent.

SRP – L – N   S – PR – L – N

If P = 3   **If P not = 3**

Comparing the diagrams briefly with the answer choices, choice B is out because L cannot be third in either of the two scenarios. Choice C is out because S must have at least four trees planted to the east of it. Choice D is out because N and R cannot be adjacent. Choices A and E are unclear and must be tested. Theoretically, it would be possible to create parallel universes from the two supplemental diagrams, but because only two answer choices are left, it is faster to test the answer choices.

Test choice A. Putting S in 3 means the rule *If P not = 3* is invoked. So spots 4 through 7 must be PRLN. Spots 1 and 2 can be O or M. There does not appear to be a rule violation. Test choice E. With N in 5, spots 1 through 4 must be either SRPL or SPRL. In both cases, S must go in 1. Choice E violates rules, and choice A is confirmed as correct.

4. **(C)** This is a *could be true* question with new information that goes in the diagram. Put M in 1. In order to fill in more of the diagram, use **General— look for most restricted**. N has only two options. However, P is equally restricted because P's placement affects R's placement. Use **General— options for player** to consider P's options. P cannot go in 2 because there would be no room for S to go before P. Spot 3 is an option. Spot 4 is an option. P cannot go any farther east than 4 because, with P not in 3, R, L, and N must follow P.

Create two universes, one with P in 3 and one with P in 4. Applying the rules, the universe with P in 3 fails, because it requires R before P, and there is no space for R. For the universe with P in 4, create two universes with the two options for N — 5 and 7. The universe with N in 5 violates rules because L must come between P and N. Spots 5 and 6 must be R/L and L/R. Spots 2 and 3 must be O/S and S/O. The answers can now be compared with the diagram.

West ——————————————————————— East
N
↙ ↘
1	2	3	4	5	6	7
M	O/S	S/O	P	L/R	R/L	N

The only viable universe

5. **(D)** This is a *must be true* question with no new information. Because there is nothing to diagram, use **Test answers—negate a must**. In general, it is sometimes useful to check the answer choices against the supplemental diagrams, but in this case, it does not help.

Test choice A by negating it. Create a diagram in which there are only four trees east of S (S is in 3). Spots 4 through 7 must include P, L, and N, and because P is not in 3, R must also be included. N cannot go in 5, so N must be in 7. R and L can go in 5 and 6 and M/O goes in 1 and 2. There do not seem to be any violations, so choice A does not have to be true.

Test choice B by finding three spots for S. Testing choice A showed that spot 3 is an option. Because S has many players after it, it is likely that S can go in 1 and 2. Two diagrams quickly show that spots 1 and 2 seem viable. Choice B does not seem to need to be true.

Test choice C by putting R next to N and putting S somewhere other than 1. The test of choice A can be used to prove that this is possible. Test choice D by putting S next to M and then trying to place L and R so that they are not adjacent. If P is in 3, S and R must be in 1 and 2. Therefore, to test choice D, P cannot be in 3. Systematically consider the options for P. If

P is in 2, S must be in 1 and so cannot be next to M. P cannot go in 1, nor can P go in 5 or 6. Put P in 4. Because P is not in 3, R, L, and N must come after P, just as in the test of choice A. Also, N cannot be in 5 because L must come between P and N, so N is in 7. R/L and L/R are in 5 and 6. Now S and M can be adjacent in 1 and 2 or in 2 and 3. These are the *only* options for S and M to be adjacent and in both cases, R and L are also adjacent. Choice D must be true. For practice, show that if M is in 7, S does not have to be in 1.

6. **(A)** This is a *must be false* question with no new information. Use **Test answers—prove a violation**. Test choice A by diagramming all of the possibilities M – P – O. Use **General—options for player** to consider the options for P. P cannot go in 1, 5, 6, or 7. P can only go in 2, 3, or 4. If P is in 2 or 3, the players for 1 and 2 are determined (S; S/R R/S, respectively). Consequently, M cannot be to the left of P. The only option for M – P – O is with P in 4.

    With P in 4, spots 5 through 7 must be L/R, R/L, and N, in that order. There is no place for O to be to the right of P. Therefore, choice A violates rules and must be false. It is not necessary to test the remaining answers, because the rule violation in choice A is clear. For practice, you can show that choices B through E are possible.

QUESTIONS 7–13

This is a one-to-one correspondence game (all one-to-one games are ordered) but it is not a sequence. It is an ONS-A game. There are six fixtures with no branches.

```
P                    1    2    3    4    5    6
R                    ─    ─    ─    ─    ─    ─
S
T        RV or VR
U        If P ≠ 3, →
V          S = 5

     Either R – P
       or R – T
         bnb
```

7. **(D)** This is the typical first question. The RV rule is violated by choice C. The *P not = 3* rule is violated by choice B. The final rule is violated by choice A, in which R is not before either P or T, and by choice E, in which R is before both P and T.

8. **(A)** This is a *must be true* question with new information that goes in the main diagram. Put P in 1 and use **Diagram—apply rules, musts**. The second rule causes S to be in 5. Apply the RV rule. The only options for RV or VR are 2 and 3, or 3 and 4. Use **Diagram—parallel universes**. In the universe with R and V in 2 and 3, T and U are the only unassigned players and can go in either of the remaining slots, 4 or 6, which can be filled in as T/U and U/T.

   In the second universe, with R and V in 3 and 4, T must come after RV or VR and so must go in 6. U must go in 2.

1	2	3	4	5	6
P	R/V	V/R	T/U	S	U/T
P	U	R/V	V/R	S	T

   Use **Eliminate—check answers against diagram** to check the answer choices. Choice B is out because R can be in 4. Choice C is out because U can be in 4 or 6. Choice D is out because T can be in 4 (top universe) and U in 6. Choice E is out because U can be in 6.

9. **(C)** This is a *CANNOT be true* question with no new information. Because there is nothing to diagram, you must use **Test answers—prove a violation**. First, briefly check the answer choices against the rules to see if any choices stand out as likely to violate a rule. There is a relationship between P and T in the third rule, though it may not be immediately clear how to apply the relationship to choice C, so test choice C first. Find all of the options for placing the sequence PT. There are three—in 1 and 2; 2 and 3; or 3 and 4. The pair cannot be placed where one of the members is in 5 because with P not in 3, 5 must be occupied by S.

   Apply the rules to the three universes. With PT in 1 and 2, R/V and V/R must go in 3 and 4. For the universe with PT in 2 and 3, there is no place for R/V and V/R, so that universe is out. For the remaining universe, R/V and V/R must go in 1 and 2. Test the two remaining universes against the third rule. Both violate the third rule, so choice C cannot be true.

1	2	3	4	5	6
P	T	R/V	V/R	S	
~~P~~	~~T~~			~~S~~	
R/V	V/R	P	T		

NOTE: All three universes violate the third rule. The second universe is out because it does not have two adjacent slots for R and V.

10. **(E)** This is a *could be true* question with no new information. Because there is no information to put in the main diagram, you must test answers. Before doing so, check the answer choices briefly against the conditions to see which players are most limited in the number of fixtures to which they could be assigned. It has already been determined in earlier questions that neither R nor V can occupy 1 or 6. Choice A is out. U has no restrictions and so is a likely candidate. S must go in 5 in all cases in which P is not in 3, but it is unclear if that limits S's overall options. It is most reasonable to test U first.

Testing U requires trying U in all six positions to see if there are slots to which U cannot be assigned. Testing the other answer choices will require the same process. This question could potentially take a long time to solve. In testing an answer, look for restrictions that could show in which fixtures a player might cause a violation. Also, consider the fixtures that have restrictions. For example, if P is not in 3, slot 5 is determined. Try putting U in 3. S must go in 5. There is now no acceptable place for RV. To prove that U *does not* have five options, it is necessary to find one more slot to which U cannot be assigned. Try putting U in 5, taking advantage of the fact that 5 is restricted. With U in 5, P must go in 3 and again there is no place for RV. Choice B is out.

Three choices are left to test, but because of the restrictions on S, it is best to consider T or P. Starting with T, put it in 3 to see if the strategy used for U works for T as well. It does. T in 3 means S is in 5 and there is no place for RV. T in 5 has the same result, as it forces P into 3. T is reduced to only four possible slots and is out.

Test P. Putting P in 3 allows S to be anywhere. RV can go in 4 and 5. There does not appear to be a rule violation. Putting P in 5 does result in a rule violation, because the fact that P is not in 3 means that S also has to be in 5. However, it is likely that P can go in any of the remaining five slots.

As a double-check, prove that S has at least two spots into which it cannot go. Because the other answer choices have been ruled out, eliminating S will confirm that P is the answer. Putting S in 3 results in a violation because with P not in 3, S would also have to go in 5. Putting S in either 4 or 6 can be shown to cause a violation.

This is a time-consuming question. You might only have enough time to work through some of the steps and then guess.

11. **(B)** This is a *completely determined* question. There is new information that does not go in the diagram (U-S). There are multiple options for U coming before S, so it is not feasible to make universes. Instead, test the answer choices. Scan the answer choices briefly to see if any choices are more likely to result in enough restrictions that the order is completely determined. P swimming third triggers a specific result—S cannot be in 5. S swimming second also means that P swims third. V swimming fifth also means that P swims third. Because all three of these require P in 3, choices B and E are more restrictive because they add an additional element.

Test choice E. Put S in 2. Based on the new information in the stem, U is in 1. P is in 3. T must come after R/V and so must be in 6. Fixtures 4 and 5 can be either R or V. The order is not completely determined.

Test choice B. V is in 5. P is in 3. T must come after R/V, so T must go in 6. R must go in 4. U must come before S, so U is in 1 and S in 2. The order is completely determined. As practice, show that choices A and D result in multiple options.

12. **(C)** This is a *must be true* question with new information that does not go directly in the main diagram. Use **General—options for player** to see how many options there are for placing T and P. If there are fewer than five or six, it may be feasible to use parallel universes.

There must be at least two empty slots between T and P (for R/V and V/R). T could go in 1. P could go in 4 at the earliest. This means that P is not in 3, and therefore, S must be in 5. P, then, could go in either 4 or 6. That gives two universes. In the universe with P in 4, R/V and V/R must go in 2 and 3. U must go in the remaining slot, 6. In the universe with P in 6, R/V could either be in 2 and 3 or in 3 and 4. Split this universe into two universes. The placement of U is determined in each.

T could also go in 2. Use **General—options for player** to determine the options for P. There must be two slots between T and P, which leaves 5 and 6 for P. However, because P is not in 3, S must be in 5. With T in 2, the only option for P is 6. S must be in 5. R/V and V/R must be 3 and 4. U must be in 1. There are now four universes that represent all possibilities.

1	2	3	4	5	6
T	R/V	V/R	P	S	U
T	R/V	V/R	U	S	P
T	U	R/V	V/R	S	P
U	T	R/V	V/R	S	P

Use **Eliminate—check answers against diagram** to find the correct answer. Choices A, B, D, and E do not have to be true.

13. **(D)** This is a rare *how many* question, with new information that does not go in the main diagram. Use **General—options for player** to determine the options for placing PS. If P is in 3, S goes in 4. However, if P is in 3, R/V and V/R must go in 4 and 5. Therefore, P cannot go in 3.

   If P is not in 3, S is in 5. Therefore, PS must go in 4 and 5. There must be at least two slots between P and T, so T must go in 1 and R/V and V/R go in 2 and 3. U must go in 6. The exact locations of four players are known.

QUESTIONS 14–18

This is a hybrid between a sequence game and a non-sequence game that has one-to-one correspondence. The setup lacks a string of at least three relationships. However, there is information about every player, and the game functions much like a regular sequence game.

```
N              M    T    W    Th    F    Sa    Su
P              1    2    3    4     5    6     7
R                            Ⓦ
S
T      R
        ⟍P
U      N⟋
W
       N⟍
          U
       T⟋

       W = 4
    Either R – W
      or T – S
        bnb

       R
        ⟍P
       N⟋
          ⟍U
       T⟋
```

14. **(D)** This is the typical first question. The first rule is violated by choice C. The second rule is violated by choice B. No choices violate the W = 4 rule. Choices A and E violate the last rule. In choice A, R is not before W *and* T is not before S. In choice E, R is before W *and* T is before S.

15. **(B)** This is a *could be true* question with new information that does not go directly into the main diagram. The new information —R – – U or U – – R [there need to be 2 dashes between R and P to represent two players]— does not go into the supplemental diagram, either. If this were a pure sequence game, the supplemental diagram would be helpful with this type of question.

    In a testing situation, it would not be clear whether it would be faster to diagram all of the universes or to test the answer choices. Because either R or U could be first in the sequence, and because there are multiple options for where the pair can be placed, testing answers would be a reasonable first approach.

    Test choice A. Four answer choices violate rules, so use **Test answers—prove a violation**. Put S in 3. Find the options for R – – U or U – – R. There is only one—slots 2 and 5. Try both universes—one with R in 2 and one with U in 2. With R in 2 and U in 5, there are not enough slots for N and T to come before U. The same is true with U in 2. Choice A violates rules.

    Test choice B. Put N in 2. There is only one place for R/U—in 3 and 6. Test both universes. In the universe with R in 3, R is before W, so T must go after S but before U. This means S is in 1, T in 5, and P in 7. Check this order against the rules. There are no violations. This is enough information to prove that N could be assigned to Tuesday.

    As an exercise, prove that choices C through E violate rules, and then approach this question by setting up parallel universes, rather than testing answer choices.

16. **(D)** This is a *CANNOT be true* question with no new information. Because there is nothing to diagram, use **Test answers—prove a violation**. Before testing answer choices, though, use **General—count places in sequence** to determine which players cannot appear in either 1 or 2. Both P and U require two players before them. W can only be in 4. Any answer choice that includes P, U, or W is out. However, there are no such choices.

    Use **Eliminate—check previous valid assignments** to eliminate choice A, as it appears in the correct answer to question 14. Test choice B. With S in 1 and T in 2, the fourth rule dictates that R must be before W, and thus in 3. Putting N in 5 creates an order that appears valid. Remember that it is not necessary or time-effective to prove absolutely that an order is viable. If an order appears viable, move on. Because the correct answer is one that violates rules, it will be clear when you find it.

Test choice C. N and T in 1 and 2, respectively, means that T is before S and, thus, R is after W. Putting U and P at the end (6 and 7) guarantees that the first two rules are not broken. There appears to be a viable order.

Test choice D. T and R in 1 and 2, respectively, means that R is before W. The last rule dictates that T cannot be before S, but with T in 1, that rule is violated. Choice D violates rules and is therefore the correct answer.

A quick double-check of choice E shows that it appears viable. Because the violation in choice D is clear, it is not necessary to spend much time testing choice E, but it is good strategy to glance at it.

17. **(D)** This is a rare *could be false* question, with new information that goes in the diagram. Four answers choices cannot be false, meaning that they must be true. Use **Diagram—put in new information** to put P in 3. Use **Diagram—apply rules, musts** to determine that R and N must go in 1 and 2. Use **Diagram—parallel universes** to show the two options— R and N in 1 and 2 versus N and R in 1 and 2. The rules indicate that T must come after S, because R is before W. T must also come before U. That means that in both universes slots 5, 6, and 7 must be STU, respectively. The answer choices can now be compared to the two universes. Choices A, B, C, and E all must be true (cannot be false). Only choice D does not have to be true.

M	T	W	Th	F	Sa	Su
1	2	3	4	5	6	7
R	N	P	(W)	S	T	U
N	R	N	(W)	S	T	U

18. **(E)** This is a *could be true* question with new information that does not go directly into the main diagram. However, if T is before S, then the fourth rule dictates that R must be after W. Because R must be before P, there are only two options for R after W—5 or 6. If R is in 6, then P must be in 7. If R is in 5, then P can be in either 6 or 7. This leads to three universes.

T must be before S and also before U, so T must be placed so that there are at least two blank slots after it. There is only one blank slot after W in all three universes. Therefore, T cannot be in 3. The only options for T are 1 and 2.

M	T	W	Th	F	Sa	Su
1	2	3	4	5	6	7
			Ⓦ	R	P	
			Ⓦ	R		P
			Ⓦ		R	P

Partial universes

At this point, pursuing parallel universes would result in over six possibilities. Switch to testing answer choices. Doing so will be easier because of the partially filled-in universes. Test choice A. There is only one universe in which Friday is open, and placing N there violates the *N, T before U* rule.

Test choice B. Placing T in 5 violates the conditions in the question stem (T-S). Test choice C. T in 3 does not allow for both S and U after T. Test choice D. R in 3 is not allowed in any of the universes.

Testing choice E puts U in 3. N and T can go in either order in 1 and 2. S can go in whichever spot is empty after W. Choice E appears to be valid. The other answer choices have been proven to violate rules.

QUESTIONS 19–23

This is an unordered game. There is not one-to-one correspondence. At least one player must be left out. The number of fixtures is variable. There must be at least three people chosen, but there could theoretically be up to seven chosen. For this reason, the number of slots in the discard pile is also variable, from a maximum of five to a minimum of one. It is not necessary to show slots for all five possible discard slots. Simply leave enough room to add players to the discard pile if necessary. Note the use of three dots after fixture 3 to indicate that the first three fixtures are required and the subsequent fixtures are optional.

F

G

H

I

$$\begin{array}{ccccccccc} & & \underline{1} & \underline{2} & \underline{3} & \cdots & \underline{4} & \underline{5} & \underline{6} & \underline{7} \end{array} \Big| \; \underline{\quad} \; \underline{\quad} \; \underline{\quad}$$

J   If H → –F, –L

K   If I → –K

L   If H → I

M   If M → –F

If K or G → KG

19. **(A)** This is the typical first question. The first rule is violated by choice C. The second rule is violated by choice E. The third rule is violated by choice B. The fourth rule is violated by choice D.

20. **(A)** This is a *must be true* question with new information that goes in the main diagram. Put H in the assignment. Apply the rules. The first rule indicates that F and L go in the discard pile. The third rule indicates that I is in the assignment. The second rule now indicates that K is in the discard pile. The fifth rule indicates that G is in the discard pile. The only players not accounted for are M and J. J has no restrictions. M can be in because F is already out. The third, required slot can be taken by either M or J. A fourth slot could be taken by whichever of the two is not in 3.

$$\begin{array}{cccccccc} \underline{1} & \underline{2} & \underline{3} & \cdots & \underline{4} & \underline{5} & \underline{6} & \underline{7} \\ \text{H} & \text{I} & \text{M/J} & & \text{J/M/}\varnothing \end{array} \Big| \; \underline{\text{K}} \; \underline{\text{G}} \; \underline{\text{F}} \; \underline{\text{L}}$$

The fourth slot can be J, M, or empty (∅).

Use **Eliminate—check answers against diagram**. Choice A must be true. Choice B is incorrect because there cannot be five people chosen. Choice C is incorrect because Monroe does not have to be chosen. Neither choice D nor choice E must be correct, though they could be.

21. **(D)** This is a *one or both of a pair* question, with a new condition that there must be at least four players chosen. The correct answer for this type of question consists of a pair, both of which cannot be out. To test the answer choices, put both members of the pair in the discard pile and try to show that a violation results.

For choice A, F and I go in the discard pile. The rule $H \rightarrow I$ means that H must also be in the discard pile. The absence of F, however, does not trigger any rules. With only three players in the discard pile, there are most likely options for creating a viable assignment of four players. Do not take the time to prove that there is an option. When you find the correct answer, the rule violation will be clear.

Choice B functions similarly to choice A. The absence of F does not trigger any rules. The absence of G means that K is in the discard pile. There are enough players left to create a viable assignment.

For choice C, H in the discard pile does not trigger any rules. Although the presence of H affects many players, the absence of H is not a trigger. The absence of K triggers the absence of G and again there are only three players out.

For choice D, the absence of I triggers the absence of H. The absence of K triggers the absence of G. The remaining players are F, J, L, and M. However, F and M cannot occur together. One slot in the assignment is for one of F and M. Only two players remain, so it is not possible to create an assignment with four players. It is not possible to discard both members of the pair in choice D. One or both of the pair must be chosen.

As a double-check, choice E results in I, H, and M being out. Enough players are left to make a viable assignment.

22. **(E)** This is a *could be true* question with new information that goes in the diagram. Put F in the assignment and J in the discard pile. Apply the rules. The presence of F triggers the absence of H and the absence of M. The discard pile now contains H, M, and J. The assignment contains F. The remaining players are G, I, K, and L. Create two parallel universes based on the presence or absence of I.

In the universe with F and I, the presence of I triggers the absence of K. The absence of K triggers the absence of G. Only L is left. This universe consists of F, I, and L. In the universe without I, K and G must be in. If one of K and G is out, the other is out. If they are both out, there are not three players left (I is out in this universe). K and G, then, must be in, and L might or might not be in.

1	2	3	...	4	5	6	7					
F	I	L						H	M	J	K	G
F	K	G		(L)				H	M	J	I	(L)

Parallel universes. Parentheses represent optional elements.

Use **Eliminate—check answers against diagram**. Choice A cannot be true because there are always at least four employees not selected. Choice B cannot be true because there can only be three or four employees selected. Choice C cannot be true because the presence of I triggers the absence of K, which triggers the absence of G. The diagram reflects this.

Choice D cannot be true because if I is selected, the only remaining option for a third player is L. Choice E can be true, as is shown in the bottom universe.

23. **(B)** This is a rare *maximum/minimum* question. There is no new information. To find the maximum number of players, try to find the smallest possible number of players in the discard pile. Create two universes, one with H in the discard pile and one with H in the assignment. With H in the discard pile, F and M cannot both be in, so one of them goes in the discard pile (F/M). I and K cannot both be in. If K is out, G is also out, so put I in the discard pile to keep the discard pile as small as possible. The remaining five players can all be in without violating any rules. Choice A is out because there is a viable assignment with more than four players.

In the universe with H in the assignment, F and L are in the discard pile. I and K cannot both be in. Putting I in the discard pile results in three players in the discard pile again. It is not possible to have two or fewer members in the discard pile, so the maximum number of players in an assignment is five, and answer choice B is correct.

Section IV: Logical Reasoning

1. **(E)** This is a *resolve a paradox* question that is worded in terms of explaining a phenomenon, and the phenomenon is a contradiction or paradox. In this question, the paradox is that staying open later, given that there are customers in the store during the additional hour, should bring in more money, and yet the net profit has decreased. Choice E explains how there could be additional sales, but if the cost of operating the store for an extra hour is greater than the sales, there is a net loss.

Choice A is incorrect because, among other reasons, buying fewer items is not the same as spending less. Choice B is incorrect because by itself it does not explain how the net profit decreased. Choice B does go in the right direction, but without including the fact that staying open costs money, as choice E states, choice B does not work. Choice C is incorrect because it is irrelevant and does not explain why there is an ongoing decrease in net profit. Choice D is irrelevant because the issue is not the popularity of the store but rather the net profit.

2. **(B)** This is a *main conclusion* question. It asks you to find the main idea of the passage. Although the passage begins by discussing Ed, its conclusion is about patients in general. For this reason, choices C, D, and E are incorrect. The conclusion is that nagging can prevent or slow down the healthful changes that a patient may make. Choice B correctly states this. Choice A is a premise that supports the conclusion about nagging.

3. **(A)** This is a *sufficient assumption* question. The correct answer is one that, if true, causes the conclusion to be true. The negation of choice A is that there has been interbreeding between the butterfly species on the two islands. This destroys the argument that the long tongues are the result of *independent* adaptation.

   The negation of choice B is that the two flower species are related. This does not affect the argument. The negation of choice C is that, if the butterflies had not developed long tongues, they would not have had any food. This is irrelevant to the conclusion. The negation of choice D is that there is another animal that is better adapted. This does not affect the conclusion that the adaptation of the butterflies is an example of independent adaptation. The negation of choice E is that the butterflies are not capable of long-distance flight. This would strengthen the conclusion, so choice E itself actually weakens the conclusion, by implying that there could have been interbreeding.

4. **(D)** This is a *conclusion* question that asks for information that can be inferred from the premises in the passage. The passage contains a deductive premise:

   If want to please → make unrealistic promises

   It also contains an inductive premise:

   If unrealistic promises → voters unlikely to vote for you

   This is inductive because the conclusion of the if/then statement refers to a probable action, not an inevitable one. Combining these two premises gives:

   If want to please → voters unlikely to vote for you

   Choice D expresses this conclusion.

Choice A is incorrect because it states:

If realistic promises → likely to vote for you

This does not follow from the premise:

If unrealistic promises → voters unlikely to vote for you

Choice B is incorrect because, even though the passage implies that it is natural to want to please voters, there is no information to support that *most* candidates want to please voters. Choice C is incorrect because there is no support for the conclusion that voters will not vote in the election at all. Choice E is incorrect because its logic is invalid. The original logical conclusion, as stated in choice D, is:

If want to please → voters unlikely to vote for you

The logic in choice E is:

If –want to please → voters –unlikely to vote for you

In other words, choice E negates both sides of the actual conclusion, which does not result in a valid statement.

5. **(C)** This is a *strengthen by principle* question. The answer choices are general principles. The correct answer strengthens the argument. Choice C is a principle that matches the argument and strengthens it.

    Choice A is incorrect because the argument is not that only certain people should use OYSTER but that no one should. Choice B is incorrect because the argument is not based on finding OYSTER more powerful than necessary, but rather on finding OYSTER more difficult to use. Choice D is incorrect because the argument is not based on the fact that the people writing the language are more advanced than those modifying programs, but rather that the people modifying programs—as well as people writing programs—will find it harder to use. It does not necessarily follow that a less-advanced programmer will have a hard time working with a program written by a more-advanced programmer. Choice E is incorrect because the argument is not based on less-advanced programmers not understanding OYSTER programming but rather on less-advanced programmers having a hard time working with it. It is possible to understand programming but still have a hard time working with it.

6. **(C)** This is a *parallel reasoning* question. The basis of the original argument is that the sample surveyed is not representative of the population that the survey attempts to evaluate. Choice C establishes that the people surveyed outdoors in the evening were not representative of all dog owners.

Choice A is incorrect because the sample—visitors to the museum—is the same as the population about which the survey makes a conclusion. Choice B is incorrect because the flaw in the survey is that its terms were not defined. Choice D is incorrect because the survey makes its conclusion about journalists—not about physicians—and the sample consists of journalists. Choice E is incorrect because it criticizes the survey on grounds other than that the sample was not representative.

7. **(E)** This is a *necessary assumption* question. The negation of choice E is that even without vitamin D, calcium can be made available for the body. This destroys the conclusion that people need vitamin D.

   The negation of choice A is that there are as many dietary sources of vitamin D as there are of calcium. This does not affect the argument. The negation of choice B is that calcium from foods is not better than calcium from supplements, which does not affect the argument. The negation of choice C is that it is possible to have strong bones without a healthy diet. This does not affect the argument because the argument is based only on the intake of calcium, not on a balanced diet. The negation of choice D is that it is not necessary to have the same amounts of vitamin D and calcium. This does not affect the argument.

8. **(A)** This is a *committed to agree/disagree* question. Choice A is correct because Phuong is committed to agreeing with it and Jacob is committed to disagreeing with it.

   Choice B is incorrect because both agree with it. Choice C is incorrect because both agree that such a garden *may* have fulfilled its purpose. Choice D is incorrect because both disagree with it (and thus agree with each other). Choice E is incorrect because Jacob agrees with it, and Phuong does not express an opinion about it, thus the two do not disagree.

9. **(E)** This is a *strengthen* question based on a cause-and-effect argument. The argument concludes that being watched causes some drivers to get into an accident. Choice E strengthens the argument by explaining the mechanism by which being watched leads to an accident, namely that frequent monitoring of the speedometer can block out peripheral vision, which means that drivers are temporarily unaware of the other drivers around them.

   Choice A is incorrect because there is no clear reason why nervousness would lead to less-safe driving. Choice B is incorrect because there is no evidence that any drivers are speeding as they pass the visible patrol cars. Choice C is incorrect for the same reason as choice A. Nervousness alone does not necessarily lead to less-safe driving. Choice D is incorrect because it has not been established that the drivers passing the patrol cars are nervous. Choice D would be stronger if it said *Drivers passing patrol cars become nervous and nervous drivers change lanes frequently*. Even then, changing lanes is not necessarily unsafe, whereas losing peripheral vision, as in choice E, inherently cuts the driver off from important information about nearby cars.

10. **(C)** This is a *match a principle to a concrete example* question, in which the passage presents the principle and the answer choices are concrete examples. The principle involves two deductive statements:

If –one positive review from professional critic → –significant
If two or more curators praise AND if one positive review from critic → significant

The first statement establishes that a positive review from a professional critic is *necessary* for the work to be significant. Without the positive review, it is not possible for the work to be significant. However, a positive review from a critic is not *sufficient* for guaranteeing that the work is significant.

The second statement—which requires that the work has received at least one positive review from a professional critic—establishes that the fact that two or more curators have praised the work is *sufficient* to guarantee that the work is significant. Choice C meets both of these criteria, because one of the curators is also a professional critic.

Choice A is incorrect. Its logic is:

If two or more curators praise AND if one positive review from critic →
significant (original condition)
∴ *If –two or more curators praise AND if one positive review from critic →*
–significant (negation of both sides)

Although the occurrence of certain conditions guarantees *significant*, the absence of those conditions does not guarantee the absence of *significant*.

Choice B is incorrect because, even though the situation meets the criterion of two or more curators, it is not known whether it meets the criterion of one professional art critic. Therefore, it cannot be concluded that the work is significant. Choice D is incorrect. It meets the criterion of one art critic but does not meet the second criterion, even though one curator has praised the work. The conclusion is that because the work has met some of the criteria, it has higher odds of being significant. The original principle does not support this conclusion because it does not discuss a partial satisfying of criteria. Choice E is incorrect. Consider what rules are triggered by the fact that the work is not significant. In the first rule,

If –one positive review from professional critic → –significant

the factor *not significant* does not trigger any rules. In the second rule,

If two or more curators praise AND if one positive review from critic → significant

the contrapositive is:

–significant → – (If two or more curators praise AND if one positive review from critic)

and the factor *not significant* triggers the conclusion that the combination of events shown in parentheses is not true. However, this does not mean that no critics gave the work a positive review. It includes the possibility that some critics gave a positive review but there were not two curators who praised it.

11. **(B)** This is a *sufficient assumption* question. If choice B is assumed to be true—that eyewitnesses often have characteristics that make them seem unreliable—then the conclusion of the argument inevitably must follow—that jurors often do not believe eyewitnesses.

The other choices are incorrect because they do not lead inevitably to the conclusion of the argument. Choice A leads to the conclusion that most eyewitnesses believe they can reliably report what they have seen. Choice C is irrelevant because eyewitnesses are not necessarily people who have committed crimes. Choice D would only lead to the conclusion that jurors ignore circumstantial evidence. Choice E leads to the conclusion that jurors sometimes must rely on eyewitness reports but does not lead to the conclusion that such jurors reject most eyewitness reports.

12. **(E)** This is a *weaken* question. Choice E is correct because it results in all students in a coeducational class performing better on tests and quizzes, and performance on tests and quizzes directly measures the amount that the students have learned.

Choice A is incorrect because the fact that a female teacher teaches a class of boys does not directly influence how much the boys learn. Choice B is incorrect because it is not clear whether there is a net increase in learning. Choice C is incorrect because it does not necessarily lead to an increase in learning. Choice D is incorrect because less-aggressive behavior among boys does not necessarily lead to more learning.

13. **(B)** This is a *resolve a paradox* question that does not use the word *paradox* in its stem. The paradox is that the Old Town voters voted for a measure that they were warned would not benefit them. Choice B is correct because it explains that the Old Town voters considered themselves middle class, even if they did not meet the economic criteria for actually being middle class.

    Choice A does not explain why the seemingly non-middle-class residents voted for the measure. Choice C is incorrect because it would only explain why some voters considered middle class because of their incomes might have voted against the measure. Similarly, choice D only explains why some middle-class people might have voted against the measure. Choice E is irrelevant.

14. **(B)** This is a *necessary assumption* question. Choice B is correct because the negation of choice B—that Edgar does not have any infection at all—destroys the argument. The surgeon would then have no reason for not operating.

    The negation of choice A is that Edgar's infection can be cured by the day of surgery. This does not affect the argument because the requirement for favorable conditions is that the patient be free of infection the day before surgery. The negation of choice C is that if the conditions were favorable, the surgeon still might not operate. This does not affect the argument. The negation of choice D is that the protocol includes measures for avoiding infection. This does not affect the fact that Edgar has an infection. The negation of choice E is that there are other days on which the surgeon could operate on Edgar. This does not affect the argument.

15. **(A)** This is a *complete the sentence/argument* question. Choice A is correct because it is analogous to hearing the words of a story when there is no one present to tell the story.

    Choice B is incorrect because it would be analogous to writing a story, not to hearing a story. Choice C is incorrect because it is analogous to hearing the excitement or drama behind a story, rather than simply hearing the story itself. Choice D is incorrect because it is analogous to seeing the letters of which a story is composed, rather than reading the story itself. Choice E is incorrect because it is analogous to using the imagination to make up a story, rather than reading the story.

16. **(C)** This is a *main conclusion* question. Choice C correctly identifies the main point of the argument as rebutting the hypothesis that the lower mortality rate is due to an understanding of history.

Choice A is incorrect because it misses the point that the argument rebuts a hypothesis. In addition, combat technology is only one possible alternative explanation. Choice B is incorrect because it is the point that the argument rebuts. Choice D is incorrect because the fact that modern wars seem less destructive in one way is not the main point of the argument. Choice E is incorrect because it is simply a premise that is used to defend the main point—that knowledge of history is not the cause of reduced mortality.

17. **(B)** This is a *relevant information* question. Four of the answer choices are not relevant to the effectiveness of the biologist's argument. Choice B is relevant because the rancher's argument is that there is no benefit in return for the potential loss of livestock. Clarifying choice B would determine whether or not there was any benefit.

Choice A is incorrect because it does not compare the ranchers' loss with the ranchers' gain. Choice C is incorrect because comparing the relative values of the two benefits that the biologist names is not relevant to the rancher's argument. Choice D is incorrect because the rancher's argument does not depend on receiving a benefit that is equal to the loss, but simply on receiving any benefit at all. Choice E is incorrect because the benefit to ranchers does not necessarily need to be economic.

18. **(A)** This is a *weaken* question based on a cause-and-effect argument. The argument establishes a correlation between reading the summary and voting for the bond issue and then concludes that the summary caused people to vote for the bond issue. Choice A weakens the conclusion by indicating that the cause-and-effect relationship is the reverse—being in favor of the bond issue caused people to want to read the summary.

Choice B is incorrect because it is possible that the people had read or not read the summary before deciding how to vote. Choice C is incorrect because the existence of some exceptions to the correlation does not change the fact that there is a strong correlation. Choice D is incorrect because it does not change the correlation that was demonstrated by those who did vote on election day. Choice E would only weaken the argument if many more opponents than proponents refused to talk with pollsters.

19. **(C)** This is a *conclusion* question that asks what can be inferred from the premises in the passage. Choice C is correct because the average speed is the same for cars during the first and second hours of rush hour, but the second hour is subject to stop-and-go conditions that lower the mileage.

Choice A cannot be concluded from the information in the passage. It is possible that stop-and-go traffic occurs at other times. Choice B is incorrect because it is not known whether the reduced gas mileage due to stop-and-go conditions is enough to cancel out the increased mileage from driving at an average of 30 miles per hour. Choice D is incorrect because nothing is known about maximum speed, only about average speed. Choice E is incorrect because it contradicts the information in the passage that states that the average speed is the same throughout rush hour.

20. **(E)** This is a *flaw* question that uses the wording *vulnerable to criticism*. Choice E is correct because, if there were other ways to obtain the information about the behavior of corporations, the conclusion—that if the courts will not order disclosure, there is no way to obtain the information—falls apart.

Choice A is incorrect because the argument does not assume that corporations violate ethics, only that they might. Choice B is incorrect because the argument is not based on changing the behavior of corporations but on simply judging their behavior. Choice C is incorrect because the argument is not concerned with whether corporations can judge their own behavior but rather with the ability of the public to do so. Choice D is incorrect because failing to back up a premise with a rationale is not a flaw in logic.

21. **(B)** This is a *strengthen* question. The argument claims that avoiding disease will help people live longer. Choice B strengthens this conclusion by establishing that avoiding diseases is a significant factor in living longer. It this were not the case, the conclusion would fall apart.

Choice A is incorrect because the conclusion concerns an event in the future, not in the present. The argument has already established that modern medicine has increased life expectancy. Choice C is incorrect because it is irrelevant to the future scenario. Choice D is incorrect because it weakens the argument, suggesting that people who have recovered from a disease may be healthier than people who avoided the disease. Choice E is incorrect because, although it supports the premise that people who have avoided a disease are healthier than people who have recovered from the disease, it does not support the conclusion that people who have avoided diseases will live longer. A statement such as choice B is needed to make the logical leap from healthier people to people who live longer.

22. **(B)** This is a *flaw* question that uses the rare wording *in that it takes for granted*. With this type of question, the argument is flawed because it takes

something for granted that may in fact not be true. Choice B correctly points out that the argument assumes that because there have been more sightings of UFOs, there must be more visitations of UFOs. This is not a valid assumption because there could be other explanations for more sightings, such as increased awareness or better reporting of sightings.

Choice A is incorrect because the argument does not depend on an ongoing increase in the frequency of sightings. Choice C is incorrect because, although the argument assumes this, it does not represent a logical flaw. Choice D is incorrect because the argument does not assume this. The argument does not depend on the fact that the UFOs are not piloted by humans. Choice E is incorrect because the argument does not assume that UFOs are harmless.

23. **(A)** This is a *parallel flaw* question that does not use the word *parallel*. The flaw in the original argument is that, even though the odds of any individual new small business succeeding for a year are only 30 percent, the odds of one out of fifteen surviving are much higher. Choice A contains the same error. Even though the odds of any individual greyhound winning are low, the odds of one out of six winning are higher.

Choice B is incorrect because it is not flawed. Choice C is incorrect because it is a cause-and-effect argument. Choice D is incorrect because its error is in failing to consider the possibility that the man bribed the juries that acquitted him. Choice E is incorrect because it is not flawed.

24. **(D)** This is a *role of a claim* question. Choice D is correct, in that the quoted statement is a conclusion defended by the specific facts in the second sentence. The fact that the silvery minnow is endangered is then used as a premise to support the conclusion in the last sentence.

Choice A is incorrect because the quoted statement is not the main conclusion. Choice B is incorrect because the argument does not rebut the quoted statement. Choice C is incorrect because the quoted statement supports the main conclusion directly, not through supporting an intermediate conclusion. Choice E is incorrect because the quoted statement is not a hypothesis. It is a fact.

25. **(E)** This is a *flaw* question. Choice E is correct because adequate food and shelter is necessary for people to pursue the truth—without it, people cannot pursue the truth. However, the argument concludes that once adequate food and shelter is provided, that people will pursue the truth. That is a logical flaw because people still may not pursue the truth. Food and shelter is necessary but not sufficient.

Choice A is incorrect because there is no individual case given. Choice B is incorrect because the information about the group of people who do not have food or shelter is not based on the characteristics of some people in the group. Choice C is incorrect because it is not necessarily probable that once people have food and shelter, they will pursue the truth. Choice D is incorrect because the argument does not claim that the group of people without food or shelter is representative of the population as a whole.

Writing Sample: Example of a Superior Response to the Essay

Slotown ("ST") chooses RoadRail ("RR") over Green Bus ("GB") because RR affords sufficient routing flexibility while minimizing ST's fuel use and hydrocarbon footprint. ST uses two criteria, which are that ST wants flexibility to make routing changes, and that ST wants to minimize the fuel consumption and hydrocarbon emissions of its public transportation system. RR is ST's superior alternative because RR is more efficient and environmentally friendly than GB and offers a changeable routing system. GB is ST's inferior alternative because GB brings greater fuel consumption and larger hydrocarbon emissions. RR is therefore ST's superior alternative because RR better meets ST's selection criteria.

ST uses two criteria to choose between RR and GB. One criterion says ST wants to minimize fuel use and reduce hydrocarbon emissions. The second criterion says ST wants to maximize its transportation flexibility if a HugeGro factory closes or moves. These criteria may be combined into a single rule that says ST wants to use less fuel and generate minimal pollution, as well as to be able to change routes quickly. Over the long term, ST's goal to reduce its fuel use and hydrocarbon emissions outweighs its needs for routing flexibility.

RR is ST's superior alternative because RR's trains are fuel efficient and emit low amounts of pollutants into ST's atmosphere. RR's modular tracks may be moved around ST's streets to provide routing changes. Unfortunately, the city where RR's tracks are already installed remains quiet about RR's actual routing flexibility. Even so, RR is ST's better alternative because RR uses less fuel and emits fewer hydrocarbons than does GB.

GB is ST's inferior choice. GB's buses are less fuel efficient and therefore emit more air pollution than RR's trains. Over the long term, GB's buses could be more costly to operate than RR's trains. The increased air pollution GB's buses bring could become irreversible. Although GB's buses could provide easy routing changes and are becoming more efficient, GB's greater fuel consumption and harmful emissions point to RR as ST's superior alternative. Therefore, ST rejects GB as ST's inferior alternative.

RR is ST's superior alternative. RR uses less fuel than GB and emits fewer hydrocarbons. RR's modular track system allows GB to make routing changes. GB's buses use more fuel and pollute ST's air more than do RR's trains. Therefore, ST chooses RR because RR is more fuel efficient, emits fewer hydrocarbons, and provides routing flexibility.